AFRICA-CHINA LINKAGES

Building Deeper and Broader Connections

Editors

ABEBE AEMRO SELASSIE
ANDREA RICHTER HUME
ALFRED SCHIPKE

Cover design: IMF Creative Solutions

Cataloging-in-Publication Data
IMF Library

Names: Abebe Aemro Selassie, editor. | Hume, Andrea Richter, editor. | Schipke, Alfred, 1959- , editor. | International Monetary Fund, publisher.
Title: Africa-China linkages : building deeper and broader connections / Editors Abebe Aemro Selassie, Andrea Richter Hume, Alfred Schipke.
Other titles: Building deeper and broader connections.
Description: Washington, DC : International Monetary Fund, 2025. | 2025. | Includes bibliographical references.
Identifiers: ISBN:
9798400239182 (paper)
9798400237652 (ePub)
9798400237713 (WebPDF)
Subjects: LCSH: Africa–International economic relations–China. | China–Internation economic relations–Africa.
Classification: LCC HF1359.A4 2025

DISCLAIMER: The views expressed in this book are those of the authors and do not necessarily represent the views of the IMF's Executive Directors, its management, or any of its members. The boundaries, colors, denominations, and any other information shown on the maps do not imply, on the part of the International Monetary Fund, any judgment on the legal status of any territory or any endorsement or acceptance of such boundaries.

Recommended citation: Selassie, Abebe Aemro, Andrea Richter Hume, and Alfred Schipke, eds. 2025. Washington, DC: International Monetary Fund.

ISBN: 9798400239182 (paper)
9798400237652 (ePub)
9798400237713 (PDF)

Please send orders to:

International Monetary Fund, Publication Services
PO Box 92780, Washington, DC 20090, USA
Tel: (202) 623-7430 Fax: (202) 623-7201
E-mail: publications@imf.org
Internet: www.elibrary.imf.org
www.bookstore.imf.org

Contents

Foreword

In 2023, the International Monetary Fund and the World Bank Group held their Annual Meetings in Morocco—their first such gathering in Africa in 50 years. The event highlighted the continent's pivotal role in the global community. Indeed, the continent is rich with opportunities. With its population set to double to about 2.5 billion by 2050, Africa will account for more than half of global population growth through the mid-21st century. This human potential is complemented by natural resource wealth—Africa's metal and mineral resources make it critical for the green transition, and its agricultural potential is vast. Africa's development will therefore clearly have profound implications for the global economy. The meetings in Morocco not only marked a milestone for international financial institutions but also served as a powerful reminder of Africa's growing importance and impact on the world stage. Indeed, this may be the African Century.

Africa's economic and financial linkages with China have played a vital role in the region's growth story. These ties are multifaceted, encompassing trade, foreign direct investment, and financing. They are also mirrored in institutional arrangements that aim to foster these ties, such as the Forum on China–Africa Cooperation.

Given the importance of the Africa–China economic relationship, it features increasingly in the IMF's work. Based on the IMF's *October 2024 World Economic Outlook*, China's economy is projected to contribute about a quarter of global economic growth over the next five years; this highlights its continued importance for Africa and the world. At the same time, China's economic slowdown and continued structural transformation will present both opportunities and challenges for African countries.

This book brings together a diverse set of research studies focusing on the evolution of economic and financial linkages between Africa and China and explores how current trends in China could impact Africa in the period ahead. It includes chapters on official financing and a comprehensive overview of the Chinese government agencies entrusted with the China–Africa economic partnership. Another chapter focuses on the evolution of fintech in Africa and China—including financial inclusion—which contributes to higher growth and lower income inequality. Here, the book offers insightful lessons for fintech advances in other emerging markets and developing countries. This book also includes a dedicated chapter on China's economic relations with the Maghreb countries of Africa. A discussion of the international experience of strengthening policy frameworks and building capacity provides valuable lessons for enhancing the institutional structures that underpin successful international economic and financial relations.

This book provides a notable complement to the IMF's regular policy dialogue and lending to African countries. The IMF's deep experience in analyzing spill-overs is particularly relevant for the book's assessment of the channels through which developments in China affect Africa. An additional important part of the IMF's engagement with both Africa and China involves capacity development, which is delivered by the IMF's technical departments and through capacity development centers in Africa and the China-IMF Capacity Development Center. The IMF remains steadfast in its commitment to working closely with both Africa and China in all areas of IMF expertise to foster high, sustainable, inclusive, and green growth.

Antoinette M. Sayeh
Former Deputy Managing Director
International Monetary Fund

Acknowledgments

This project was initiated in 2019 after a visit by Abebe Aemro Selassie, Director of the IMF African Department, to Beijing, China. Given the significant engagement between Africa and China, it was clear that producing a set of analytical studies on various aspects of this dynamic economic and financial relationship would be of wider benefit. Over the years, and despite interruptions caused by the COVID-19 pandemic, this project has received enthusiastic guidance, support, and input from many individuals, notably Dominique Desruelle and Vivek Arora, who in turn led the African Department's work on Africa–China relations.

The project brought together economists from across the IMF, including the African, Asia and Pacific, and Middle East and Central Asia departments, as well as functional departments such as Strategy and Policy Review, Fiscal Affairs, Monetary and Capital Markets, Research, and the Institute for Capacity Development. We extend special thanks to the many IMF staff who contributed thoughtful and constructive inputs and comments throughout the review process.

This book benefited from inputs from officials in African member countries, especially in the context of a lending survey, as well as Chinese interlocutors, especially the People's Bank of China.

Our thanks go first and foremost to Xiangming Li, for her outstanding work during the editorial process and her steadfast commitment to seeing this book through to completion and beyond. We are also incredibly grateful to Kaihao Cai, Yadian Chen, and Cecilia Prado for their outstanding research and editorial support.

We extend our deepest appreciation to Lorraine Coffey of the IMF Communications Department, who not only managed copyediting but also expedited the book's production in record time. We are also extremely grateful to her colleagues Linda Kean and Patricia Loo, who from the outset played pivotal roles in helping the project come to fruition.

Contributors

Steven Barnett is the IMF's Senior Resident Representative in China. Before that, he was the Advisor to IMF Deputy Managing Director Tao Zhang. For much of his career, he has covered Asia. His positions have included Chief of the China Division in the IMF's Asia and Pacific Department, Assistant Director of the IMF Office for Asia and the Pacific in Tokyo, Resident Representative to China, and Resident Representative to Thailand. Before joining the IMF in 1997, he earned his PhD in economics from the University of Maryland. He has a BA in economics and an MA in Russian and East European studies from Stanford University.

Mariya Brussevich is a Professor of Economics at Ibmec in Rio de Janeiro, Brazil. Before this position, she was an economist in the IMF's Research Department. Her research interests center around international trade, inequality, and structural transformation. She holds a PhD in economics from Purdue University.

Diego A. Cerdeiro is the Deputy Chief of the Regional Studies Unit of the IMF's European Department. Before this, he worked in the IMF's Asia and Pacific Department's Regional Studies Division, was the Senior Desk for China, and was the Mission Chief for Tuvalu. Other previous assignments covered Honduras, Panama, and the United States while also contributing to various *World Economic Outlook* and *External Sector* reports. His research interests include capital flows, capital controls, trade, firm-level productivity, and network theory. He holds a PhD from the University of Cambridge.

Eugenio Cerutti is Chief of the Macrofinancial Unit in the Strategy, Policy, and Review Department of the IMF. Before this, he served as the Assistant to several Directors of the IMF Research Department (Olivier Blanchard, Maurice Obstfeld, and Gita Gopinath), in the Macrofinancial Division of the Research Department, and on several IMF country teams, including Maldives (as Mission Chief), Indonesia (as Deputy Mission Chief), Philippines (as Deputy Mission Chief), Sweden, Turkey, Venezuela, Lithuania, Bolivia, and Barbados. His research interests fall in the general field of international macroeconomics, with a particular focus on capital flows, financial regulation, and macrofinancial linkages. He holds a PhD in Economics from Johns Hopkins University.

Wenjie Chen is the Mission Chief for Mali and Deputy Division Chief of the Regional Studies Division in the IMF's African Department. She started her career as an Assistant Professor of International Business at the George Washington University. Upon joining the IMF's African Department as a mid-career economist in 2014, she worked on South Sudan, Eswatini, and South Africa while also contributing to several *Regional Economic Outlook* chapters. She then worked in the Research Department, where she coauthored and co-led chapters for the *World Economic Outlook*. She has also worked on the China team and participated in missions to Timor-Leste. She has published extensively in academic and policy journals on global value chains, trade competitiveness, market power, and China–Africa relations. She received her MA and PhD in economics from the University of Michigan and a BA in economics and mathematics from Lawrence University.

Seung Mo Choi is Executive Vice President at Samsung Global Research. While at the IMF, he was a Deputy Division Chief in the Statistics Department, leveraging big data and innovative statistical techniques to enhance the IMF's surveillance and research efforts. Previously, he contributed to program negotiations and reviews in the African Department, including Rwanda's Resilience and Sustainability Trust program, and led analytical projects encompassing GDP nowcasting, climate change, inflation, and debt. He also worked in the European Department and the Institute for Capacity Development. He holds a BA in economics from Seoul National University and a PhD in economics from the University of Chicago.

Mattia Coppo is a consultant at the World Bank Prospect Group where he participates in the production of the flagship report *Global Economic Prospects*. He previously worked at the IMF as a research officer in the Research Department and the Institute of Capacity Development. He completed his graduate studies at University College London and Higher School of Economics, Moscow.

Michele Fornino is an Economist in the Regional Studies Division of the African Department. He joined the IMF in September 2021 through the Economist Program, after completing a PhD in economics at the Massachusetts Institute of Technology. His first IMF assignment was in the Financial Institutions Division of the Statistics Department, where he worked extensively on the impact of climate change on the financial sector. During this time, he also participated in Article IV missions to Kiribati and Luxembourg. Since joining the African Department in March 2023, he has coauthored the October 2023 *Regional Economic Outlook* Analytical Note on the economic relationship between sub-Saharan Africa and China and served on the Mali country team. His research interests include fiscal policy, issues at the intersection of macroeconomics and labor economics, automation, and the future of work.

Shushanik Hakobyan is a Senior Economist in the Multilateral Surveillance Division of the IMF's Research Department. Before this, she was a Senior Economist in the African Department of the IMF where she covered Lesotho and Rwanda and co-led the department's Trade Group. She previously worked on regional surveillance in the African Department, on strategic issues (also covering

Kosovo) in the Strategy, Policy and Review Department, and in academia (Fordham University, Georgetown University, and Middlebury College). Her research interests include trade policy, trade and labor markets, and preferential market access. She holds a PhD in economics from the University of Virginia.

Ben Hunt served as an Adviser in the IMF's Research Department.

Alexei Kireyev is a Senior Economist at the IMF and former IMF Representative to the World Trade Organization. He leads advance IMF missions to member countries; provides advice on macroeconomic policies to countries with IMF-supported programs; and reviews IMF policy advice, financing, and technical assistance. His degrees include an MA in economics from George Washington University and a Doctor of Science in economics from Moscow State Institute of International Relations. Before his IMF career, he served as an Economic Advisor to President Gorbachev, economist at the World Bank, and a Professor of international economics at Moscow State Institute of International Relations. He teaches applied macroeconomics and policy, and he publishes extensively on international economics, trade, principles of economics, and economic problems of low-income countries.

Jiawei Li is an Economist at the Federal Energy Regulatory Commission (FERC) and a former Research Analyst at the International Monetary Fund. At FERC, he leads efforts in assessing and regulating the wholesale electricity market and interstate transmission. During his tenure in the IMF's Middle East and Central Asia department, he worked on various country teams including Algeria, Djibouti, and Somalia. His efforts contributed to Somalia's debt relief, multiple departmental research projects and cross-departmental initiatives. He is fluent in multiple languages.

Xiangming Li is an Advisor in the IMF's African Department. Before this, she was the Director of the IMF's Regional Technical Assistance Center for East Africa. She has held operational and policy positions across the IMF, including in the African Department and previously in the European, Strategy Policy and Review, Fiscal Affairs, and Monetary and Capital Markets Departments, as well as in the Institute for Capacity Development. Her work on surveillance, lending, training, and technical assistance spans Africa, Europe, Asia, and the Caribbean. She has also worked with development partners across the world on supporting IMF capacity development. She earned a PhD in economics and economic development from the Massachusetts Institute of Technology and an MA in urban planning and a BS from Peking University.

Yibin Mu is a Senior Economist in the Western Hemisphere Department of the IMF, working on Dominica and Antigua and Barbuda. His previous experience includes roles in the African Department covering South Africa, Lesotho, and Sierra Leone. Before joining the IMF, he served as a Senior Financial Economist in various departments (Asia, Europe, and Financial Vice Presidency) of the World Bank for 11 years. Preceding his tenure at the World Bank, he worked at the Hong Kong Monetary Authority and the People's Bank of China for eight years, where he was responsible for regulating and supervising foreign banks in China and played a key role in formulating China's financial reform strategies and policies. His professional expertise spans a wide range of topics, including macro-financial policy, monetary and exchange rate policy, fiscal policy, prudential supervision and regulation, and financial sector and financial/capital market development. He holds an Executive MPA from Harvard University and a PhD in economics and an MA in finance from Tsinghua University, China. He was also a Chartered Financial Analyst (2006–13).

Papa N'Diaye is Deputy Director in the IMF's Finance Department. Prior to this, he held various positions at the Fund, as Assistant Director in the African Department, Mission Chief for South Africa and Botswana, Chief of the Regional Studies Division of the African Department, and Deputy Division Chief in the Strategy, Policy, and Review Department. He also worked on the China, Japan, and Malaysia desks at the IMF. He studied at Sorbonne University, specializing in macroeconomics and econometrics. He has numerous publications on various topics, including monetary policy, asset prices, macroprudential policies, fiscal policy, and rebalancing growth in China.

Chris Papageorgiou is the Mission Chief for Bangladesh in the Asia and Pacific Department of the IMF. Since joining the Fund in 2006, he has done country work across Africa, the Western Hemisphere, and the Asia and Pacific regions, and he has led IMF policy work on structural, monetary, and climate-related topics. His analytical work primarily focuses on growth and macroeconomic development. He received his PhD from the University of Pittsburgh.

Andrea Pescatori is the Chief of the Commodities Unit in the IMF's Research Department and Mission Chief for Tonga. He previously was a Senior Economist on the Chile, US, and Canada teams in the IMF's Western Hemisphere Department and, before that, an Economist in the World Economic Studies Division of the IMF's Research Department. He has written extensively on a variety of macroeconomic topics including monetary and fiscal policy and had published work in well-established peer-reviewed journals. Before joining the IMF, he was an economist at the Federal Reserve Bank of Cleveland and at the Board of Governors of the Federal Reserve System. He holds a PhD in economics from Universitat Pompeu Fabra.

Henry Rawlings joined the IMF as a Research Analyst in 2020. For over three years, he worked in the Regional Studies Division of the African Department, where he contributed to seven editions of the *Regional Economic Outlook: Sub-Saharan Africa*. He also published research on the COVID-19 pandemic and fiscal policy. He earned his MA in international economics at the Johns Hopkins University School of Advanced International Studies and his BS in economics and international relations at the University of Wyoming.

Ivohasina Fizara Razafimahefa is the Director of the IMF's African Regional Technical Assistance Center in West Africa 2. Before that, he was the IMF's Mission Chief for The Gambia. He is also a lead member of the working group on debt-related issues in the IMF's African Department. Previously, he was mission chief for Togo and economist on countries including Guinea, Republic of Congo, Burundi, Romania, and Greece. Prior to joining the IMF, he was Minister of Economy in Madagascar, worked at UNIDO in Austria, and was a Research Fellow at the Institute of Developing Economies in Japan. He earned a Maitrise in economics from the University of Antananarivo, Madagascar, and a PhD in economics from the University of Kobe, Japan. He has published a book and several research papers on international economics, exchange rate, fiscal decentralization, and other topics.

Andrea Richter Hume is a Deputy Director in the IMF's African Department, where she supervises country teams working on Southern and Eastern Africa. She also leads departmental teams working on Africa–Asia economic and financial relations; fragile and conflict-affected states; economic diversification; artificial intelligence; data and knowledge management and statistics; and vulnerability and enterprise risk. With over 25 years of operational and policy experience at the IMF, she has held leadership positions in economic policy, budget and planning, donor relations, human resources, knowledge and data management, technology, and communications. She has worked on country teams in Africa, Asia and the Pacific, Eastern Europe, and Latin America. Before joining the IMF, she worked on international economic policy issues in the US government as an Economist at the Council of Economic Advisers. She holds an MPhil and a DPhil in economics from the University of Oxford (UK), and a BA in economics from Princeton University.

Alfred Schipke is the Director of the East Asian Institute and a Professor of the Practice of International Finance at the National University of Singapore. He is also Adjunct Professor at the National School of Development at Peking University and has been teaching international finance at Harvard Kennedy School of Government. Before that, he held several senior positions at the IMF, including as Director of the IMF–Singapore Regional Training Institute for Asia and the Pacific; Assistant Director and Mission Chief for India; and Senior Resident Representative and Mission Chief for China, where he provided policy advice, spearheaded research, and coordinated capacity development. He was also Division Chief in the IMF Asia and Pacific Department and was Mission Chief for Vietnam. In the IMF's Western Hemisphere Department, he negotiated several successful IMF programs including for El Salvador and St. Kitts and Nevis. He has authored and edited several books and articles, including *India's Financial*

System: Building the Foundation for Strong and Sustainable Growth, *The Future of China's Bond Market*, and *Modernizing China: Investing in Soft Infrastructure*. He holds a PhD from Duisburg-Essen University, an MPA from Harvard, and a BA from Indiana University of Pennsylvania.

Abebe Aemro Selassie is the Director of the African Department, where he oversees the IMF's operations and engagement with 45 countries across sub-Saharan Africa. Under his leadership, the IMF has disbursed some $51 billion to support the post pandemic recovery and foster greener, more inclusive growth. Working alongside the region's leaders, he strives to strengthen the region's financial architecture and support Africa reaching its true potential. Before taking up his current position in 2016, he gained extensive experience in a wide-ranging career at the IMF. He held various senior positions, including Deputy Director in the African Department, Mission Chief for Portugal during the Euro Area Crisis, and Mission Chief for South Africa. He has served as the IMF's Senior Resident Representative in Uganda and earlier in his career, he worked on the Fund's lending programs with Turkey, Thailand, Romania, and Estonia. While in the Strategy, Policy and Review Department he was deeply involved in low-income country and emerging-market programs and policy design issues. Before joining the IMF in 1994, he worked for the Government of Ethiopia as Principal Economist in the Office of the President and at the Economist Intelligence Unit in London. He also serves as an advisor to the Global Commission for the Economics of Water. He did his graduate studies at the London School of Economics.

Y. Modeste Somé joined the IMF in 2018 and has worked on a range of assignments covering low-income and emerging market economies. He is currently the IMF Resident Representative in Benin and worked as an economist in the Asia and Pacific Department. Before that, he worked in the IMF's Strategy, Policy, and Review Department. Prior to joining the IMF, he worked at the World Bank Group and at the University of Johannesburg as a Senior Lecturer. He has conducted extensive research, including on drivers of international financial market access for countries across regions, debt sustainability analysis, macro financial issues, fiscal policy, monetary policy and inflation dynamics, and international trade.

Tao Sun has a PhD in economics and has worked in the International Department and then the Financial Stability Bureau of the People's Bank of China. In May 2007, he started work as an economist in the Monetary and Capital Markets Department of the IMF. He then worked as a Senior Economist in the IMF's Asia and Pacific Department. He also worked as a Senior Director at Ant Group during 2015–2019. He is now a Deputy Division Chief of Payment, Currencies, and Infrastructure Division in the Monetary and Capital Markets Department at the IMF. His recent work has focused on fintech, digital currencies, and cross-border payments.

Katsiaryna Svirydzenka is the Deputy Mission Chief for Sri Lanka at the IMF. Before that, she was the Mission Chief for Bhutan and Tuvalu. Since joining the IMF in 2010, she has contributed to the work of multiple country teams, including Japan, India, Russia, Malaysia, Mongolia, Serbia, the Solomon Islands, and others. Her research interests include financial cycles, network analysis and systemic risk, financial spillovers, financial development, diversification, firm-level productivity, and zombie firms. She holds a PhD in economics from the Graduate Institute of International and Development Studies (Geneva, Switzerland), an MA in international economics and international relations from the Johns Hopkins School of Advanced International Studies (Bologna, Italy, and Washington DC), and a BA in economics from the American University in Bulgaria.

Amadou Sy is an Assistant Director in the IMF's African Department and Mission Chief for Angola. He was previously an Advisor in the African Department and co-led the department's Financial Sector and Monetary Policy Network. He is a former Director of the Africa Growth Initiative at the Brookings Institution. He holds a PhD in finance from McGill University and is a Chartered Financial Analyst as well as a Financial Risk Manager.

Ling Hui Tan served at the IMF for over 25 years, working mainly in capacity development for the Asia Pacific region, including as the inaugural Director of the China–IMF Capacity Development Center. She also served as an Adviser in the IMF's Independent Evaluation Office and as Group Head and Lead Economist for regional surveillance in the ASEAN+3 Macroeconomic Research Office (on secondment). She holds a PhD in economics from Harvard University. Her research publications include papers on trade and structural policy issues in various academic journals.

Nico Valckx joined the Fund in 2010 after having worked for eight years at the European Central Bank in Frankfurt and the ECB's Washington office. Previously, he worked in research departments of De Nederlandsche Bank and Bank of Finland and was lecturer in international macroeconomics. At the Fund, he has worked on euro area monetary and financial/crisis management policies in the European Department, as team leader of the Global Financial Stability Report, as Deputy Lead for the Hong Kong Financial Stability Assessment Program team and Mission Chief for the Financial Statistics Stability Report team for Uganda. He was also an energy commodity expert in the IMF's Research Department and a country economist for Malta and Kiribati. Currently, he is Senior Desk on Mali and contributes to climate work in the African Department. He holds an MSc from KU Leuven and Ghent University and a PhD in applied economics from the University of Antwerp.

Geneviève Verdier is an Advisor and Mission Chief for the Central African Economic and Monetary Community in the IMF's African Department. Before that, she served as Mission Chief for Algeria in the Middle East and Central Asia

Department, and Deputy Division Chief in the Fiscal Affairs Department where she worked on public expenditure issues and their fiscal and macroeconomic implications. In her 18 years at the IMF, she has held various positions on country desks and capacity development teams in a range of countries in Africa, Emerging Europe, and Asia. Before joining the IMF, she was an Assistant Professor of economics at Texas A&M University and an Economist in the Research Department of the Bank of Canada. She earned a PhD from the University of British Columbia. Her work and publications in IMF publications, books, and peer-reviewed journals cover macroeconomic issues related to public spending efficiency, public investment, sovereign debt restructuring, economic growth, and digitalization.

Fan Zhang is an Economist in the Research Department of the IMF. Before this, he worked in the China team of the Asia Pacific Department. He has contributed to the IMF's technical assistance to the Reserve Bank of India and the Bank of Thailand on monetary policy issues. His research focuses mainly on international macroeconomics, monetary policy, and model developments. He has been a contributor to IMF publications such as *World Economic Outlook* and several working papers. He holds a PhD in applied mathematics from the University of Warwick (UK).

Longmei Zhang is a Senior Economist in the IMF's Strategy, Policy, and Review department. Since joining the IMF, she worked on a diverse set of countries, including Australia, New Zealand, China, the Philippines, Romania, and Uganda. She also served as the IMF Deputy Resident Representative in Beijing from 2017 to 2020. In this capacity, she provided policy advice, co-led the IMF office's analytical work, and engaged with academia and think tanks. She has served as a Senior Fellow at Harvard Kennedy School and the Citi Visiting Chair in International Finance at Schwarzman College, Tsinghua University. She has published research in areas including long-term growth/middle-income trap, macroprudential policies, corporate leverage, capital flows and asset prices, digital economy, and fintech, and co-edited the book, *The Future of China's Bond Market.* She holds a PhD in Economics from Goethe University Frankfurt.

Abbreviations

ADF	African Development Fund
AfCFTA	African Continental Free Trade Area
AfDB	African Development Bank
AGTF	Africa Growing Together Fund
AIIB	Asian Infrastructure Investment Bank
AML/CFT	anti-money laundering and combating the financing of terrorism
ASEAN	Association of Southeast Asian Nations
ATM	automated teller machine
BRI	Belt and Road Initiative
BRITACOF	BRI Tax Administration Cooperation Forum
BRITACOM	Belt and Road Initiative Tax Administration Cooperation Mechanism
CAD	China–Africa Development
CARI	China–Africa Research Initiative
CBDC	central bank digital currency
CDB	China Development Bank
CICDC	China–IMF Capacity Development Center
CIDCA	China International Development Cooperation Agency
CLA	Chinese loans to Africa
COVID-19	coronavirus disease 2019
CPC	The Communist Party of China
DRS	Debtor Reporting System
DSA	Debt Sustainability Analysis
DSSI	Debt Service Suspension Initiative
EU	European Union
EXIM	Export–Import Bank of China
FDI	foreign direct investment
FOCAC	Forum on China–Africa Cooperation
FSB	Financial Stability Board
GBRIC	Green Belt and Road Initiative Center

GDP	gross domestic product
GVAR	global vector autoregressive
GVCs	global value chains
HS	Harmonized System
ICP	International Comparison Program
ICT	information and communication technology
IDS	International Debt Statistics
IMF	International Monetary Fund
IP	industrial production
ITC	International Trade Center
JHU CARI	Johns Hopkins University China–Africa Research Initiative
JVs	joint ventures
LICs	low-income countries
MDB	multilateral development banks
MENA	Middle East and North Africa
MTBFs	medium-term budgetary frameworks
MTRS	medium-term revenue strategy
ODI	outward direct investment
OECD	Organisation for Economic Co-operation and Development
OLS	ordinary least squares
P2P	peer-to-peer
PBC	People's Bank of China
PFRAM	PPP Fiscal Risk Assessment Model
PIMA	Public Investment Management Assessment
PPG	public and publicly guaranteed
PPP	public-private partnership
PRC	People's Republic of China
RCA	revealed comparative advantage
SAFE	State Administration of Foreign Exchange
SDG	Sustainable Development Goals
SDR	Special Drawing Rights
SINOSURE	China Export & Credit Insurance Corporation
SMEs	small and medium enterprises
SMS	Short Message Service
SOEs	state-owned enterprises

SPVs	special purpose vehicles
SSA	sub-Saharan Africa
TADAT	Tax Administration Diagnostic Assessment Tool
TIR	Transports Internationaux Routiers
UNCTAD	United Nations Conference on Trade and Development
VAR	vector autoregression
VAT	value-added tax
VITARA	Virtual Training to Advance Revenue Administration
VIX	equity market volatility
WAEMU	West African Economic and Monetary Union
WB	World Bank
WCO	World Customs Organization
WTO	World Trade Organization

CHAPTER 1

The Africa-China Economic Partnership

Abebe Aemro Selassie, Andrea Richter Hume, and Alfred Schipke

INTRODUCTION

Africa's progress in recent decades—across all development metrics—has been remarkable. Improvements in life expectancy, literacy, health, and education have all profoundly reshaped the continent and its potential. With Africa's population set to double to about 2.5 billion by 2050, the economic performance of the continent will become increasingly important for the success of the global economy.

International trade and finance have played a key role in driving Africa's economic growth. Engagement with China has become increasingly important in this regard because deepening trade, investment, and financing ties have allowed African countries to benefit from China's economic dynamism over the past half-century. China's success in eliminating extreme poverty through sustained high growth and government policies has also been an inspiration to many countries in Africa.

Although economic contacts between China and Africa date back over 2,000 years, it was only in the latter part of the 18th century that Chinese laborers and traders came to several regions of Africa (Shinn 2019). More formal economic relations between China and Africa began developing after the founding of the People's Republic of China in 1949, picking up speed after the historic visit of Ethiopia's Emperor Haile Selassie to Beijing in 1971 and as China's external orientation increased. Today, the relationship is multifaceted, with strong economic linkages mirrored in the development of new institutional partnerships, such as the Forum on China–Africa Cooperation (FOCAC).

A few indicators capture how much economic and financial engagements between Africa and China have grown. Over the past decades, China has become sub-Saharan Africa's single largest bilateral trading partner, accounting for about 13 percent of its exports and 16 percent of its imports. In the financial sphere, China's lending grew rapidly starting in the early 2000s, such that more than half of bilateral official debt at the aggregate level is now owed to China. On the equity side, Chinese foreign direct investment (FDI) in Africa is a more recent phenomenon, reaching a little over 4 percent of the total stock of FDI in Africa in 2021.

Because China's economy changes, so will its economic and financial engagements with Africa. In this regard, China's slower pace of growth and ongoing structural transformation present both challenges and opportunities for African countries.

The Africa–China relationship is clearly multifaceted, and the key issues will continue to evolve. Although a comprehensive coverage of these issues would require several volumes, this book presents a set of studies that assess the Africa–China relationship from selected economic and financial vantage points. It seeks to provide a fuller picture of how these ties have developed over time and how China has contributed to the continent's growth. In this regard, it contributes to broadening the discussion of China's impact on Africa, which in recent years has focused heavily on issues related to debt. A discussion of the institutions entrusted with fostering China's relationship with Africa helps enrich our understanding of these developments.

Given the significant interest in China's lending to Africa, the book presents a novel survey-based data set of official debt owed to China. It also discusses how Africa and China have leveraged financial technology (fintech) to foster economic development and increase financial inclusion; lessons from these experiences could be useful for other countries.

Looking ahead, the book analyzes how changes in China's growth and investment patterns could affect Africa in the coming years and decades. The international experience with strengthening policy tools and frameworks provides useful lessons in how to help maximize the benefits to all parties from continued financial engagement by China in Africa while mitigating risks. Although the book focuses primarily on sub-Saharan Africa, a dedicated chapter on China's engagement with Maghreb countries provides new insights into its rapidly developing economic and financial relationship.

The key issues and findings of the chapters are summarized in the following section.

GROWING INSTITUTIONAL RELATIONSHIPS

China's economic engagement with Africa has expanded over time, along with its own economic growth. Initially, the engagement focused on projects that required relatively small investment, reflecting the fact that China itself was among the least developed countries and a recipient of significant foreign assistance. From the mid-1990s, China's foreign assistance put more weight on supporting trade and investment, reflecting its "opening-up" reforms and increasing integration with the world economy. During this phase, foreign assistance promoted exports and facilitated imports of natural resources to support China's economic development and to help its companies develop abroad as part of the "going-out" strategy. With the establishment of the China Export and Import Bank and the China Development Bank (CDB) in 1994 and FOCAC in 2000, financial support to Africa increased. A series of official China–Africa policy papers also provide valuable insights into the country's evolving priorities in its relationships with Africa, as do statements by Chinese leaders.[1] South–South cooperation (among developing countries), mutually beneficial and equal partnerships, and nonconditionality are mentioned throughout these policy documents.

Institutionally, relationships have also been evolving and encompass many levels of the Chinese government and associated agencies. Overall, the Central Committee of the Communist Party, particularly the Foreign Affairs Committee,[2] holds ultimate authority over China's strategic direction abroad. Major initiatives are approved at the State Council level (China's cabinet), with interministerial consultation, especially with the Ministries of Foreign Affairs, Commerce, and Finance, as well as the People's Bank of China, the National Development and Reform Commission, and the China International Development Cooperation Agency (CIDCA). In addition, the Export–Import Bank is the official policy-related financial institution, the only institution receiving state interest subsidies for lending externally. Other state-owned entities, such as the CDB and China Export Credit Insurance Corporation, state-owned banks, and state-owned enterprises are also active in Africa. China engages with Africa as a member of the African Development Bank, the Asia Infrastructure and Investment Bank, the New Development Bank, the African Import and Export Bank, and the World Bank Group.

FOCAC has become a key platform for policy announcements and action plans. China and African countries meet every three years and conclude with a declaration and an action plan that guides cooperation in the subsequent three years.[3] To implement the action plan, China set up a follow-up action committee and its members represent almost all the Chinese ministries and agencies involved in African affairs.

CIDCA, founded in 2018, is a sub-ministerial-level executive agency directly under the State Council that is tasked as the lead agency for China's foreign aid. Implementation and ultimate accountability for foreign aid, however, still rest with the respective ministries, Export–Import Bank, and China Development Bank (CDB). A range of other efforts are underway to strengthen institutions for engagement with Africa; these are discussed in the chapter.

NAVIGATING SHIFTS IN AFRICA-CHINA ECONOMIC ENGAGEMENT

After China's accession to the World Trade Organization in 2001, trade with Africa increased sharply, such that China has become Africa's largest trading partner. Benefiting from China's high economic growth, the relationship produced prolonged growth spurts and boosted incomes in African countries. As of 2022, Africa's exports to China amounted to approximately 13 percent of total exports. Imports

[1] The first China–Africa white paper was issued in 2006. The most recent such paper, "China and Africa in the New Era: A Partnership of Equals," was issued by the State Council of the People's Republic of China in November 2021.

[2] Previously the Foreign Affairs Leading Group.

[3] Through 2024, 53 African countries and China have signed the declaration.

from China increased even more rapidly, to 16 percent of total African imports in 2022. In trade composition, Africa primarily exports natural resources (for example, crude oil, unprocessed minerals) as well as intermediate goods. For several African countries, exports to China account for more than 50 percent of their total (Angola, Democratic Republic of Congo, Eritrea, the Republic of Congo, and South Sudan). At the same time, Africa's imports are primarily manufactured goods and machinery. Here, China's share of African countries' imports is similar across countries. While Ghana, Guinea, and Nigeria import about 30 percent of the total from China, even countries outside of the top 10 still import about 10 percent from China.

China's FDI globally has increased significantly over the past two decades, reaching almost $2.8 trillion in 2021, with the largest share going to Asia and Latin America. Although China's FDI to Africa increased as well, the stock of Chinese investments as a share of the region's total FDI is still relatively small—at about 3.6 percent in 2021.

China's investments in Africa have primarily been in construction, mining, and manufacturing, and in these areas, state-owned enterprises have often played a critical role. Investments have also been concentrated in a small number of countries, especially those rich in natural resources. Chinese FDI and the establishment of Chinese companies in Africa contributed to an increase in the number of Chinese workers living there. Chinese workers in Africa include both those working for Chinese companies and those working for local companies providing labor services. In 2019, Algeria, Angola, Kenya, Nigeria, and Zambia were the top five countries, accounting for about 50 percent of all Chinese workers in Africa. Over the past decade, however, and especially since COVID-19, the number of workers fell from 250,000 in 2015 to about 90,000 in 2021. China has also been backing vocational training programs and workshops and, since 2016 (initiated under the Belt and Road Initiative), educating local students. In April 2023, the Chinese government formed a special committee to help plan new workshops.

China has gradually emerged as the largest bilateral official creditor in Africa. Key areas of financing include infrastructure, mining, and energy projects. In more recent years, total official loans have fallen significantly from a peak of 1.2 percent of the region's GDP in 2016. This reflects the effect of several external shocks, including commodity and oil-price shocks and the COVID-19 pandemic.

Compared with official financing, China's foreign aid is still relatively small but has been increasing steadily. During the 2024 FOCAC, for example, in addition to its contributions through international organizations, China pledged $12 billion in aid to Africa—a quarter of its total commitment to the region.

Going forward, China's slowdown and continued changing economic structure with less reliance on investment and the real estate sector will affect its economic relationship with Africa. Indeed, it is estimated that a 1 percentage point decline in China's growth may lead to a growth slowdown of 0.25 percentage points in sub-Saharan Africa on average. Of course, linkages differ across countries, and in the case of oil-exporting countries such as Angola and Nigeria, the effect would likely be more pronounced, with growth declining by about 0.5 percentage points (Abdel-Latif and others 2023).

SPILLOVERS: EXAMINING THE ECONOMIC AND FINANCIAL LINKS BETWEEN CHINA AND AFRICA

Given China's important role in the global economy, including in Africa, it is not surprising that economic and financial shocks from China have a significant impact on the latter, mainly transmitted through trade, with large effects for net commodity exporters. Although economic and financial developments in China typically reverberate in global financial markets, so far the effects mainly reflect China's important role in trade and commodity markets, rather than its integration into global financial markets or the direct financial linkages it has with other countries.

To assess spillovers from China to Africa, several methods are used. The chapter illustrates how shocks in China affect Africa in a general equilibrium setting where the initial effect through trade linkages could be amplified through other transmission channels, including relative price changes, demand, and financial channels. Also, the study updates and extends previous empirical findings on the effect of China on commodity prices. Finally, it empirically estimates financial spillovers from China to foreign exchange and equity markets in Africa.

The IMF's G20 Model is used to simulate the potential effect on Africa of three different Chinese policy scenarios: (1) a large fiscal stimulus in response to a "global financial crisis"; (2) a moderate fiscal package, as observed during the COVID-19 crisis; and (3) a continued rebalancing from investment to consumption. The results suggest that a large fiscal stimulus in China would boost growth in African countries, with a particularly large effect in low-income and fragile economies. Furthermore, a rebalancing from investment to consumption would have minor negative growth effects in most African economies in the short term while benefiting eastern and fragile economies and hurting commodity exporters in the medium term.

The analysis also zooms in empirically to examine the effects of Chinese industrial production growth on commodity prices, covering 1992–2020. It uses quantile regression techniques to account for extreme commodity price movements and a small vector autoregression model to allow for dynamic interactions between the model variables. The findings suggest that China's industrial production has a major effect on commodity prices and that this effect is even larger in times of extreme volatility in commodity markets. Furthermore, from the vector autoregression model, Chinese industrial production shocks appear to have a more significant and longer-lasting effect on commodity prices than industrial production shocks in the euro area or the United States.

The chapter also sheds light on how economic and financial developments in China affect foreign exchange and equity markets in Africa. Although the magnitude of financial spillovers from China has increased over time, the effect is still lower than that from the developments in the euro area or those related to global equity market volatility and is often lower than the effect of the larger African countries. This is consistent with the fact that financial linkages between China and Africa are considerably less established than trade linkages.

SUB-SAHARAN AFRICAN PUBLIC DEBT TO CHINA

China's engagement with sub-Saharan Africa includes being a major bilateral lender and being a source of significant infrastructure financing. In the wake of global shocks and a rise in debt service pressures for many African countries, their debt to China has received significant attention, in particular, as the global community has sought to improve existing mechanisms to support debt restructuring.

This chapter seeks to shed light on the various aspects of sub-Saharan Africa's debt to China, considering stocks, flows, and composition. It is based on data self-reported by debtor countries, combined with iterations between IMF staff and country authorities to ensure accuracy and consistency with the standard IMF–World Bank Debt Sustainability Framework.[4] Hence, the analysis fills a gap in the literature by providing a set of China–sub-Saharan Africa debt data that are consistent with the statistical concepts used in public debt sustainability analysis and complements information provided by others, including the Chinese Loans to Africa database by the Johns Hopkins University China–Africa Research Initiative (see also Acker and Brautigam, 2021), AidData (William and Mary Global Research), and International Debt Statistics (World Bank).

The analysis shows that China accounts for a relatively small share of sub-Saharan Africa's total public debt but a significant share of the region's official bilateral debt. This in part reflects the decline of official development assistance from the traditional bilateral donors, particularly in proportion to sub-Saharan Africa's GDP. Given that official bilateral debt is an important component in debt treatments, China has an important role in negotiations related to public debt. The data also show that China's share in official bilateral debt differs markedly across sub-Saharan Africa, with five countries accounting for about two-thirds of the total. The analysis does not find a clear pattern between sub-Saharan African countries' public debt owed to China and their debt vulnerabilities.

The data set compiled for this chapter can provide a basis for a deeper analysis of issues discussed in the literature. Future work could include examining the association of public debt to China with macroeconomic performance in sub-Saharan Africa, for example, using Dollar (2016) as a starting point. A potential area for investigation is the relationship between sub-Saharan Africa's debt to China and trade or FDI with China. In addition, although this data set lacks information on collateralization and debt restructuring patterns, future work can seek to collect more information on these trends.

[4] The analysis uses aggregated data to ensure confidentiality. The aim is to update the data periodically.

STRENGTHENING POLICY FRAMEWORKS AND CAPACITY

For the many countries globally grappling with high debt levels and high gross financing needs, recent shocks—most notably COVID-19 in 2020–2022—further complicated efforts to attract the investments they need to foster growth and reduce poverty. In sub-Saharan Africa, 18 of 35 low-income countries were either in debt distress or at high risk of distress as of September 2024 based on the IMF–World Bank Debt Sustainability Framework for Low-Income Countries. As such, future financing strategies in these economies need to account for new vulnerabilities and potential exposures to shocks. African countries with limited fiscal space would benefit from highly concessional support, FDI rather than debt financing, and other flexible and innovative financial arrangements to reduce reliance on public sector funding.

Yet, in every challenge, there is an opportunity: authorities can redouble efforts to strengthen policy frameworks to maximize the benefits of investments while minimizing risks. President Xi Jinping spoke to this opportunity in his remarks at the Second Belt and Road Forum;[5] the Belt and Road Debt Sustainability Framework of 2019 (Chinese Ministry of Finance 2019) also captures this objective.

To aid in the design of fiscal policy frameworks, the IMF has developed several fiscal toolboxes and principles aimed at reducing vulnerabilities and improving allocation of resources. These are informing efforts by African countries to enhance their institutions and processes. The fiscal toolboxes and principles cover the following:

- Effective budgetary institutions
- Public investment management assessment frameworks
- Institutional arrangements for fiscal risk management
- Effective public-private partnership regulatory frameworks
- Tax administration cooperation mechanisms
- Tax administration reform
- Medium-term revenue strategy
- Fiscal rules

No single model is sufficient for guiding good practices for lending abroad. However, it is clear from international experience that strong lending frameworks are critical, especially because they relate to governance and oversight of lending agencies, procedures for internal risk assessment and controls, and monitoring and reporting. For collateralized transactions, specifically, the G-20 Operational Guidelines and a 2023 joint IMF–World Bank note make clear that improved

[5] Speech at the Belt and Road Forum for International Cooperation in April 2019.

governance frameworks and enhanced technical capacity are critical to ensure their benefits outweigh their costs.

Amid current heightened vulnerabilities, strengthening policy frameworks and institutions and capacity development are more important than ever. And IMF practices and international experiences are providing guidance in Africa–China relationships, including in the context of the Belt and Road Initiative. In many of these areas, the IMF has been working with authorities in African countries and China through technical assistance and training, including through six regional capacity development centers in Africa; the African Training Institute and the China-IMF Capacity Development Center; and technical assistance from the IMF Fiscal Affairs, Legal, Monetary and Capital Markets, Strategy and Policy Review, and Statistics Departments.

MAGHREB AND CHINA: STRENGTHENING RESILIENCE AND GROWTH THROUGH COLLABORATION

In contrast to China's long association with sub-Saharan Africa, the Maghreb countries and China have only recently been discussed in a mutual context. The Maghreb—which means "the land where the sun sets" in Arabic—is a vast region of North Africa of some 100 million people, including Algeria, Libya, Mauritania, Morocco, and Tunisia. To a large extent, these countries share a common history, culture, and language. All Maghreb countries are maritime economies strategically located between the advanced economies of Europe across the Mediterranean Sea to the north and the high-potential, developing economies of sub-Saharan Africa to the south. Economically, the Maghreb is a relatively small region, with limited links between its countries. At the same time, China is the second-largest economy in the world, with strong economic linkages globally, including with the Maghreb countries.

The Maghreb and China have been at the periphery of each other's economic interests for years, and mutual interest has picked up only recently. Their cooperation has been limited to commodity trade, mainly exports of energy and other raw materials by the Maghreb to China, and imports of consumer and investment goods from China. Bilateral tourism has increased, and China has become more involved in infrastructure projects in the region. However, COVID-19 severely disrupted these activities. The Maghreb trades substantially less with China than with a comparator group of other G20 countries (European Union, India, Japan, United States, United Kingdom), mainly reflecting long distances between the Maghreb countries and China and the lack of historical ties.

Nevertheless, the economic structures of the Maghreb and China are broadly complementary, suggesting their trade could increase, even based on the current structure of comparative advantages. In addition, domestic reforms and active policies could help Maghreb countries strengthen their position in China's global value chains. Efforts by Maghreb governments to improve the business climate and negotiate mutually beneficial trade agreements would help the region's countries attract additional investment, advance technologies, integrate into China's global value chains, and diversify exports into new products and services. The ensuing export expansion to China, in both traditional goods through regular trade channels and new products through global value chains, could be an additional source for export-led growth, resilience, and job creation in the region.

The obstacles to trade relate to macroeconomic vulnerabilities in some Maghreb countries, such as trade barriers (both natural and policy related), low openness to foreign investment, small national markets, and differences in business practices. The regulatory and institutional framework for trade, although improved in recent years, is limited and could be complemented by carefully designed and balanced trade agreements between each Maghreb country and China. Increased cooperation with China is not without risks, including competition from low-cost imports from China and debt sustainability pressures if debt financing from China grows. Potential risks can be mitigated by carefully designed and well-balanced trade liberalization agreements with China that would preserve the integrity of domestic markets in Maghreb countries while prompting local producers to upgrade competitiveness. Also, an improved business environment would be a key factor in replacing debt financing with direct investment.

FINTECH IN CHINA AND AFRICA

Fintech has developed rapidly in both China and Africa in recent decades, because new applications have helped emerging markets and developing countries leapfrog technology. This has helped to bring hundreds of millions of underserved people into financial systems. These experiences can inform other developing countries as they develop their digital and fintech infrastructure. No one-size-fits-all approach exists, of course, and the right path depends—among other things—on a country's digital infrastructure, level of development, and the type of companies that could provide fintech services. China's and Africa's experiences nonetheless display commonalities in their success.

China's fintech industry started with mobile payments for emerging e-commerce firms to facilitate online transactions. The two third-party payment platforms combined—Alipay founded in 2004 (Alibaba Group) and WeChat Pay in 2013 (Tencent Group)—accounted for 90 percent of the market, with each serving over one billion customers in 2023. Although they mainly focused on payments (on- and offline), both companies expanded operations into financial services ranging from wealth management to microlending, digital banking, insurance, and credit scoring. Ant Group, formerly known as Ant Financial (an affiliate company of Alibaba), launched an online money market fund in 2013, which is now one of the largest money market funds in the world. Benefiting from the large number of existing users on their payment platforms, the fintech firms established digital banks serving mostly underserved small firms and consumers—most without credit history—including MYbank of Ant Group, WeBank of Tencent Group, and XWBank of Xiaomi Group. Peer-to-peer platforms were another segment that initially grew rapidly in China; however, a subsequent tightening of regulation led to the demise of the sector.

Both China and some countries in Africa have been developing digital currencies. Starting in 2015, China has been researching and running pilots of a retail central bank digital currency, the e-CNY, gaining valuable experience that can be shared globally. In Africa, the Central Bank of Nigeria officially launched the eNaira in 2021; Ghana has started pilot studies. Given advances in domestic payment systems through fintech, central bank digital currencies could potentially offer significant benefits in cross-border payments (Ricci and others 2024).

Fintech in Africa has been driven by mobile payments, although in Africa mobile network operators rather than third-party payment platforms spearheaded the effort. In particular, the privatization of telecommunication companies has spurred use of new technology in financial systems over the past two decades. Mobile money accounts now exceed those of traditional bank accounts in 17 countries for which data are available, such as in Kenya, South Africa, and Tanzania.

The spectacular fintech revolution in Africa has not only allowed consumers and merchants to make low-cost and instantaneous domestic payments but also allowed governments to better deliver targeted financial support to those in need. Even so, a big untapped potential still exists to foster delivery of financial services such as loans, savings, insurance, and wealth management through fintech. In this regard, insights from China's experience can be useful.

Despite their differences, experiences in the two regions illustrate how countries can leverage technology and foster their fintech development path based on the level of digital infrastructure and development stage. In both China and Africa, surging fintech has been changing the structure of the financial system, forcing traditional financial institutions such as commercial banks to adjust and in many cases to collaborate with fintech companies. And across all countries, it is important to strengthen regulatory frameworks and consumer protection and to address money laundering and cybersecurity risks.

Given that Africa's fintech is still in an early stage of expanding beyond payments, China's experience in fintech for lending, wealth management, and e-commerce might be helpful for African countries. But this will require further investment in digital infrastructure and financial and digital literacy, among other things.

CONCLUSION

As discussed in the previous section, Africa has made remarkable strides across many development metrics, significantly improving life expectancy, literacy, health, and education. With its population expected to double to about 2.5 billion by 2050, the continent's economic performance will play an increasingly crucial role globally. China's engagement with Africa, spanning trade, investment, and financing, has deepened since the latter half of the 20th century and has helped support Africa's economic growth. The relationship between Africa and China will likely continue to evolve, reflecting the ongoing economic development and changing structures in the respective countries, and guided by the interests of both African nations and China.

The chapters that follow examine the evolving Africa–China relationship from multiple economic and financial perspectives, highlighting the importance of policy frameworks, capacity building, and fintech in fostering sustainable development.

REFERENCES

Abdel-Latif, Hany, Wenjie Chen, Michele Fornino, and Henry Rawlings. 2023. "China's Slowing Economy Will Hit Sub-Saharan Africa's Growth." In *Regional Economic Outlook: Sub-Saharan Africa*. Washington, DC: IMF. https://www.imf.org/en/News/Articles/2023/11/09/cf-chinas-slowing-economy-will-hit-sub-saharan-africas-growth.

Acker, Kevin, and Deborah Brautigam. 2021. "Twenty Years of Data on China's Africa Lending." SAIS-CARI Briefing Papers 04/2021, China Africa Research Initiative, School of Advanced International Studies, Johns Hopkins University, Washington, DC.

Chinese Ministry of Finance. 2019. "Debt Sustainability Framework for Participating Countries of the Belt and Road Initiative." April 25. https://view.officeapps.live.com/op/view.aspx?src=http%3A%2F%2Fwjb.mof.gov.cn%2Fywwz_14955%2FCooperation%2Fmulid%2F202011%2FP020201104575791004623.docx&wdOrigin=BROWSELINK.

Dollar, David. 2016. "China's Engagement with Africa: From Natural Resources to Human Resources." John L. Thornton China Center, Brookings Institution, Washington, DC.

Ricci, Luca, Calixte Ahokpossi, Anna Belianska, Khushboo Khandelwal, Sunwoo Lee, Grace Li, Yibin Mu, and others. 2024. "Central Bank Digital Currency and Other Digital Payments in Sub-Saharan Africa: A Regional Survey." IMF Fintech Note. https://www.imf.org/en/Publications/fintech-notes/Issues/2024/03/26/Central-Bank-Digital-Currency-and-Other-Digital-Payments-in-Sub-Saharan-Africa-A-Regional-546859.

Shinn, David H. 2019. "China–Africa Ties in Historical Context." In *China-Africa and an Economic Transformation*, edited by Arkebe Oqubay and Justin Yifu Lin, 61–83. Oxford: Oxford University Press.

State Council Information Office of the People's Republic of China. 2021. "China and Africa in the New Era: A Partnership of Equals." http://www.news.cn/english/2021-11/26/c_1310333813.htm.

CHAPTER 2

Growing Institutional Relationships

Steven Barnett and Xiangming Li

INTRODUCTION

In October 1971, Ethiopian Emperor Haile Selassie made a historic state visit to Beijing.[1] He met with Chairman Mao Zedong and presided over the signing of an economic and technical cooperation agreement between China and Ethiopia. That was the beginning of a new era in China–Africa cooperation.

This chapter reviews China–Africa cooperation, focusing on economic issues. The first section examines the evolution of relations, largely from a Chinese perspective, and thus relies heavily on statements from China's leaders and official documents. The second section, building on the first, describes China's current institutional structure for China–Africa economic relations.

EVOLUTION OF CHINA-AFRICA RELATIONS

The modern China–Africa cooperation dates to the founding of the People's Republic of China in 1949.[2] Soon after the new regime solidified its position, it started to establish diplomatic relations with independent African states in the 1950s, when African countries were gaining independence (Shinn 2019). The depth and breadth of the relations have evolved, as well as the institutional structure that supports the relations.

The authors gratefully acknowledge input from Ms. Ming Ai, deputy director general, International Department, People's Bank of China (PBC), and research support from Yuqing Wang, Chunlin Zheng, Yanyang Tao, and Kaihao Cai.

[1] *New York Times*. 1971. "Haile Selassie of Ethiopia Arrives in China for Visit." October 6, p. 5. https://www.nytimes.com/1971/10/06/archives/haile-selassie-of-ethiopia-arrives-in-china-for-visit.html. Reuters. 1971. "People's Republic of China: Ethiopia's Haile Selassie Given Tumultuous Welcome in Peking." https://reuters.screenocean.com/record/622592.

[2] While the precise commencement of China's involvement with Africa remains a topic of debate, historical records suggest that Chinese envoys and merchandise reached Northern Africa before the second century BC. In addition, the visit of Zheng He, a celebrated Chinese explorer, to East Africa during the Ming Dynasty (1368 and 1644), along with visits from envoys representing East Africa, is well documented in historical literature (Gao 1984).

Notwithstanding its own rapid development, China continues to emphasize that it is still a developing country and describes its relations with Africa as South–South cooperation—a form of mutual assistance between developing countries (Ministry of Foreign Affairs [MOFA] 2015). In what follows, the chapter focuses on institutional aspects of China's economic relations with Africa.

Relations during the 1950s-70s

Since the founding of the People's Republic of China, the government has sought to support African countries in their fight for independence. Chinese Premier Zhou Enlai attended the Bandung Conference with 29 governments of Asian and African nations in 1955. The core principles of the Bandung Conference evolved around political self-determination, mutual respect for sovereignty, nonaggression, noninterference in internal affairs, and equality. Economic relations in the early period reflected that China was still poor and developing. During the first high-level Chinese visit to Africa in 1964, Premier Zhou Enlai announced the following eight principles of Chinese foreign aid:[3]

- Pursuing mutual benefit
- Respecting the recipient's sovereignty and, specifically, not attaching any conditionality to aid
- Favorable lending, with no- or low-interest-rate loans and extension of loan terms when needed
- Improving capacity and economic independence
- Prioritizing projects with low investment and quick returns to help recipient countries to generate revenue
- Using the best Chinese equipment and products, valued at international prices
- Ensuring that technology used could be learned and mastered by locals
- Treating Chinese and local experts equally, with no extra benefits or special amenities for Chinese.

From the beginning, China clearly emphasized mutual benefit as a principle of its relations with Africa. It characterized its economic assistance as focusing on building capacity and self-reliance while stressing the principle of noninterference in each other's internal affairs.

According to China State Council (2011), China's foreign aid to Africa started in 1956, soon after the Bandung Conference. The first large Chinese foreign aid project, iconic in China, was the construction of the Tanzania–Zambia Railway. In 1967, China committed to building this railway, spanning nearly 1,860

[3] In 1963–64, Premier Zhou visited 11 African countries; Guinea received China's first foreign aid, an interest-free loan of renminbi (RMB) 100 million (about $25 million) (Bartke 1975, p. 116). The eight principles can be found at http://fangtan.china.com.cn/zhuanti/2009-03/18/content_17464417.htm.

kilometers, and provided an interest-free loan of RMB 988 million (approximately $406 million) for its realization (https://www.tazara.co.tz).

Relations during the 1980s-90s

In the 1980s, China adjusted its aid policy to support its own transition from a planned to a more market-based economy, which started in 1978. More prominence was given to economic considerations, particularly on efficiency and mutual benefit (Bräutigam 2009; Huang and Liu 2013). The establishment of China–US diplomatic relations in 1979 facilitated this new emphasis. As one of the world's 25 least developed countries, with a per capita income of $208 in the early 1980s, China also had significant internal needs and was itself a large recipient of foreign assistance. The forms of the country's economic cooperation with other developing countries have been expanded beyond interest-free loans (Box 2.1). Technical assistance, managerial cooperation, and joint ventures were also used, and the focus on long-term issues grew.

China stressed that its support for African economic development represented South–South cooperation. In December 1982, Premier Zhao Ziyang, on an 11-country tour of Africa, announced that foreign aid would be guided by four principles: (1) quality and mutual benefit, (2) an emphasis on practical results, (3) diversity in form, and (4) common progress. He did not use the word "aid." He emphasized, instead, "South–South cooperation" and that cooperation could "take a variety of forms, including cooperative production and joint ventures." He noted that the goal of cooperation was to build capacity and promote growth in both China and Africa and that the two sides could complement each other (Lou 2020).

The emphasis on improving the efficiency and effectiveness of aid was also prompted by a 1983 Chinese study, which found that many former Chinese turnkey aid projects built in the 1960s and 1970s in Africa were failing due to poor management and lack of maintenance. Throughout the 1980s and into the 1990s, the country's aid focused on rehabilitating former aid projects. This was sometimes used as compensatory trade,[4] whereby Chinese loans to African companies were used to buy spare parts and equipment that would be paid back from proceeds of product exports (such as cattlehides).

To facilitate China's involvement in managing and rehabilitating these projects, a new policy was issued, which clarified that management cooperation did not constitute a violation of the principle of "no interfering in internal affairs" as perceived previously and, instead, helped recipients "build self-reliance" (another principle of its foreign aid). With the policy change, completed aid projects could hire Chinese experts and managers to improve project sustainability. The country

[4] The country first experienced this as a recipient of support from Japan and other Western economies. The practice can help borrowers constrained by a lack of foreign exchange or collateral.

Box 2.1. Forms of China's External Assistance

Foreign assistance financing includes grants, interest-free loans, and concessional loans (Figure 2.1.1.).

According to the China State Council, "Grants are mainly used to help recipient countries to build hospitals, schools, and low-cost houses, and support well-digging or water-supply projects, and other medium and small projects for social welfare. In addition, grants are used in projects in the fields of human resources development cooperation, technical cooperation, assistance in kind, and emergency humanitarian aid.

"Interest-free loans are mainly used to help recipient countries to construct public facilities and launch projects to improve people's livelihood. The tenure of such loans is usually 20 years, including five years of use, five years of grace, and ten years of repayment. Currently, interest-free loans are mainly provided to developing countries with relatively good economic conditions.

Figure 2.1.1. Average Annual Chinese Foreign Aid Composition
(In billion yuan)

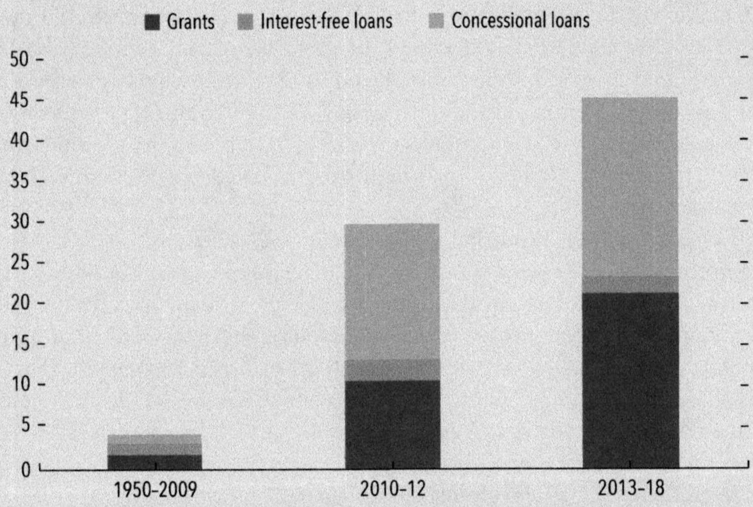

Source: China State Council (2011, 2014, 2021).

"Concessional loans are mainly used to help recipient countries to undertake productive projects generating both economic and social benefits and large and medium-sized infrastructure projects, or to provide complete plant, mechanical and electrical products, technical services, and other materials. Concessional loans are raised by the Export–Import Bank of China on the market, and since the loan interest is lower than the benchmark interest of People's Bank of China, the difference is made up by the

State as financial subsidies. At present [in 2011], the annual interest rate of China's concessional loans is between 2 percent and 3 percent, and the period of repayment is usually 15 to 20 years (including five to seven years of grace). By the end of 2009, China had provided concessional loans to 76 foreign countries, supporting 325 projects, of which 142 had been completed. Of China's concessional loans, 61 percent are used to help developing countries to construct transportation, communication, and electricity infrastructure, and 8.9 percent are used to support the development of energy and resources such as oil and minerals" (China State Council 2011).

Over time, the share of interest-free loans has declined substantially.

China's foreign aid projects are in eight forms: complete projects, goods and materials, technical cooperation, cooperation in human resources development, South–South Cooperation Assistance Fund, medical teams, outbound volunteers, emergency humanitarian aid, and debt relief (China State Council 2021).

also experimented with using Chinese companies to implement aid projects (Bräutigam 2009).[5]

Since 1990, the country has diversified the sources of its financing for external aid, in line with its shift to a more market-based economy. This included providing medium- and long-term low-interest loans and expanded technical training programs. In addition, since the mid-1990s, China's foreign assistance started to put more weight on supporting trade and investment (Bräutigam 2009; Huang and Liu 2013), which coincided with China's ongoing reforms to be more open and integrated with the global economy. The country still emphasized economic cooperation for mutual benefit and fostering development in recipient countries. Foreign assistance, however, was also expected to promote exports, facilitate the import of resources to support China's economic development, and assist its companies in developing abroad as part of the "going-out" strategy. The strategy was first advocated by the government in 1992. As reported by the Export–Import Bank of China (EXIM), "the extension of Chinese Government Concessional Loans has supported the export of products . . . and facilitated Chinese companies' entry into the market of developing countries" (EXIM 2006, p. 21; Kobayashi 2008).

[5] This was made possible by a law passed in 1979 that permits enterprises to invest overseas (the Ministry of Commerce). Since then, Chinese companies have contracted both Chinese aid-financed projects and projects financed by other donors. China's membership in the World Bank and the African Development Bank (AfDB) since 1980 enables its companies to participate in the bidding process for projects funded by these institutions (Bräutigam 2009).

In 1995, China further reformed its aid program to align it with the "market-oriented" principle for use of public money. This drew on the lessons from both China's aid in the 1980s and China's own experiences as an aid recipient. In May 1995, the State Council issued "Decisions Regarding Issues on Reforming Foreign Assistance Program," which included (1) increasing government-subsidized preference loans and grants; (2) promoting joint ventures; (3) combining on-budget government aid, bank loans, and company resources in foreign assistance projects; and (4) stopping new zero-interest-rate loans (Liu 2002).

In 1994, China had established EXIM and the China Development Bank (CDB), two policy banks that became key players in lending to Africa. Following the "Decisions" of 1995, EXIM began to offer concessional loans, for which it received government subsidies. It also raised financing by issuing domestic bonds. Around this time, China also began to use the build–operate–transfer model. By the end of the period, China's trade with Africa started to increase rapidly.

Relations since 2000

The Forum on China–Africa Cooperation (FOCAC), established in October 2000, ushered in a new era of rapid development of economic ties between China and Africa. Bilateral trade expanded rapidly, as did foreign aid (Figures 2.1 and 2.2). The forum's objective is to serve as a consultative platform for diplomatic dialogue and constructive multilateral interactions. It is hosted alternately by China and an African country every three years. China and African countries have pledged to operate within the framework of South–South cooperation and build "a long-term and stable partnership based on equality and mutual benefit" to "deepen dialogue, broaden consensus, continue to harmonize our positions on international affairs and enhance mutual support so as to uphold the legitimate rights and interests of China and African countries" and to facilitate "the establishment of a new international order" (FOCAC 2006).

The forum's broad agenda focuses strongly on trade and development cooperation, particularly in infrastructure. At the opening ceremony of the 2018 Beijing Summit, President Xi Jinping noted: "Since the 2015 FOCAC Johannesburg Summit . . . a large number of railways, highway, airport, port, and other infrastructure projects as well as a number of economic and trade cooperation zones have been built or are under construction. Our cooperation on peace and security, science, education, culture, health, poverty reduction, and people-to-people interactions has deepened" (http://www.xinhuanet.com/english/2018-09/03/c_129946189.htm).

China has used the FOCAC summits to announce new commitments (Table 2.1). During the 2000 FOCAC, it committed to step up development assistance and emphasized trade and investment but made no specific financial commitments (Annex 2.1). In the 2003 FOCAC in Addis Ababa, it committed to forgive the debt of 31 African nations. Although debt forgiveness was featured in subsequent forums, it has been overshadowed by rising financial pledges. In the November 2006 FOCAC, China, for the first time, explicitly committed $10

Figure 2.1. Trade Between China and Africa Has Grown Rapidly Since 2000
(In billions of US dollars)

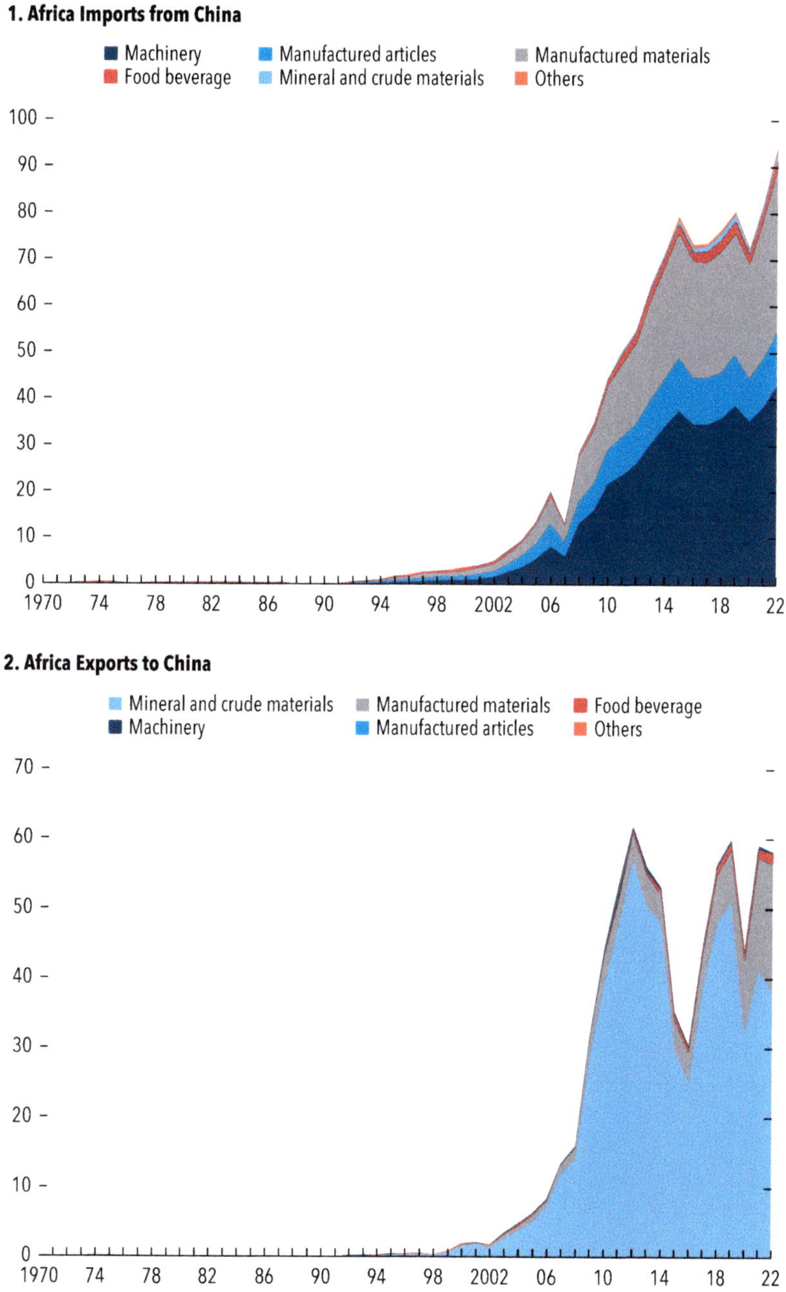

Source: UN Comtrade.

Figure 2.2. China's Foreign Aid Increased Rapidly since 2000, with Africa Receiving the Highest Share

1. China's Foreign Aid

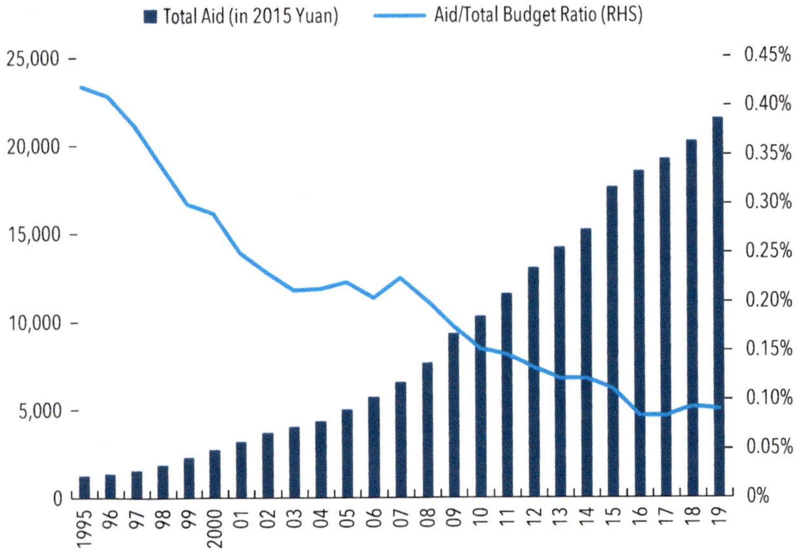

Sources: Kobayashi (2008); CEIC; and IMF staff calculations.
Note: RHS = Right-hand scale.

2. China's Foreign Aid Geographic Distribution

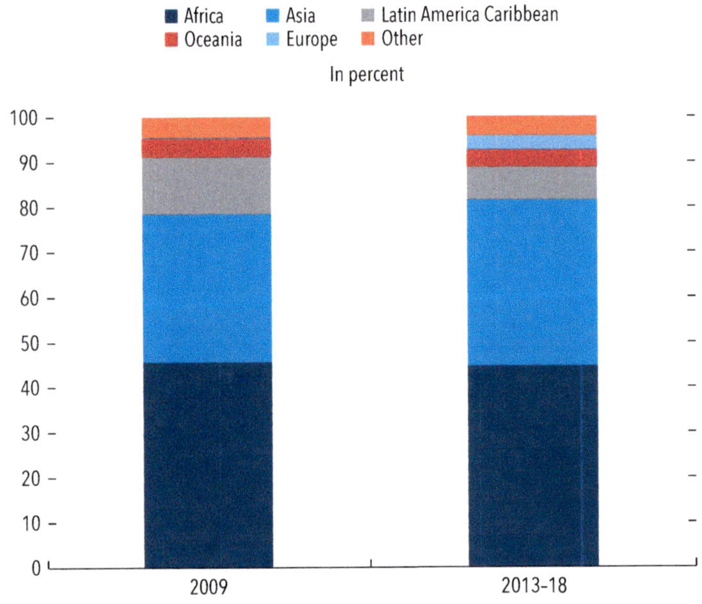

Source: China State Council (2011, 2021).

TABLE 2.1.

China's Financial Pledges at the Forum on China-Africa Cooperation
(In billion US dollars)

	2000	2003	2006	2009	2012	2015	2018	2021	2024[4]
Total	**...**	**...**	**10**	**37**	**25**	**60**	**60**	**40**	**51**
Supported by government	**...**	**...**	**10**	**37**	**25**	**60**	**50**	**30**	**41**
Grants	...	...	...	...	...	5	15	...	12[5]
Concessional loans	...	...	5	11	20	40	20	10[2]	30
Special funds	...	...	5	26	5	15	15	10[3]	...
SDR rechanneling	...	...	...	...	...	...	...	10	...
From private investment announcement[1]	**...**	**...**	**...**	**...**	**...**	**...**	**10**	**10**	**10**
HIPC	1.3	...	...	...	...	...	...	...	...
Cancellation of zero-interest loans to LICs	...	...	yes	yes	...	yes	yes	yes	yes

Source: FOCAC, 2000–24.
Note: FOCAC = Forum on China-Africa Cooperation; HIPC = Heavily Indebted Poor Countries Initiative; LICs = Low-income countries; SDR = Special Drawing Rights ...= not applicable as the category does not exist.
[1] In 2003, FOCAC noted that debt relief promised in 2000 was implemented; 2000–12 called for implementation of debt relief. China also canceled noninterest loans in 2020 to mitigate the COVID-19 effect.
[2] Trade finance.
[3] Credit line to African financial institutions to support small- and medium-sized African enterprises.
[4] Excluding facilities supporting African countries in international organizations.
[5] Announced as aid of various kinds.

billion in loans and special funds for the following three years. Since then, the commitments grew to $60 billion in 2015 and 2018. Notably, from the very start, FOCAC stressed diversity of content in the cooperation and encouraged trade and participation of Chinese enterprises in a continuation of the going-out policy. Besides loans, funds were established for investing in Africa. And in 2018, for the first time, total commitments included expected investment from China's private sector. Subsequently, the total commitment declined to $40 billion during the FOCAC of 2021 and rebounded to $51 billion in the latest FOCAC of 2024.

Over the years, FOCAC action plans have been adapted to changing circumstances. At the beginning, a large portion of Chinese investment was associated with natural resource extraction. Over time, the goals were broadened to manufacturing, including developing export processing zones, processing of primary products, and more recently to green growth and digitalization. At the same time, generating local employment and technology transfer to African counterparts also gained prominence. During President Hu Jintao's visit to four African nations (Mali, Mauritius, Senegal, Tanzania) in February 2009, he pledged to support Africa to face the challenge of the financial crisis and asked Chinese investors to promote greater employment opportunities for local African communities and technology transfer.[6] To promote more balanced trade between China and Africa, tariffs on African goods were reduced steadily, and efforts were made to facilitate finance and trade, such as sponsoring trade exhibitions. In FOCAC 2015, China pledged to implement 50 trade-promotion programs across the continent, aiming to gradually change the composition of trade. The Minister of Trade and Industry in South Africa, Rob Davies, told news agencies at the 2015 FOCAC ministerial meeting that "to grow the trade, we need to move beyond just supplying raw materials, into us also supplying some value-added products" (Independent Online 2015).

More recently, sustainable economic development, managing climate change, and environmental protection have gained prominence, with practical smaller projects gaining traction. The FOCAC 2021 focused on three key areas: green growth, marked by the issuance of the first-ever Declaration on China–Africa Cooperation on Combating Climate Change; state-supported private sector investment; and digital innovation. Besides the $40 million financial pledge and cancellation of interest-free Chinese government loans due by the end of 2021, China pledged an additional 1 billion doses of COVID-19 vaccines, increased concessionality of loans, and the initiation of numerous new assistance projects. These themes were highlighted again in the 2024 FOCAC summit that took place in Beijing, attended by 53 African countries, the African Union Commission, and other forum members, as well as observers from some international and regional organizations. In addition, the 2024 FOCAC summit aimed to promote the participation of African countries in the global industrial production chain, granted zero tariffs on all items to all least-developed countries with diplomatic relations with China (including 33 African countries), and pledged $51 billion in financing for the FOCAC action plan of 2025–28. The concept of "small and beautiful projects," introduced during FOCAC 2021, was once again emphasized.

During this period, China's economic relations with Africa are also guided by China's Africa Policy Papers. The first Africa Policy Paper was issued in 2006 and updated in 2015 (China State Council 2006, MOFA 2015). Over the years, the relationship had advanced from the "new type of strategic partnership" in 2006 to a "comprehensive strategic and cooperative partnership" in the 2015 Africa Policy Paper, emphasizing the economic complementarity of the two sides, linking China's "two centenary goals" with the African Union Agenda 2063 (https://au.int/en/agenda2063) and aspiring to make win–win cooperation a new model for international cooperation. China committed to help Africa overcome the two major bottlenecks constraining its development—backward infrastructure and inadequate professional and skilled personnel—to promote industrialization, agricultural modernization, and regional integration.

In addition, China's relations with Africa are supported by other global initiatives, particularly the Belt and Road Initiative (BRI). As infrastructural

[6] See President Hu Jintao's speech on February 16, 2009 in Dar es Salaam: "Together we will write a new chapter in China–Africa friendship." http://www.chinanews.com.cn/gn/news/2009/02-17/1565573.shtml.

development is a key component of China–Africa cooperation, the FOCAC action plan of 2018–21 is linked explicitly to the BRI, which aims to promote the connectivity of the Asian, European, and African continents and their adjacent seas to promote trade and sustainable development. The 2018 action plan stated that China and Africa "pledge to leverage the strengths of the [FOCAC] Forum . . . in jointly building the Belt and Road," which will help "speed up African regional integration." The FOCAC action plan of 2021–24 continues to promote the use of BRI platforms, including the green and sustainable development standards under the framework of the BRI. Except for Mauritius and Eswatini, all African countries have joined the BRI and, therefore, will benefit from the recently announced funding of 430 billion yuan ($60 billion) at the third BRI forum in October 2023.

China's relationship with Africa is also intricately linked to its broader foreign aid policy. The white paper on foreign aid was initially issued in 2011, with subsequent updates in 2014 and 2021. This document reaffirms China's enduring principles of external assistance, emphasizing equality, mutual trust, and the South–South nature of its engagements. Notably, the 2021 paper shifts the focus from aid to development cooperation, underscoring China's dedication to multilateralism in development cooperation and the promotion of global public goods. It advocates for international cooperation and an expanded role for the private sector, nongovernmental organizations, and various social groups.

Aligned with government support, China's foreign direct investment (FDI) in Africa has witnessed both growth and diversification (see Figures 2.3 and 2.4). During 2003–22, China's accumulated direct investment in Africa surpassed $70.6 billion, establishing China as the fourth-largest source of investment for the continent. Notably, China's new direct investment in Africa amounted to $1.38 billion in the initial four months of 2023, marking a 24 percent year-over-year increase. Presently, over 3,000 Chinese enterprises are actively investing in Africa. Over the decade spanning from 2012 to 2022, Chinese enterprises signed new construction contracts in Africa exceeding $700 billion, with a turnover surpassing $400 billion. In 2022, Chinese enterprises secured contracts valued at $740 million from the

Figure 2.3. Annual Chinese Foreign Direct Investment in Africa
(In millions of US dollars)

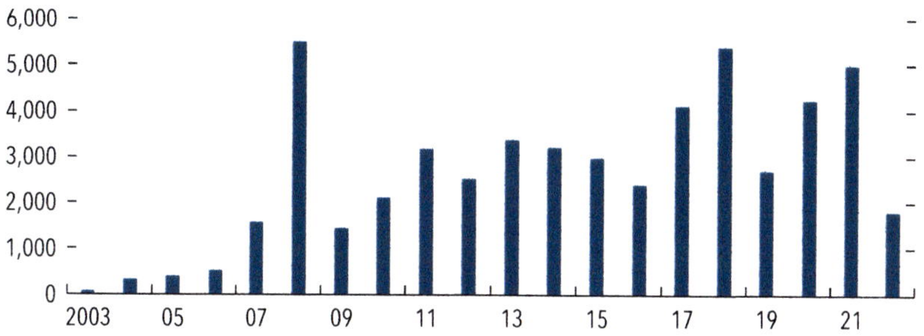

Source: CEIC.

African Development Bank (AfDB), constituting 42 percent of the total and securing the top position. China's contributions to Africa's infrastructure are noteworthy, including the construction of over 6,000 kilometers of railways, 6,000 kilometers of roads, almost 20 ports, and more than 80 large-scale power facilities. In the mining sector, Chinese companies collectively hold less than 7 percent of the continent's total output. However, in strategic mining areas, such as copper production (30 percent) and cobalt production (50 percent), their share is notably larger.

Besides construction and mining, Chinese FDI goes to manufacturing, finance, and business services (Figure 2.4). The China–Africa Entrepreneurs Conference, integrated into the FOCAC since 2013, serves as a pivotal component. Collaboratively, the Ministry of Commerce (MOFCOM) and Chinese embassies have initiated the preparation of the "Guide for Foreign Investment and Cooperation by Country (Region)" for individual countries, facilitating FDI.

It is worth noting that while China's financial assistance to Africa for major infrastructure projects has contributed to the debt burden of African countries, the growth in bilateral borrowing by African countries, including from China, has been comparatively smaller than the escalation in domestic and eurobond borrowing, as illustrated in Figure 2.5.

The deepening connection is evident in the expanding trade relationship. Since 2000, China has imported $1.42 trillion from Africa and exported $1.58 trillion to the continent. Maintaining its position as Africa's primary trading partner from 2012 to 2022, China has consistently bolstered economic ties with the region. The annual trade volume between China and Africa surged by 42 percent,

Figure 2.4. Composition of the Stock of Chinese Foreign Direct Investment in Africa

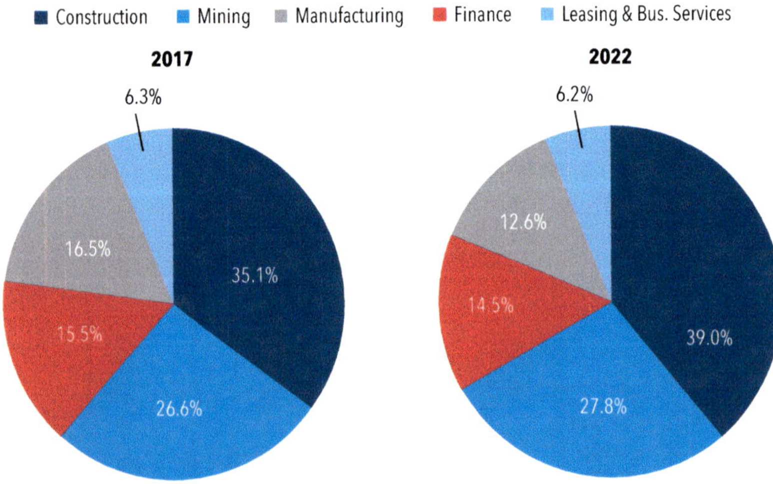

Sources: China's Outward FDI Bulletin, 2017 and 2022 (China Ministry of Commerce, National Bureau of Statistics, and State Administration of Foreign Exchange, 2018 and 2023).

Figure 2.5. Sub-Saharan Africa: Composition of General Government Debt, 2000–22
(Percentage of GDP in Sub-Saharan Africa)

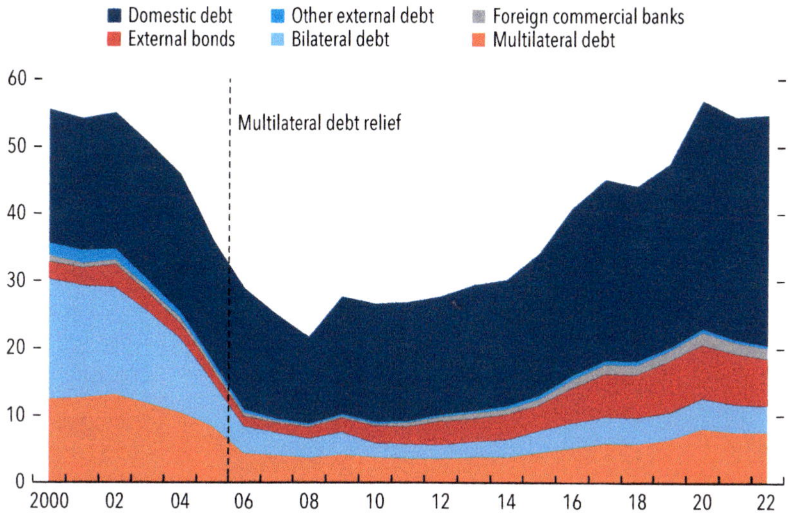

Sources: World Bank, International Debt Statistics; and IMF, World Economic Outlook database.
Note: Excludes Equatorial Guinea, Namibia, Seychelles, and South Sudan due to data availability in the World Bank, International Debt Statistics database.

reaching $282 billion in 2022, marking an 11.1 percent year-over-year increase. This notable figure includes $164.5 billion in exports to Africa and $117.5 billion in imports from the continent. The rising trade volumes underscore the robust and mutually beneficial economic alliance between China and Africa.

CHINA'S INSTITUTIONS FOR INTERNATIONAL COOPERATION

China's engagement with Africa spans numerous domestic and international agencies. This section reviews the domestic agencies involved in lending to Africa and then surveys international organizations that China belongs to that also engage with Africa.

Domestic Institutions

On the domestic front, many central government agencies are involved in Africa, as are many financial and nonfinancial enterprises (Figure 2.6). For government units, ultimately, the Central Committee of the Communist Party of China (CPC) and the State Council have decision-making authority. But below them, many ministries, agencies, and other institutions play a role. This section reviews the roles and responsibilities of these various bodies.

Figure 2.6. China's Institutional Framework for Collaboration with Africa

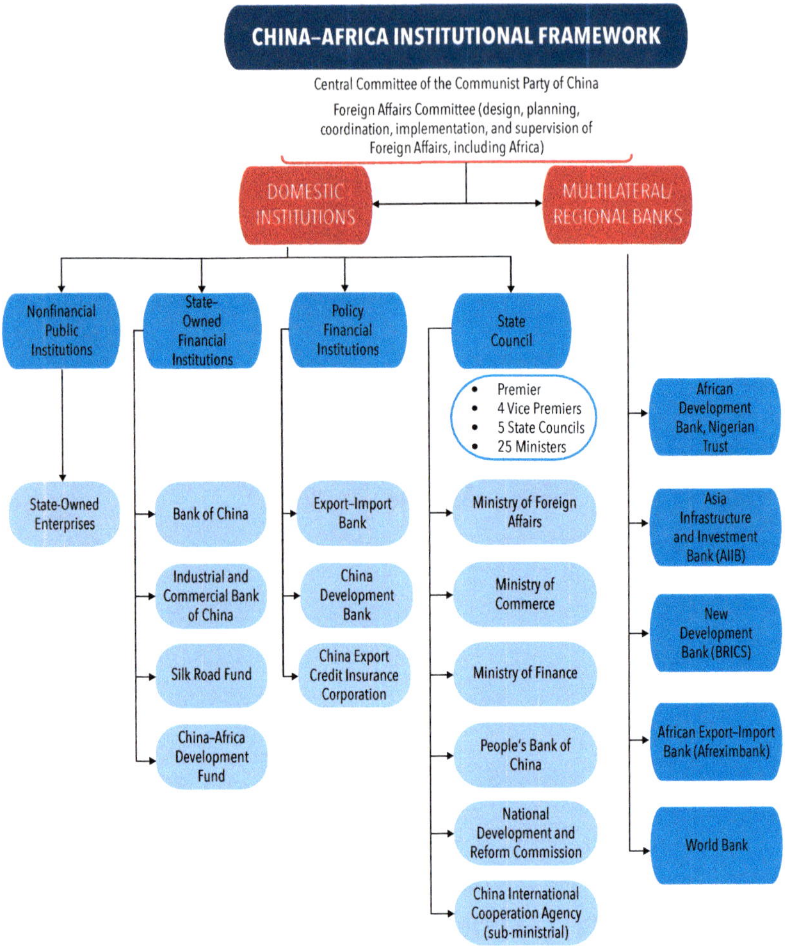

Source: Authors.

Central Government Level

Foreign Affairs Committee, Central Committee of the Communist Party of China

The Central Committee comprises the top leaders of the CPC. Under it, the Foreign Affairs Leading Group exercises general oversight of foreign affairs, including for Africa. In 2018, the group was reorganized into the Foreign Affairs Committee, which was empowered to design, plan, coordinate, implement, and supervise foreign affairs.

The State Council

The State Council is the chief administrative authority. As of early 2025, the council consists of one premier, four vice premiers, three state councilors, and

26 ministers in charge of the council's constituent ministries. Under the unified leadership of the State Council, every ministry is responsible for leading and administering a certain aspect of administrative affairs and exercising specific state administrative powers. In African affairs, the most involved ministries and agencies are the MOFA, MOFCOM, the China International Development Cooperation Agency (CIDCA), the National Development and Reform Commission (NDRC), the Ministry of Finance, and the People's Bank of China (PBC).

Follow-Up Action Committee, FOCAC

As noted previously, in 2000, China and the African countries jointly established FOCAC, and every three years, leaders from China and 53 African countries meet. The meeting concludes with one "declaration" and one "action plan," guiding cooperation between China and Africa for the following three years. Since its establishment, FOCAC has become the most important China–Africa cooperation mechanism.

To implement the action plan, China set up a Follow-up Action Committee, its 36 members representing nearly all the Chinese ministries and entities involved in African affairs (Figure 2.7). The committee is cochaired by the deputy ministers from the Ministries of Foreign Affairs and of Commerce, and the secretariat consists of the MOFA, MOFCOM, Ministry of Finance, Ministry of Culture and Tourism, International Department Central Committee of the CPC, and CIDCA. The general office of the committee's secretariat, responsible for daily work, is in the MOFA, Department of African Affairs.

Ministries and Central Agencies

The Ministry of Foreign Affairs (MOFA)

The MOFA's primary responsibility is diplomatic affairs, including with Africa. Its responsibilities include implementing the government's diplomatic policies, handling relations with foreign leaders, and providing analytical and strategic input on foreign affairs to the government. The ministry also leads all Chinese diplomatic missions abroad.

The Ministry of Commerce (MOFCOM)

MOFCOM plays an important role in China–Africa relations. It is responsible for China's foreign trade, overseas direct investment, and international economic cooperation. For foreign trade, MOFCOM oversees the import and export of commodities and services. This includes responsibility for strategy, policy, and negotiations related to multilateral and bilateral trade and economic cooperation agreements. For foreign investment, it guides China's outward investment and approves Chinese enterprises to invest in and set up overseas establishments (excluding financial companies). In economic cooperation, the ministry guides and monitors overseas project contracting and labor service cooperation. Finally, regarding foreign aid, the establishment of CIDCA reduced MOFCOM's responsibility to either policymaking or project implementation.

Figure 2.7. China FOCAC Follow-Up Action Committee

Sources: Forum on China-Africa Cooperation. http://www.focac.org; authors.

China International Development Cooperation Agency (CIDCA)

In the 2018 reform of party and state institutions, a sub-ministry-level executive agency directly under the State Council was established to integrate China's foreign aid resources. The new agency, CIDCA, is tasked with being the lead agency for China's foreign aid. However, the implementation of foreign aid is still carried out by relevant departments. The reform's aim is to give full play to the role of foreign aid as an important means of major country diplomacy; strengthen the strategic planning, coordination, and management of foreign aid; and better support China's foreign affairs, including the BRI.

China National Development and Reform Commission (NDRC)

The NDRC has broad power over domestic economic issues, which also extends to overseas issues. It is responsible for the comprehensive coordination of major strategic plans, reforms, and projects that span departments, regions, industries, and fields in China. For example, the commission has a leading role in the "Going Global Strategy" and the BRI. Thus, the NDRC also plays an important role in China–Africa relations.

The Ministry of Finance

The Ministry of Finance administers the government budget, which includes the budgets for the Ministry of Foreign Affairs, MOFCOM, and CIDCA. It also takes the lead in the formulation of tariff and import tax policies. The Ministry of Finance undertakes the investor responsibilities of central, state-owned financial capital, which include policy financial institutions such as EXIM, the China Export & Credit Insurance Corporation (SINOSURE), and government investment funds, as discussed in the following section. It also participates on the board of the Asian Infrastructure Investment Bank (AIIB) and New Development Bank (NDB) on behalf of China. The Ministry of Finance also has international exchanges and cooperation in finance and economics, including with African countries.

Other Agencies

The Ministry of Culture and Tourism guides and administers foreign exchanges and promotes culture and tourism. It is a member of the FOCAC Follow-up Action Committee's Secretariat, which reflects the important role of people-to-people exchanges in China–Africa exchanges.

The State-owned Assets Supervision and Administration Commission of the State Council (SASAC) performs the functions of investor on behalf of the central government to manage state-owned enterprises. This includes guiding the enterprises to formulate and implement international business strategies and supervising their overseas investments. The SASAC oversees 98 centrally state-owned enterprises, not including centrally owned financial enterprises, which are under the Ministry of Finance's purview and several other special central enterprises.

Nongovernment Entities

People's Bank of China (PBC)

The PBC has typical central bank responsibilities for formulating and implementing monetary and exchange rate policy. With China and African countries expanding and deepening financial cooperation, the PBC plays a growing role in China–Africa relations. It holds and manages international foreign exchange reserves, which are a key source of capital for outward investment funds such as the Silk Road Fund. It formulates and implements the cross-border RMB business system, promotes the cross-border and international use of RMB, and enhances monetary cooperation between central banks. As of the end of 2024, the PBC has signed bilateral swap agreements totaling RMB 80.6 billion with more than 30 foreign central banks, including with South Africa, Nigeria, and Mauritius (http://www.pbc.gov.cn/huobizhengceersi/214481/5546061/5575771/index.html). It also participates on the board of the AfDB.

Policy Financial Institutions

EXIM, CDB, and SINOSURE are the three main policy financial institutions of China involved in international economic and commercial cooperation. They are all state-funded and state-owned financial institutions directly under the leadership of the State Council. EXIM and SINOSURE are established to support China's foreign trade, investment, and international economic cooperation. CDB provides medium- to long-term financing facilities that serve China's major long-term economic and social development strategies. But among the country's strategies of going global and the BRI, CDB also plays a key role. EXIM, CDB, and SINOSURE operate according to market principles and are responsible for their own profit and loss.

The ownership structures of EXIM, CDB, and SINOSURE differ. For EXIM, the Ministry of Finance owns 11 percent and Buttonwood Investment the remaining 89 percent. Buttonwood Investment, in turn, is owned by the State Administration of Foreign Exchange. CDB is owned by the Ministry of Finance (37 percent), Central Huijin Investment Co., Ltd. (35 percent), Buttonwood Investment (27 percent), and the National Council for Social Security Fund (SSF) (2 percent). For SINOSURE, Central Huijin Investment Co., Ltd. owns 74 percent and Buttonwood Investment 26 percent.

EXIM is the only institution considered official bilateral lender and designated to implement the Chinese Government Concessional Loan and Preferential Export Buyer's Credit. By the end of 2023, its concessional business had covered more than 90 countries in the Association of Southeast Asian Nations, South Asia, Central Asia, West Asia, Africa, Latin America, Central and Eastern Europe, and the Pacific island countries. At the end of 2023, EXIM assets totaled RMB 6.4 trillion. Of this, the outstanding balance of foreign trade loans was RMB 3.0 trillion, overseas investment loans were RMB 0.2 trillion, and international cooperation loans and loans for supporting greater openness were RMB 2.3 trillion (EXIM 2024). Such a loan scale makes EXIM China's most important lender in this market. Foreign trade loans are provided to its clients to support trade of goods, labor, and technology between China and overseas markets. Overseas investment loans are provided to Chinese-funded companies (registered in China or overseas) to support their investment in the overseas market. International cooperation loans are provided to clients to support their cooperation with foreign governments, financial institutions, and companies with sovereign guarantees. The loans are also provided to Chinese companies for overseas contracting projects.

EXIM also has a 20 percent stake in the China–Africa Fund for Industrial Cooperation. At the FOCAC Johannesburg Summit in December 2015, President Xi announced the establishment of the first batch of $10 billion for China–Africa Fund for Industrial Cooperation. It is a medium- and long-term development investment fund and cooperates with domestic and foreign enterprises and financial institutions to invest in market-oriented manufacturing and infrastructure projects. It can invest through equity or debt.

CDB is the world's largest development finance institution but is more focused on domestic lending. By the end of 2023, CDB assets were RMB 18.7 trillion (CDB 2024), about three times of EXIM. However, international lending accounts for a small share of CDB's activities and stood at about $287 billion at the end of 2015 (https://www.cdb.com.cn/English/ywgl/xdyw/gjhzyw), about 10 percent of its assets. CDB also participated in the establishment of government investment funds, including the Silk Road Fund (CDB has 5 percent of the capital). CDB wholly owns the China–Africa Development Fund, which is established to support Chinese enterprises investing in Africa and developing the African market. By 2023, the China–Africa Development Fund had completed decisions on $7.3 billion of investments in 39 African countries.

SINOSURE's main products and services include medium- and long-term export credit insurance, overseas investment insurance, short-term export credit insurance, domestic trade credit insurance, bonds and guarantees, and reinsurance related to export credit insurance, accounts receivable management, and information consultation services. By the end of 2021, SINOSURE had provided credit insurance and related services to more than 240,000 enterprises, paid compensation of $17.84 billion to enterprises, and led more than 300 banks in raising more than RMB 4 trillion for export enterprises (https://eng.yidaiyilu.gov.cn/z/230720-2/index.shtml).

In addition, Silk Road Fund is committed to promoting high-quality development of the BRI. Its investments span key BRI regions, including North Africa, and a wide spectrum of fields such as infrastructure, energy and resources, industrial cooperation, financial cooperation, and sustainable development. The State Administration of Foreign Exchange established the SiYuan Investment Co., Ltd. in early 2019 (https://www.cmcapital.com.cn/list/712). It provides professional and multilevel investment and financing support to international cooperation projects in Africa and Latin America, including managing the China–LAC Industrial Cooperation Investment Fund and the China–Africa Fund for Industrial Cooperation.

Commercial Banks

The two large state-owned commercial banks most involved in overseas lending are the Bank of China (assets of $4.8 trillion) and the Industrial and Commercial Bank of China ($6.6 trillion) at the end of June 2024 (Bank of China 2024; Industrial and Commercial Bank of China 2024). The Bank of China's 546 overseas institutions cover 64 countries and regions in the world, including 44 countries along the BRI. The Industrial and Commercial Bank of China has 410 overseas branches in 49 countries and regions in the world and, in 2008, took a 20 percent stake (with a $5.5 billion investment) in the South Africa Standard Bank.

Other State-Owned Enterprises

State-owned enterprises have been a major force in China's overseas investments. By the end of 2020, they accounted for 46 percent of the total stock of the country's outbound nonfinancial direct investment (https://www.gov.cn/xinwen/2021-09/29/content_5639984.htm). State-owned enterprises can make their own decisions based on cost–benefit analysis to invest overseas. But the investment should be in line with the state provisions and the requirements of the Assets Supervision and Administration Committee. The NDRC, MOFCOM, and the PBC set regulations over outbound investment, which apply to state-owned enterprises and private firms. The regulations have been simplified and relaxed in recent years. The current main limitation relates to investment in sensitive countries, regions, or industries.

Multilateral Organizations

China's engagement with both multilateral and bilateral development agencies has undergone significant expansion over time. Its tripartite projects with international organizations trace back to the 1980s and have since grown through co-financing initiatives and trust funds within international bodies, notably the United Nations Fund for South–South Cooperation. These collaborations aim to support sustainable development, poverty reduction, and environmental protection. Beyond this, China has extended its tripartite cooperation programs to include bilateral donors such as Australia, France, Portugal, Switzerland, the United Kingdom, and the United States, as well as philanthropic organizations like the Bill & Melinda Gates Foundation (China State Council 2021).

In addition to joining existing multilateral financial institutions, China took the lead in establishing AIIB and NDB in 2016, both headquartered within its borders. These two multilateral financial institutions focus on assisting emerging economies and developing countries in mobilizing resources for infrastructure and sustainable development projects. This section provides a summary of China's involvement with several multilateral financial institutions pertinent to African countries.

African Development Bank (AfDB)

The AfDB Group seeks to spur sustainable economic development and social progress in its regional member countries and comprises the AfDB (founded in 1964), the African Development Fund (ADF), and the Nigeria Trust Fund.

China has been actively involved with AfDB for many decades. It joined both the ADF and AfDB as a nonregional member country in 1985. As of the end of 2023, China ranked 10th in voting power—with a 1.3 percent share—among the 27 Non-Regional Member Countries. China's share of subscribed capital was also 1.3 percent, with paid-in capital in the unit of account 93 million ($123 million) and callable capital in the unit of account $1756 million ($2300 million).[7]

It has supported AfDB's concessional lending. Concessional lending is financed through the ADF, which is usually replenished every three years through donor contributions. There have been 15 replenishments through the end of 2022[8] (ADF-1 to ADF-15). China's total contributions to ADF replenishments amounted to unit of account 688 million ($951 million), which is 2 percent of the total share.

Other lending agencies in China have also partnered with the AfDB. EXIM signed a memorandum of understanding with the AfDB in 2008; CDB in 2008; and the Agricultural Bank of China in 2011. These memorandums of understanding promote co-financing, knowledge sharing, and joint analytical work in trade finance, the private sector, agribusiness, and clean energy.

---

[7] The unit of account of the AfDB is equal to one special drawing right of the International Monetary Fund (IMF) or any unit adopted for the same purpose by the IMF. The conversion rate in 2019 was 1 unit of account to $1.38.

[8] ADF-15 covers 2020–22.

In 2014, China established the Africa Growing Together Fund (AGTF) with the AfDB Group. AGTF is a $2 billion facility sponsored by the PBC and administered by the AfDB. The money is to be provided over a 10-year period and to be used alongside the AfDB's own resources to support development projects. By the end of 2023, the total financing from AGTF had reached $1.73 billion.

Asian Infrastructure Investment Bank (AIIB)

AIIB is a multilateral development bank with a mission to improve social and economic outcomes in Asia. It began operations in 2016 and now has 110 approved members from around the world as of the end of 2024, of which 21 are from Africa. AIIB's approved African members are responsible for over 60 percent of Africa's gross domestic product and represent over 46 percent of Africa's population.

China is the largest shareholder in AIIB. It holds nearly 31 percent of the subscribed capital (equivalent to about $30 billion). Voting power largely depends on capital share, so China also has the largest share of votes (at 26.6 percent), giving it effective veto power over decisions that require a 75 percent majority, such as changes to AIIB's capital base or the board of directors. Loans, however, require only a simple majority.

As a multilateral development bank committed to financially sustainable lending practices, the bank offers African members access to affordable capital and infrastructure expertise to help address Africa's infrastructure financing gap. By the end of 2022, AIIB had projects in Egypt (five projects totaling $1280 million), Côte d'Ivoire (one project of $100 million), and Rwanda (two projects totaling $200 million).

AIIB also collaborates with other multilateral banks. It signed a memorandum of understanding with the AfDB to enhance collaboration on sustainable economic development in April 2018. The mandates and comparative advantages of the two institutions converge around infrastructure development, particularly energy and power, transportation, and communication. These key activity areas will provide a framework to foster collaboration in developing programs, co-financing, and other forms of financial assistance, knowledge, and staff exchange.

New Development Bank (NDB)

NDB is a multilateral development bank established by Brazil, Russia, India, China, and South Africa (so-called BRICS) in 2014, and it became fully operational in February 2016. It is headquartered in Shanghai and has a regional office in Johannesburg, South Africa. The initial authorized capital is $100 billion, of which $50 billion has been subscribed equally by the initial five founding members (Brazil, China, India, Russian Federation, and South Africa). By March 2023, Bangladesh, Egypt, and the United Arab Emirates had joined with 2–3 percent of share. Meanwhile, approved projects in South Africa total $5 billion (New Development Bank Investor Presentation, August 2023 [https://www.ndb.int/wp-content/uploads/2023/04/Investor-Presentation_2023.pdf]). The projects focused on infrastructure and sustainable development sectors like clean energy, transportation, environmental protection, and public health.

NDB also collaborates with the AfDB. In October 2019, it signed a memorandum of understanding with it to jointly identify, prepare, and co-finance projects in countries of mutual interest. Projects to be targeted cut across clean energy, transport infrastructure, irrigation, water resource management and sanitation, sustainable urban development, and economic cooperation and integration.

Also, as a member of the African Export–Import Bank, China contributes to trade financing and as an important shareholder in the World Bank; China supports the bank's activities in the region.

CONCLUSION

China's economic involvement with Africa spans several decades, evolving in tandem with its own development trajectory. While the forms of this engagement have shifted over time, the emphasis on mutual benefits and a South–South orientation has been a constant.

The evolution reflects insights gained from its external aid program and China's own experiences with foreign assistance during its transition to a market economy. Initially, financial support primarily took the form of interest-free loans, exemplified by the funding of the Tanzania–Zambia Railway in the late 1960s. This has been broadened to encompass concessional loans while the share of grants also grew relative to interest-free loans. The establishment of the China Exim Bank in the 1990s marked a pivotal moment, introducing concessional loans that further supported China's heightened focus on promoting trade with Africa.

Since the 2000s, the volume of China's assistance to Africa has seen significant growth, bolstered by the establishment of FOCAC. Gradually, Chinese investment has broadened from natural resource extraction to manufacturing, including developing export processing zones, processing of primary products, and more recently to green growth and digitalization as reflected in the FOCAC action plans. Generating local employment and technology transfer to African counterparts has also gained prominence. In addition, global initiatives such as the BRI contribute to enhancing China–Africa cooperation, particularly in the realm of infrastructural development.

Regarding China's institutional structure, its relations with Africa involve various government ministries and agencies, government policy banks, commercial banks, and both private and state-owned companies. China's participation in numerous multilateral institutions further underscores its commitment to engaging with Africa on multiple fronts.

ANNEX 2.1.

CHRONICLE OF THE FORUM ON CHINA-AFRICA COOPERATION

The First Ministerial Conference (Beijing, October 12-14, 2000)

Attendees of the First Ministerial Conference included President Jiang Zemin, four presidents from Africa, more than 80 ministers from China and 44 African countries, representatives of 17 regional and international organizations, and people from business communities in China and Africa. The conference aimed to foster a new, stable, and long-term partnership based on equality and mutual benefit. It also aimed to promote political dialogue and economic cooperation. The Forum on China–Africa Cooperation (FOCAC) was designed to be consistent with the Five Principles of Peaceful Coexistence that underpin China's foreign policy, including participants' recognition of a one-China policy.

Participating countries characterized the cooperation as essential for influencing the establishment of a new world order to overcome the perceived bias against developing countries, which were facing "more challenges and risks than opportunities" in the process of increased globalization. It envisaged that enhanced cooperation would be wide-ranging and include trade, investment, agriculture, transportation, medical care, extraction of natural resources, and financing. Specifically, the cooperation:

- Stressed equality and mutual benefit; it could take a diversity of forms and content, aim to strengthen existing bilateral consultation mechanisms, increase high-level visits and dialogue, and promote private sector exchanges.
- Encouraged preferential market access for products from African countries into China to move toward balanced and enhanced trade; and encouraged Chinese enterprises to give preference to the import of African products in light of market conditions.
- Noted that China's government would provide development assistance to African countries within the framework of South–South cooperation in the form of grants, concessional loans, and interest-free loans.
- Called for trade and investment promotion to gradually play a leading role in the China–Africa economic partnership.
    - The Chinese side would set aside special funds to support and encourage investment by well-established Chinese enterprises in Africa to set up joint ventures to build infrastructure, transfer technologies, promote and diversify local industries, and generate employment.
    - The Chinese side agreed to share with African countries its experience in investment promotion relating to the establishment and management of free and special economic zones.

    - The Chinese side would also consider accepting various forms of payment, such as payment in kind, to ease African countries' financial burden and help increase their exports to China.
    - A China–Africa Joint Business Council and China–Africa Products Exhibition Centre were established to promote bilateral trade and to facilitate African products accessing the Chinese market.
- Increased financial cooperation, including parallel and co-financing arrangements and cooperation with multilateral financial institutions.
- Committed China to provide debt relief and cancellation amounting to RMB 10 billion to the heavily indebted poor countries and least developed countries in Africa in the following two years.
- Enhanced cooperation in natural resources exploration based on the principle of mutually benefit and sound environmental practices.
- Promoted cooperation in other areas, including health care, agriculture, education and training, environmental management, and arms control. In particular, China committed to grant more scholarships to African students to study in China, continue to send teachers to Africa to help local institutions of higher learning, and establish an African Human Resources Development Fund.

The Second FOCAC Ministerial Meeting (Addis Ababa, Ethiopia, December 15-16, 2003)

Chaired by Chinese Premier Wen Jiabao, the meeting was attended by six African presidents and high-level officials from most African countries and the African Union (AU). China committed to:

- Continue to increase support to Africa.
- Train 10,000 Africans in three years, enhance medical assistance, and provide technical support on agriculture.
- Open market and eliminate tariffs on some products from underdeveloped African countries.
- Expand tourism cooperation with Africa and increase cultural exchange.

The first "China–Africa Entrepreneurs Conference" took place in parallel, with more than 500 entrepreneurs in attendance and contracts of $1 billion signed.

The Beijing Summit and the Third Ministerial Conference (November 3-5, 2006)

President Hu Jintao, heads of government from 35 African countries, and senior officials from 48 African countries and the AU participated. The main commitments by China included the following:

- Double Chinese assistance to Africa by 2009 from the 2006 level.
- Provide $3 billion in preferential loans and $2 billion in preferential buyer credits to Africa over the following three years.

- Establish a China–Africa Development Fund, valued at $5 billion, to encourage Chinese companies to invest in Africa.
- Build an African Unity conference center in Ethiopia to assist in advancing African unity.
- Further cancel debt, specifically the interest-free loans due by 2005 of heavily indebted poor countries.
- Expand from 190 to 440 the number of export products receiving zero-tariff treatment.
- Establish five new trade and economic cooperation zones in Africa.
- Double scholarships to African students by 2009 (to 4,000 persons), build 100 rural schools, open 23 Confucius Institutes, and train 15,000 African professionals.
- Establish 10 agricultural technology demonstration centers, send 100 senior experts, and build 30 hospitals and 30 malaria-prevention centers; strengthen cooperation within the framework of the Special Program for Food Security of the Food and Agriculture Organization (FAO) of the United Nations.
- Collaborate in energy and resources for mutual benefit.

The Fourth Ministerial Conference (Sharm El-Sheikh, Egypt, November 8-9, 2009)

Chinese Premier Wen Jiabao, Egyptian President Hosni Mubarak, other heads of state and senior officials from 49 African countries, and officials of the AU attended. The conference explored the theme "Deepening the New Type of China–Africa Strategic Partnership for Sustainable Development." China made the following promises (FOCAC 2009):

- Provide $10 billion in concessional loans to African countries.
- Increase the size of China–Africa Development Fund to $30 billion to support Chinese companies' investment in Africa and support Chinese financial institutions in setting up a special loan of $1 billion for small- and medium-sized African businesses.
- Further cancel debt for heavily indebted poor countries and least developed countries in Africa having diplomatic relations with China, interest-free government loans due to mature by the end of 2009.
- Contribute $30 million to trust fund to support South–South cooperation under United Nations FAO's food security framework, send 50 agricultural technician delegations, build 20 additional agricultural technology demonstration centers, and train 2,000 agricultural technicians in the next three years.
- Build clean energy projects in Africa; carry out joint scientific and technological demonstration projects with Africa; train agricultural technology personnel for Africa; and offer assistance on medical care, health, human resources development, and education (including $1.5 million to support training of nurses).

The Fifth Ministerial Conference (Beijing, China, July 19-20, 2012)

Ministers in charge of foreign affairs and economic cooperation from 50 African countries attended. The meeting developed a plan to strengthen relations with the AU, supporting regional integration and sustainable development. The plan emphasized the importance of agriculture and food security. It also considered the need to establish a China–Africa energy forum and enhanced capacity for improving energy production and efficient resource use. Chinese commitments were as follows (FOCAC 2012):

- Provide $20 billion in credit to African countries for developing infrastructure, agriculture, manufacturing, and small- and medium-sized enterprises; gradually scale up China–Africa Development Fund to $5 billion.
- Increase assistance in agriculture, including through sending more agro-technology teams, stepping up training, building technology demonstration centers, and cooperating with the FAO.
- Prioritize infrastructure in the cooperation, including transnational and trans-regional infrastructure development, and continue to support development of overseas business cooperation zones.
- The two sides highlighted once again the significance of promoting balanced development of China–Africa trade. The Chinese side would actively extend aid-for-trade to African countries, provide technical support for the intensive processing of African agro-produce and industrial raw materials, and further open Chinese market to African countries by phasing in zero tariff to 97 percent of all tariff items from the least developed countries in Africa that have diplomatic relations with China.
- Support the currency swap cooperation with African central banks and encourage local currencies for trade and investment settlement; support Chinese financial institutions to lend in RMB in Africa.
- Deepen cooperation with the AU and African countries and launch the "Initiative on China–Africa Cooperative Partnership for Peace and Security."
- Cooperate on climate change issues, scaling up assistance and training to Africa in disaster prevention and reduction and environment management. Help African countries enhance meteorological infrastructure and forest protection. The two sides will explore a consultation mechanism on climate change, actively advance cooperation in clean energy and renewable resources projects for sustainable development.
- Implement the "African Talents Program" to train 30,000 personnel in various sectors, provide 18,000 scholarships, and build cultural and vocational training facilities.
- Deepen medical and health cooperation, send 1,500 medical personnel to Africa, and continue to carry out the "Brightness Action" campaign to provide free treatment for cataract patients. Help provide safe drinking water.

- Boost people-to-people friendship and promote exchanges. Set up a "China–Africa Press Exchange Center" in China to encourage exchanges and visits between Chinese and African media, and sponsor 100 programs for research, exchange, and cooperation by academic institutions and scholars of the two sides.

The Johannesburg Summit and the Sixth Ministerial Conference (December 3-5, 2015)

Cochaired by Chinese President Xi Jinping and South African President Jacob Zuma, the forum's theme was "Africa–China Progressing Together: Win-Win Cooperation." Heads of states, senior officials from 50 African states, and the chairperson of the African Union Commission participated. President Xi pledged to implement "10 major cooperation plans," covering industrialization, agricultural modernization, infrastructure, finance, green development, trade and investment facilitation, poverty reduction, public health, cultural and people-to-people exchanges, and peace and security. Key commitments included the following:

- Provide $60 billion in funding support:
    - $5 billion of grants and interest-free loans
    - $35 billion of preferential loans and export credit on favorable terms
    - $5 billion of additional capital for the China–Africa Development Fund
    - $5 billion additional funding for the "Special Loan for the Development of African SMEs" fund
    - $10 billion in capital for a new China–Africa production capacity cooperation fund
- Exempt the outstanding intergovernmental interest-free loans due by the end of 2015 owed by the least developed, landlocked, and small island developing countries in Africa.
- Increase China's stock of direct investment in Africa to $100 billion by 2020 from $32.4 billion in 2014.
- Provide a total of $60 million in aid to the AU to improve Africa's peacekeeping ability and $156 million of emergency food aid to countries hit by El Niño.
- Continue to support Africa in agricultural development and food security, including by sending 30 expert teams, helping African countries develop water conservancy and irrigation projects, and encouraging and supporting Chinese enterprises to invest in agriculture in Africa.
- Support Africa to build industrial capacity, as well as develop and operate special economic zones. Encourage Chinese businesses and financial institutions to expand investment, including through public-private partnership and build–operate–transfer, particularly in infrastructure; cooperate in information and communication technology, thereby helping African countries to build "smart cities."

- Cooperate in the exploitation of resources, enhancing African countries' capacity for intensive processing of energy and natural resource products, raising local employment while protecting the local environment.
- Elevate the China–Africa trade volume to $400 billion in 2020 from $220 billion in 2014, support the establishment of logistics centers, and implement 50 trade-promotion assistant programs. Continue to facilitate travel and tourism between China and Africa.
- Encourage both Chinese and African enterprises to invest and trade in local currencies.
- Continue to send medical teams to Africa and train doctors, nurses, public health workers, and administrative personnel for African countries.
- Offer 2,000 degree-education opportunities in China and 30,000 government scholarships to African countries, establish regional education centers and colleges in Africa and train 200,000 local African vocational and technical personnel, and provide Africa with 40,000 training opportunities in China.
- Introduce the "China–Africa Green Envoys Program" for wildlife protection, water resources management, and rehabilitation of disused mines. Provide 20 billion RMB to fund the China South–South Cooperation Fund to support other developing countries to combat climate change and improve cooperation in disaster mitigation and relief.

The 2018 Beijing Summit and the Seventh Ministerial Conference (September 2–4, 2018)

Heads of state and senior officials from 53 African countries and the chairperson of the AU participated. Mr. Xi noted that China (the largest developing country) and Africa (the continent with the most developing countries) should seize the opportunity created by the complementarity and the BRI to strengthen multidimensional, wide-ranging, and in-depth cooperation for mutual benefit and common development. The theme of the forum was "China and Africa: Toward an Even Stronger Community with a Shared Future through Win-Win Cooperation." Mr. Xi launched eight major initiatives on (1) industrial development, (2) infrastructure connectivity, (3) trade facilitation, (4) green development, (5) capacity-building, (6) health care, (7) people-to-people exchange, and (8) peace and security. Key commitments were as follows (FOCAC 2018):

- Provide financial support of $60 billion:
  - $20 billion in new loans
  - $15 billion in foreign aid (grants, interest-free loans, and concessional loans)
  - $5 billion special fund for financing imports from Africa
  - $10 billion special fund for development financing
  - At least $10 billion of investment by Chinese companies

- Cancel interest-free Chinese government loans maturing by the end of 2018 for Africa's least developed countries that have diplomatic relations with China.
- Promote cooperation on agricultural modernization, including by implementing 50 agricultural assistance programs, providing RMB 1 billion of emergency humanitarian food assistance, sending 500 senior agriculture experts, setting up a China–AU Agriculture Cooperation Commission, holding regular China–Africa Agriculture Cooperation Forums, and establishing a China–Africa Research Center for the Development of Green Agriculture.
- Support industrial capacity cooperation to boost the industrialization of Africa in line with the BRI and the Agenda 2063, including the development of special economic zones and industrial parks and basic vocational training for African workforce.
- Jointly formulate an infrastructure cooperation plan with the AU, focusing on energy, transport, information, telecommunications, and cross-border water resources; support Africa in developing the Single African Air Transport Market; and strengthen exchanges and cooperation between seaports.
- Advance cooperation in new technologies, including cloud computing, big data, the mobile internet, "smart cities," and cybersecurity.
- Enhance cooperation on energy and resources, establishing a China–Africa Energy Cooperation Center in Africa and developing renewable energy, mainly solar energy in Africa.
- Expand the use of local currencies in bilateral trade, investment, and financing, and support RMB settlement in Africa. China would facilitate the issuance of Panda bonds by African sovereigns and facilitate African countries holding RMB as international reserves.
- Continue to promote tourism.
- Continue to scale up medical assistance to African countries and upgrade 50 medical and health aid programs for Africa.
- Implement the China–Africa cultural and people-to-people cooperation plan, carrying out a tailor-made program to train 1,000 high-caliber Africans; provide Africa with 50,000 government scholarships and 50,000 training opportunities for seminars and workshops; and train more professionals in a variety of disciplines.
- Implement the China–Africa green development policy, including 50 projects for green development and ecological and environmental protection in Africa, forest management, and wildlife protection. Continue to provide meteorological satellite data and remote-sensing application equipment and training; cooperate on strengthening drought resistance, emergency response, and post-disaster reconstruction.
- Jointly establish a China–Africa media cooperation network and continue to run the China–Africa Press Exchange Center program.

The Eighth Ministerial Conference of the Forum on China-Africa Cooperation (FOCAC) in Dakar (November 29-30, 2021)[9]

China signaled an increased focus on three areas during the FOCAC 2021 (November 29–30) in Dakar: green growth with the first-ever Declaration on China–Africa Cooperation on Combating Climate Change, state-supported private sector investment, and digital innovation. The theme was "Deepen China–Africa Partnership and Promote Sustainable Development to Build a China–Africa Community with a Shared Future in the New Era." China pledged an additional 1 billion doses of COVID-19 vaccines to Africa, $40 billion of new financing, cancellation of interest-free Chinese government loans due as of the end of 2021, increased concessionality of its loans, and many new assistance projects. The action plan, which is in support of the China–Africa Cooperation Vision 2035, was also adopted during the forum. The announced financial package in this FOCAC was lower than the previous two forums. However, the action plan has more concrete assistance projects and intends to increase concessionality of loans, which are for trade financing and lending to small and medium enterprises (SMEs). The forum was attended by 55 members (53 African countries plus the AU and China).

A key output was the Dakar Action Plan, which outlined the following nine China–Africa Cooperation Programs:

1. Medical and health. China is committed to delivering an additional 1 billion doses of COVID-19 vaccine to Africa, including 600 million donated doses and 400 million doses to be jointly produced by Chinese companies and African countries. In addition, China will undertake 10 medical and health assistance projects for African countries and send 1,500 medical personnel and public health experts to Africa.
2. Agriculture, food security, and safety. China will open "green lanes" for African agricultural exports to China, send 500 agricultural experts to Africa, and strengthen support in sustainable agriculture, water-saving irrigation, grain loss reduction, and climate response in agriculture.
3. Trade-promotion program. This includes raising total imports from Africa to $300 billion in the next three years, including through a $10 billion trade financing facility for African exports, "green lanes" mentioned earlier, further expanding zero-tariff coverage, and building in China a trade and economic cooperation zone and a China–Africa industrial park for Belt and Road cooperation. It will also explore the possibility of establishing e-commerce hubs in Africa dedicated to African exports to China.
4. Investment promotion program. Chinese enterprises will be encouraged to invest in medium- and high-technology manufacturing, energy and

[9] Thanks to Yibin Mu for this summary.

electricity, digital infrastructure development, digital economy, and aviation and aerospace sectors, including through a platform for China–Africa private investment promotion. China will encourage its businesses to invest no less than $10 billion in Africa in the next three years. In addition, China will implement 10 connectivity assistance projects for Africa, in support of African Continental Free Trade Area, and encourage the participation of Chinese enterprises, including through public-private partnerships and trilateral and multilateral cooperation. It will also provide credit facilities of $10 billion to African financial institutions to support African SMEs.

5. Other financial commitments include increasing the concessionality of its loans; canceling interest-free loan payments to the Chinese government due by the end of 2021; welcoming Panda bond issuance by eligible African sovereign, multilateral, and financial institutions; implementing the G20 debt-related initiatives in support of African countries in difficulties; channeling to African countries $10 billion from its share of the IMF's new special drawing rights allocation (1/4 of China's total new allocation), and establishing a China–Africa cross-border RMB center. African countries commended China for its full implementation of the G20 Debt Service Suspension Initiative.
6. The digital innovation program. China commits to 10 digital economy assistance projects for Africa, setting up centers for China–Africa cooperation on satellite remote sensing, and supporting the development of joint laboratories, partner institutes, and scientific and technological innovation cooperation bases. It will also hold online shopping festivals promoting African products and a campaign to market 100 African stores and 1,000 African products on e-commerce platforms.
7. The green development program. China will undertake 10 green development, environmental protection, and climate action projects for Africa, support the development of the "Great Green Wall," and build centers of excellence on low-carbon development and climate change adaptation in Africa.
8. The capacity-building program. Projects will include the building or upgrading of 10 schools in Africa, invite 10,000 high-level Africans to training programs, and promote vocational training.
9. The cultural and people-to-people exchange program. Chinese tourism in African countries will be promoted and facilitated.
10. The peace and security program. China will implement 10 peace and security projects for Africa, continue to deliver military assistance to the AU, establish a China–Africa police cooperation mechanism, support African countries' efforts to independently maintain regional security and fight terrorism, and conduct joint peacekeeping exercises.

The 2024 Summit of the Forum on China-Africa Cooperation (FOCAC) in Beijing (September 4-6)

The 2024 FOCAC Summit (9th Forum) in Beijing was attended by 53 African nations. During the three-day summit, President Xi Jinping conducted bilateral meetings with 51 heads of state, underlining China's commitment to individual partnerships. The Forum produced the Beijing FOCAC Action Plan (2025–27), which envisions an "all-weather China–Africa community with a shared future."

China backed this vision with a 360 billion yuan (approximately $51 billion) commitment, comprising:

- $30 billion in credit lines
- $10 billion in Chinese company investments
- $12 billion in various other assistance over three years

Additional financial measures include:

- Waiving intergovernmental interest-free loans for least-developed African countries due by the end of 2024
- A $50 million contribution to the China–World Bank Group Partnership Facility supporting inclusive economic growth
- Calls for multilateral financial institutions and commercial creditors to participate in debt relief

Building on the Dakar Action Plan (2022–24), the new Action Plan (2025–27) continues emphasizing "small and beautiful projects," reflecting China's shift from large infrastructure to targeted initiatives in digital technology and environmental sustainability.

Key economic initiatives included in the Plan include:

- Zero-tariff treatment for all goods from least developed countries with Chinese diplomatic relations, benefiting 33 African nations
- Integration of African countries into global industrial chains through China–Africa economic zones and small-and medium-enterprise development
- Development of 30 infrastructure connectivity projects supporting the African Continental Free Trade Area
- Agricultural modernization focusing on productivity, export value addition, and job creation

The plan also encompasses government cooperation, health, education, cultural exchanges, security, and environmental protection, including meteorological systems, disaster prevention, and biodiversity conservation.

REFERENCES

Bank of China. 2024. *2024 Interim Report*. Beijing. https://pic.bankofchina.com/bocappd/report/202408/P020240829626275183368.pdf.

Bartke, W. 1975. *China's Economic Aid*. New York: Holmes and Meier.

Bräutigam, D. 2009. *The Dragon's Gift: The Real Story of China in Africa*. Oxford: Oxford University Press.

China Development Bank. 2024. *2023 Annual Report*. Beijing. https://www.cdb.com.cn/English/bgxz/ndbg/ndbg2023.

China Ministry of Commerce, National Bureau of Statistics, and State Administration of Foreign Exchange. 2018. "2017 Statistical Bulletin of China's Outward Foreign Direct Investment."

China Ministry of Commerce, National Bureau of Statistics, and State Administration of Foreign Exchange. 2023. "2022 Statistical Bulletin of China's Outward Foreign Direct Investment."

China State Council. 2006. "China's Africa Policy Paper." Beijing. https://www.gov.cn/gongbao/content/2006/content_212161.htm.

China State Council. 2011. "China's Foreign Aid." Beijing. http://english.www.gov.cn/archive/white_paper/2014/09/09/content_281474986284620.htm.

China State Council. 2014. "China's Foreign Aid." Beijing. https://english.www.gov.cn/archive/white_paper/2014/08/23/content_281474982986592.htm.

China State Council. 2021. "China's International Development Cooperation in the New Era." Beijing. https://english.www.gov.cn/archive/whitepaper/202101/10/content_WS5ffa6bbbc6d0f72576943922.html.

Export–Import Bank of China (EXIM). 2006. "Annual Report." Beijing. http://www.eximbank.gov.cn/aboutExim/annals/2006/201806/P020191119544945938142.pdf.

Export–Import Bank of China (EXIM). 2024. "2023 Annual Report." Beijing. http://english.eximbank.gov.cn/News/AnnualR/2023.

Forum on China–Africa Cooperation (FOCAC). 2000. China–Africa Economic and Social Development Cooperation Program. http://www.china.org.cn/english/features/focac/185182.htm.

Forum on China–Africa Cooperation (FOCAC). 2003. "Forum on China–Africa Cooperation-Addis Ababa Action Plan (2004–2006)." http://www.china.org.cn/english/features/focac/185197.htm.

Forum on China–Africa Cooperation (FOCAC). 2006. "Forum on China–Africa Cooperation Beijing Action Plan (2007–2009)." http://www.focac.org/eng/zywx_1/zywj/200611/t20061116_7933564.htm.

Forum on China–Africa Cooperation (FOCAC). 2009. "Forum on China–Africa Cooperation Sharm El-Sheikh Action Plan (2010–2012)." http://www.focac.org/eng/zywx_1/zywj/200911/t20091112_7933571.htm.

Forum on China–Africa Cooperation (FOCAC). 2012. "The Fifth Ministerial Conference of the Forum on China–Africa Cooperation Beijing Action Plan (2013–2015)." http://www.focac.org/eng/zywx_1/zywj/201207/t20120723_8079762.htm.

Forum on China–Africa Cooperation (FOCAC). 2015. "The Forum on China–Africa Cooperation Johannesburg Action Plan (2016–2018)." http://www.focac.org/eng/zywx_1/zywj/201512/t20151225_7933575.htm.

Forum on China–Africa Cooperation (FOCAC). 2018. "Forum on China–Africa Cooperation Beijing Action Plan (2019–2021)." http://www.focac.org/eng/zywx_1/zywj/201809/t20180912_7933578.htm.

Forum on China–Africa Cooperation (FOCAC). 2021. "Forum on China–Africa Cooperation Dakar Action Plan (2022–2024)." http://www.focac.org/eng/zywx_1/zywj/202201/t20220124_10632444.htm.

Gao, J. 1984. "China and Africa: The Development of Relations over Many Centuries." *African Affairs* 83 (331): 241–50.

Huang, M., and A. Liu. 2013 "Economic Motives and Economic Benefits in China's Foreign Aid." Xiamen University Forum on International Development. https://core.ac.uk/download/pdf/41448799.pdf.

Independent Online (IOL). 2015. "Raw Materials: Africa 'Pushing to Curb Exports.'" https://www.iol.co.za/business-report/economy/raw-materials-africa-pushing-to-curb-exports-1955196.

Industrial and Commercial Bank of China. 2024. *2024 Interim Report.*

Kobayashi, T. 2008. "Evolution of China's Aid Policy." JBICI Working Paper 27, JBIC Institute, Tokyo.

Liu, X. 2002. "Continue to Promote Overseas Economic and Technical Assistance." Beijing, China. http://liuxiangdong.mofcom.gov.cn/aarticle/Nocategory/200912/20091206663380.html.

Lou, J. 2020. "The Model of China's Foreign Aid: Theory, Practice and Global Significance." *International Forum* 22 (6): 39–63.

Ministry of Foreign Affairs (MOFA). 2015. "China's Africa Policy Paper." http://www.china.org.cn/world/2015-12/05/content_37241677.htm.

Shinn, David H. 2019. "China–Africa Ties in Historical Context." In *China-Africa and an Economic Transformation*, edited by Arkebe Oqubay and Justin Yifu Lin, 61–83. Oxford: Oxford University Press.

CHAPTER 3

Africa-China: Navigating Economic Shifts

Wenjie Chen, Michele Fornino, and Henry Rawlings

INTRODUCTION

China and Africa have forged strong economic ties over the past two decades, especially after China's accession to the World Trade Organization (WTO) in 2001.[1] Although political ties between China and several African nations date back to the Mao Zedong era (Shinn 2019), economic interactions have surged only after China's growth takeoff. In this context, this chapter examines the key aspects of this economic relationship, focusing on trade, lending, and foreign direct investment (FDI).

The first part of this chapter outlines key findings regarding the evolving economic relationship between Africa and China. First, China has emerged as Africa's largest individual country trading partner, with African countries mainly exporting raw commodities and primary goods while importing Chinese manufactured products. However, the trade pattern exhibits a higher concentration in exports to China than in imports, leading to higher exposure for certain African countries. Second, China's role as a major credit provider in the region is significant, but the debt African governments owe to China remains a small fraction of their total public debt. Recent data have shown a significant scaling back in Chinese lending activities. Finally, although China has been a notable source of FDI in Africa, it only accounts for a small proportion of the total FDI stock.

In recent years, several factors, including US–China trade tensions, changing patterns in China's capital outflows, shifts in its economic policies, and rising debt vulnerabilities in Africa, have gradually altered this long-standing relationship. China's economic growth, particularly affected by a slowdown in its real estate sector and demographic changes due to an aging population, as well as other factors, has decelerated since the early 2010s. These developments are poised to reshape trade and growth dynamics between China and African nations.

[1] In this chapter, we refer to Africa as the group of 54 countries in the continent. Sub-Saharan Africa refers to the group of 45 countries that are under the purview of the IMF's African Department. A list is provided in the appendix of the *Regional Economic Outlook for Sub-Saharan Africa*, October 2023 (https://www.imf.org/en/Publications/REO/SSA/Issues/2023/10/16/regional-economic-outlook-for-sub-saharan-africa-october-2023) (IMF 2023b).

Therefore, the second part of the chapter assesses the effect of China's economic slowdown on African economies, focusing on changes in Chinese lending and investment patterns. Key findings include reduced Chinese lending to African countries due to the COVID-19 pandemic and heightened risk aversion amid debt sustainability concerns. Likewise, China's foreign investment strategy in the continent is shifting toward green and digital infrastructure, involving more local collaboration in project selection. The analysis shows that African oil and resource exporters are most vulnerable to a Chinese economic slowdown, facing deteriorating terms of trade as China's economy rebalances away from investment toward consumption, thus reducing the demand for commodities.

The chapter starts by documenting the channels of economic engagement between China and African countries, including bilateral trade, Chinese loans and investments in African countries, and other linkages such as construction projects and Chinese workers in Africa. We then assess recent developments and the outlook of Africa–China economic relations, considering both short-term conjunctural shifts and long-term structural factors (see Chapter 5 on economic linkages). Finally, we conclude with a discussion of policies that could help African countries navigate the evolving landscape of economic engagements with China.

THE MAKINGS OF A STRONG ECONOMIC PARTNERSHIP

The economic relationship between Africa and China is complex and multifaceted. Understanding this relationship is more challenging because of the relative scarcity of reliable and comprehensive data on trade and investment with low-income countries, including those in Africa. Drawing on a variety of data sources, the following few sections aim to provide an overview of significant patterns in the historical economic engagement between China and Africa. This includes an examination of trade dynamics, lending activities, and FDI.

Trade: Where It All Began

The most important channel of economic engagement between China and Africa is trade. China is Africa's largest individual country trading partner (Figure 3.1), rivaling the combined flows of the entire euro area block. Between 2020 and 2022, about 13 percent of the region's total goods exports have found their way to China, a stark contrast to the 1990s—before China's accession to the WTO in 2001—when western countries dominated as the primary destinations of the continent's exports. Since then, China's robust economic growth and substantial demand for raw materials have propelled African goods exports, witnessing a more than fourfold increase in nominal US dollar terms between 2000 and 2022.[2]

[2] According to WEO data, total goods exports increased by about 60 percent in this period in terms of volume. The large difference stems not only from the cumulative inflation since 2000 but also from the positive evolution of terms of trade for the region's exports.

Figure 3.1. Africa: International Trade Partners, 2000-22

(Percentage of total exports, period average)

1. Exports of Goods

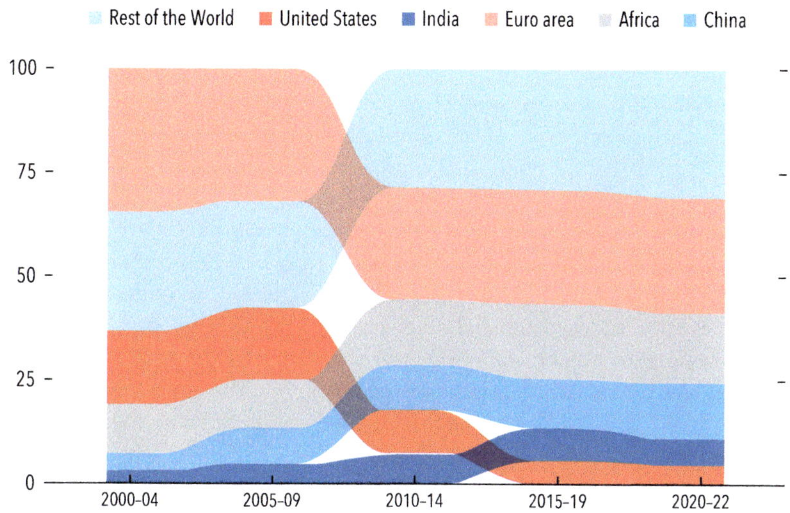

2. Imports of Goods

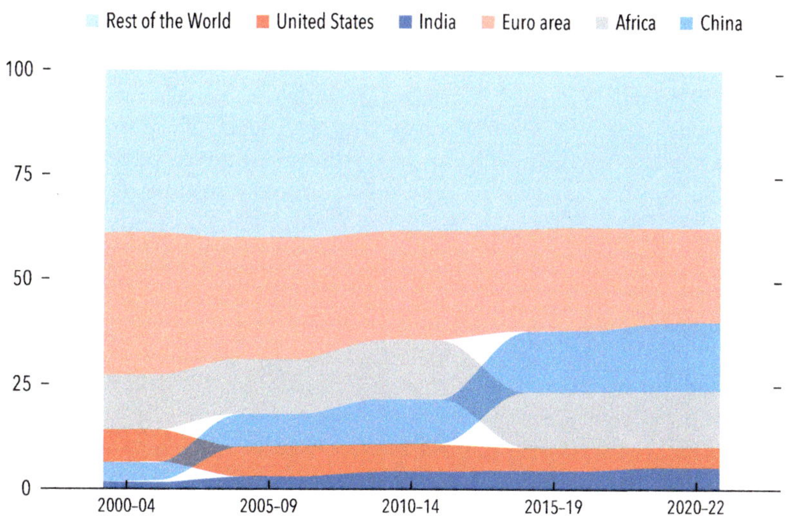

Sources: IMF, Direction of Trade Statistics database; and IMF staff calculations.

Note: The chart depicts five-year averages of the share of exports from and imports to sub-Saharan Africa for the top five destinations and origins, with the remainder combined in a residual category. Regions are listed from the largest (top) to the smallest (bottom). Euro area's definition excludes Croatia.

Conversely, African imports from China have surged in value twentyfold between 2000 and 2019 and averaged 16 percent of the total between 2020 and 2022.

Despite intermittent declines during global crises—the Global Financial Crisis in 2009 and the commodity downturn in 2015—trade has played an important role in boosting regional incomes, primarily through increased export revenues.

Africa, however, does not play as big of a role as a trading partner to China, although its importance has been increasing in the past two decades. In 2022, Africa received 4.6 percent of China's total exports and, after peaking in 2012, China's imports from Africa constituted about 4.3 percent of its total imports in the same year. Other Asian countries, as well as euro area countries and the United States, play more relevant roles as China's bilateral trading partners.

A distinctive feature of China and Africa's trade relationship is the composition of exports and imports, illustrated in Figure 3.2 using UN Comtrade data. Africa predominantly exports natural resources, especially crude oil and other fossil fuels as well as raw unprocessed minerals and other intermediate goods to China. In contrast, imports from China are primarily manufactured goods and machinery, and other items that are generally further along in the global value chain. Moreover, UN Comtrade data show that Africa consistently runs a bilateral trade deficit with China. In all, this persistent trend is a result of the relative abundance of natural resources posing challenges for economic diversification in African countries.

Figure 3.3 portrays the African countries ranked by the share of China in both imports and exports. As it can be gleaned from Figure 3.3 (panel 1), China's share of imports to African countries is relatively homogeneous across countries, with the top 3, including Ghana, Guinea, and Nigeria, standing at just over 30 percent compared with slightly less than 20 percent on average for countries outside of the top 10. When looking at the share of exports to China, portrayed in Figure 3.3 (panel 2), we see a strikingly different pattern emerge. Indeed, the top five countries by exposure to China in this metric, including South Sudan, Democratic Republic of the Congo, Angola, Eritrea, and the Republic of Congo, all have shares above 50 percent, with countries outside the top 10 exporting, on average, less than 15 percent to China. This fact has important implications, both because countries that have been exporting intensively to China may be more exposed to a deceleration in Chinese economic activity and because the relatively large demand for raw materials during China's unprecedented growth spell in the past two decades may have created incentives not to diversify some of the economies that benefited the most from its spectacular rise.

Loans and Debt: It Is Complicated

This section delves into the lending dynamics between China and African countries, highlighting China's growing role as a key creditor in the region. However, the data indicate that the debt owed to China is relatively minor within the broader spectrum of African debt. Notably, there has been a recent downtrend in

Figure 3.2. Africa: Composition of Trade with China, 2000-22
(Billions of US dollars)

1. Exports of Goods

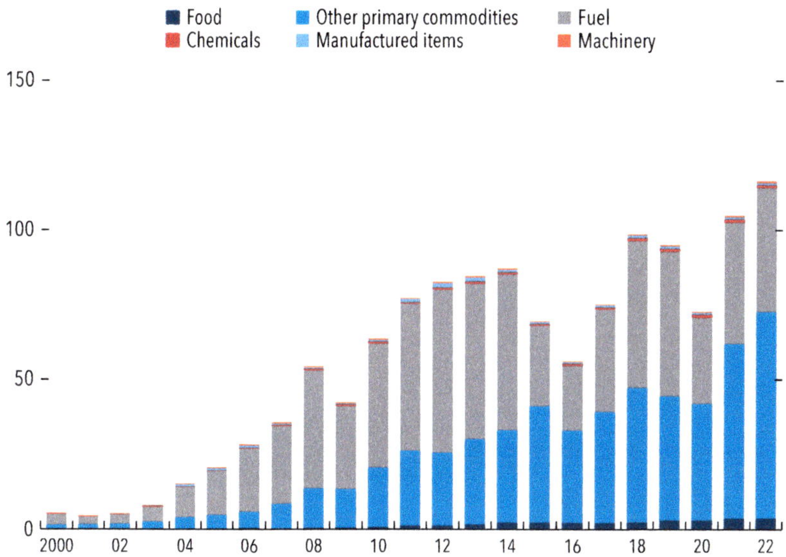

2. Imports of Goods

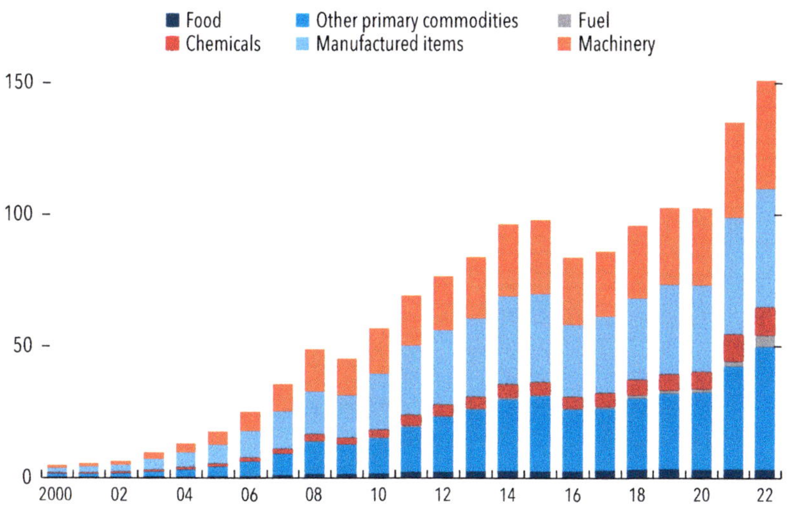

Source: UN, Comtrade database.

China's lending. The analysis also sheds light on the framework of China's institutional lending, particularly emphasizing state-owned enterprises' significant role in offering loans to foreign governments.

Figure 3.3. African Trade Concentration with China, 2018–22

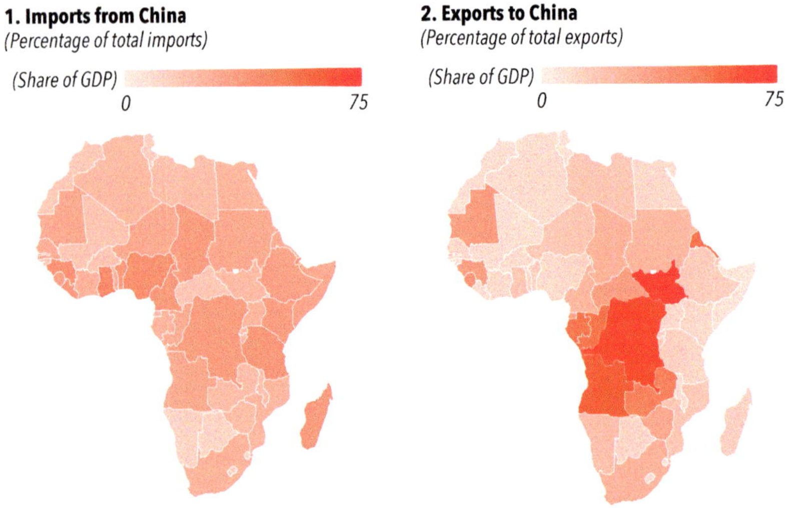

Source: IMF, Direction of Trade Statistics database.
Note: Maps depict Chinese trade flows as a share of total trade flows with the world. Darker shades imply higher shares. The boundaries and colors shown on the maps do not imply, on the part of the IMF, any judgment on the legal status of any territory or any endorsement or acceptance of such boundaries.

Methodological Considerations

The second main channel of engagement between Africa and China is lending. Quantifying this aspect of the relationship is challenging, given that Chinese lending agencies do not typically reveal their loan amounts or terms publicly. It has been reported that confidentiality clauses have been included in some debt contracts (Gelpern and others 2022). Furthermore, China is not a member of the Paris Club of government lenders, which tries to coordinate debt forgiveness among its members and systematically discloses the terms surrounding the debt. In this context, it is difficult to assess the full extent of China's lending to African countries. Despite these challenges, China's loan programs in Africa have attracted considerable media attention, especially in debt distress situations for specific countries. Discrepancies in reports on the size and growth of African debt to China can be attributed to two main issues.

First, available data often comprise debt *commitments*, which reflect *promised* lending arrangements. The main benefit of focusing on commitments is their relative ease of compilation from various sources. This approach is exemplified by Horn and others (2021) who show that up to 50 percent of Chinese foreign lending may not be captured by "gold standard" sources like the World Bank International Debt Statistics. However, commitments might not lead to actual disbursements, or they may take longer than initially projected. The discrepancy between commitments and disbursements can be significant, as illustrated in Figure 3.4.

Second, data coverage and the choice of statistical concepts significantly affect the reported magnitudes. Our main data source for disbursements is the International Debt Statistics database, maintained by the World Bank. This data set is assembled based on External Debtor Reporting System (DRS) data submissions from country authorities directly to the World Bank, which then aggregates these data according to multiple criteria. These include the type of creditor (bilateral, multilateral, commercial, and so on), the specific counterparty (that is, country, MDB, or international organization), classification of the creditor as official or commercial, and, of course, the degree of involvement of the public sector from the debtor side (general government debt, public and publicly guaranteed debt, which among the central government, central bank, or other government agencies owes the debt). However, not all countries submit data to the World Bank through the DRS, and it has been documented that, at times, loans extended by Chinese agencies and commercial banks will be formally recorded as owed by private entities, even when there is a parallel arrangement whereby the ultimate responsibility for repayment lies with the debtor government (Malik and others 2021). These kinds of arrangements complicate, at times, an accurate estimation of the existing stock of debt obligations.

Figure 3.4. Africa: Inward Chinese Lending, 2000–22
(Percentage of GDP)

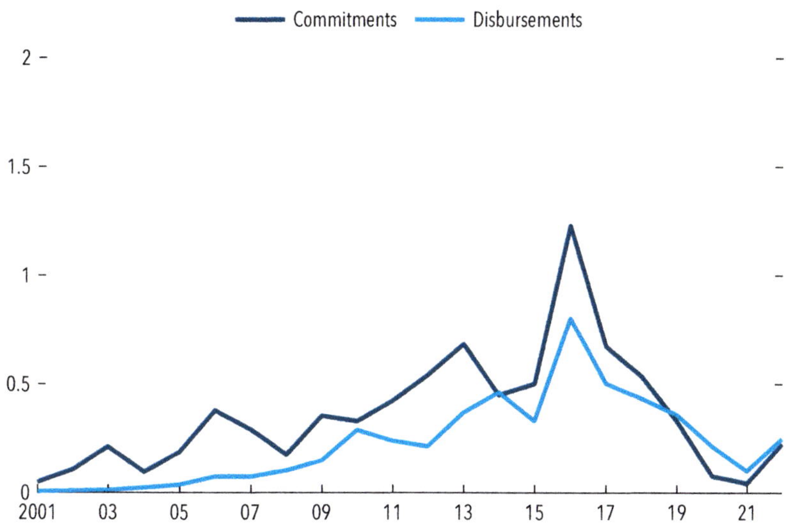

Sources: Boston University, Chinese Loans to Africa database for commitments; World Bank, International Debt Statistics database for disbursements; and IMF, World Economic Outlook database for GDP.
Note: Aggregate GDP for Africa excludes South Sudan.

External Lending Trends

Despite these data limitations, key facts emerge regarding the trajectory of China's lending to African countries. First and foremost, China has gradually emerged as the largest bilateral official creditor of African governments in the past two decades, serving as a significant source of infrastructure, mining, and energy financing for the continent (Figures 3.5 and 3.6). Although concessional loans, as defined in the DRS, initially formed a substantial portion of China's loans to Africa, their share has decreased to less than 10 percent by the end of 2020 (Figure 3.7). The region's total external interest payment attributable to China's official bilateral loans is 10 percent as of 2019 (Figure 3.8).[3]

In the past five years, however, Chinese official total loan disbursements to African countries have fallen, constituting in 2021 about one-eighth of their peak value of 1.2 percent of the region's GDP in 2016. Total loan commitments also contracted dramatically from their peak in 2016.

Examining the debt-service cost of Chinese loans compared with other external creditor types reveals a middle-of-the-road positioning. China's loans fall between low-cost, concessional loans from multilateral development banks

Figure 3.5. Africa: Loan Commitments from China, 2000–20
(Billions of US dollars)

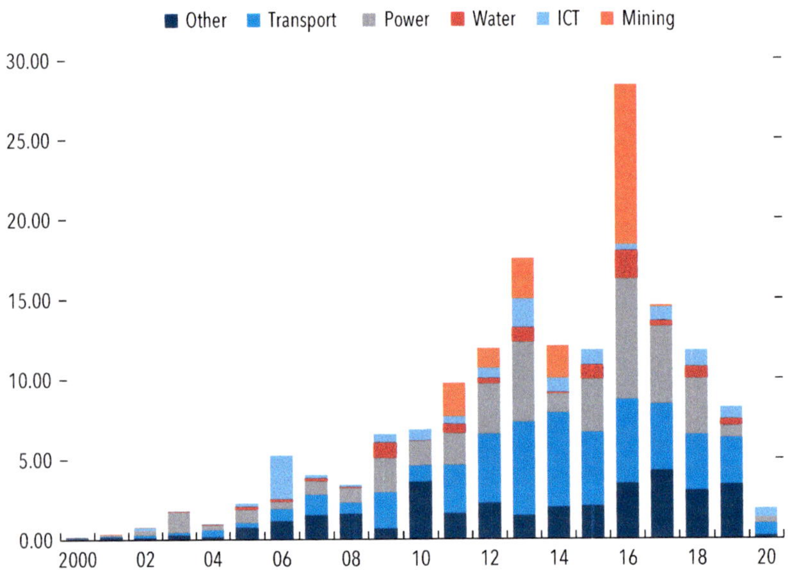

Source: Boston University, Chinese Loans to Africa Database.
Note: Other includes agriculture, business, budget, education, defense, food, government, health, trade, and unallocated.

[3] We focus on 2019 data because in 2020, as discussed in the following sections of the chapter, a significant portion of interest payments on bilateral debt was frozen in the context of the Debt Service Suspension Initiative, spearheaded by the World Bank and the IMF.

Figure 3.6. Africa: External Debt, End of 2021
(Percentage of total external debt)

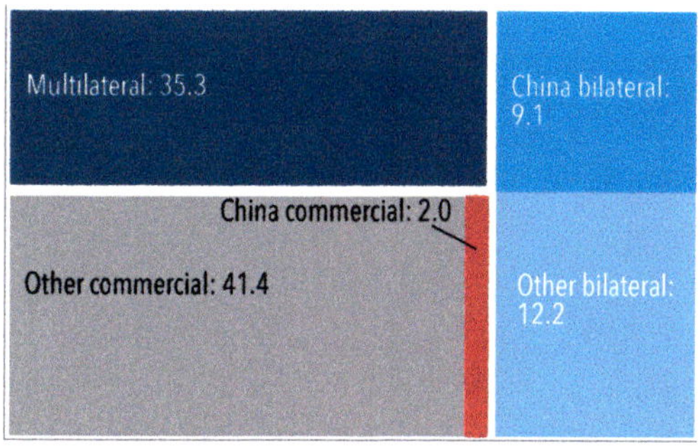

Sources: World Bank, International Debt Statistics; IMF, World Economic Outlook database; and IMF staff calculations.
Note: Multilateral includes regional development banks. China Development Bank is included in China bilateral debt but not in China commercial debt.

Figure 3.7. Africa: Share of General Government External Debt Owed to China Extended on Concessional Terms, 2005–21
(Percent)

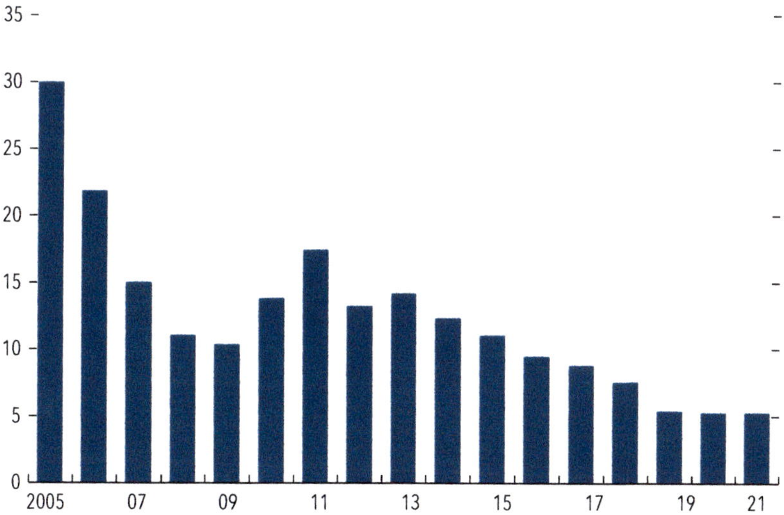

Sources: World Bank, International Debt Statistics database; and IMF staff calculations.

(MDBs) and traditional Paris Club lenders and the more expensive loans from commercial entities like Eurobonds and syndicated loans (Figure 3.9). Concessional loans from MDBs and traditional Paris Club lenders have stringent safeguards, making qualification more challenging, but they offer lower interest rates and longer grace periods. However, loans from commercial entities, such as Eurobonds and syndicated loans, come with higher debt-service costs. Chinese loans, as per International Debt Statistics data, offer terms that lie somewhere in

Figure 3.8. Africa: Share of Interest Payments on General Government External Debt, by Creditor Type, 2019
(Percent)

Sources: World Bank, International Debt Statistics database; and IMF staff calculations.
Note: Interest payments are actual amounts of interest paid by the borrower in currency, goods, or services in the year specified (World Bank 2000).

Figure 3.9. Africa: Implicit Interest Rate on General Government External Debt, by Creditor Type, 2006–22
(Percent)

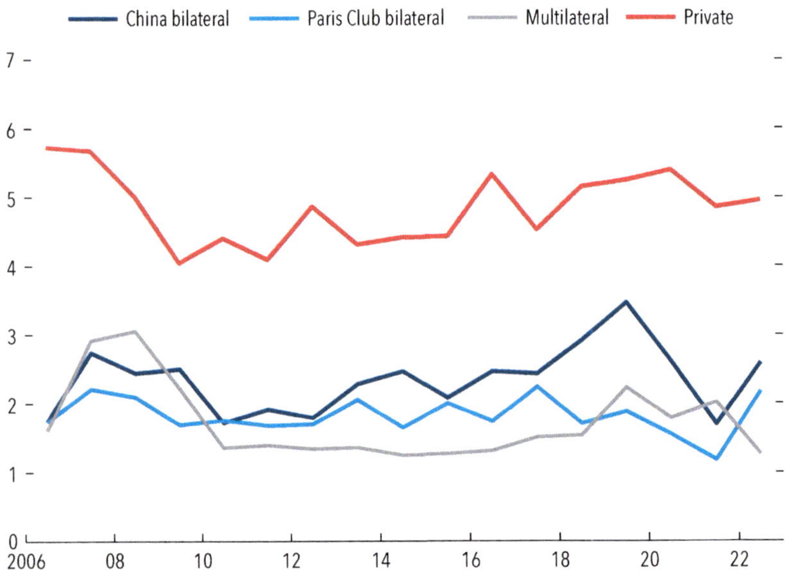

Sources: World Bank, International Debt Statistics database; and IMF staff calculations.
Note: Interest payments are actual amounts of interest paid by the borrower in currency, goods, or services in the year specified (World Bank 2000). The implicit interest rate is calculated as the ratio of interest payments to existing stock of debt for each creditor type. This concept may differ from the interest rate agreed upon because of many factors, including grace periods, repayment schedules, missed interest payments, or arrears.

between. While featuring a more streamlined qualification process that might elevate the risk of debt distress, they also offer a relatively higher return for China.

A Closer Look at China's Lending Agencies

According to Acker, Brautigam, and Huang (2020), China's two largest overseas lenders include the Export–Import Bank of China (China Exim Bank) and the China Development Bank (CDB), with China Exim Bank holding the bulk of outstanding loans to African countries (Figure 3.10). China Exim Bank provides

Figure 3.10. Africa: Loan Commitments from China, 2000–20
(Billions of US dollars)

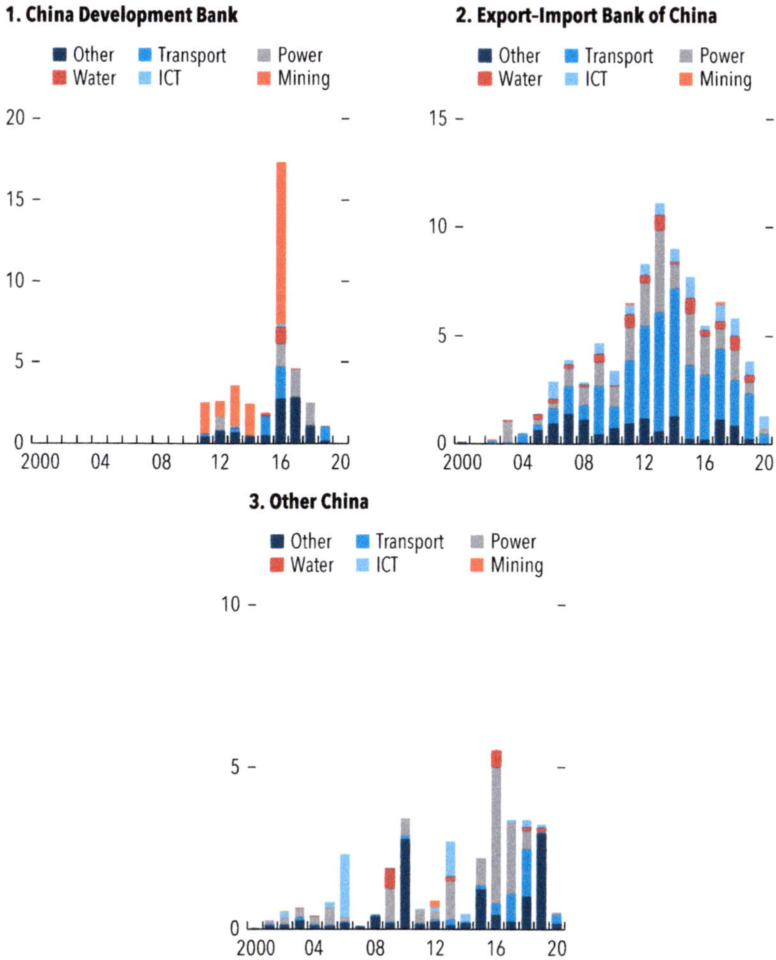

Source: Boston University, Chinese Loans to Africa Database.
Note: Other includes agriculture, business, budget, education, defense, food, government, health, trade, and unallocated. The large loan commitment granted by China Development Bank in 2016 corresponds to the well-documented loan to Angola's government to recapitalize Sonangol (https://china.aiddata.org/projects/53063/). ICT = Information and Communications Technology.

three main types of loans. *Export seller's credits* are loans extended to Chinese companies or "export sellers" seeking funds to boost their business abroad, whereas *export buyer's credits* are loans provided to buyers of exported Chinese goods and services. Both types are negotiated at commercial rates based on prevailing rates in international capital markets.

China Exim Bank also operates a third category known as *preferential loans*—preferential export buyer's credits and concessional foreign aid loans. Both loan instruments have interest rates that are subsidized by annual appropriations from the Chinese budget and are exclusively provided to other developing-country governments or their state-owned firms. China Exim Bank also has a 20 percent share in the China–Africa Fund for Industrial Cooperation, which was announced in December 2015 by President Xi Jinping and officially launched the following January with an initial cash injection of $10 billion, with the State Administration of Foreign Exchange owning the remaining 80 percent share (Li 2020). In recent years, this fund has been merged with the China–LAC Industrial Cooperation Fund that focuses on investments into Latin America as part of a big revamp to form a joint investment vehicle for the Belt and Road Initiative (see the following section for more details).

Like China Exim Bank, CDB is a state-owned policy arm of the Chinese government. CDB's main mission is the development of China, with a focus on domestic projects related to public infrastructure, highways, and electric power. Unlike China Exim Bank, CDB is more commercialized and domestically oriented, with most of its lending directed toward supporting domestic projects. It is the second-largest bond issuer in China after the Ministry of Finance, accounting for about one-quarter of China's bond market (Global Infrastructure Hub 2019, Annex D). Both China Exim Bank and CDB have been reported to rely on collateralized lending, specifically through a model referred to as "resource-secured infrastructure finance," which essentially relies on future receivables to secure the loan. Although about a quarter of 2020 loan commitments were secured in this way, this model is different from the practice of using existing assets as collateral (Brautigam, Huang, and Acker 2020).

Although China Exim Bank and CDB are the major agencies tasked to fund development loans, Chinese President Hu Jintao announced the formation of China–Africa Development Fund (CAD Fund) during the Forum on China–Africa Cooperation (FOCAC) as an initiative to strengthen China–Africa cooperation in 2006. The CAD Fund became operational in 2007 with an initial capital amount of $10 billion. The CAD Fund, a wholly owned private-equity subsidiary of the CDB, focuses on Africa, investing in projects through equity, quasi-equity (for example, preferred shares, convertible bonds), or funds. Although it evaluates many of its projects independently, the CDB may recommend some of its loan projects to the CAD Fund for equity financing (Centre for Chinese Studies 2013). This fund also encourages and supports Chinese enterprises that have set up operations in Africa or plan to invest in Africa, especially those that facilitate infrastructure construction and enhance the social and economic development of African countries (Centre for Chinese Studies 2013).

Finally, commercial banks in China also hold an increasingly significant share of the debt stock of African countries (Figure 3.11). However, as per IDS definitions (World Bank 2000), commercial banks that are creditors for public debt reporting will be considered as such regardless of whether they are privately or publicly owned.[4] Therefore, for China, this share is mostly attributable to China Exim Bank and CDB, and it may also include several other state-owned enterprises.

The Currency Composition of Chinese Lending to Africa and Currency Swap Agreements

The currency composition of Chinese lending has become a notable aspect in recent years, particularly in relation to bilateral swap line agreements that have been signed by the People's Bank of China over the past decade. Beyond

Figure 3.11. Africa: Outstanding Debt Owed to Chinese Entities by Creditor Type, 2005–21
(Billions of US dollars)

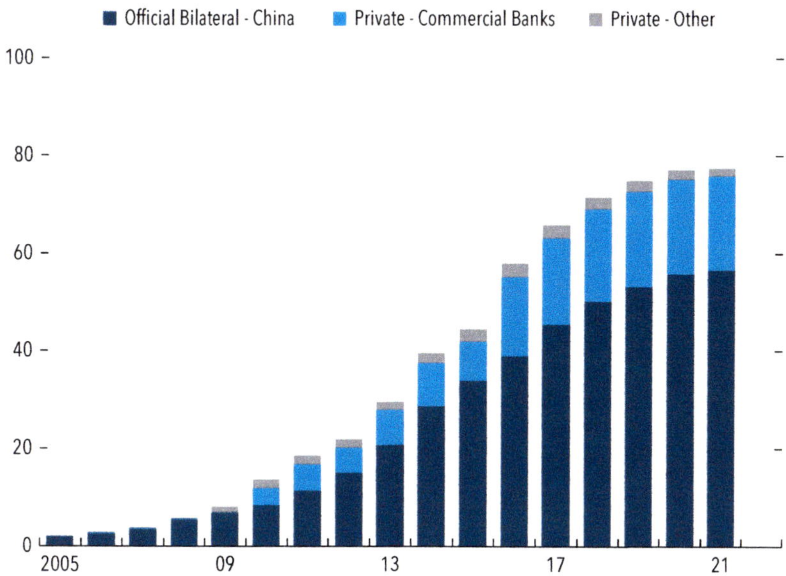

Sources: World Bank, International Debt Statistics database; and IMF staff calculations.

[4] The World Bank's DRS Manual (https://databankfiles.worldbank.org/public/ddpext_download/site-content/kb/debt/DRS_Manual_English.pdf, on page 9) defines commercial banks for public debt reporting as "[including] all commercial banks, whether or not publicly owned, as well as other financial institutions, such as finance companies, merchant banks, insurance companies, and the like. Note the asymmetry in definitions with regards to commercial banks: as debtors, publicly owned commercial banks are in the public sector; as creditors all commercial banks are classified as private, whether publicly or privately owned."

multilateral debt owed to the IMF and the World Bank, which is denominated in special drawing rights, most of the external worldwide debt recorded in the IDS data is denominated in US dollars and euros, which together account for about 70 percent of the total. Although the World Bank's IDS database details the share of public and publicly guaranteed debt denominated in US dollars, euros, and a few other currencies, it does not specifically isolate renminbi-denominated debt, grouping it instead with other currencies.[5]

Figure 3.12 presents the currency decomposition of total public and publicly guaranteed debt owed by African DRS-reporting countries to China. This analysis divides the debt into three currency groups: the US dollar, the euro and other traditional advanced economies' currencies, and the renminbi along with other local currencies, with the latter being combined in a residual category in IDS. The data reveal that most African external debt owed to China is denominated in US dollars, with no clear pattern indicating a decrease, aside from normal fluctuations likely because of exchange rate movements.

Figure 3.12. Africa: Currency Decomposition of Public and Publicly Guaranteed Debt in Africa, 2010–22
(Percentage of total)

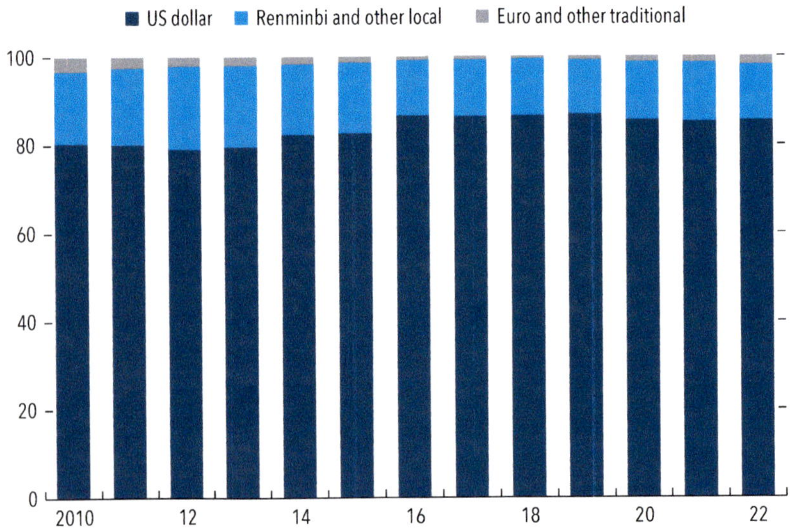

Sources: World Bank International Debt Statistics; and IMF staff calculations.
Note: Euro and other traditional currencies comprise the euro, yen, UK pound sterling, Swiss franc, and multiple-currency loans, whereas the renminbi and other local comprise all remaining currencies not included elsewhere in the totals. No special drawing right-denominated debt is owed to China.

[5]To be specific, the World Bank's IDS public-facing data portal shows the shares of public and publicly guaranteed debt denominated in US dollars, euros, UK pound sterling, Swiss franc, Japanese yen, special drawing rights, and two residual categories—namely "Multiple Currencies," for debt which explicitly is due in more than one currency, and "Other," which captures the (offshore) renminbi as well as all other currencies not explicitly mentioned in other categories.

Horn and others (2023) report that between 2008 and 2021, the People's Bank of China signed 40 bilateral swap agreements with major central banks worldwide. In general, these agreements are designed for swift currency swaps between two central banks, primarily to provide liquidity support to commercial banks needing foreign currency in challenging market conditions. Swap lines are increasingly used worldwide as a crucial tool to stabilize capital markets and facilitate trade.

However, Horn and others (2023) note that the People's Bank of China's swap line agreements, especially when systematically rolled over an extended period, may complicate the calculation of the foreign exchange reserves in countries facing balance of payment crises. They suggest these swaps might serve as an alternative way for China to support debtor countries to which it has significant exposure. It is important to note that in Africa, only Egypt and Nigeria have been documented in tapping and rolling over bilateral swap lines.

Investment Linkages

This section examines FDI in Africa, focusing on both Chinese contributions and the African perspective. The analysis reveals that although Chinese FDI flows have constituted a significant portion of total recent inflows to Africa, they remain relatively small compared with the total FDI stock from more traditional investors. Conversely, Africa's share in China's total outward FDI is modest in both flow and stock terms. The Belt and Road Initiative, launched in 2013, is discussed as a key framework for China's foreign economic activities, especially in terms of FDI.

Foreign Direct Investment: It Is Small, but Also Big

Over the years, China has become a major overseas investor, with outward direct investment (ODI) flows peaking at about $200 billion in 2016 and reaching approximately $180 billion in 2021, as reported by the National Bureau of Statistics of China. From 2014 to 2021, Chinese cumulative ODI nearly tripled in value, growing from almost $900 billion to about $2.8 trillion. Despite this substantial growth, Africa's share as a destination remains relatively small, constituting less than 3 percent of China's overall ODI flows and less than 2 percent of its overall ODI stock as of 2021, with the latter on a steady decline from a high of 4 percent in 2012 (Figure 3.13). The key destinations for Chinese ODI are overwhelmingly located in Asia and Latin America, which together account for almost all the ODI stock as of 2021. The data, however, might not be complete, because almost half of China's ODI flows to Hong Kong, but this is likely not the ultimate destination for most of these investments.

From Africa's perspective, FDI *flows* from China have been playing an increasingly important role over the years (Figure 3.14, panel 1). The rise of China's FDI flows was impressive, hovering between 6 percent and 12 percent of the total annual FDI inflows in recent years and amounting to approximately $4.8 billion in 2021. However, when compared with the size of investments from other parts

Figure 3.13. China: Outward Direct Investment, 2000–20
(Billions of US dollars; percent on right scale)

1. Flows

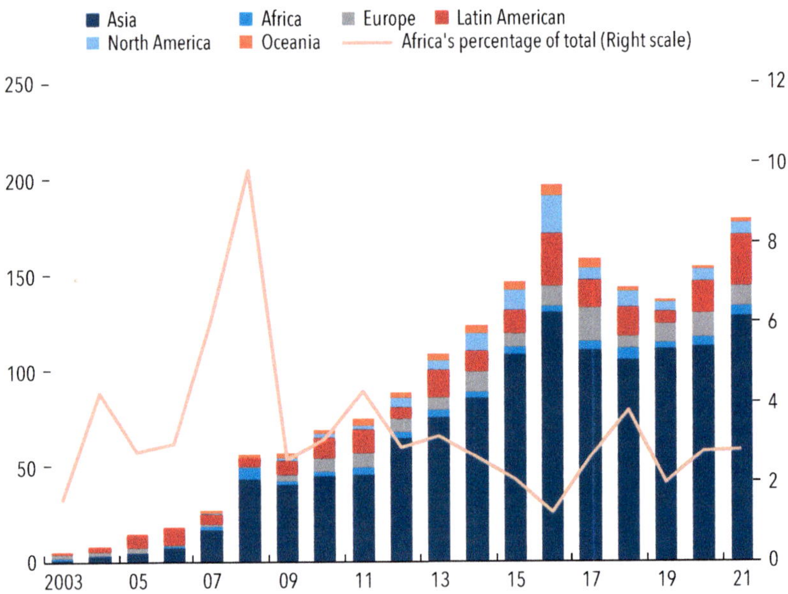

2. Stock

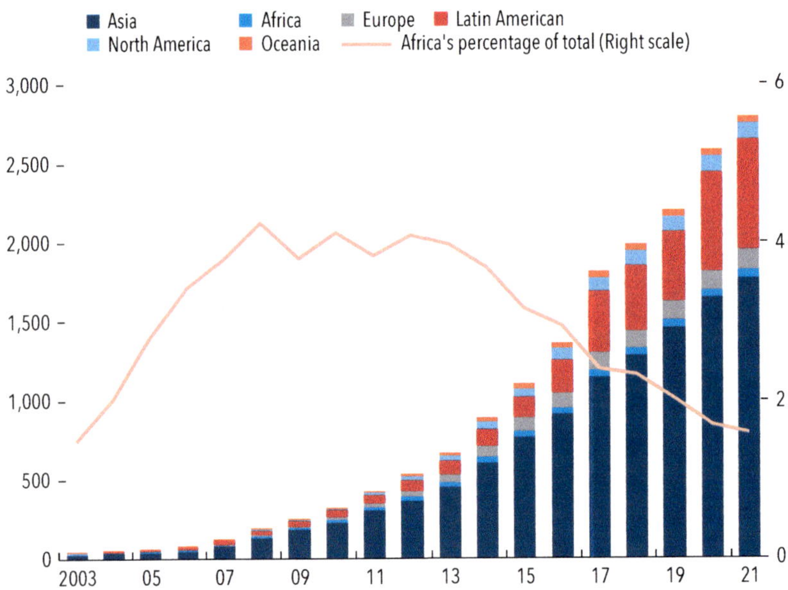

Source: The National Bureau of Statistics of China.

Figure 3.14. Africa: Inward Direct Investment, 2003-21

1. Flows

(Billions of US dollars; percent on right scale)

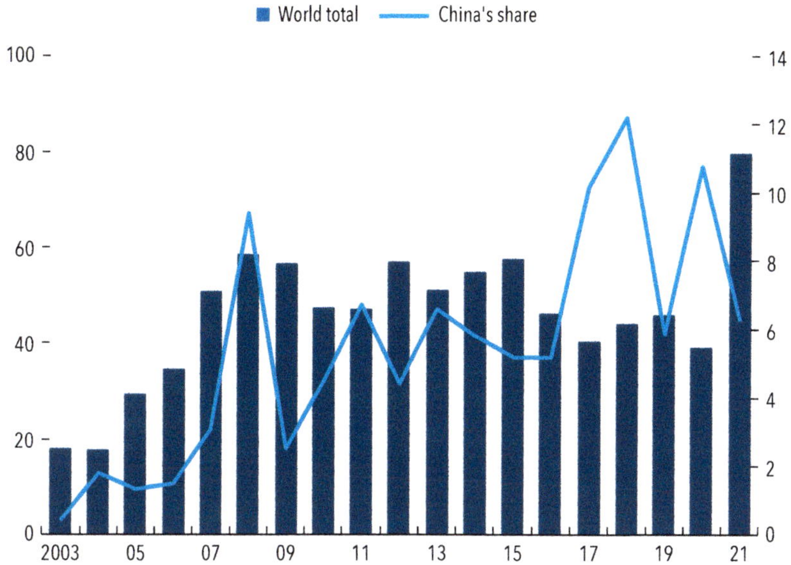

2. Stock

(Billions of US dollars)

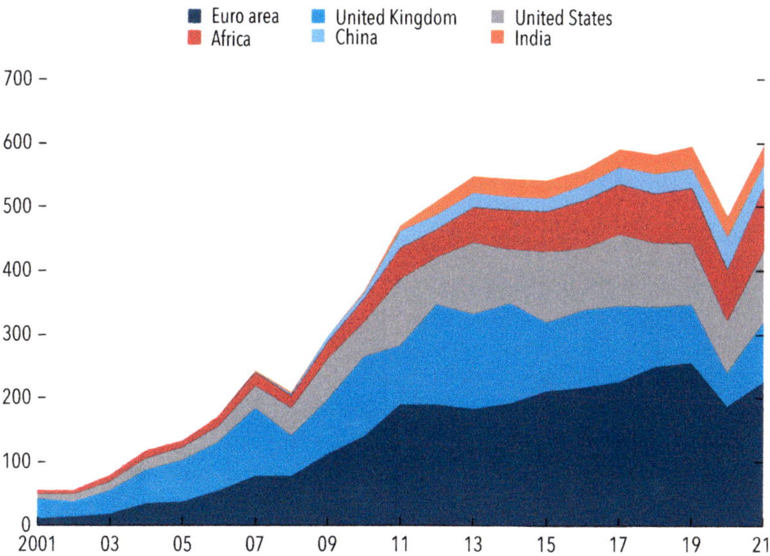

Sources: The National Bureau of Statistics of China; UNCTADstat; and IMF staff calculations.

of the world, the *stock* of Chinese investments as a share of the region's total FDI is still relatively small—at about 3.6 percent in 2021 (Figure 3.14, panel 2). The latter increased almost tenfold between 2004 and 2018, albeit from a very low base.

This relatively small magnitude might be surprising given the large media attention surrounding Chinese investments in Africa. Even if these numbers might not reflect the full extent of Chinese investments and miss parts that come through roundabout channels, a doubling of the Chinese ODI stock to Africa would still be a relatively small share of the total existing stock of FDIs.

Chinese ODI to Africa can be construed as relatively big compared with its investments in advanced economies. In general, FDI tends to flow more to advanced economies than to developing countries. As of 2021, the United States received more than eight times the amount of direct investment from the world compared with the amount that Africa received. However, China's stock of investment to the United States is only about two times bigger than its investments to Africa in 2021. Hence, China's relative interest in Africa is large, even if it plays a small role in terms of attracting overall investment (Chen, Dollar, and Tang 2016).

Chinese ODI in Africa is concentrated in specific sectors, including construction, mining, and manufacturing (Figure 3.15, panel 1). These official statistics based on the value of the stock of investments are often dominated by large investments made by Chinese state-owned companies. The geographic concentration is notable, with investments focused on a limited number of countries, particularly those rich in natural resources (Figure 3.15, panel 2). Primary products and oil-exporting countries in Africa are major recipients of Chinese FDI, with a significant share of investments going to a handful of countries. This concentration has persisted, with diversification to other countries plateauing after 2015 (Figure 3.15, panel 3). Similar to the case of trade and lending, concentration of FDIs in a few key countries may constitute a source of vulnerability should Chinese investors decide to divest.

The Belt and Road Initiative

The Belt and Road Initiative (BRI), launched by China in 2013, is a collection of global development and infrastructure investments aimed at enhancing connectivity and fostering economic cooperation.[6] Since its inception, most of the FDI originating from China has been under the umbrella of the BRI. Initially aimed at improving linkages between East Asia and Europe, the BRI encompasses projects such as railways, major road networks, and maritime infrastructure. As of 2023, over 150 countries and 30 international organizations have signed cooperation agreements with China under the BRI, with a cumulative engagement surpassing $1 trillion (Nedopil 2023).

[6] This section takes stock of the Belt and Road Initiative-related engagements, given the wide-ranging nature of this initiative as an organizing framework for Chinese foreign economic policy. In practice, this results in some overlap with the results presented in previous sections.

Figure 3.15. Africa: Chinese Inward Direct Investment
(Billions of US dollars)

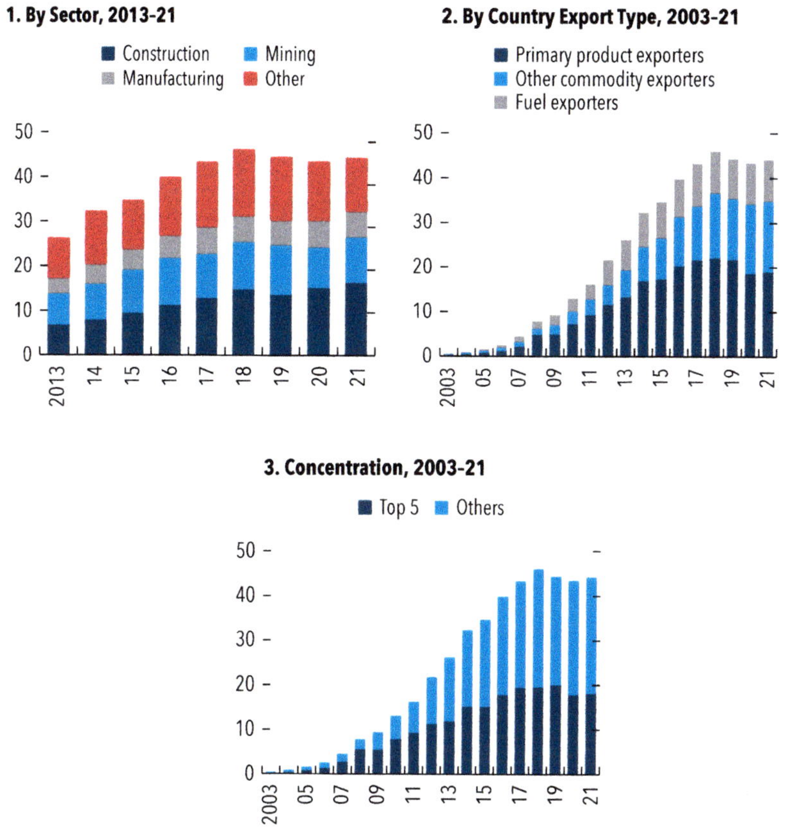

Sources: The Johns Hopkins University SAIS China Africa Research Initiative; China Statistical Yearbook: "Overseas Direct Investment by Countries or Regions."

Although the initial focus was on the Eurasian continent, BRI investments have been significantly extended to Africa and South America (Figure 3.16). In Africa, key sectors financed through the BRI include transportation, energy, and mining infrastructure, aligning with the sectoral composition of Chinese loan commitments to African countries (Figure 3.17). This underscores the BRI's role as a prominent framework for Chinese engagements in development finance in the region. Notably, the retrenchment in BRI-related engagement since 2020 has affected all regions, indicating that the slowdown in Chinese investment is not necessarily specific to Africa. This observation is supported, for example, in a recent report by Myers and Ray (2023), which examines BRI-related engagements between China and Latin American and Caribbean countries.

The BRI offers African countries opportunities to address infrastructure bottlenecks, evident in the Chinese share of projects, job creation, and the involvement

Figure 3.16. The Belt and Road Initiative Engagement by Region, 2013–23
(Percentage of GDP)

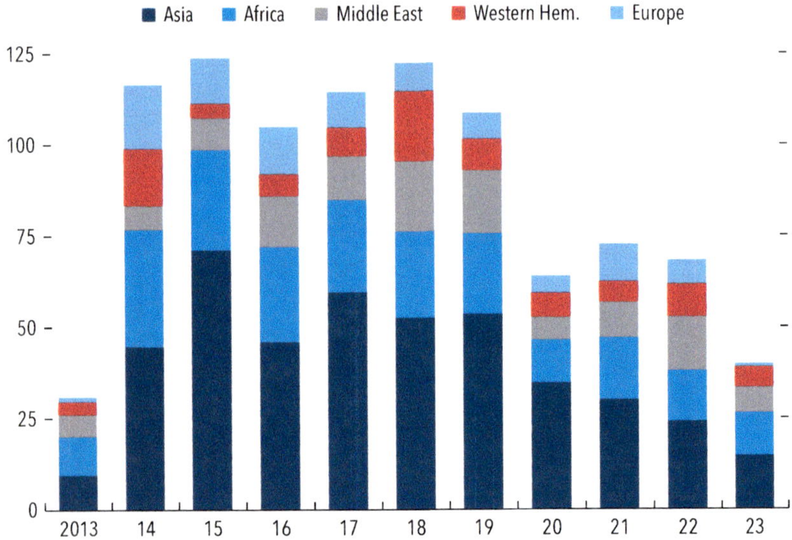

Sources: American Enterprise Institute, China Global Investment Tracker; and IMF staff calculations.

Figure 3.17. Africa: Total Belt and Road Initiative Engagement in Africa, by Sector
(Percentage of GDP)

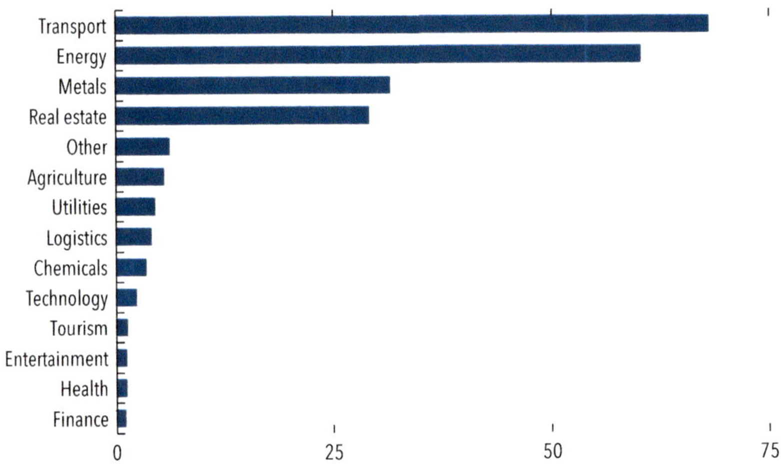

Sources: American Enterprise Institute, China Global Investment Tracker; and IMF staff calculations.

of companies in FDIs (see Figure 3.18). However, some aspects of the initiative remain opaque, particularly details on specific projects and their terms. Most BRI loans are in dollars and provided on commercial terms more generous than those

Figure 3.18. Africa: Chinese Share of Announced Greenfield Foreign Direct Investment Projects, 2009–21

(Percentage of total)

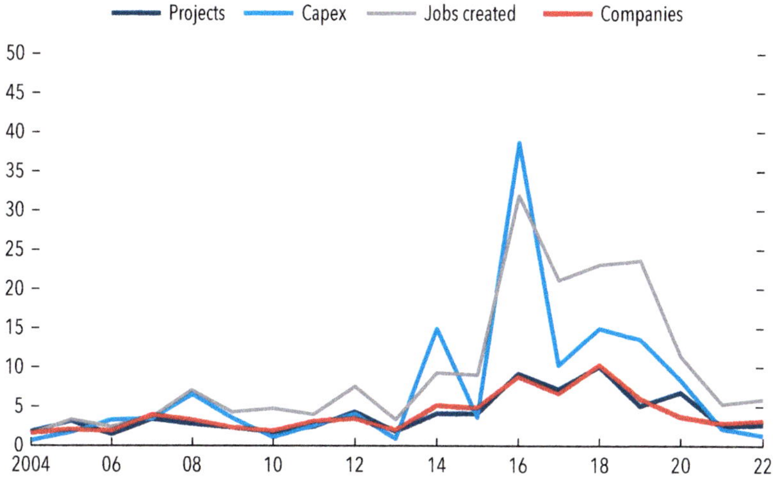

Sources: FDI Markets; and IMF staff calculations.

from private investors, but they are costlier than funds from western lenders or MDBs. Chinese investment projects, although less bureaucratically demanding than those financed by MDBs, present trade-offs for African authorities seeking swift infrastructure deployment (Dollar 2019). A 2019 study emphasized the potential benefits of reducing transport costs through improved infrastructure but highlighted that policy impediments, such as import tariffs, investment restrictions, customs delays, bureaucracy, and corruption, often increase trade costs significantly (World Bank 2019). The key message, then, is that improving the investment climate is a necessary complement to investing in infrastructure. These findings will put a premium on careful project selection to ensure maximum effect.

Labor Flows Associated with Chinese FDI in Africa

Increased Chinese investment in Africa facilitated the significant expansion of Chinese construction companies on the continent. The gross annual revenues of Chinese companies engaged in engineering and construction projects in Africa have steadily risen until their peak in 2015, with the latest number totaling about $37 billion in 2021, a 3 percent reduction from the year prior (Figure 3.19). The top five countries in 2021 are Nigeria, Algeria, Kenya, Angola, and the Democratic Republic of the Congo, accounting together for about 40 percent of all Chinese companies' gross annual revenues from 2021 construction projects in Africa. Nigeria alone accounts for about 11 percent. Notably, the gross annual revenues of Chinese construction projects have risen in other Asian countries

Figure 3.19. Gross Annual Revenues of Chinese Companies' Construction Projects by Region, 1998–2021
(Billions of US dollars)

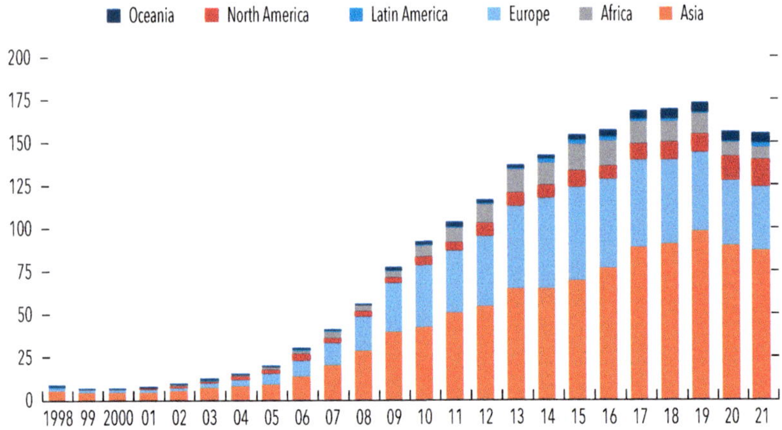

Sources: The Johns Hopkins University SAIS China Africa Research Initiative; and The National Bureau of Statistics of China.

while seemingly plateauing or declining in Africa during the pre-COVID-19 period, a trend that persisted and intensified amid the pandemic.

The presence of Chinese companies in Africa goes hand in hand with the presence of Chinese workers in Africa. There is a positive correlation between the number of Chinese workers and the gross revenues of Chinese companies in Africa, especially before the pandemic. Like the trend in gross annual revenues of Chinese companies' construction projects in Africa, the number of Chinese workers in Africa has also declined since 2015, reaching less than 200,000 by the end of 2019. The data on Chinese workers include those who were sent to work on Chinese companies' construction contracts in Africa ("workers on contracted projects") and Chinese workers sent to work for local companies in Africa ("workers doing labor services"). They are reported by Chinese contractors and do not include informal migrants such as private traders, investors, and shopkeepers, and likely underestimate the total presence of Chinese migrants in Africa. In 2019, the top five countries with Chinese workers were Algeria, Angola, Nigeria, Zambia, and Kenya, which together accounted for 52 percent of all Chinese workers in Africa. Algeria alone accounted for almost a quarter of the total (Figure 3.20).

Based on official data, the COVID-19 pandemic has severely reduced the presence of Chinese workers in Africa amid a reduction of overall Chinese economic activity on the continent, but possibly also because of public health reasons and travel restrictions. At the end of 2021, the official number of Chinese workers in Africa stood at about 93,000, a 64 percent reduction from the 2015

Figure 3.20. Africa: Number of Chinese Workers, 2009-21
(Number of workers, thousands)

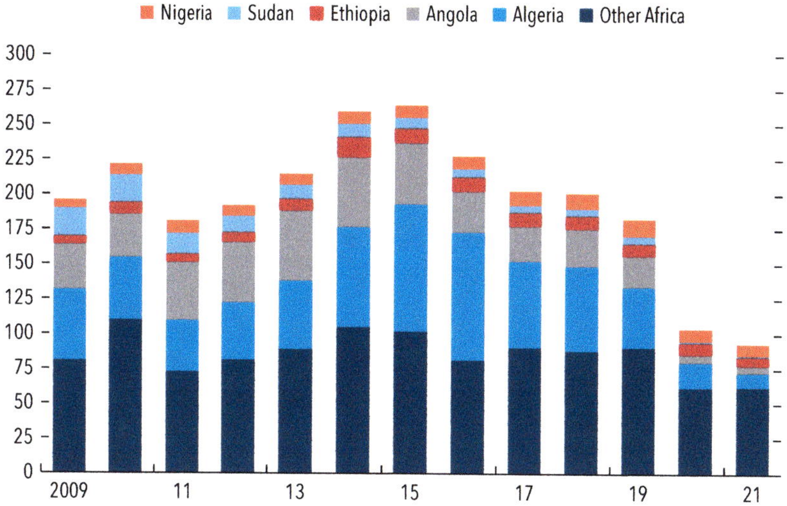

Sources: The Johns Hopkins University SAIS China Africa Research Initiative; and The National Bureau of Statistics of China.

peak. Algeria and Angola both stand out in this metric, with an almost 90 percent reduction in the number of registered Chinese workers in 2021 compared with 2015.

One hypothesis that has been raised is that the influx of Chinese workers in Africa could impede job and training opportunities for locals (Dollar 2016). Research on the effect of Chinese projects in Africa has shown that these may be associated with positive employment effects (Guo, An, and Jiang 2022) and increased employment stability as workers transition from the primary to the secondary or tertiary sectors (Zhang and others 2023). In terms of training and upskilling, we note the recent emergence of the so-called Luban Workshop, a Chinese-backed vocational training program initiated in 2016 under the BRI highlights this change in trend. These workshops, spanning more than 30 locations in 25 countries largely in Asia, the Middle East, and Africa, focus on educating local students in servicing Chinese electric-vehicle engines, operating commercial drones, and assembling robots according to Mahtani and Irwandi (2023). They contribute to educational advancement by constructing schools, introducing technology, and organizing trips to Chinese vocational schools for local educators. Tens of thousands of young people have graduated from them, with Beijing having announced in April 2023 the formation of a special committee to help plan and construct new workshops. On balance, it may be argued that while the reduction in the presence of Chinese workers in African countries has been declining because of both the reduction of Chinese projects and the direct effect of the COVID-19 pandemic, there are also signs that Chinese companies engage in meaningful training activities to employ locals in construction projects.

Foreign Aid

China's *global* foreign aid is relatively small compared with that of other nations of comparable economic size, but it is rising (Figure 3.21). For comparison, US aid in fiscal year 2021 totaled approximately $28 billion, compared with about $3 billion for China. To put these numbers in context, however, it is important to note that China is still an emerging market and its per capita income, at roughly $9,000 in nominal terms, is only about a quarter of the Organisation for Economic Co-operation and Development average according to World Bank data. This consideration, in turn, affects the way China approaches aid. According to the State Council Information Office of the People's Republic of China (2014), aid includes grants (aid gratis), interest-free loans, and concessional loans. Unfortunately, it is not clear how much of China's global aid flows to Africa. During the 2018 FOCAC, China pledged $15 billion in aid amount to African countries out of the total $60 billion commitment (Shepherd and Blanchard 2018). However, data on actual disbursements out of that total envelope are not publicly available.

The bulk of Chinese financing to Africa falls under the category of development finance rather than aid. According to Dreher and others (2017), China provides relatively little aid in the strictest sense of the term, that is, development projects with a grant element of 25 percent or higher. A large proportion of the financial support that China provides to other countries comes in the form of

Figure 3.21. China: Foreign Aid Expenditure, 2003–21
(Billions of US dollars)

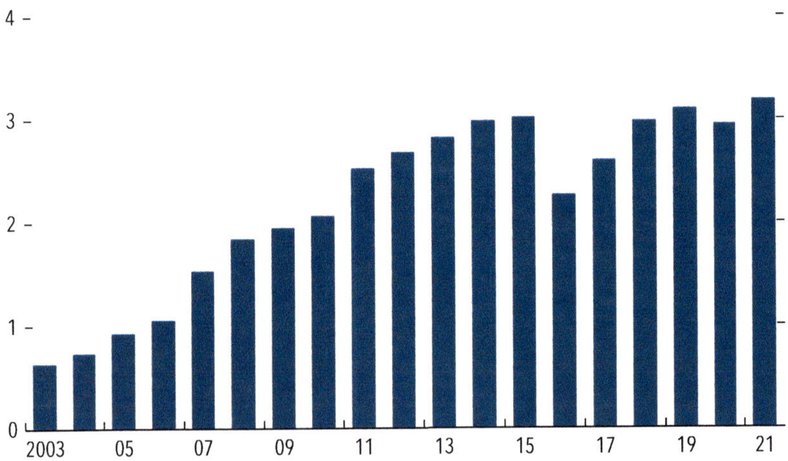

Sources: The Johns Hopkins University SAIS China Africa Research Initiative; and The Ministry of Finance of China.

export credits, and market rate or close-to-market rate loans. Western donors and lenders, on the other hand, generally provide development finance on highly concessional terms and have less aggressive export credit programs.

China is also not a member of the Organisation for Economic Co-operation and Development Assistance Committee, and it classifies itself as a South–South cooperation development partner or provider rather than a "donor." As aid and loans have increased in volume and significance in recent years, China has recognized the importance of aid (Sun 2015). In 2018, it formally established its first independent foreign aid agency, known as China International Development Cooperation Administration. It was designed to manage China's rising development cooperation in a more intentional and streamlined manner and was a response to the increasingly complex and fragmented landscape of Chinese development cooperation. So far, China International Development Cooperation Administration's budget still appears small in comparison with China's overall foreign aid spending, which could be a sign of slow progress in consolidating China's aid efforts (Sun 2019). However, the establishment of the foreign aid agency signals an emphasis on strategic planning, interagency coordination, monitoring, and evaluation, and, therefore, it reflects efforts and progress in modernizing China's foreign aid, its pursuit of better practice, and engagement with traditional donors.

RECENT DEVELOPMENTS AND CHINA'S GROWTH SLOWDOWN

Lending: Evolving Priorities and Risk Appetite

Chinese loan commitments to African countries peaked at about 2016, with disbursements following a similar pattern. Since then, however, and notably already before the COVID-19 pandemic, lending activities have significantly subsided (Figure 3.5). The reasons for this retrenchment are manifold. However, it is notable that the earlier surge in loan arrangements slowed down after the commodity price collapse of 2015, coinciding with the rise in debt sustainability and solvency concerns for some of the hardest-hit African countries. The slowdown in Chinese lending is also not isolated to Africa. Myers and Ray (2023) document a precipitous decline in Chinese loan commitments to Latin American and Caribbean countries between 2015 and 2020. They cited as reasons China's efforts to align outward engagement with domestic growth objectives, which has led to a focus on specific, often high-tech, sectors.

The pandemic further intensified the strain on many African economies, which were hit hard by the collapse in international trade and the need to address demanding public health challenges. In light of increased debt sustainability concerns for low- and lower-middle-income countries, the World Bank and the IMF urged G20 countries to establish the Debt Service Suspension Initiative (DSSI) at the onset of the pandemic (IMF 2021; World Bank 2022). Out of the 73 countries that were eligible for a temporary suspension of debt-service payments owed to their official bilateral creditors, 38 are in Africa and, out of those, 32 participated in the initiative. The DSSI helped countries concentrate their resources on fighting the pandemic and safeguarding the lives and livelihoods of millions of the most vulnerable people. According to the World Bank, the initiative delivered potential savings of about $12.9 billion to 48 participating countries in 2021 (World Bank 2022). Moreover, in anticipation of the need for deeper debt restructurings in some cases, the G20 agreed on a Common Framework for Debt Treatments beyond the DSSI, which should help facilitate debt restructuring on a case-by-case basis and burden sharing across creditors (Group of Twenty 2020).

For many African countries, the multiyear shocks culminated in a funding squeeze after Russia's invasion of Ukraine and the tightening in global monetary policy conditions. The decline in Chinese lending, coupled with reduced support from traditional financing sources, has made it challenging for African countries to refinance public debt and meet repayment obligations. Indeed, external borrowing costs have soared to new highs in many African countries, with the ratio of public interest payments to revenue (excluding grants) more than doubling over a decade, at 10 percent for the median African economy, and at three times the level prevailing in advanced economies (IMF 2023a).

China has been a key player in recent debt restructuring and negotiations, unlike in negotiations leading to the Heavily Indebted Poor Countries Initiative, during which Chinese lending to low-income countries was minimal. China also contributed to the DSSI, providing 63 percent of suspensions in 2020 and 2021, though owning just 30 percent of the claims (Brautigam and Huang 2023). However, debt restructuring for some countries (including under the Group of Twenty Common Framework) has been slow and challenging because of several factors, such as many different debt instruments and a more diverse creditor base, which requires adaptation and coordination. China's involvement in the debt restructuring process is further complicated by its varying entities participating in the creditor negotiations. For instance, whereas China Exim Bank is part of the Official Creditor Committee in the case of Ghana, the CDB is classified as a private creditor in the case of Zambia.

Chinese authorities have started addressing debt sustainability concerns by strengthening risk assessment frameworks and adopting formal debt sustainability frameworks. For example, China Exim Bank has strengthened its risk assessment framework. A formal debt sustainability framework has also been adopted, which could contribute to explain the relative slowdown in lending activity in recent years as risks are better evaluated.

Looking at the entire period since the commodity price decline in 2015, it is apparent that notwithstanding the difficulties associated with the COVID-19 pandemic and the resulting wave of sovereign debt sustainability concerns in many African countries, appetite for lending to these countries has been on a declining trend for some time. This trend is unlikely to change in the near future given China's sluggish domestic growth and the decreased risk appetite, especially in light of the complexity of the existing debt restructuring cases.

Investment: Shrinking Financing Envelope and Evolving Framework

Recent data, spanning the pre- and post-COVID-19 periods, highlight a notable decline in China's financial commitments to FDI directed toward Africa. The shift was evident at the 2018 FOCAC, where China's historical pattern of doubling or tripling previous FOCAC pledges experienced a break (Shepherd and Blanchard 2018). Although this trend was unlikely to continue indefinitely, China's nominal financing pledge of $60 billion at the 2018 Beijing Summit remained flat compared with the pledge three years prior. It actually decreased in terms of the contribution of the Chinese government, considering that Chinese private companies were encouraged to contribute $10 billion in investment projects out of the total package (Brautigam 2018).

The 2021 FOCAC marked an even more significant departure, when China announced for the first time a reduction in the *nominal envelope* of its financial commitments to Africa, from $60 billion to $40 billion over a three-year period, with half of the decrease attributed to a fall in infrastructure lending. The composition of the commitments showed a shift away from direct infrastructure financing toward more trade credit. Although it is not clear how binding the total FOCAC commitments are likely to be in practice, the decline is mirrored in the sharp declines in Chinese companies' African construction gross revenues and presence of Chinese workers on the field as discussed in the previous section. More recently, the 2023 China–Africa Economic and Trade Expo saw a 50 percent drop in signed projects compared with 2019 (Africanews 2023), despite high-profile attendance. These developments are not, by themselves, definitive evidence of a permanent retrenchment of Chinese activity in the region. However, they may indicate that Chinese authorities have decided to recalibrate their strategy and reduce their direct involvement in favor of greater reliance on local governments for practical decision-making. For example, African banks have recently been given more leeway to select projects to be carried out in the context of the FOCAC commitments.

At the third BRI Forum, held in October 2023, the Chinese president, Mr. Xi, called for "high quality and well-targeted projects, promoting a multidimensional (land, sea, air) Belt and Road connectivity network, 'small and smart' livelihood projects, green development, digital economy, and technopolitical innovation," which may signal a move away from large infrastructure projects to green energy and high-tech investments. This shift aligns with China's pledge to halt new overseas coal-fired power stations and joint initiative involving several African countries—Comoros, Ethiopia, the Gambia, Kenya, and São Tomé and Príncipe—to cooperate to improve digital infrastructure such as telecommunications, satellite navigation, and cloud data centers. China also launched a Global AI Governance Initiative to contain potential risks of emerging AI technologies, while harnessing their potential. Taken together, these statements of intent from Chinese authorities signal a potential evolution of the BRI, away from the more traditional focus on transport, energy, and mining, and toward new potential sources of growth.

Despite these shifts, the long-term trajectory of Chinese FDI in Africa will ultimately hinge on China's broader growth path. With China's aging population and its quest to move up to higher-value-added supply chains and diversification into high-tech and green sectors, Africa's youthful population, and expanding markets offer potential. On their own, however, these factors are not enough to continue to attract FDI to the region. Indeed, significant roadblocks emerge in the form of poor infrastructure, institutions, and productivity, combined with insufficiently developed human and physical capital.

China's Conjunctural and Structural Growth Slowdown

China has experienced a deceleration in economic growth since the early 2010s, a trend expected to persist into the medium term (Figure 3.22). This is due to a confluence of factors—curbing of its real estate sector, demographic trends from an aging population, and, more recently, volatility in the external environment including trade tensions, and geoeconomic fragmentation (IMF 2024). Whereas China's annual growth rate averaged about 10 percent in the 2000s, it grew by less than 8 percent per year on average in the 2010s. Since the COVID-19 pandemic, China's growth has declined even further, and the latest IMF projections show average annual growth below 4 percent for 2023–28, with notable trends pointing to a reduction in investment. Demographic pressures are now starker than ever for China (IMF 2024). In 2022, the country saw its population decline for the first time in decades, and it is projected to face a dramatic reduction in working-age population before the middle of the century (Figure 3.23). Beyond its direct effect on long-run growth, a shrinking working-age population will have to support a growing elderly population, similar to what has been observed in some advanced economies.

Next, we examine China's relationship with Africa, which reveals that shifts were underway before the pandemic. Indeed, China's reduced demand for commodities significantly affected African countries heavily reliant on fuel and

Figure 3.22. China: Average Annual Growth Rates, 2000–28
(Percent)

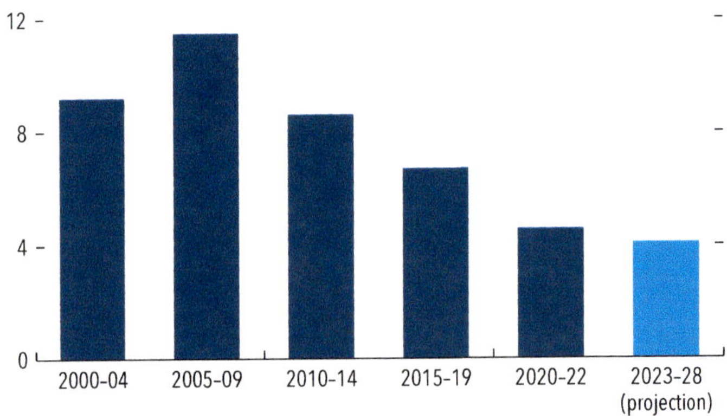

Source: IMF, World Economic Outlook database.

Figure 3.23. China: Working-Age Population, 2000–50
(Millions)

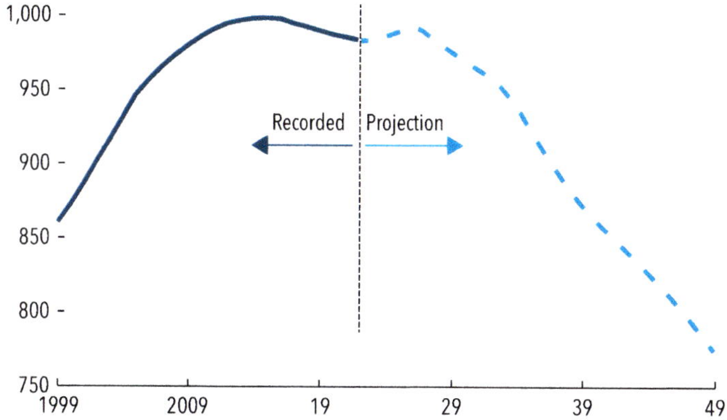

Source: UN, World Population Prospects, 2023.

commodity exports. The fuel component of total African exports to China fell dramatically after 2015 and contracted further during the pandemic, reflecting global oil price dynamics (Figure 3.2).

As economic activity faced an unprecedented fall in 2020 and 2021, trade, lending, and investment from China to Africa experienced a retrenchment. The key question now is whether the ongoing recovery will prompt renewed engagement from China in Africa. Given the deep economic ties, a potential slowdown in China's growth in the medium to long term will likely affect economic activity negatively in sub-Saharan Africa. These negative spillovers would primarily emerge from trade links, encompassing both a deceleration in export volumes and commodity price declines.

To delve into the potential effect, the main results from complementary approaches in evaluating the effect of a Chinese deceleration on the economy of *sub-Saharan Africa* are presented.[7] First, the analysis from Abdel-Latif and El-Gamal (2023)—also featured in the first analytical note of the October 2023 *Regional Economic Outlook for sub-Saharan Africa*—shows that a 1 percentage point decline in China's real GDP growth rate leads to about 0.25 percentage points decline in sub-Saharan Africa's total GDP growth within a year (Figure 3.24).[8]

[7] The analytical work mentioned here was carried out for the *Regional Economic Outlook developed by the African Department*, which comprises 45 sub-Saharan African countries. Northern African countries are under the purview of the Middle East and Central Asia Department and are not included in this analysis.

[8] The empirical model consists of a large 70-block GVAR model with real GDP growth and inflation as key domestic endogenous variables, and the US interest rate and oil prices as global variables. Each country's endogenous variables depend on their lagged values, because it is standard for autoregressive models, but also on the lagged value of a trade-weighted aggregate of all other countries' endogenous variables and global variables. The model includes 43 sub-Saharan African countries for which data are available, as well as several, mostly advanced, economies. The key shock of interest is a negative GDP shock to the Chinese economy, which then propagates to all other countries.

Figure 3.24. Sub-Saharan Africa: GDP Response to China's Growth Slowdown
(Percentage points of GDP)

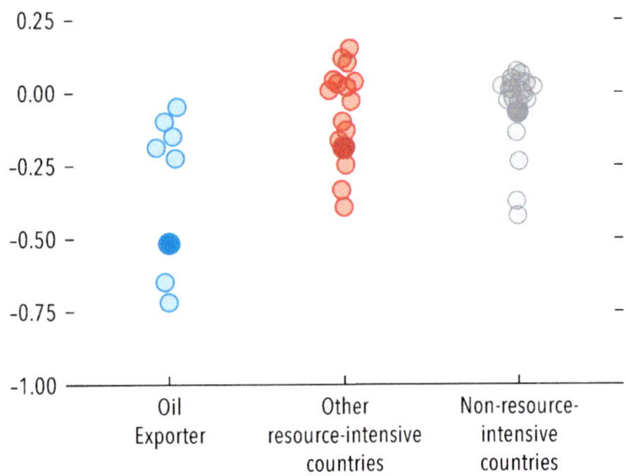

Source: Abdel-Latif and El-Gamal (2023).
Note: Lighter shade dots denote individual countries. Darker shades represent group GDP-weighted averages. Country groupings are detailed in Annex 3.1.

When considering the effect on oil-exporting countries, the growth shortfall rises to more than 0.5 percentage points on average. For other resource-intensive countries, the growth loss averages 0.2 percentage points.[9] Therefore, countries that export relatively more to China are more likely to be more susceptible to negative effects resulting from a slowdown in China.

In the second approach, a scenario analysis is conducted similar to one of the downside scenarios of Chapter 1 of the World Economic Outlook, October 2023 (https://www.imf.org/en/Publications/WEO/Issues/2023/10/10/world-economic-outlook-october-2023) using the IMF AFRMOD model, an open-economy general equilibrium model specifically tailored for sub-Saharan Africa.[10] The shock envisions a contraction in the real estate sector in China and assumes no swift policy actions to restructure property developers. This, in turn, leads to weaker consumption because of subdued confidence. The scenario also assumes no meaningful countercyclical policy support on the fiscal side. The effect of this shock on China's growth, projected over six years from 2023 to 2028, is portrayed in Figure 3.25. Notably, the effect of the shock is felt throughout the region, with a more pronounced effect on fragile and low-income countries, as well as oil exporters (Angola and other sub-Saharan African oil exporters). One of the key

[9] The regional or group average of the response of GDP growth to the shock to Chinese GDP growth was calculated using the share of each country's cumulative GDP between 2018 and 2022 as a weighting factor.

[10] Annex 3.1 provides more information on the model and on the definitions of the regions included therein.

Figure 3.25. Sub-Saharan Africa: GDP Response to China's Growth Slowdown, 2003–28

(Deviation from steady state, percent)

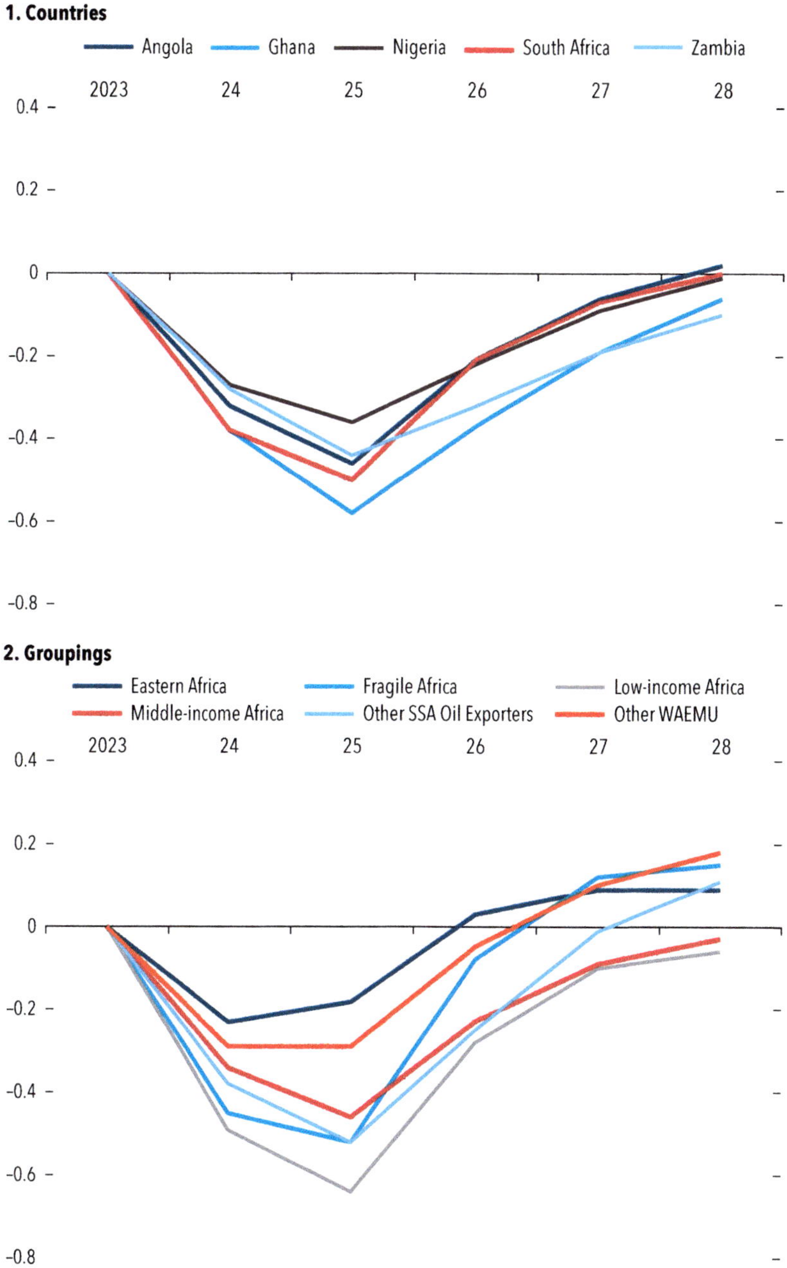

Source: IMF (2023c).

Note: The figure portrays the percent deviation of GDP from the steady-state growth path in the absence of the shock to the Chinese economy. Country groups are detailed in Annex 3.1. WAEMU = West African Economic and Monetary Union, SSA = sub-Saharan Africa.

advantages of using a model-based approach is that this allows for better understanding of the evolving effect over time. Notably, some groups of countries, in particular Eastern Africa, Fragile countries, and West African Economic and Monetary Union countries not included in other regions, fare relatively better toward the end of the projection horizon, with GDP surpassing the steady state before converging in the long term.

Other analyses of spillover effects from China's growth to Africa and to the rest of the world economy have highlighted complementary aspects to those outlined in the previous section (Cashin, Mohaddes, and Raissi 2016; Furceri, Jalles, and Zdzienicka 2017; Lakatos and others 2017; Hakobyan and others 2023). While the focus in individual studies is sometimes placed on specific issues, such as fiscal or monetary policy in China, the channels highlighted are usually very similar and encompass primarily trade and the effect of China's economy on global commodity prices. A common finding is that spillovers from China will primarily affect African countries that are more heavily reliant on commodities exports, including both oil and fuels, and minerals. Crucially, however, the extent of the spillover effects depends on the way in which authorities in China use economic policy to respond to shocks. For example, Hakobyan and others (2023) focus on the differential effect of a slowdown in Chinese economic activity, showing that the effect on African economies ultimately largely depends on whether the response of fiscal and monetary policy is accommodative or not. In addition, the chapter shows that a rebalancing scenario, that is, a situation in which public infrastructure investment is permanently reduced in favor of transfers to households, and thus, private consumption, will generally have muted effects on African economies as the import content of consumer goods in China is relatively higher than the import content of investment goods—providing offsetting effects on net imports.

CONCLUSION

The economic relationship between Africa and China is undergoing a significant shift. After 2001, with China's WTO entry and investment-heavy growth model, its demand for raw materials, especially from Africa, surged, affecting global commodity prices and trade volumes. However, changes are afoot in China's growth model, now veering toward less resource-intensive practices due to factors like an aging population and a deceleration in the real estate sector. This change is expected to temper China's demand for fossil fuels, diverging from the peak of its economic boom.

This shift poses notable implications for Africa, particularly for oil-exporting and resource-intensive countries. Yet, it also opens avenues for new collaboration as China recalibrates its economic trajectory. China's shrinking working-age population, resulting in tighter labor markets and higher domestic wages, could prompt Chinese firms to seek alternative markets, with Africa's abundant labor force becoming increasingly attractive. Proper economic and social policies in Africa can strategically position the continent within this evolving landscape. This study draws tentative conclusions and recommendations on China's engagement with Africa in trade, investment, and lending.

- ***Trade dynamics:*** China has become Africa's largest trading partner, reshaping the continent's export landscape. African exports to China, mainly natural resources, have increased significantly. However, with China's waning appetite for raw materials, African nations must adapt, emphasizing diversification and sustainable trade strategies, including those involving regional trade integration, such as the African Continental Free Trade Area (AfCFTA), to boost competitiveness (El-Ganainy and others 2023).
- ***Lending:*** China plays a big role in the region, but, collectively, other multilateral and official creditors often play an even more important role in lending to Africa. The recent funding squeeze has adversely affected many African countries, leading to debt distress or high risk of debt distress. While China's participation in the DSSI is a positive step, it remains a small first step as interest accrues, and debt burdens rise. Further progress on the specifics of debt restructuring plans, including private creditors, is crucial for a sustained recovery of African economies.
- ***Foreign direct investment:*** China's role in African FDI has been modest but holds potential, especially as China seeks to diversify its investments. Africa's young population and competitive labor market make it an appealing destination for foreign capital and technology. Attracting investment requires African countries to enhance their investment climates.

Going forward, *China's economic slowdown* presents both challenges and opportunities for Africa. Adapting to this new reality requires resilience and structural reforms in Africa. These include diversifying the economy, increasing regional trade, and enhancing competitiveness. Building financial buffers and strengthening policy frameworks will reduce vulnerabilities. For Africa to offset China's reduced economic presence, it is essential to focus on sustainable growth through economic diversification, leveraging the green energy transition, and enhancing local processing capabilities. Implementing reforms in mining laws, financial management, private sector growth, and human capital development, combined with infrastructure improvements, will broaden Africa's economic horizons.

ANNEX 3.1.
DETAILS OF GVAR AND AFRMOD MODELS

AFRMOD

The IMF G20 Model is a version of the Flexible System of Global Models—FSGM (Andrle and others 2015). This model is particularly suitable for running short- to medium-term scenario analyses in an internally consistent way in general equilibrium. Its rich setup, in terms of both sectors and of interlinkages between countries, allows for rich dynamics and for the analysis of the joint response of key parts of the world economy to shocks of interest.

AFRMOD, which is the version used for the analysis carried out in this chapter, is a specific version of the FSGM framework tailored to sub-Saharan Africa, in the sense that it specifically focuses on a few regions and countries in Africa. The complete definition of the groups is provided in Annex Table 3.1.1. It consists of 13 individual countries, of which 5 are relatively large sub-Saharan African economies and 8 advanced economies, together with 8 country groups, of which 6 consist of sub-Saharan African countries and 2 of other important groups of mostly advanced economies and emerging markets.

GVAR Model

As detailed in Abdel-Latif and El-Gamal (2023), the 44 sub-Saharan African countries included in the study are grouped as detailed in Annex Table 3.1.2.

ANNEX TABLE 3.1.1.

Country Groupings in the AFRMOD Model

Type	Group Name	ISO3 Codes
Individual	N/A	USA, CHN, FRA, DEU, IND, ITA, JPN, GBR, AGO, GHA, NGA, ZAF, ZMB
SSA Group	Eastern Africa	KEN, RWA, TZA, UGA
SSA Group	Fragile Africa	BFA, BDI, CIV, CAF, COM, ERI, GIN, GNB, STP, SLE, TGO, LBR, ZWE
SSA Group	Low-Income Africa	ETH, GMB, MDG, MWI, MOZ
SSA Group	Middle-Income Africa	BWA, CPV, LSO, MUS, NAM, SEN, SYC, SWZ
SSA Group	Sub-Saharan Africa Oil Exporters	CMR, COD, TCD, COG, GNQ, GAB, SSD
SSA Group	West African Economic and Monetary Union, WAEMU	BEN, MLI, NER
Non-SSA Group	Other Advanced Economies	AUS, CAN, DNK, HKG, ISL, ISR, KOR, NZL, NOR, SGP, SWE, CHE, TWN
Non-SSA Group	Other Oil Exporters	DZA, BHR, BRN, ECU, IRN, KAZ, KWT, OMN, QAT, RUS, SAU, TTO, ARE, VEN, YEM

Source: IMF staff.
Note: Table uses International Organization for Standardization country codes. SSA = sub-Saharan Africa.

ANNEX TABLE 3.1.2.

Country Groupings in the GVAR Model

Group Name	ISO3 Codes
Oil Exporter	AGO, CMR, TCD, COG, GNQ, GAB, NGA
Other Resource-Intensive	BWA, BFO, CAR, DRC, ERI, GHA, GIN, LBR, MLI, NAM, NER, SLE, ZAF, TZA, ZMB, ZWE
Non-Resource Intensive	BEN, BDI, CPV, COM, CIV, SWZ, ETH, GMB, GNB, KEN, LSO, MDG, MWI, MUS, MOZ, RWA, STP, SEN, SYC, TGO, UGA

Source: Abdel-Latif and El-Gamal (2023).
Note: Table uses International Organization for Standardization country codes.

REFERENCES

Abdel-Latif, H., and M. El-Gamal. 2023. "Chinese Economic Deceleration and Sub-Saharan Africa." Unpublished.

Acker, K., D. Brautigam, and Y. Huang. 2020. "Debt Relief with Chinese Characteristics." Working Paper No. 2020/39, China Africa Research Initiative, School of Advanced International Studies, Johns Hopkins University, Washington, DC.

Africanews. 2023. "The China–Africa Trade Biennale Bears Fruitful Results." July 3. https://www.africanews.com/2023/07/03/the-china-africa-trade-biennale-bears-fruitful-results.

Andrle, M., P. Blagrave, P. Espaillat, K. Honjo, B. Hunt, M. Kortelainen, R. Lalonde, and others. 2015. "The Flexible System of Global Models—FSGM." IMF Working Paper WP/15/64, International Monetary Fund. https://www.imf.org/en/Publications/WP/Issues/2016/12/31/The-Flexible-System-of-Global-Models-FSGM-42796.

Brautigam, D. 2018. "China's FOCAC Financial Package for Africa 2018: Four Facts." China–Africa Research Initiative Blog, September 3. http://www.chinaafricarealstory.com/2018/09/chinas-focac-financial-package-for.html.

Brautigam, D., and Y. Huang. 2023. "Integrating China into Multilateral Debt Relief: Progress and Problems in the G20 DSSI." SAIS-CARI Briefing Paper 9, April. https://www.econstor.eu/bitstream/10419/271579/1/1847106269.pdf.

Brautigam, D., Y. Huang, and K. Acker. 2020. "Risky Business: New Data on Chinese Loans and Africa's Debt Problem." Briefing Paper 2020/3, China Africa Research Initiative, School of Advanced International Studies, Johns Hopkins University, Washington, DC.

Cashin, P., K. Mohaddes, and M. Raissi. 2016. "China's Slowdown and Global Financial Market Volatility: Is World Growth Losing Out?" IMF Working Paper 16/63, International Monetary Fund, Washington, DC.

Centre for Chinese Studies. 2013. "The China–African Development Fund (CAD Fund)." Policy Briefing, Stellenbosch University, July.

Chen, W., D. Dollar, and H. Tang. 2018. "Why Is China investing in Africa? Evidence from the Firm Level." *World Bank Economic Review* 32 (3): 610–32.

Dollar, D. 2016. *China's Engagement with Africa: From Natural Resources to Human Resources.* Washington, DC: Brookings.

Dollar, D. 2019. *Understanding China's Belt and Road Infrastructure Projects in Africa.* Washington, DC: Brookings.

Dreher, A., A. Fuchs, P. Bradley, A. Strange, and M. Tierney. 2017. "Aid, China, and Growth: Evidence from a New Global Development Finance Dataset." AidData, October. https://docs.aiddata.org/ad4/pdfs/WPS46_Aid_China_and_Growth.pdf.

El-Ganainy, A., S. Hakobyan, F. Liu, H. Weisfeld, A. Abbas, C. Allard, H. Balima, and others. 2023. "Trade Integration in Africa: Unleashing the Continent's Potential in a Changing World." Departmental Paper 2023/003, International Monetary Fund, Washington, DC.

Furceri, D., J. T. Jalles, and A. Zdzienicka. 2017. "China Spillovers: New Evidence from Time-Varying Estimates." *Open Economies Review* 28 (3): 413–29.

Gelpern, A., S. Horn, S. Morris, B. Parks, and C. Trebesch. 2022. "How China Lends: A Rare Look into 100 Debt Contracts with Foreign Governments." *Economic Policy* 2022: eiac054.

Global Infrastructure Hub. 2019. "Guidance Note on National Infrastructure Banks and Similar Financing Facilities." July. Toronto, Canada.

Group of Twenty. 2020. "Common Framework for Debt Treatments beyond the DSSI." https://clubdeparis.org/sites/default/files/annex_common_framework_for_debt_treatments_beyond_the_dssi.pdf.

Guo, S., J. An, and H. Jiang. 2022. "Chinese Aid and Local Employment in Africa." November 20. https://ssrn.com/abstract=3718578.

Hakobyan, S., M. Brussevich, D. Cerdeiro, E. Cerutti, M. Coppo, B. Hunt, P. N'Diaye, and others. 2023. "Spillovers: Examining the Economic and Financial Links between China and Africa." Unpublished.

Horn, S., B. C. Parks, C. M. Reinhart, and C. Trebesch. 2023. "China as an International Lender of Last Resort." NBER Working Paper w31105, National Bureau of Economic Research, Cambridge, MA.

Horn, S., C. M. Reinhart, and C. Trebesch. 2021. "China's Overseas Lending." *Journal of International Economics* 133: 103539.

International Monetary Fund (IMF). 2021. "Questions and Answers on Sovereign Debt Issues." Washington, DC, April 8. https://www.imf.org/en/About/FAQ/sovereign-debt.

International Monetary Fund (IMF). 2023a. "Africa. Special Issue: In Pursuit of Stronger Growth and Resilience." Regional Economic Outlook: Africa. Washington, DC, October. https://www.imf.org/-/media/Files/Publications/REO/AFR/2023/October/English/africa-special-issue.ashx.

International Monetary Fund (IMF). 2023b. "At a Crossroads: Sub-Saharan Africa's Economic Relations with China." Regional Economic Outlook: Sub-Saharan Africa—Light on the Horizon? Washington, DC, October. https://www.imf.org/-/media/Files/Publications/REO/AFR/2023/October/English/africa-special-issue.ashx.

International Monetary Fund (IMF). 2023c. "Global Prospects and Policies." In *World Economic Outlook: Navigating Global Divergences.* Washington, DC, October.

International Monetary Fund (IMF). 2024. "People's Republic of China: 2023 Article IV Consultation-Press Release; Staff Report; and Statement by the Executive Director for the People's Republic of China." Country Report No. 2024/038, IMF, Washington, DC.

Lakatos, C., M. Maliszewska, I. Osorio-Rodarte, and D. Go. 2017. "China's Slowdown and Rebalancing: Impacts on Sub-Saharan Africa." *Journal of Economic Integration* 32 (4): 759–803.

Li, H. 2020. "From Politics to Business: How a State-Led Fund Is Investing in Africa? The Case of the China–Africa Development Fund." GCI Working Paper 001, Boston University Global Development Policy Center.

Mahtani, S., and J. Irwandi. 2023. "Winning Friends by Training Workers Is China's New Gambit." *Washington Post*, July 10. https://www.washingtonpost.com/world/interactive/2023/china-luban-workshops-global-influence.

Malik, A., B. Parks, B. Russell, J. Lin, K. Walsh, K. Solomon, S. Zhang, and others. 2021. *Banking on the Belt and Road: Insights from a New Global Dataset of 13,427 Chinese Development Projects.* Williamsburg, VA: AidData at William & Mary. https://www.aiddata.org/publications/banking-on-the-belt-and-road.

Myers, M., and R. Ray. 2023. "At a Crossroads: Chinese Development Finance to Latin America and the Caribbean, 2022." China LAC Report March 2023, The Dialogue and Boston University Global Development Policy Center.

Nedopil, C. 2023. "China Belt and Road Initiative (BRI) Investment Report 2023 H1." Green Finance and Development Center, FISF Fudan University Shanghai.

Shepherd, C., and B. Blanchard. 2018. "China's Xi Offers Another $60 Billion to Africa, but Says No to 'Vanity' Projects." Reuters. https://www.reuters.com/article/us-china-africa/chinas-xi-offers-another-60-billion-to-africa-but-says-no-to-vanity-projects-idUSKCN1LJ0C4.

Shinn, D. H. 2019. "China–Africa Ties in Historical Context." In *China–Africa and an Economic Transformation*, edited by Arkebe Oqubay and Justin Yifu Lin, 61–83. Oxford: Oxford Academic.

Sun, Y. 2015. "Xi and the 6th Forum on China–Africa Cooperation: Major Commitments, but with Questions." Brookings Institution. https://www.brookings.edu/articles/xi-and-the-6th-forum-on-china-africa-cooperation-major-commitments-but-with-questions.

Sun, Y. 2019. "One Year on, the Role of the China International Development Cooperation Administration Remains Cloudy." Brookings Institution. https://www.brookings.edu/articles/one-year-on-the-role-of-the-china-international-development-cooperation-administration-remains-cloudy/.

The State Council Information Office of the People's Republic of China. 2014. "China's Foreign Aid (2014)." http://english.www.gov.cn/archive/white_paper/2014/08/23/content_281474982986592.htm.

World Bank. 2000. *Debtor Reporting System Manual.* Washington, DC: World Bank.

World Bank. 2019. *Belt and Road Economics: Opportunities and Risks of Transport Corridors.* Washington, DC: World Bank.

World Bank. 2022. "Debt Service Suspension Initiative." Washington, DC, March 10. https://www.worldbank.org/en/topic/debt/brief/covid-19-debt-service-suspension-initiative.

Zhang, L., Y. Zhuang, Y. Ding, and Z. Liu. 2023. "Infrastructure and Poverty Reduction: Assessing the Dynamic Impact of Chinese Infrastructure Investment in Sub-Saharan Africa." *Journal of Asian Economics* 84: 101573.

CHAPTER 4

The Maghreb and China: Strengthening Resilience and Growth through Cooperation

Alexei Kireyev, Jiawei Li, Modeste Some, and Geneviève Verdier

INTRODUCTION

The Maghreb and China are increasingly discussed in a mutual context. The Maghreb—"the land where the sun sets" in Arabic—is a vast region in North Africa, stretching across almost 6 million square kilometers. With a total population of 100 million, its five countries—Algeria, Libya, Mauritania, Morocco, and Tunisia—share a common history, culture, and language to a large extent. All Maghreb countries are maritime economies strategically located between the advanced economies of Europe across the Mediterranean Sea to the north and the high-potential, developing economies of sub-Saharan Africa to the south. In terms of economic size, the Maghreb is a relatively small region with limited economic links among its countries. At the same time, China is the second-largest economy in the world, with economic linkages globally, including with Maghreb countries.

The Maghreb has been hit hard by multiple shocks in recent years, including the COVID-19 crisis, drought, and geopolitical tensions. These recent crises exacerbated existing structural weaknesses (macro imbalances, social unrest, youth unemployment, and so on). Strengthening the recovery will be critical to help the region address its persistent unemployment problem. Domestic reforms aimed at raising growth and its inclusiveness should be the main driving force to improve resilience, growth, and ultimately, job creation. Policies that strengthen international cooperation to increase foreign direct investment, infrastructure financing, and trade, including with China, could be an additional source of growth, job creation, and improved resilience for the Maghreb.

In this chapter, we assess the cooperation between the Maghreb and China—particularly in trade—as a potential opportunity to strengthen resilience and support the Maghreb's growth. Increased cooperation could improve the quality of the recovery and resilience to shocks and gradually restore economic growth and inclusion. The chapter takes stock of existing relationships in trade, investment, financing, and other cooperation. With a focus on trade in goods, the chapter identifies new opportunities for the Maghreb in its relationship with China and suggests reforms to tap these strategic opportunities and accelerate growth while mitigating the associated risks.

The chapter concludes the following:

- *Economic cooperation between the Maghreb and China has been below potential.* The Maghreb and China have been at the periphery of each other's economic interests for years, and mutual interest has only recently increased. Cooperation has been limited to commodity trade, mainly exports of energy and other raw materials by the Maghreb to China and imports of consumer and investment goods from China. Bilateral tourism has increased, and China has become more involved in infrastructure projects in the region, but the pandemic severely disrupted these activities.
- *More active participation by Maghreb countries in China's global value chains (GVCs) could help them accelerate their growth, strengthen resilience, and create jobs.* The Maghreb trades substantially less with China than with a comparator group of other G20 countries (the European Union, India, Japan, the United States, the United Kingdom), mainly reflecting the long distances between the Maghreb countries and China and the lack of historical ties. Nevertheless, the economic structures of the Maghreb and China are broadly complementary, suggesting that their trade could increase, even with the current structure of comparative advantages. In addition, this analysis suggests that domestic reforms and active policies could help Maghreb countries strengthen their position in China's GVCs. Efforts made by Maghreb governments to improve the business climate and negotiate mutually beneficial trade agreements would help the region's countries attract more investment and advanced technologies, integrate into China's GVCs, and diversify their exports into new products and services. The subsequent export expansion to China—both in traditional goods through regular trade channels and in new products through GVCs—could be an additional source for export-led growth, resilience, and job creation in the region.
- *Obstacles to cooperation with China are surmountable, but action is needed to mitigate risks from increased engagement.* In some Maghreb countries, the obstacles to trade include macroeconomic vulnerabilities, trade barriers—both natural and protectionist barriers—low openness to foreign investment, small national markets, and differences in business practices. Although improved in recent years, the still-limited regulatory and institutional framework for trade could be complemented by carefully designed and balanced trade agreements between each Maghreb country and China. Increased cooperation with China is not without risks, including increased competition (from low-cost imports from China) and debt sustainability (if debt financing from China increases). Potential risks can be mitigated by carefully designed and well-balanced trade liberalization agreements with China that would preserve the integrity of domestic markets in Maghreb

countries while spurring local producers to improve competitiveness. Furthermore, an improved business environment would be a key factor in replacing debt financing with direct investment.

This chapter first reviews the experience of Maghreb–China cooperation in recent years, then presents evidence of untapped potential for additional trade with China, and finally presents some concluding thoughts.

MAGHREB'S COOPERATION WITH CHINA REMAINS LIMITED

Institutional Arrangements

The history of Maghreb–China economic cooperation is relatively recent. In the wake of the 2008 global financial and euro area crisis, Maghreb countries, which have historically relied on trade, remittances, tourism, and investment from Europe and the United States, started searching for new opportunities to diversify their markets and economic partners (Lafargue 2018; Ghafar and Jacobs 2019). China's economy maintained an impressive momentum during this period, boasting high growth rates, albeit lower than earlier.

The institutional framework of cooperation with China reflects the economic diversity of the Maghreb. Maghreb countries are geographically close but economically diverse. *Algeria,* an important gas- and oil-exporting upper-middle-income country, is the region's largest economy. Highly dependent on hydrocarbons, it faces macroeconomic challenges posed by large oil-price fluctuations. *Libya*, also a major oil and gas exporter and an upper-middle-income country, has been mired in civil war for the past decade. The war has led to a power vacuum and instability, with serious economic and social consequences. *Mauritania*, a lower-middle-income country, is an important iron ore producer and has been growing relatively fast but faces volatile metal prices. *Morocco*, the second-largest economy in the region, is a relatively well-diversified middle-income country. Being an important regional producer of agricultural products, cars, and fertilizers, and an active participant in GVCs (mainly with Europe), the country is vulnerable to volatile agricultural output and external demand. Finally, *Tunisia* is a small middle-income country in transition. A producer of electrical components, light machinery, equipment parts (also as part of European GVCs), olive oil, and garments, the country is seeking to resume broad-based growth and restore macroeconomic stability after several domestic and external shocks.

China has traditionally focused on bilateral relations with Maghreb countries. As in other regions, most Chinese activities in the Maghreb are embedded in broader public policy initiatives, with private sector interests often playing a secondary role. Zoubir (2019, 2020) notes that China has no specific regional policy for the Maghreb, but a broader approach to Arab countries focused on infrastructure building, trade, and investment by facilitating cooperation in various sectors, including energy, petrochemicals, agriculture, manufacturing, and services. China is also interested in high-technology fields, such as nuclear energy, space satellites, and renewable energy.

China has upgraded its relationship with the Maghreb to a strategic partnership. In 2013, China designated the Middle East and North Africa a key geostrategic zone, singling out Morocco and Algeria. China's 2016 Arab Policy Paper suggested building relations with Arab countries, including those in the Maghreb region, through strategic partnerships (Zoubir 2020). Among Maghreb countries, this "partnership diplomacy" (Ghafar and Jacobs 2019) has led to agreements with Algeria in 2014 and with Morocco in 2016, primarily focusing on infrastructure and development projects.[1]

China's 2013 Belt and Road Initiative (BRI) provided an additional institutional framework for cooperation, and all Maghreb countries have signed BRI memorandums of understanding with China (GBRIC 2021). Although the focus has been on strengthening economic cooperation through infrastructure investment, including roads, railways, and power grids, the BRI also covers broader cooperation, such as trade facilitation and technical assistance. Participation in the BRI is meant to strengthen bilateral cooperation in five areas: policy coordination, interconnection of infrastructure, trade facilitation, financial integration, and mutual understanding.

Maghreb countries cooperate with China in several international fora. For example, since the early 2000s, China has been working with all Maghreb countries within the Forum on China–Africa Cooperation (FOCAC 2021) (see Chapter 2). The China–Arab States Cooperation Forum, a formal dialogue initiative between China and the Arab League, most recently focused on China helping Arab League members overcome the COVID-19 pandemic (CASCF 2021). Algeria joined the Asian Infrastructure Investment Bank, a multilateral development bank launched in 2015; China is the largest shareholder and has the largest voting power. Libya, Morocco, and Tunisia are listed as prospective nonregional members (AIIB 2021). China's Ministry of Commerce does not list any Maghreb country among those with which China has concluded, is currently negotiating, or considering a free trade agreement (FTA) (Ministry of Commerce, PRC 2021).

China's interest in the Maghreb has evolved. China previously saw the Maghreb as a source of natural resources and a regional market for its export products (Lafargue 2018; Ghafar and Jacobs 2019; Zoubir 2019, 2020). However, reflecting its maturing global strategy, China started viewing the Maghreb as a northern gateway to sub-Saharan Africa about a decade ago, with an initial focus

---

[1] According to Ghafar and Jacobs (2019), China engages in two main types of partnerships in the Maghreb: strategic partnerships and comprehensive strategic partnerships. Strategic partnerships usually go beyond typical diplomatic relations and involve regular meetings between government officials to develop communication and trust. Strategic partnerships do not fall within the confines of treaty-based alliances or coalitions; they are more goal driven and focus on economic, cultural, security, and technological cooperation. Comprehensive strategic partnerships involve a higher level of institutional communication, including regular high-level meetings between top leaders.

on natural resources. With the development of GVCs, Zoubir (2020) argues that the Maghreb has become important for China as a gateway to Northern Africa because of its important role in the Arab world and its proximity to Europe.

Maghreb countries view China as a promising potential partner—a source of foreign investment, an expanding export market, and a partner in infrastructure projects that could stimulate economic growth, create jobs, and reduce inequality (Lafargue 2018; Ghafar and Jacobs 2019; Zoubir 2019, 2020). All Maghreb countries established diplomatic relations with China shortly after gaining independence in the 1960s.

China's interest in the Maghreb increased during the COVID-19 pandemic. Since mid-2020, Google Trends consistently shows increased searches by Maghreb internet users for terms such as "China," "vaccines," and "vaccination" (Box 4.1). This trend partially reflects the tradition of cooperation in health care between China and the Maghreb. Since independence, most Maghreb countries have received assistance from China in the form of medical personnel, medicine, and training. Health issues have also been on the BRI agenda, and amid vaccine shortages, some Maghreb countries received support from China in the form of vaccination doses and equipment.[2]

Irrespective of mutual interest, cultural barriers could constrain relations between China and the Maghreb. Significant Chinese migration to the Maghreb region, particularly in Algeria, which hosts up to 80,000 Chinese citizens, has occasionally caused local conflicts because of cultural barriers (Zoubir 2020). China is addressing the issue of cultural and language barriers by setting up Confucius Institutes in Morocco and Tunisia, and providing emergency humanitarian support during the COVID-19 pandemic.

Box 4.1. Text-Mining Techniques Confirm an Increase in Mutual Interest in Recent Years

The number of searches in each Maghreb country for "China" as the keyword or topic and the number of searches in China for individual Maghreb countries have risen steadily since 2004 (Figure 4.1.1). During this period, the number of searches in China for Maghreb countries more than tripled. Morocco exceeded the number of searches by far in China relative to other countries in the region, suggesting that Morocco is China's main point of interest in the Maghreb (reflecting Morocco's higher integration in global value chains), with Algeria a distant second.

[2] For example, Morocco signed a convention to produce the vaccine developed by China and distribute it to other African countries. Morocco procured over 40 million doses of Sinopharm, a COVID-19 vaccine developed in China (Duke Global Health Innovation Center 2021). Algeria started producing China's Sinovac vaccine in September 2021. It also benefitted from visits of Chinese medical experts (Rudolf 2021). In addition to the immediate benefits, such partnerships presented an opportunity for countries in the region to upgrade production capabilities and benefit from technology transfers.

Figure 4.1.1. Maghreb and China: Evolution of Mutual Interest, 2004–21

(Six-month moving average Google Trends search volume index[1])

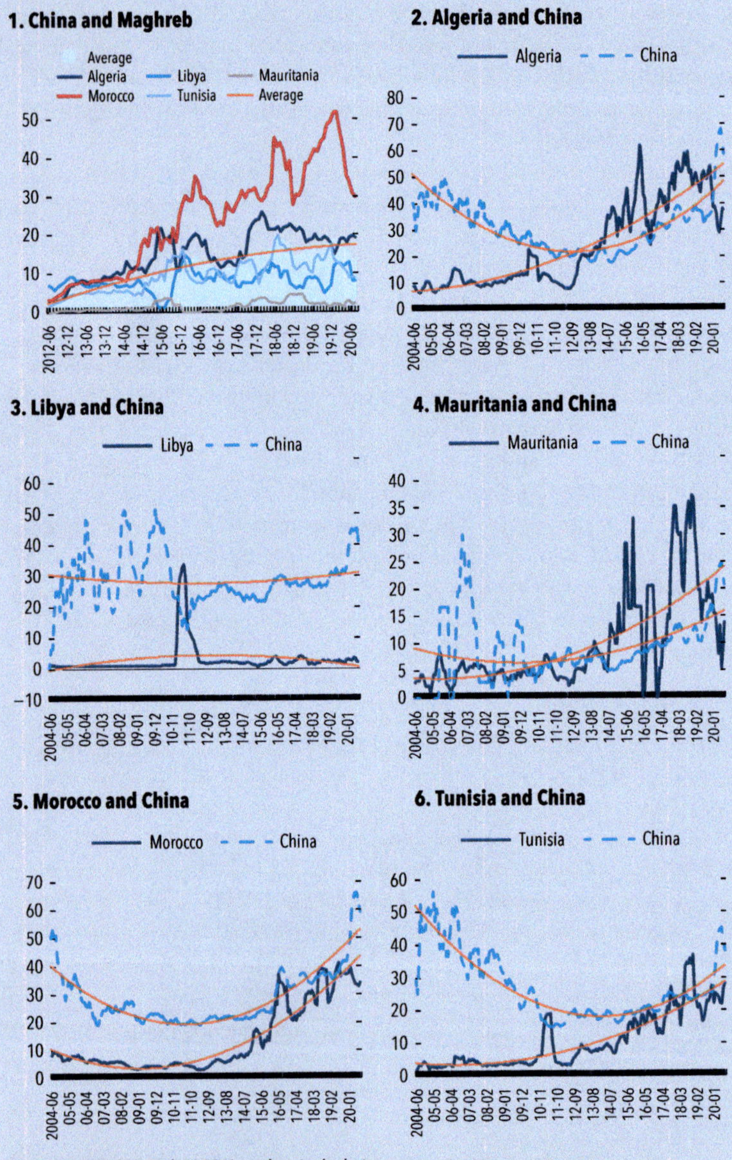

Sources: Google Trends (2021); authors' calculations.

[1] The Google Trends search volume index represents the number of searches of a keyword or a topic relative to the total number of searches rescaled on a range of 0–100. Second-order polynomial trends are included.

Trade in Goods and Services

Maghreb countries' trade with China is rising, although from a low base. Since the early 2000s, Maghreb countries' exports to China have never exceeded 1 percent of their GDP, whereas imports from China during this period quadrupled, from 1 to 4 percent of GDP. As a result, the trade balance of Maghreb countries with China turned from slightly negative in the early 2000s to strongly negative in the past decade, averaging about 3 percent of GDP in 2019 (Figure 4.1).

Trade patterns with China mirror the economic structure of individual Maghreb countries. For example, only Libya and Mauritania have recorded trade surpluses with China, mainly reflecting Chinese demand for natural resources and the limited purchasing power of local populations for China's exports. Mauritania's trade surplus with China reached almost 18 percent of GDP at its peak in the mid-2010s but turned into a deficit in recent years. Trade patterns differ for Algeria and Libya but mainly reflect the evolution of oil and gas prices, although the former imports much more from China than the latter. For Morocco and Tunisia, trade deficits with China have been large and persistent, mainly reflecting China's role as a supplier of consumer goods. Tunisia's trade deficit with China represents one-third of its total trade deficit.

China's importance in trade is not homogeneous across Maghreb countries. Despite large fluctuations, Libya has historically been the region's lead exporter to China (representing 40 percent on average of total Maghreb exports to China). Algeria, Mauritania, and Morocco follow with 15–20 percent of total exports to China; Tunisia is a distant last with a 5 percent share on average. Algeria has been the lead importer, with a share exceeding 40 percent in the past two decades. Morocco ranks second, with a 30 percent share, followed by Libya, Tunisia, and Mauritania, each with shares below 15 percent (Figure 4.2).

Maghreb peer countries trade more with China.[3] Maghreb countries export less and import more from China than their peers of a comparable development level (Figure 4.3). Relative to other Middle East and North Africa (MENA) countries, Maghreb exports to China were lower in 2000–11 and somewhat higher thereafter, whereas imports from China were consistently higher than other MENA countries. Finally, Maghreb exports to China have been substantially lower relative to sub-Saharan African countries; their imports from China have been comparable. Until 2012, overall trade between Maghreb countries and

[3] This paper identifies two comparator groups for the Maghreb, its peer countries and other MENA countries. Both comparator groups are selected based on the purchasing-power-parity (PPP) exchange rates used in the *World Economic Outlook* databases for cross-country comparisons and derived from the International Comparison Program (ICP 2021). In this paper, the "peer" comparator group includes six countries (Armenia, Dominica, Eswatini, Jamaica, Moldova, and Ukraine) with a nominal GDP per capita close to the average GDP per capita of the Maghreb for 2007–19, that is, about $10,700 in PPP terms +/– $500. Also, the relative shipping distance between these countries and the Maghreb to China is comparable. The "other MENA" comparator group consists of five MENA oil importers, excluding Maghreb countries, which also have per capita GDP comparable with that of the Maghreb (about $9,000 in PPP terms).

Figure 4.1. Maghreb and China: Trade in Goods, 2019
(Percentage of GDP)

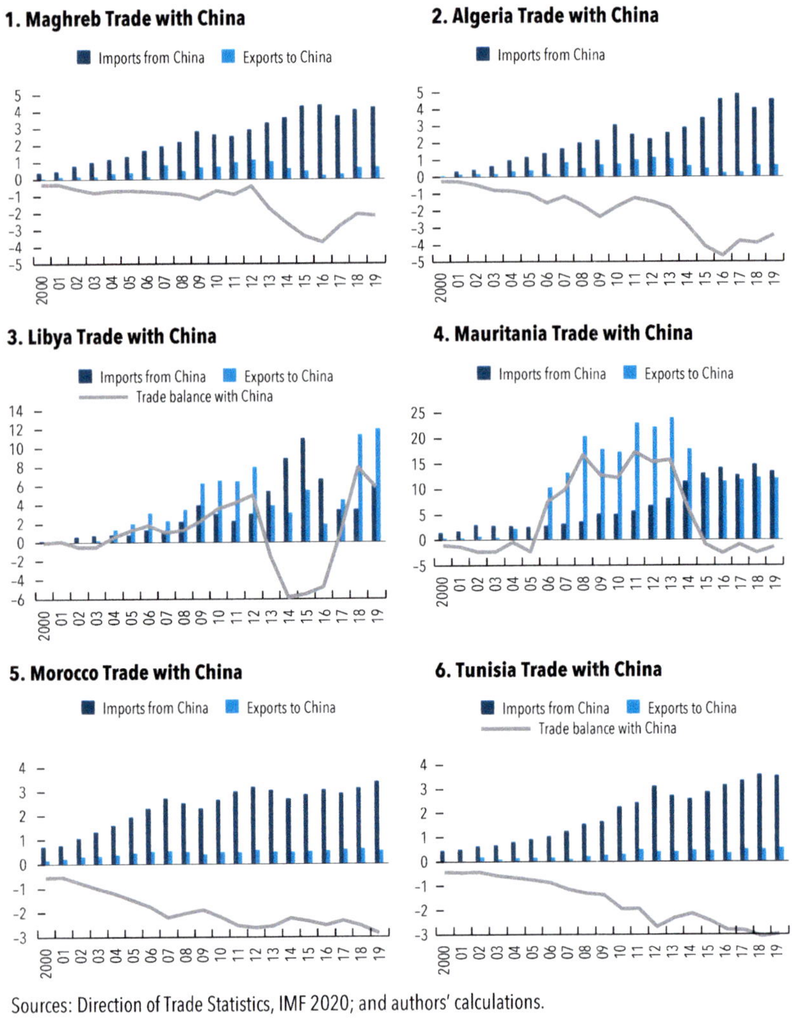

Sources: Direction of Trade Statistics, IMF 2020; and authors' calculations.

China was broadly balanced but has turned to a deficit over the past decade because imports picked up substantially, pointing to increased consumption of Chinese products in the Maghreb. Nevertheless, the Maghreb's trade deficit with China has remained relatively lower than that of international peers, except during the 2014–15 oil shock and the 2020 COVID-19 crisis.

Maghreb exports to China are low relative to other trade partners. Europe is the Maghreb's main trading partner, reflecting historical linkages, geographical proximity, and bilateral trade agreements with the European Union. In 2019, roughly 62 percent of Maghreb exports went to Europe (Figure 4.4). Although

Figure 4.2. China's Share in Maghreb Trade in Goods, 2019
(Percentage)

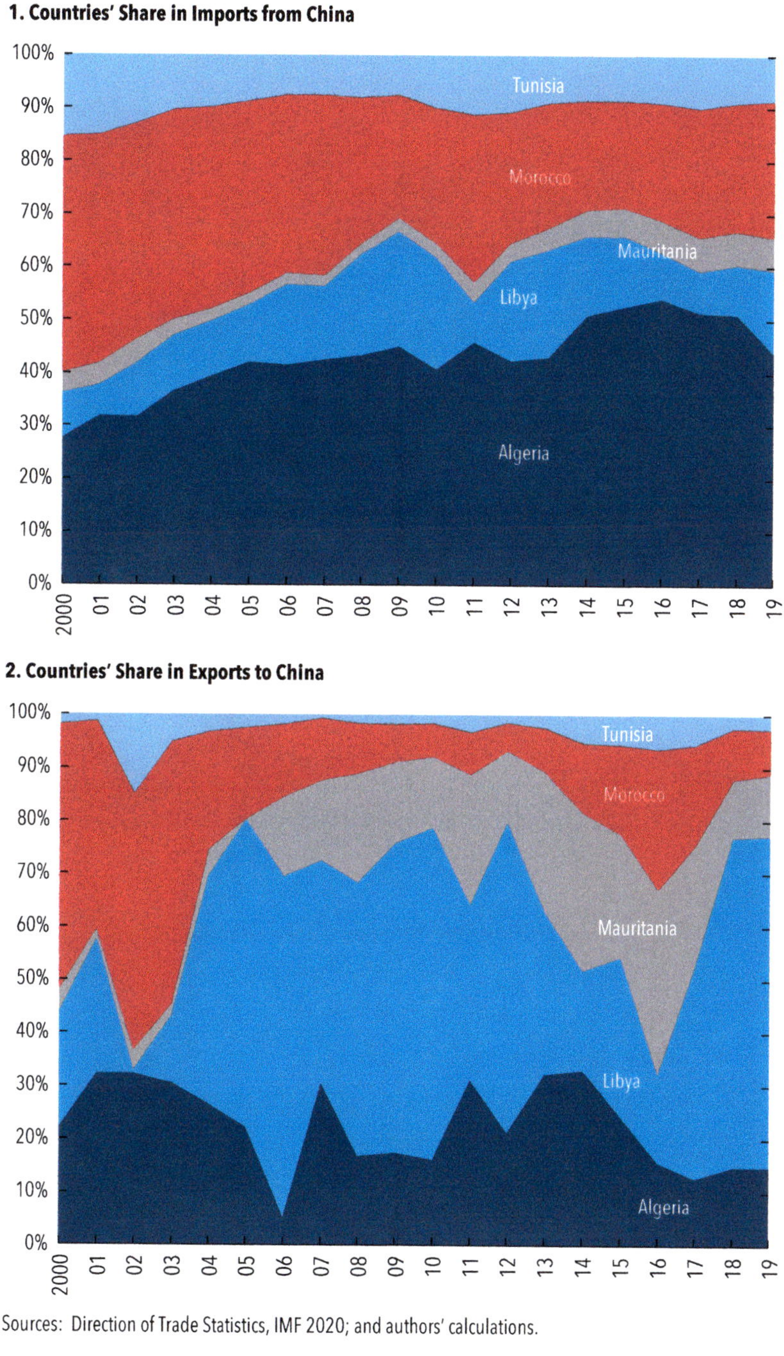

Sources: Direction of Trade Statistics, IMF 2020; and authors' calculations.

Figure 4.3. Maghreb and Peers: Trade with China
(Percentage of GDP)

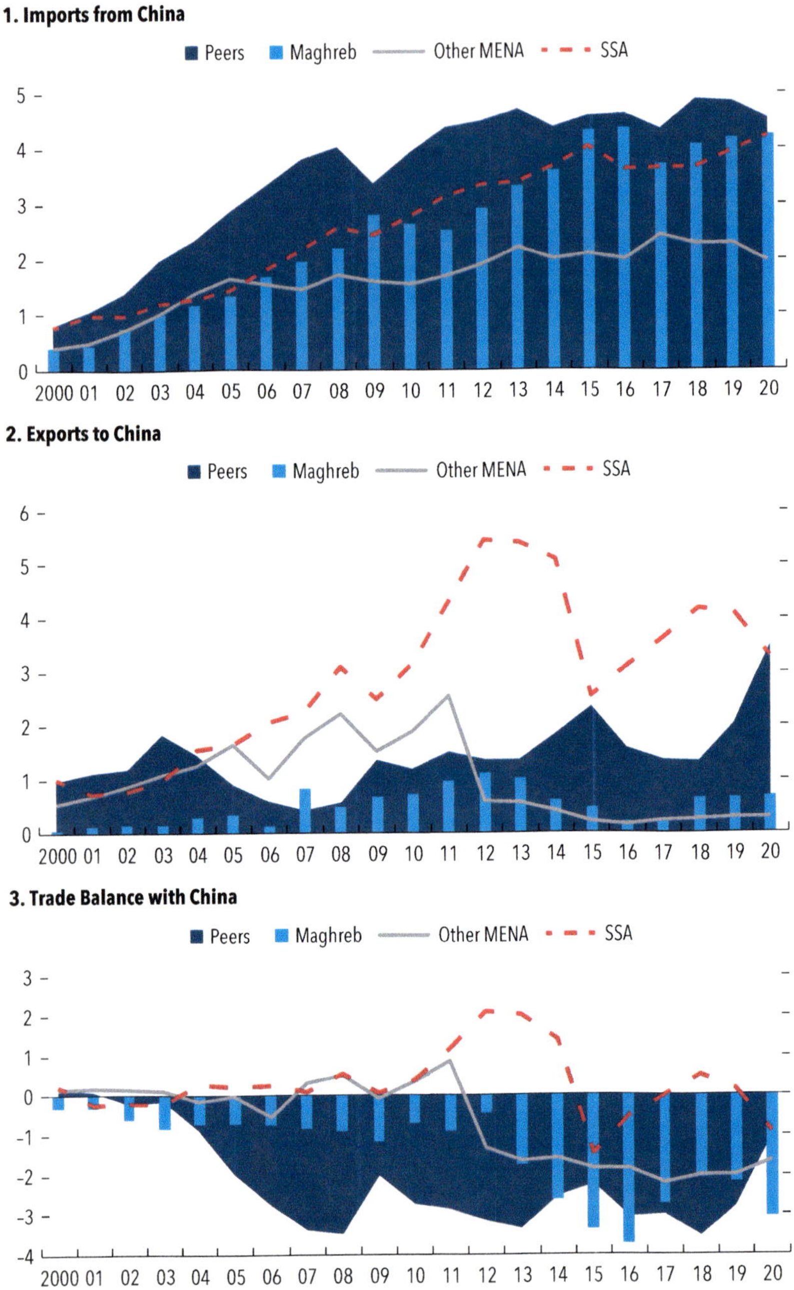

Source: IMF Direction of Trade Statistics (2021).
Note: Peer countries are Armenia, Dominica, Eswatini, Jamaica, Moldova, and Ukraine. Other MENA countries are Djibouti, Egypt, Jordan, Lebanon, and Sudan. MENA = Middle East and North Africa; SSA = sub-Saharan Africa.

Figure 4.4. Maghreb Countries: Export Destination, 2003–19
(Percent of total exports)

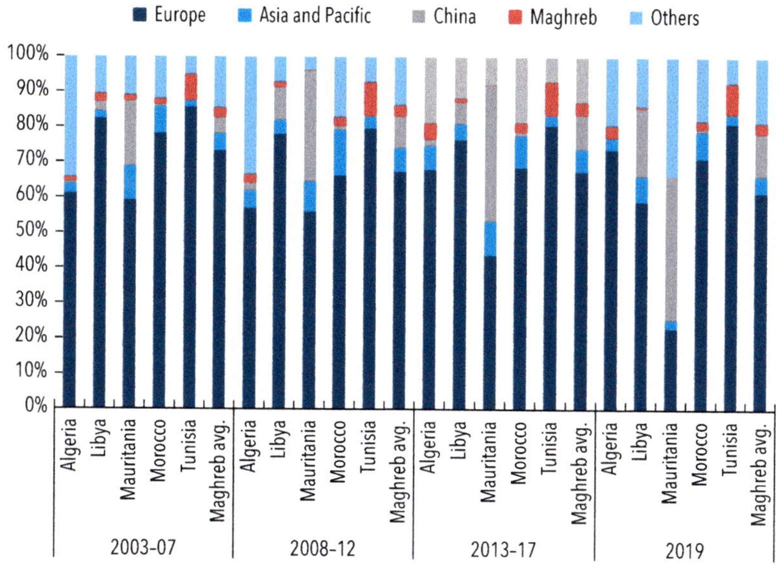

Sources: Direction of Trade Statistics, IMF (2020); and authors' calculations.
Note: "Others" refers to countries in Africa, the Western Hemisphere, and the Middle East and Central Asia.

exports to other regions are minimal, a substantial share of exports from Mauritania and Libya are destined for China.

A few countries dominate Maghreb–China trade flows. The main trade flows are exports from China to Algeria, Morocco, and Tunisia, and exports from Libya to China (Figure 4.5). China is Algeria's main source of imports (16 percent of its total), the third-largest source of imports for Morocco and Tunisia, and the eighth for Mauritania. China is Mauritania's main export destination, receiving about 35 percent of the country's total exports. However, for Algeria, Morocco, and Tunisia, China remains a very secondary export market, with its share not exceeding 1–2 percent of their exports (see Box 4.2 and Annex Figure 4.1.1 for a description of the structure of commodity trade).

Beyond commodity trade, tourism is a new area of exchange between the Maghreb and China. The number of tourists in both directions increased after the Arab Spring. To attract tourists from China, Morocco and Tunisia lifted visa requirements for Chinese citizens, and Mauritania introduced a simplified visa-on-arrival procedure. Algeria and Libya still require visas from travelers from China, and China requires visiting visas for tourists from all Maghreb countries. Morocco is the only country in the Maghreb that operates direct flights to China. In 2018, Tunisia also signed an agreement with China to start direct flights between Tunis and Beijing as part of its participation in the BRI.

Tourism remains limited despite some pickup before the pandemic. Morocco and Tunisia are the prime Maghreb destinations for Chinese tourists. The number of

Figure 4.5. Maghreb and China: Trade in Goods, 2019
(Main flows each direction, millions of US dollars)

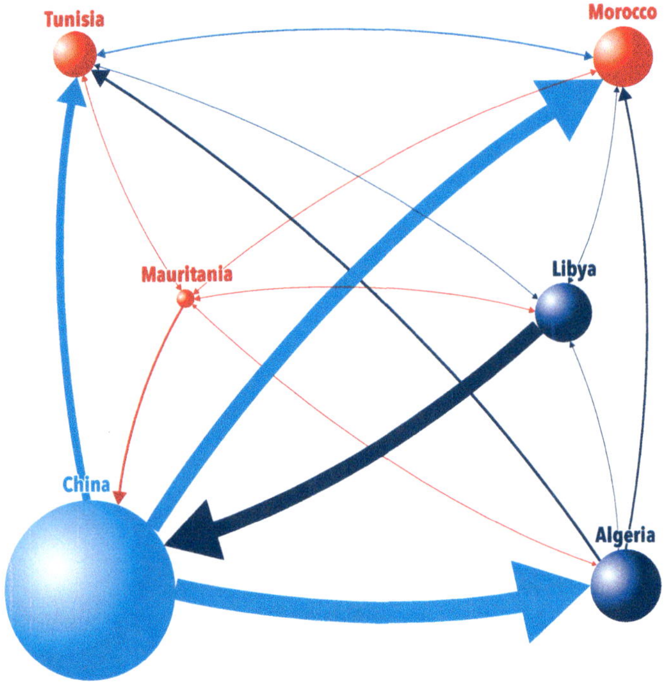

Sources: Direction of Trade Statistics, IMF 2020; and authors' calculations.
Note: Node areas are proportional to the country's total exports and decupled for Maghreb countries; link weights are proportional to the largest value of a trade flow; arrows indicate the direction of the largest flow.

Chinese tourists visiting Morocco has grown significantly in recent years. Based on partial information, in 2015–19, Chinese tourist arrivals to Morocco increased tenfold, from 20,000 to 200,000, which is still insignificant relative to the total number of tourists, nearly 8 million, visiting Morocco in 2019. Chinese tourism in Tunisia has also increased tenfold, from 2,000 in 2016 to 20,000 in 2019, although this represents an even smaller share of the 5 million tourists who visited Tunisia in 2019. Other Maghreb countries remain marginal destinations for Chinese tourists.

Investment and Infrastructure Projects

Mutual investment between Maghreb countries and China is limited. China's foreign direct investment stock in the region in 2018 was close to $1 billion (about 0.1 percent of Maghreb's GDP at PPP), mainly in Algeria. At the same time, the Maghreb's direct investment (mainly from Libya and Tunisia) amounted to just below $100 million, a tiny share of China's GDP (Figure 4.6). Portfolio investment is even smaller. Chinese companies purchased some equity and debt securities in Morocco and Tunisia. There is no reported portfolio investment by Maghreb companies in China.

Box 4.2. Maghreb and China: Commodity Structure of Trade (2019)

Maghreb countries export a limited number of products—mostly raw materials and semi-processed products—but import a diverse range of products, including consumer and investment goods (Annex Figure 4.1.1). Of the 99 product groups captured by the Harmonized System HS, an average Maghreb country exports to China only 38 product groups, most in minuscule quantities, whereas it imports 86 product groups, most in substantial quantities. For China, supplies from individual Maghreb countries—even of oil, gas, and ores—represent no more than 1 percent of China's imports of the respective product (Figure 4.2.1).

Maghreb commodity producers mainly export oil and metal-related products to China. Algeria, Libya, and Mauritania almost exclusively export extractive industry products to China, largely reflecting their mono-product structures. Algeria's exports to China almost exclusively consist of oil and petroleum gas (99.5 percent), with the remainder comprising cork, wool, and plastics. Algeria imports nearly all groups of commodities from China, including substantial quantities of mechanical and electrical machinery and equipment, including military equipment, iron and steel, vehicles, plastics, clothing, rubber, and a broad range of other consumer and investment products. Oil dominates Libya's exports to China (99.99 percent), with salt and zinc exported in tiny amounts. Libya imports a wide range of products from China, including mechanical and electrical machinery and equipment, apparel and clothing, furniture, iron and steel, rubber products, ceramic, plastics, and, broadly, most other industrial commodity groups. Mauritania's exports to China consist almost exclusively of ores, slag, and ash, and a few other products. Mauritania imports a broader range of products from China, including apparel and clothing, staple fibers, iron and steel, and electrical and mechanical machinery.

The trade structure of Maghreb non-oil exporters with China is substantially more diversified. Morocco's exports to China include electrical machinery, apparel and clothing, ores (copper, zinc, and lead), food products, aircraft parts, and a broad range of other agricultural and industrial products. Morocco imports many products from China, including machinery and equipment, cars, plastics, iron and steel, furniture, and a broad range of other products. Similarly, Tunisia's exports to China comprise mainly parts of electrical machinery, apparel and clothing, plastics, leather, and medical equipment. Tunisia imports substantially more from China than it exports, including electrical and mechanical machinery and equipment, vehicles, plastics, iron and steel, fabrics, furniture, filaments, chemicals, and a broad range of other products.

Figure 4.2.1. Products Traded Between Maghreb Countries and China

(Number of products at two-digit harmonized system level)

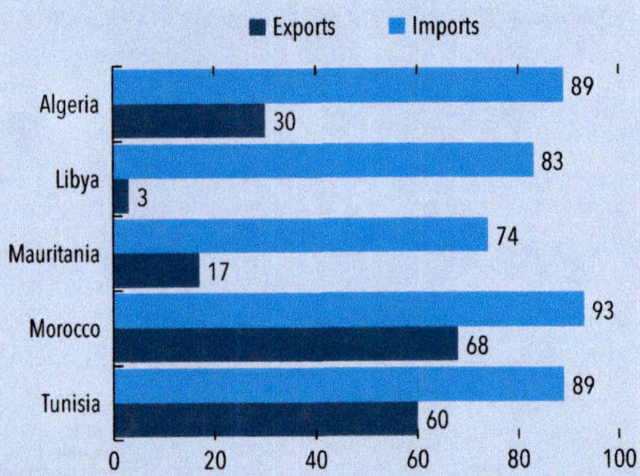

Sources: IMF DTS 2021; and authors' calculations. At the two-digit chapter level of the HS of tariff nomenclature, an internationally standardized classification of traded products. HS chapters are arranged in order of a product's degree of manufacture or in terms of its technological complexity. Natural commodities, such as live animals and vegetables, are classified in the early chapters, whereas more evolved goods, such as machinery and precision instruments, are classified in later chapters.

Chinese investment in the Maghreb is concentrated in a few countries, with Algeria receiving the largest share of direct investment. In addition to infrastructure, the Chinese have invested mainly in the construction, housing, oil and gas, and tourist sectors. In Mauritania, China's second-largest investment recipient in the Maghreb, investment is relatively sizable and focused mainly on ports, hospitals, roads, urban infrastructure, stadiums, and office buildings. In Morocco, Chinese direct investment is concentrated in tax-free zones and infrastructure projects. In Libya, most of China's government investors have discontinued operations because of instability but may resume when postconflict reconstruction opportunities arise. China's investments in Tunisia are marginal.[4]

[4] Some examples of China's investment in the Maghreb include the following: In Algeria, about 4 million dwellings and several high-profile projects, such as the East–West Highway, Opera House, Sheraton hotel, Grand Mosque, El Qods shopping mall, the Oran hospital, the port, and the El Hamdania industrial zone (Lafargue 2018). In Morocco, direct investment in the Atlantic Free Zone in Kenitra, Casablanca Finance City, and the Tanger Tech City; residential zones in the Tangier region; extending the Jerada power plant; setting up a China–Morocco industrial park (Zoubir 2020); and a high-tech sock, hosiery and lingerie facility (The North Africa Post 2020). In Tunisia, there are just 10 Chinese companies, including Huawei, an active supplier of telecoms, with a combined annual revenue of about $10 million (Zoubir 2020). During the FOCAC summit in Beijing in 2018, Tunisia signed agreements with China for several new projects, including port renovation and construction of a railway and a car plant (FOCAC 2021). Also, China is building a hydraulic dam, a solar power plant, a diplomatic academy, and a hospital, mainly on grant funding, which allows China's contractors to supply their own personnel, materials, and equipment.

Figure 4.6. The Maghreb and China: Mutual Investment
(Millions of US dollars, on right scale; percentage of GDP at PPP on left scale)

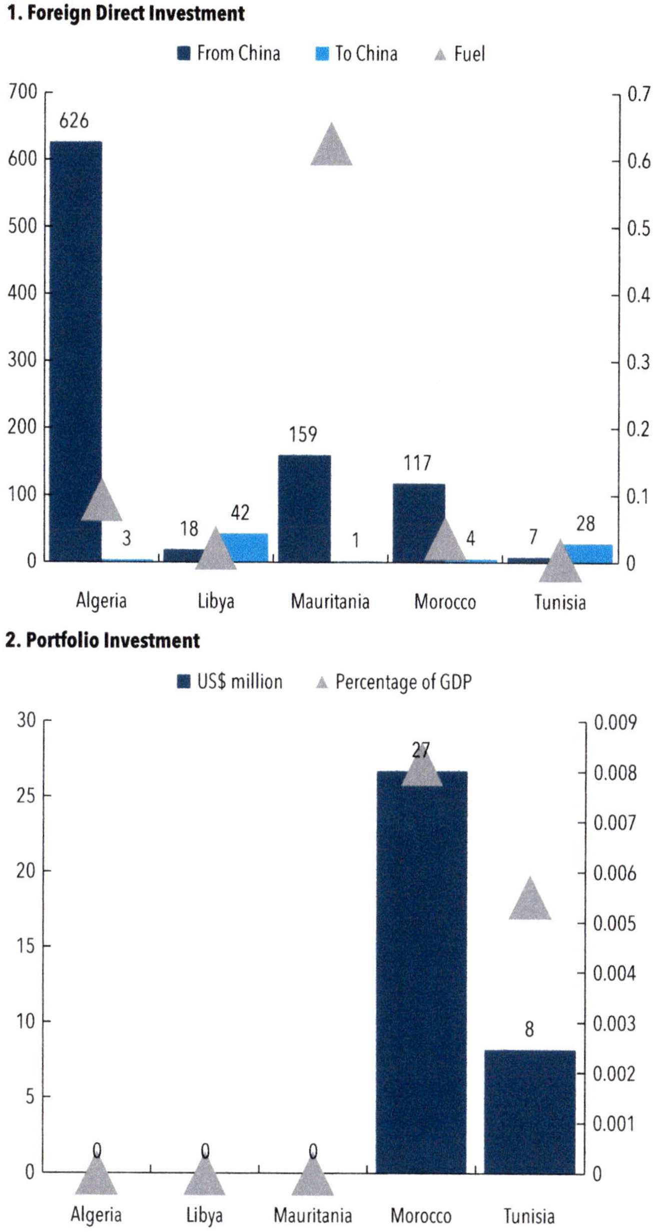

Source: Coordinated Direct Investment and Portfolio Surveys, IMF 2020.
Note: PPP = purchasing power parity.

Lending and Debt

Maghreb's debt to China is not significant (averaging just 0.3 percent of regional GDP) and has remained relatively steady over the past decade (Figure 4.7). At the end of 2020, Mauritania had the highest debt to China as a share of GDP (4.3 percent of GDP, or $337 million), having fallen from its 2015 peak. Morocco had the highest debt to China in nominal terms (about $422 million or 0.3 percent of GDP). Tunisia's debt to China amounted to $7 million (0.02 percent of GDP) at the end of 2020, and Algeria's totaled $68 million (0.04 percent of GDP) at the end of 2019.

Lending by China to Maghreb countries is limited (Figure 4.7). Mauritania and Morocco have been the main recipients of Chinese lending, but this was mostly before 2015. China's loans to Algeria and Tunisia are very small, and there

Figure 4.7. Debt and Lending

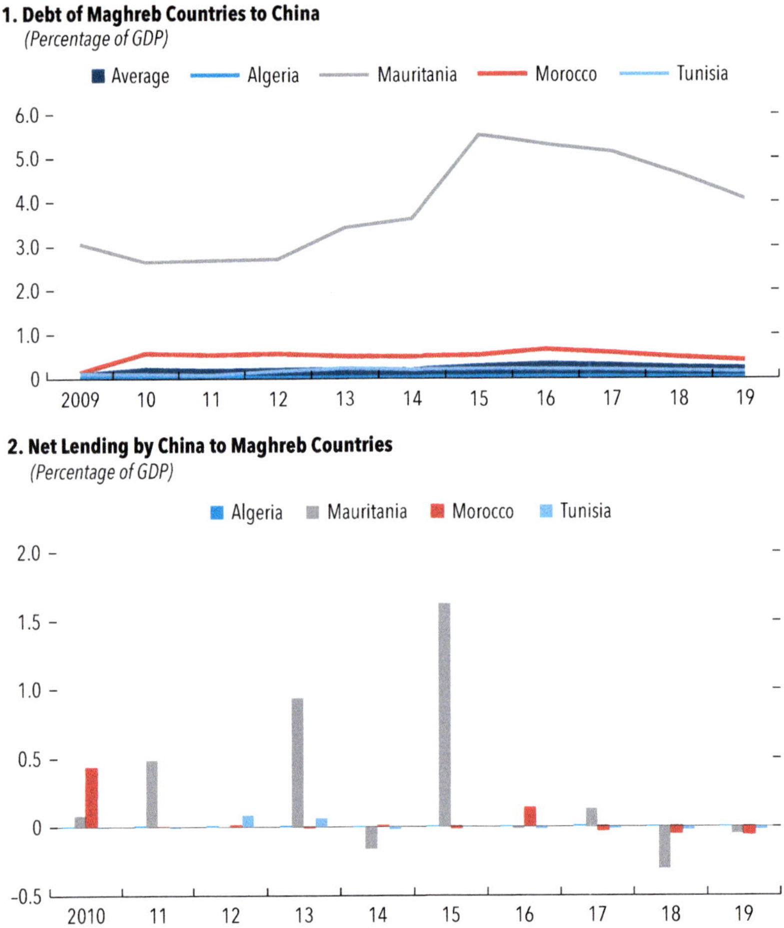

Sources: World Bank 2021; and authors' calculations.

are no data on China's loans to Libya in the past decade. According to the School of Advanced International Studies (SAIS) China–Africa research initiative, China's loans to the Maghreb in 2000–18 cumulatively totaled about $2 billion, less than 2 percent of China's lending to Africa. Most loans have been provided by China's Export–Import Bank to the governments of Morocco and Mauritania for the transport and energy sectors (Johns Hopkins SAIS China–Africa Research Initiative 2020).

IS THERE SCOPE FOR GREATER COOPERATION?

Quantifying the Missing Trade

The relatively modest level of economic cooperation between the Maghreb and China raises questions about the scope to expand it. If Maghreb's trade with China is below potential, there may be opportunities to strengthen cooperation and trade, even in currently traded commodities. Moreover, there may be some new sectors, unexploited so far, where Maghreb countries could develop a competitive advantage and enhance their trade with China. Such "missing trade" may be substantial and, if properly developed, could become an important source of growth and job creation in the Maghreb.

High trade complementarity between some Maghreb countries and China suggests unused trade opportunities. Trade complementarity can be measured by an index, indicating to what extent the export profile of Maghreb countries matches or complements the import profile of their trading partners, including China (World Bank 2013). Complementarity suggests that the China–Maghreb trade potential may exceed observed trade (Figure 4.8). In Tunisia and Mauritania, trade complementarity with China exceeds their trade complementarity with any of their six top export partners. For Tunisia, China is not a main export destination, although for Mauritania, it is among the top partners. For Morocco, trade complementarity with China is below the average for the top-six export partners and lower than with France, Italy, Spain, and the United States, all of which are already its main export markets. Algeria's trade complementarity with China is at about the average for the top-six export partners and lower than with Brazil and Spain (its main export markets). Although this analysis suggests that exports to traditional trading partners (mainly Southern Europe and the United States) should be preserved because they reflect high complementarity between the export structure of Maghreb countries and their import needs, more exports to China could be a substantial source of untapped trade potential, particularly for Tunisia, Mauritania, and somewhat less for Morocco.

The order of magnitude of this trade potential can be assessed with a gravity model of trade. This model predicts that trade flows correlate with the economic size of countries and trade impediments between them, including distance (see a detailed review of references in Yotov and others 2016). A reduced-form gravity model specification, widely used in the literature, takes into account countries' size (as measured by GDP and population), distance, and trade impediments to

Figure 4.8. Maghreb and China Trade Complementarity, 2018[1]

(Index, China, and top export partners)

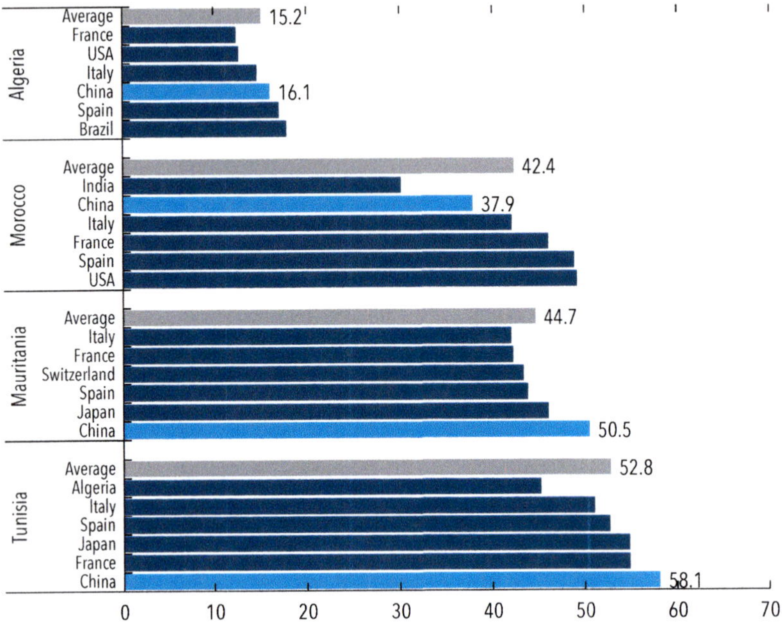

Sources: World Bank 2020; and authors' calculations.

Note: No data are available for Libya.

[1] The trade complementarity index indicates to what extent the export profile of the reporting country matches, or complements, the import profile of the partner country. Calculated the four-digit level of the Harmonized System product classification, a score of 100 indicates ideal trading partners, whereas a score of 0 indicates that the two countries are perfect competitors. A high index may indicate that the two countries would stand to gain from increased trade (World Bank 2013).

explain bilateral trade flows (Eaton and Kortum 2002; Anderson and van Wincoop 2003; Allard and others 2016):

$$\ln X_{ijt} = \beta_1 \ln M_{it-1}^{EX} + \beta_2 \ln M_{jt-1}^{IM} + \delta_1 \ln D_{ij} + \delta_2 RD + \mu_t + \varepsilon_{ijt},$$

where $\ln X_{ijt}$ is the logarithm of exports from country i to country j at time t; $\ln M_{it}^{EX}$ and $\ln M_{jt}^{IM}$ denote vectors of exporter and importer attributes, respectively (for example, GDP). Factors that affect trade costs between i and j are captured by (for example, distance). To capture global trends affecting trade, a year effect is added in the regression. RD is a set of regional or country-specific pairs with dummy variables added to capture regional and country-specific pairs' trade heterogeneity.[5] The regression is conditioned on a one-year lag of all-time varying regressors to minimize the bias from potential endogeneity and reverse causality. The data for the model are collected from international and national sources

[5] In this specification, the exponential of the coefficient of a dummy variable is the ratio of the geometric means of the dependent variable between the category $RD = 1$ and the base category.

Box 4.3. Gravity Model: Regional Dummies Definitions

1. Exporter and importer are both Maghreb	= 1 if both countries are from the Maghreb = 0 otherwise
2. Exporter and importer are non-Maghreb	= 1 if neither country is from the Maghreb = 0 otherwise
3. Exporter is Maghreb; importers are EU, US, UK, Japan, India	= 1 if the exporting country is from the Maghreb and the importer is from the EU, US, UK, Japan, India = 0 otherwise
4. Exporter is Maghreb; importers are other countries, excluding EU, US, UK, Japan, India, China	= 1 if the exporting country is from the Maghreb and the importer is from the rest of the world, excluding EU, US, UK, Japan, India, China = 0 otherwise
5. Exporter is non-Maghreb, excluding EU, US, UK, Japan, India, China; importer is Maghreb	= 1 if the exporting country is from the rest of the world, excluding EU, US, UK, Japan, India, China, and the importer is from Maghreb = 0 otherwise
6. Exporter is Maghreb, importer is China	= reference group, implicit dummy

Source: Authors' presentation.

(Annex Figure 4.1.2). Bilateral trade data used in the estimation are from the IMF's Direction of Trade Statistics database covering 183 countries over 1980–2019. Time-invariant trade-cost factors are from the Centre d'Études Prospectives et d'Informations Internationales.[6]

This model can be used to estimate possible gaps in bilateral trade between Maghreb countries and China. The dummy variables presented in Box 4.3 describe the universe of potential bilateral trade groups. Excluding the last dummy from the equation (exporter—Maghreb/importer—China), regression coefficients can be interpreted as measuring the size of bilateral trade relative to the trade between Maghreb countries and China. In other words, by introducing regional/country dummies, the equation can capture whether trade between the Maghreb and China tends to be lower than between other bilateral country pairs even after controlling for importer and exporter attributes and trade costs (see Allard and others 2016).

The estimation strategy is as follows. First, we compare Maghreb–China trade with that of other regions (Figure 4.9, column 1). Second, we seek to establish

[6] See Annex Figure 4.1.2 for variable definitions.

the role of GVCs in promoting exports. Third, we control for the effect of the size, level of development, distance, and other frictions on Maghreb's trade with China.

Maghreb countries are less integrated into GVCs with China than their peers (Figure 4.9, column 2). By adding the variables that capture the foreign value-added content of exports (backward GVC participation) and domestic value-added content of exports (forward GVC participation) to the model with regional dummies, the model can assess the role of both backward and forward participation in GVCs in trade. Because, in this specification, exports from Maghreb countries to China remain the implicit reference category, the model suggests that Maghreb countries participate less in GVCs with China than other countries by about 38 percent. However, the gap is smaller for the backward participation (28 percent) than for the forward participation (47 percent).[7] Notably, the coefficient on the dummy capturing bilateral trade between the Maghreb and the European Union, India, Japan, the United Kingdom, and the United States remains positive but becomes less statistically significant, pointing more prominent role of GVCs in export creation relative to regional partnerships.

Current bilateral trade links with main trading partners partly reflect geography and historical ties, which becomes clear when controlling for the effect of the size, level of development, distance, and other frictions on Maghreb's trade with China (Figure 4.9, column 3). This includes exporter- and importer-relative attributes, such as population, GDP, and trade-cost measures (bilateral distance, common official and second language, former colonial relationship, and sea access). The model explains exports reasonably well; all their determinants are statistically significant and have the expected sign. For example, export flows tend to be higher between larger, more developed countries with a common language or former colonial links. Large distances, trade impediments, and landlock status all harm trade. The large and negative coefficient on distance could reflect the lack of direct transport routes.[8]

GVC participation appears to trump geographical and regional ties once gravity variables are included. The effect of the backward GVC participation increases, whereas the coefficient for the forward participation declines, but coefficients on GVC participation remain statistically significant. This suggests a more important role for backward GVCs when countries acquire inputs for their exports closer to the source and a less significant role for forward GVCs, which are more dependent on the distance to and the income level of partner countries. Second, the coefficient on the regional dummy—that sets aside Maghreb's trade with the European Union, India, Japan, the United Kingdom, and the United States—becomes statistically insignificant, suggesting that regional ties (as captured in Figure 4.9, column 1) are largely the result of GVC participation, size, distance, and other gravity attributes.

[7] For backward GVC participation: 100–100/(exp 0.329) = 28. For forward GVC participation: 100–100/(exp 0.627) = 47. Average is 38.

[8] There are only two means of transportation between Maghreb countries and China: air and sea, both insufficiently developed. There are no direct cargo flights between the Maghreb and China, other than from Morocco, and no direct sea routes. The BRI does not include Maghreb countries in its main maritime transport corridors (World Bank 2019).

Figure 4.9. Gravity Trade Model Estimates

Dependent variable = bilateral exports	(1)	(2)	(3)	(4)	(5)	(6)	(7)
Regional dummies[1]							
Exporter is Maghreb; importer is Maghreb	−1.857*** (0.707)	−1.461* (0.768)	−1.527* (0.843)			−1.444 (1.222)	−1.497 (1.247)
Exporter is non-Maghreb; importer is non-Maghreb	−4.465*** (0.330)	−4.117*** (0.584)	−0.849 (0.762)			−0.929 (1.131)	−0.947 (1.143)
Exporter is Maghreb; importers are EU, US, UK, Japan, India	1.140** (0.465)	1.189* (0.637)	−0.007 (0.792)			−0.645 (1.153)	−0.679 (1.166)
Exporter is Maghreb; importers are other countries, excl. EU, US, UK, Japan, India, China	−5.232*** (0.352)	−5.031*** (0.597)	−1.914** (0.769)			−2.177* (1.138)	−2.104* (1.150)
Exporter is non-Maghreb, excl. EU, US, UK, Japan, India, China; importer is Maghreb	−4.235*** (0.356)	−3.846*** (0.591)	−1.285* (0.765)			−1.012 (1.134)	−1.01 (1.146)
Participation in GVCs							
Backward GVC participation		0.329*** (0.021)	0.422*** (0.018)	0.436*** (0.020)	0.542*** (0.020)	0.507*** (0.023)	0.482*** (0.023)
Forward GVC participation		0.627*** (0.023)	0.322*** (0.027)	0.354*** (0.029)	0.195*** (0.028)	0.305*** (0.030)	0.225*** (0.031)
Gravity variables							
Exporter population (log)			0.510*** (0.022)	0.479*** (0.023)	0.574*** (0.021)	0.521*** (0.023)	0.630*** (0.024)
Importer population (log)			0.869*** (0.008)	0.904*** (0.008)	0.902*** (0.008)	0.947*** (0.010)	0.950*** (0.010)
Exporter GDP per capita (log)			0.325*** (0.023)	0.282*** (0.025)	0.278*** (0.024)	0.084*** (0.030)	0.160*** (0.031)
Importer GDP per capita (log)			0.734*** (0.011)	0.792*** (0.011)	0.770*** (0.010)	0.590*** (0.018)	0.586*** (0.019)

Figure 4.9. (*continued*)

Distance (log)			−1.445*** (0.017)	−1.450*** (0.017)	−1.391*** (0.019)	−1.429*** (0.020)	−1.351*** (0.021)
Common official language			0.685*** (0.073)	0.688*** (0.078)	0.634*** (0.081)	0.780*** (0.092)	0.772*** (0.093)
Common second language			0.299*** (0.071)	0.305*** (0.075)	0.309*** (0.079)	0.176** (0.087)	0.164* (0.089)
Former colonial relationship			0.586*** (0.057)	0.659*** (0.060)	0.673*** (0.064)	0.481*** (0.075)	0.619*** (0.078)
Landlocked exporter			−0.587*** (0.040)	−0.580*** (0.042)	−0.601*** (0.045)	−0.797*** (0.050)	−0.684*** (0.053)
Landlocked importer			−1.088*** (0.038)	−1.032*** (0.040)	−1.034*** (0.042)	−1.113*** (0.047)	−0.983*** (0.048)
Policy variables							
Average tariffs in importing country				−0.011*** (0.001)			
Trade agreements					0.218*** (0.024)		0.196*** (0.027)
Exporter infrastructure quality						0.187*** (0.016)	0.177*** (0.018)
Importer infrastructure quality						0.197*** (0.015)	0.220*** (0.017)
Exporter labor market efficiency						0.035 (0.023)	0.047* (0.025)
Importer labor market efficiency						0.028 (0.021)	0.048* (0.025)
Exporter regulatory quality						0.061** (0.028)	0.112*** (0.032)
Importer regulatory quality						0.227*** (0.026)	0.253*** (0.028)
Number of observations	5,48,391	4,29,890	4,17,759	3,09,310	1,20,519	1,39,835	59,120
Time fixed effects	Yes	Yes	Yes	Yes	Yes	Yes	Yes

Source: IMF staff estimates.
Note: Robust standard errors in parentheses. ****, **, and * highlight significance at 1%, 5%, and 10%, respectively. GVC = global value chain.
[1]"Exporter is Maghreb, importer is China" an implicit reference dummy.

The Role of Policy

What policies can boost Maghreb exports to China? To answer this question, we add a policy variable block to the model while controlling for GVC and gravity-related attributes (Figure 4.9, columns 4–7). As a starting point, the effect of import tariffs and trade agreements on trade in general is assessed (that is, excluding regional dummies). As expected, higher import tariffs constrain exports, whereas trade agreements boost them because the coefficients on average tariffs in importing countries and the existence of trade agreements between countries have the expected sign and are statistically significant (Figure 4.9, columns 4 and 5). The coefficients on GVC participation and all gravity coefficients remain broadly unchanged and statistically significant, suggesting that trade policies can be an important additional factor in improving export performance in all countries.

Generally, mutual tariff liberalization could help increase Maghreb exports, including to China. The average applied tariff is 14 percent in Maghreb countries and 10 percent in China. In both cases, it is higher than in advanced economies, suggesting potential for its reduction in Maghreb countries and China. But bilateral tariffs between Maghreb countries and China are even higher. China imposes an average 12 percent tariff on imports from the Maghreb. Moroccan and Tunisian tariffs on imports from China are about 35–40 percent, and Algerian and Mauritanian tariffs are 20–30 percent. Only Libya imposes no tariffs on imports from China (Figure 4.10). Therefore, a proportional tariff reduction in the Maghreb and China could potentially help increase trade in both directions.

Mutually beneficial tariff reductions could be made in the context of trade agreements, but such agreements are not without risks. On average, members of trade agreements trade about 20 percent more than countries that do not have trade agreements (Figure 4.9, column 5).[9] Countries in FTAs with China trade close to 18 percent more relative to countries that are not (Figure 4.9, column 7).[10]

Figure 4.10. Maghreb and China: Trade Tariffs
(Simple average applied tariffs, percentage)

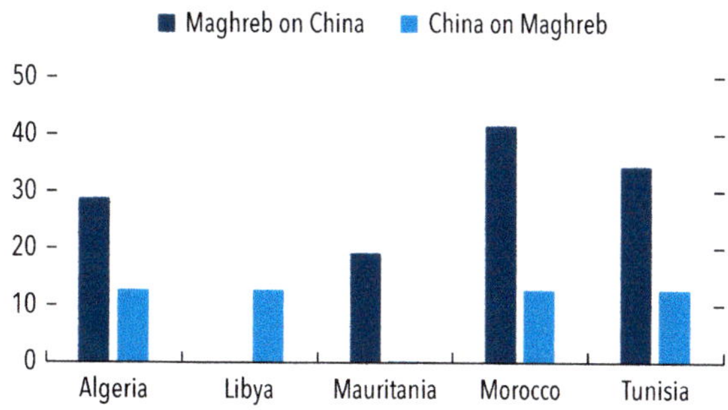

Source: World Bank 2020.

[9] 100–100/exp(0.218) = 20 percent.

[10] 100–100/exp(0.196) = 18 percent.

Currently, Maghreb countries do not have FTAs with China.[11] Although these results are indicative, they do not control for trade agreement design. The main objective of Maghreb countries should be to benefit from their existing comparative advantages and create new areas of competitive advantage while preventing increased imports from harming existing industries, in particular those with large employment multipliers.[12]

Designing trade agreements that benefit all will be important. China's trade agreements with Chile, Costa Rica, Georgia, and several other middle-income countries have led to substantial growth of bilateral trade and, after initial fine-tuning, seem to be functioning reasonably well and to mutual benefit. A few countries with a level of development comparable with the Maghreb (Cambodia, Mauritius, Sri Lanka, Moldova) have recently concluded or are negotiating trade agreements with China (China FTA Network 2021), suggesting that these countries see benefits in such agreements. At the same time, some cases suggest that trade agreements between China and smaller countries can increase their trade deficits. For example, a trade agreement between Tunisia and China signed in 2005 was suspended by Tunisia in 2018 after an inflow of Chinese goods widened Tunisia's trade deficit (Meddeb 2021). The Pakistan–China FTA signed in 2006 was renegotiated in 2019 for the same reason, allowing Pakistani products improved access to the Chinese market (Ali 2020). The FTA between China and Peru, signed in 2010, is being renegotiated mainly to address environmental concerns in the mining industry (Custodio 2020).

Other domestic policies can also play a role in bilateral trade. Controlling for several additional policy variables, such as infrastructure quality, labor market efficiency, and regulatory quality (Figure 4.9, column 6), suggests that although labor market efficiency has little effect on trade, infrastructure and regulatory quality are all statistically significant.

Infrastructure quality is positively associated with trade and could contribute to promoting trade between Maghreb countries and China. Poor infrastructure quality in the Maghreb may be related to its low openness to foreign investment. The investment climate in most Maghreb countries remains unfavorable to foreign investment in general and in the infrastructure area in particular. Operations in some natural resource sectors that could attract Chinese investors (for example,

---

[11] As of July 2021, China had 22 bilateral and regional FTAs in operation, with 10 more under negotiation and 8 more under consideration (China FTA Network 2021).

[12] The experience of other trade agreements shows that multiple instruments can be used to achieve this balance: initially, trade liberalization may cover only the sectors where both partners are equally competitive; transition periods can be established for achieving gradual liberalization in more sensitive products; some products may be exempt from liberalization altogether. Trade liberalization does not necessarily mean the removal of all trade restrictions: customs duties may be reduced, equalized, or left asymmetric. Trade agreements can go beyond the reduction of customs duties and include commitments on trade in services, including common rules for intellectual property, competition, origin, and dispute settlement. Finally, in some cases, trade agreements also embed the rules on e-commerce, investment protection, and capital movements and may even contain development provisions requiring the more developed partner to invest in certain areas of the less developed partner.

phosphates in Tunisia) remain inherently difficult because of social tensions and technical constraints. Discouragingly, many Maghreb countries have numerous capital account restrictions and insufficiently transparent business practices (Fernández and others 2015).

Deficiencies in the regulatory environment in the Maghreb may also explain the region's limited engagement with China. Reports suggest that governance issues may damage cooperation. In Algeria, for example, the China Railway Construction Corporation faced criticism after allegations of unfair wage withholding (Ghafar and Jacobs 2019). At the same time, Chinese construction companies are generally perceived favorably in the Maghreb because they build quickly and are relatively cheaper than most competitors (Ghafar and Jacobs 2019).

In Which Sectors Can Trade Increase?

An assessment of comparative advantage can reveal those sectors where—with good policies—trade in final goods can increase. Available data suggest that Maghreb countries may have a comparative advantage relative to China in several sectors. The revealed comparative advantage (RCA) index measures a product's competitiveness by comparing its share in exports to its share in world trade (Balassa and Noland 1989; World Bank 2020). A country is said to have an RCA in product *X* when its ratio of exports of *X* to its total exports exceeds the same ratio for the world as a whole (UNCTAD 2021). Products with a high RCA are competitive and can be exported to countries with a low RCA. If estimated at high levels of product disaggregation, the RCA can focus attention on nontraditional products that might be successfully traded.[13]

Maghreb countries have the potential to increase their exports to China in some sectors. However, this additional potential is unequal across countries, as indicated by the RCA index at the six-digit level of the HS product disaggregation (Figure 4.11). When the RCA index is calculated for Maghreb countries relative to China only, some indices are substantially above 1. For example, Morocco has a strong comparative advantage over China in phosphates and natural aluminum, gypsum, anhydride, plasters, fats, plants, and zinc ores, among others. Tunisia has some comparative advantage over China in used clothing, suits, tubes, and pipes. These "unused" advantages over China are more limited for other countries. For example, Algeria has some comparative advantage only in natural cork and petroleum oil, whereas Libya has some marginal advantage in petroleum oils. Mauritania has advantage in flours, meals and pellets, fats, and copper and iron ores. A more granular analysis points to individual products where trade can increase (see Box 4.4).

[13] In the case of Maghreb countries, the analysis can be performed at the two, four, and six digits of the Harmonized Commodity Description and Coding System (Harmonized System, HS) product disaggregation, in the 2012 HS classification, and for 2017–18, except for Libya, where the latest available trade data are for 2009–10 and is presented in the HS 2002 classification.

Figure 4.11. Maghreb Comparative Advantages Relative to China

(Revealed comparative advantage index, HS 2012)[1]

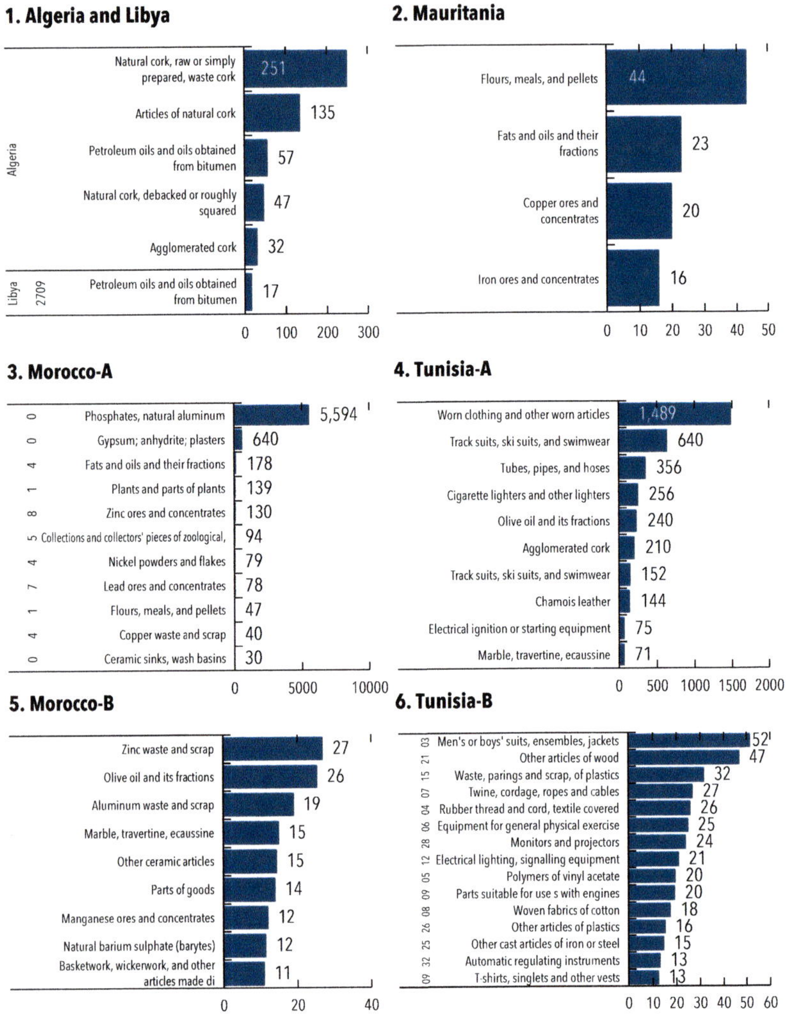

Sources: World Bank 2020; and authors' calculations.

Note: HS = Harmonized Commodity Description and Coding System.

[1] The revealed comparative advantage index measures how competitive a product is in countries' exports compared with the product's share in world trade. An index above unity indicates that a country's share of exports in that sector exceeds the partner's export share of the same sector. If this is the case, the country has a comparative advantage in that sector (World Bank 2013).

The results suggest that policy action could help the region increase trade with China. Diversifying beyond traditional trading partners would help strengthen the region's resilience to the vagaries of individual trading partners' import demand. Our analysis suggests that the region can mitigate the effect of distance

Box 4.4. Export Potential in Maghreb–China Trade

The International Trade Center Export Potential Indicator calculates the potential export value of individual products given their supply in the exporting country, demand in the importing country, and the ease of trade, including market access and trade tariffs, between these two countries (Annex Figure 4.1.3). Based on this indicator, several products have the greatest export potential.

Algeria to China. Anhydrous ammonia, rare gases, and methanol. Algeria has the highest supply capacity in anhydrous ammonia, whereas China is strongly interested in its medicaments.

Libya to China. Methanol, whole raw bovine hides and skins, and anhydrous ammonia. Libya has the highest supply capacity in raw skins, and demand in China is particularly high for these products.

Mauritania to China. Flours of fish or crustaceans, whole and frozen fish, rock lobster, and sea crawfish. Mauritania has the highest supply capacity in octopus, whether frozen, smoked, dried, salted, or in brine, and China has excess demand for flours of fish or crustaceans.

Morocco to China. Passenger motor vehicles, flours of fish or crustaceans, cobalt mattes, and cobalt powder. Morocco has the highest supply capacity in phosphoric and polyphosphoric acids, and China has strong demand for its motor vehicles.

Tunisia to China. Virgin olive oil, accessories of motor vehicles, and electronic conductors. Tunisia has the highest supply capacity in virgin olive oil and its fractions, and China has demand for its smart cards, electronic integrated circuits, and light-emitting diodes (LEDs).

China to the Maghreb. Telephone sets and other voice/image transmission apparatus and data-processing machines. China has the highest supply capacity in piles of man-made fibers, and Maghreb countries are strongly interested in telephone sets and other voice/image transmission apparatus.

Source: ITC (2020).

and geography, at least in part, by improved governance, infrastructure, and regulations supported by carefully designed bilateral trade liberalization. Finally, the empirical analysis shows that stronger integration in China's GVCs—backward and forward—would benefit bilateral trade.

Integrating the Maghreb in China's GVCs

Maghreb countries could increase their trade with China by participating in its GVCs. GVCs—production processes for which different stages of production are located across countries (OECD 2021)—have been a distinct feature of China's companies for decades (OECD 2018b; WTO 2021). Based on standard metrics (for example, domestic and foreign value-added content of exports, direct and indirect value-added in gross exports), GVC participation is less pronounced for Maghreb companies (OECD 2018b; WTO 2021).[14] The most visible examples include Morocco's garment and car industries and Tunisia's electric cable industries, which are well integrated into European GVCs (OECD 2018a; Riera and Paerzold 2020). In the 2000s, China contributed 3 percent of foreign value-added on average to Maghreb exports, whereas Maghreb countries' value-added contribution to China's exports never exceeded 0.2 percent. However, after 2010, China's share in the Maghreb's GVCs rose sharply, tripling to 9 percent by 2019, whereas the Maghreb's contribution increased to 0.3 percent (Figure 4.12). China's contribution to Maghreb's GVCs remains small relative to Maghreb's traditional partners (France, Germany, Italy, Spain, United States), which continue to dominate their exported foreign value-added. However, China's share has increased across all Maghreb countries during the past decade, in many cases displacing traditional partners.

China's role in Maghreb GVCs differs between oil and non-oil exporters. In oil exporters, China has become one of the largest suppliers of oil-extracting equipment, chemicals, and related services. For example, in Algeria, China's share in exported value-added almost tripled, becoming the second-largest foreign contributor to Algeria's exports in value-added terms after the United States. In Libya, China's role in GVCs has also increased dramatically, rising from a marginal amount to the second-largest value-added contributor after Italy. Across other Maghreb countries, China is now the third-largest contributor to Morocco's exports and the fourth largest to the exports of Mauritania and Tunisia, reflecting mainly a more active use of China's inputs for the car, cable, garment, and extracting industries in these countries. A decade ago, China's role in the Maghreb countries' exports was much more modest. For example, China was only the 9th-largest contributor to Algeria's GVCs, 15th to Libya's, 10th to Mauritania's, 7th to Morocco's, and 10th to Tunisia's.

For China's GVCs, Maghreb countries remain marginal. Their share in China's exported value-added is negligible, with no clear pattern in the shifts in recent participation. For example, although the role of Algeria and Morocco remained broadly unchanged (50–60th among China's value-added suppliers), the share of Libya and Tunisia has dropped dramatically in the past decade, suggesting that

[14] The domestic value-added content of exports is composed of the following three elements: (1) domestic value-added sent to the consumer economy corresponds to the domestic value-added embodied in either final or intermediate goods or services that are directly consumed by the importing economy; (2) domestic value-added sent to third economies represents the domestic value-added contained in intermediates (goods or services) exported to a partner economy that reexports them to a third economy as embodied in other products; and (3) domestic value-added reimported in the economy refers to the domestic value-added of exported intermediates, or inputs, that is sent back to the economy of origin as embodied in other intermediates and used to produce exports. Foreign value-added content of exports corresponds to the value-added of inputs imported to produce intermediate or final goods/services to be exported (WTO 2020).

Figure 4.12. Maghreb and China: Global Value Change (GVC) Participation

(Foreign value added in final productshare in percentage[1])

China's Contribution to Maghreb's GVCs

Algeria	2010		2019
1. France	19.2	1. USA	26.4
2. Italy	11.3	2. China	9.7
3. Germany	9.8	3. Germany	6.6
4. USA	9.0	4. Spain	5.5
5. Spain	8.2	5. France	3.9
6. UK	4.7	6. Turkey	3.5
7. Turkey	3.5	7. India	3.3
8. Belgium	3.4	8. Canada	3.2
9. China	3.3	9. Netherlands	3.1

Libya	2010		2019
1. Italy	18.9	1. Italy	9.3
2. Germany	12.0	2. China	8.3
3. UK	11.0	3. Germany	7.8
4. Tunisia	7.0	4. UK	7.2
5. France	5.2	5. USA	5.7
6. Turkey	3.8	6. Tunisia	3.9
7. Netherlands	3.7	7. France	3.9
8. USA	3.4	8. Turkey	3.0
9. Japan	3.0	9. South Korea	3.0
10. Belgium	2.3	10. Spain	2.8
11. Switzerland	2.2	11. Netherlands	2.8
12. Spain	2.0	12. India	2.5
13. South Korea	1.8	13. Belgium	2.4
14. Iran	1.7	14. Switzerland	2.3
15. China	1.6	15. Jordan	2.3

Mauritania	2010		2019
1. France	18.6	1. France	12.1
2. Spain	8.0	2. Spain	8.4
3. USA	7.3	3. USA	7.1
4. Germany	6.6	4. China	6.1
5. Japan	3.4	5. Germany	6.0
6. UK	3.0	6. Japan	2.6
7. Belgium	2.8	7. Lithuania	2.5
8. Netherlands	2.4	8. UK	2.2
9. Italy	2.4	9. India	2.2
10. China	1.9	10. Senegal	2.1

Morocco	2010		2019
1. France	20.2	1. France	16.5
2. Spain	13.2	2. Spain	12.5
3. Italy	9.0	3. China	11.0
4. Germany	8.9	4. Germany	8.1
5. USA	6.2	5. USA	5.9
6. UK	5.2	6. Italy	5.8
7. China	3.5	7. UK	4.7

Tunisia	2010		2019
1. France	19.9	1. France	18.9
2. Italy	16.2	2. Italy	11.4
3. Germany	10.7	3. Germany	9.9
4. USA	6.3	4. China	8.8
5. Spain	5.7	5. Spain	6.2
6. UK	4.1	6. USA	5.4
7. Japan	3.1	7. India	3.7
8. Belgium	3.1	8. UK	3.2
9. Netherlands	2.9	9. Netherlands	2.2
10. China	2.6	10. Japan	2.0

Maghreb's Contribution to China's GVCs

China	2010		2019
55. Yemen	0.099	55. Algeria	0.124
56. Iraq	0.096	56. Yemen	0.123
57. Hungary	0.095	57. Iraq	0.122
58. Algeria	0.092	58. Romania	0.120
59. Morocco	0.089	59. Congo	0.120
60. Myanmar	0.086	60. Morocco	0.107
61. Congo	0.072	61. Mongolia	0.101
62. Bolivia	0.058	62. Egypt	0.089
63. Greece	0.055	63. Bolivia	0.088
64. Romania	0.050	64. North Korea	0.080
65. Egypt	0.044	65. Myanmar	0.071
66. Mongolia	0.042	66. Slovakia	0.071
67. Gabon	0.041	67. Cuba	0.069
68. Slovenia	0.038	68. Luxembourg	0.069
69. Libya	0.037	69. Greece	0.064
70. Cuba	0.037	70. Zambia	0.062
71. Luxembourg	0.036	71. Slovenia	0.060
72. Slovakia	0.033	72. Bangladesh	0.056
73. Papua New Guinea	0.028	73. Macao SAR	0.055
74. Brunei	0.028	74. Gabon	0.053
75. Colombia	0.027	75. Ecuador	0.050
76. Macao SAR	0.027	76. Belarus	0.046
77. Bahrain	0.026	77. Bulgaria	0.045
78. Uruguay	0.026	78. Papua New Guinea	0.041
79. Trinidad and Tobago	0.026	79. Brunei	0.038
80. Bulgaria	0.025	80. Bahrain	0.038
81. Ecuador	0.024	81. Colombia	0.035
82. Sri Lanka	0.024	82. Jordan	0.033
83. Bangladesh	0.023	83. Trinidad and Tobago	0.028
84. Madagascar	0.022	84. Libya	0.028
85. Armenia	0.021	85. Sri Lanka	0.026
86. Tanzania	0.021	86. Uruguay	0.022
87. Cameroon	0.019	87. Ghana	0.022
88. Zimbabwe	0.017	88. Croatia	0.021
89. Zambia	0.017	89. Malta	0.021
90. Kenya	0.016	90. Uzbekistan	0.020
91. Costa Rica	0.015	91. Lithuania	0.020
92. Uzbekistan	0.013	92. Estonia	0.019
93. Syria	0.013	93. Tanzania	0.018
94. Cambodia	0.013	94. Syria	0.017
[illegible]	[illegible]	95. Laos	0.016
96. Estonia	0.011	96. Costa Rica	0.016
97. Lithuania	0.010	97. Latvia	0.015
98. Ghana	0.010	98. Cameroon	0.015
99. Nepal	0.010	99. Azerbaijan	0.014
100. New Caledonia	0.010	100. Guyana	0.014
101. Croatia	0.009	101. Cambodia	0.013
102. Iceland	0.009	102. Kenya	0.012
103. Malta	0.008	103. Ethiopia	0.012
104. TFYR Macedonia	0.008	104. Iceland	0.012
105. Dominican Republic	0.007	105. New Caledonia	0.011
106. Latvia	0.007	106. Cote dIvoire	0.011
107. Kyrgyzstan	0.007	107. DR Congo	0.011
108. Paraguay	0.007	108. Panama	0.010
109. Laos	0.007	109. Kyrgyzstan	0.010
110. Jordan	0.007	[illegible]	[illegible]
111. Senegal	0.006	111. Turkmenistan	0.009
112. Cote dIvoire	0.006	112. Dominican Republic	0.008
113. DR Congo	0.006	113. Zimbabwe	0.008
114. Jamaica	0.005	114. Paraguay	0.007
115. Mauritius	0.005	115. TFYR Macedonia	0.006
116. Tajikistan	0.005	116. Georgia	0.006
117. Turkmenistan	0.005	117. Madagascar	0.006
118. Liberia	0.004	118. Armenia	0.005
119. Azerbaijan	0.004	119. Tajikistan	0.005
120. Namibia	0.004	120. Sudan	0.005
121. Georgia	0.003	121. Mauritius	0.005
122. Suriname	0.003	122. Namibia	0.005
123. Guatemala	0.003	123. Mauritania	0.005
124. Guinea	0.003	124. Guinea	0.005
125. Panama	0.003	125. Nepal	0.004
126. Rwanda	0.003	126. Guatemala	0.004
127. Niger	0.003	127. Bosnia and Herzegovina	0.004
128. Haiti	0.002	128. Afghanistan	0.004
129. Netherlands Antilles	0.002	129. Senegal	0.004
130. Mozambique	0.002	130. Lebanon	0.003
131. Lebanon	0.002	131. Mozambique	0.003
132. Afghanistan	0.002	132. Serbia	0.003
133. El Salvador	0.002	133. Cyprus	0.003
134. Cyprus	0.002	134. Chad	0.003
135. Guyana	0.002	135. Jamaica	0.003
136. Mauritania	0.002	136. Suriname	0.002

Source: United Nations Conference on Trade and Development (UNCTAD)-Eora Global Value Chain Database.

[1] Country-by-country matrix reporting, for each exporting country, the VA contributed by all other countries in the world. Rows show the country originating the VA, whereas columns show the country exporting that VA.

Figure 4.13. Maghreb: Forward and Backward Participation in China's Global Value Changes (GVCs)

(Value added to final product, share in percentage[1])

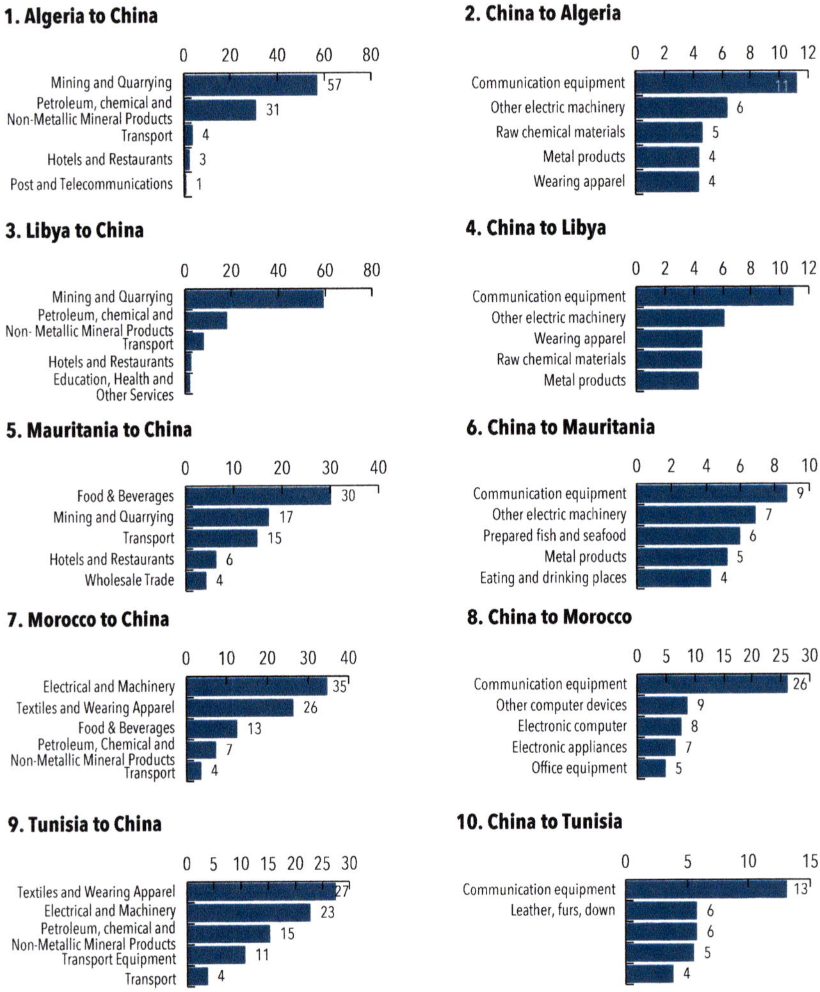

Source: United Nations Conference on Trade and Development (UNCTAD)-Eora Global Value Chain Database.

[1] Forward GVC participation refers to the share of a Maghreb country's domestic value-added in exports of a product to China. It captures Maghreb's domestic value-added contained in inputs exported to China for further processing and exports. This is the seller perspective or the supply side in GVC participation. Backward GVC participation refers to the share of China-produced value-added in a Maghreb country's exports of a particular product. It captures Maghreb's imports of intermediate goods needed to produce its exports. This is the buyer perspective or the sourcing side in GVC participation (WTO 2020).

these countries have lost their share in China's GVCs. Only Mauritania's share has increased, albeit from a very low level, mainly in the mid-2010s with the development of ore extraction.

The Maghreb's contribution to China's GVCs remains small, suggesting underused potential. Maghreb countries participate in China's GVCs by exporting domestically produced inputs to China (forward GVC participation) and by importing China's inputs to produce the goods and services for exports (backward GVC participation) (Figure 4.13). For forward GVC participation, the share of domestically produced value added in exports to China is significant only for the mining and quarrying exports from Algeria and Libya at 57 and 60 percent, respectively, and foodstuffs from Mauritania at 30 percent. All other export sectors in these three countries add domestic value to exports by less than 20 percent, with about 80 percent of their exports relying on imported value added. Morocco and Tunisia add over 20 percent of domestic value to their exports to China of electric machinery and wearing apparel, whereas the contribution of value-added in other sectors is relatively small. Regarding backward GVC participation, China provides over 10 percent in the value of communication equipment (wires and cables, and their repairs) exported by Algeria, Libya, Mauritania, and Tunisia, and 26 percent in the case of Morocco. China also supplies value-added manufactured goods in other export sectors of Maghreb countries, such as electric machinery, chemical materials, wearing apparel, and metal products.

The Maghreb has substantial untapped potential in China's GVCs. Research suggests that becoming part of GVCs, especially their middle segment, which excludes excessive reliance on both backward and forward GVC integration, is associated with positive effects on growth (Didier and Pinat 2017). So far, Maghreb countries have moved asynchronously and in different directions along GVCs. Whereas Morocco and Tunisia have increased their forward participation as contributors of intermediate inputs to other countries, Algeria and Libya have moved marginally backward using more foreign inputs in their exports. Mauritania's position has remained broadly unchanged. Based on earlier research, each Maghreb country should seek to move up GVCs, as EU countries have, and closer to the center, as ASEAN countries have using the advantages of both backward and forward GVC participation (Kireyev and others 2019). The Maghreb's deeper cooperation with China in GVCs could help achieve this goal.

CONCLUSION

Institutional arrangements for cooperation between Maghreb countries and China have strengthened over time but could be improved further. Maghreb countries have viewed China as a potentially promising partner, a source of foreign investment, a large export market, and a partner in infrastructure projects that could stimulate economic growth, create jobs, and reduce inequality. Given the diversity in the level of development, natural resource endowments, and governance structures across Maghreb countries, China may have traditionally focused on bilateral relations with individual partners. Recently, China has designated most Maghreb countries as strategic partners and signed memorandums of understanding with all of them within the BRI project. However, Maghreb countries have not yet concluded trade liberalization agreements with China. If carefully designed and well negotiated, trade liberalization agreements may open more export opportunities for the Maghreb to the Chinese market.

The Maghreb's economic cooperation with China has been confined to commodity trade, limited tourism, and investment. Most Maghreb countries trade with China less than with peer countries with a similar level of development, located at a comparable distance from China, and that have a trade deficit with China. Maghreb countries export only a limited number of products to China, mainly oil and ores, but import a broad range of diversified consumer and investment goods. Only recently, bilateral tourism has picked up, and China has become more involved in infrastructure projects in the region, but the COVID-19 pandemic severely disrupted both.

With improved policies in Maghreb countries, trade with China could increase. With technology, distance is becoming less of a constraint. Diversifying trade partners would require substantial policy reform efforts. Maghreb countries should strengthen their macroeconomic and structural policies, consider reducing impediments to trade through carefully designed and well-balanced trade agreements, enhance infrastructure investment, reform labor markets, and improve their regulatory frameworks.

Maghreb countries could expand exports to China in several sectors. For example, Morocco can further increase its exports to China of phosphates and natural aluminum, gypsum, anhydride, plasters, fats, plants and zinc ores, and a few other products. The unused comparative advantages of other Maghreb countries are more limited. For example, Algeria has some comparative advantage only in natural cork and petroleum oil, Libya has some marginal advantage in petroleum oils, and Mauritania has some advantage in flours, meals, and pellets, fats, and copper and iron ores.

Finally, Maghreb countries can increase their trade with China by participating more actively in its GVCs. China's role in Maghreb's GVCs has tripled during the past decade. In oil exporters, China has become one of the largest suppliers of oil-extracting equipment, chemicals, and related services. In oil importers, China has also become one of the largest contributors to exports, reflecting a more active use of China's inputs for the car, cable, garment, and extractive industries. More active and balanced participation of Maghreb countries in GVCs, including those with China, may be an important factor for their growth.

ANNEX 4.1.

Annex Figure 4.1.1.

Maghreb and China: Commodity Structure of Trade, 2019
(Percentage of total)

Algeria

HS	Exports	100.0	HS	Imports	100.0
27	Mineral fuels, mineral oils, and products of their distillation	99.5	84	Nuclear reactors, boilers, machinery and mechanical appliances	18.1
45	Cork and articles of cork	0.2	85	Electrical machinery and equipment and parts thereof; sound recorders	12.4
51	Wool, fine or coarse animal hair; horsehair yarn and woven fabric	0.1	73	Iron or steel articles	9.0
39	Plastics and articles thereof	0.1	87	Vehicles; other than railway or tramway rolling stock	6.6
26	Ores, slag, and ash	0.0	39	Plastics and articles thereof	5.0
25	Salt; sulfur; earths, stone; plastering materials, lime and cement	0.0	61	Apparel and clothing accessories; knitted or crocheted	4.0
22	Beverages, spirits, and vinegar	0.0	40	Rubber and articles thereof	3.6
41	Raw hides and skins (other than furskins) and leather	0.0	64	Footwear; gaiters and the like; parts of such articles	3.5
97	Works of art; collectors' pieces and antiques	0.0	94	Furniture; bedding, mattresses, mattress supports, cushions	3.1
38	Chemical products n.e.c.	0.0	62	Apparel and clothing accessories; not knitted or crocheted	3.0
0	Other	0.0	0	Other	31.8

Libya

HS	Exports	100.0	HS	Imports	100.0
27	Mineral fuels, mineral oils and products of their distillation	100.0	85	Electrical machinery and equipment and parts thereof; sound recorders	13.3
25	Salt; sulfur; earths, stone; plastering materials, lime and cement	0.0	84	Nuclear reactors, boilers, machinery and mechanical appliances	8.9
79	Zinc and articles thereof	0.0	61	Apparel and clothing accessories; knitted or crocheted	6.2
99	Commodities not specified according to kind	0.0	62	Apparel and clothing accessories; not knitted or crocheted	4.8
84	Nuclear reactors, boilers, machinery and mechanical appliances	0.0	94	Furniture; bedding, mattresses, mattress supports, cushions	4.4
22	Beverages, spirits and vinegar	0.0	73	Iron or steel articles	3.8
39	Plastics and articles thereof	0.0	40	Rubber and articles thereof	3.5
49	Printed books, newspapers, pictures, and other products	0.0	69	Ceramic products	3.5
26	Ores, slag, and ash	0.0	39	Plastics and articles thereof	3.3
40	Rubber and articles thereof	0.0	64	Footwear; gaiters and the like; parts of such articles	25.5
0	Other	0.0	0	Other	22.8

Annex Figure 4.1.1. (*continued*)

Mauritania

HS	Exports	100.0	HS	Imports	100.0
26	Ores, slag, and ash	85.9	61	Apparel and clothing accessories; knitted or crocheted	10.4
23	Food industries, residues, and wastes thereof; prepared animal fodder	9.9	55	Man-made staple fibers	9.6
3	Fish and crustaceans, mollusks, and other aquatic invertebrates	3.5	73	Iron or steel articles	7.3
41	Raw hides and skins (other than furskins) and leather	0.3	85	Electrical machinery and equipment and parts thereof; sound recorders	7.3
16	Meat, fish or crustaceans, mollusks, or other aquatic invertebrates	0.2	64	Footwear; gaiters and the like; parts of such articles	6.3
15	Animal or vegetable fats and oils and their cleavage products	0.2	9	Coffee, tea, mate, and spices	6.2
25	Salt; sulfur; earths, stone; plastering materials, lime and cement	0.0	84	Nuclear reactors, boilers, machinery and mechanical appliances	6.0
85	Electrical machinery and equipment and parts thereof; sound recorders	0.0	62	Apparel and clothing accessories; not knitted or crocheted	5.4
62	Apparel and clothing accessories; not knitted or crocheted	0.0	52	Cotton	4.8
99	Commodities not specified according to kind	0.0	54	Man-made filaments; strip and the like of man-made textile materials	4.1
0	Other	0.0	0	Other	32.6

Morocco

HS	Exports	100.0	HS	Imports	100.0
85	Electrical machinery and equipment and parts thereof; sound recorders	34.6	85	Electrical machinery and equipment and parts thereof; sound recorders	16.6
62	Apparel and clothing accessories; not knitted or crocheted	17.1	84	Nuclear reactors, boilers, machinery and mechanical appliances	13.2
26	Ores, slag, and ash	15.5	9	Coffee, tea, mate, and spices	5.8
74	Copper and articles thereof	10.8	60	Fabrics; knitted or crocheted	5.8
61	Apparel and clothing accessories; knitted or crocheted	4.9	87	Vehicles; other than railway or tramway rolling stock	5.7
23	Food industries, residues, and wastes thereof; prepared animal fodder	3.2	94	Furniture; bedding, mattresses, mattress supports, cushions	4.8
25	Salt; sulfur; earths, stone; plastering materials, lime and cement	2.8	73	Iron or steel articles	4.5
88	Aircraft, spacecraft, and parts thereof	1.5	39	Plastics and articles thereof	4.1
90	Optical, photographic, measuring, checking, medical instruments	1.4	54	Man-made filaments; strip and the like of man-made textile materials	2.8
8	Fruit and nuts, edible; peel of citrus fruit or melons	1.4	90	Optical, photographic, measuring, checking, medical instruments	2.5
0	Other	6.8	0	Other	34.2

Annex Figure 4.1.1. (*continued*)

		Tunisia			
HS	**Exports**	100.0	**HS**	**Imports**	100.0
85	Electrical machinery and equipment and parts thereof; sound recorders	34.6	85	Electrical machinery and equipment and parts thereof; sound recorders	24.7
62	Apparel and clothing accessories; not knitted or crocheted	26.8	84	Nuclear reactors, boilers, machinery and mechanical appliances	13.4
61	Apparel and clothing accessories; knitted or crocheted	8.6	87	Vehicles; other than railway or tramway rolling stock	8.5
84	Nuclear reactors, boilers, machinery and mechanical appliances	6.2	39	Plastics and articles thereof	6.4
39	Plastics and articles thereof	6.1	72	Iron and steel	3.6
25	Salt; sulfur; earths, stone; plastering materials, lime and cement	4.9	73	Iron or steel articles	3.4
87	Vehicles; other than railway or tramway rolling stock	3.2	60	Fabrics; knitted or crocheted	2.9
42	Articles of leather; saddlery and harness; travel goods, handbags	2.3	94	Furniture; bedding, mattresses, mattress supports, cushions	2.6
90	Optical, photographic, measuring, checking, medical instruments	1.9	90	Optical, photographic, measuring, checking, medical instruments	2.6
59	Textile fabrics; impregnated, coated, covered or laminated	0.8	54	Man-made filaments; strip and the like of man-made textile materials	2.2
0	Other	4.5	0	Other	29.6

Sources: IMF DTS (2021); and authors' calculations.
Note: HS = Harmonized Commodity Description and Coding System.

Annex Figure 4.1.2.

Gravity Model Variables and Sources

Variable	Description	Source
Xij	Exports from reporting country i to destination country j	IMF Direction of Trade Statistics
pop_i	Population in reporting country	World Bank WDI
pop_j	Population in destination country	World Bank WDI
gdpc_i	GDP per capita in reporting country	World Bank WDI
gdpc_j	GDP per capita in destination country	World Bank WDI
dist	Distance	Centre d'Études Prospectives et d'Informations Internationales
comlang_off	Common official of primary language	Centre d'Études Prospectives et d'Informations Internationales
comlang_ethno	A language is spoken by at least 9% of the population in both countries	Centre d'Études Prospectives et d'Informations Internationales
comcol	Common colonizer post 1945	Centre d'Études Prospectives et d'Informations Internationales
r_landlocked	reporting country is landlocked	Centre d'Études Prospectives et d'Informations Internationales
p_landlocked	Destination country is landlocked	Centre d'Études Prospectives et d'Informations Internationales
p_tariffs_avg	Average tariffs in destination country	World Bank World Integrated Trade Solution
infras_i	Infrastructure quality in reporting country	World Economic Forum database
infras_j	Infrastructure quality in destination country	World Economic Forum database
labor_eff_i	Labor market efficiency index in reporting country	World Economic Forum database
labor_eff_j	Labor market effectiveness in destination country	World Economic Forum database
regulatoryqual_i	Regulatory framework quality in reporting country	World Bank: Worldwide Governance Indicators
regulatoryqual_j	Regulatory framework quality in destination country	World Bank: Worldwide Governance Indicators
maghreb_both	Is equal to 1 if both exporter and importer are from the Maghreb region and 0 otherwise	Calculated
maghreb_none	Is equal to 1 if none of the countries involved is from the Maghreb region and 0 otherwise	Calculated
exp_maghreb_to_chn	Is equal to 1 if the exporter is from the Maghreb and importer is China and 0 otherwise	Calculated
exp_maghreb_to_EUR	Is equal to 1 if the exporter is from the Maghreb and importer is from the European Union and 0 otherwise	Calculated
exp_maghreb_to_others	Is equal to 1 if the exporter is from the Maghreb and importer is from other countries excluding China and the European Union and 0 otherwise	Calculated
exp_rw_maghreb	Is equal to 1 if the exporter is from the rest of the world (outside Maghreb) and importer is a country from the Maghreb and 0 otherwise	Calculated
fta_wto	Free trade agreement	World Bank World Integrated Trade Solution (WITS)

Source: Authors' estimates.

Annex Figure 4.1.3. Potential for Maghreb Countries in Trade with China

(Export Potential Indicator)[1]

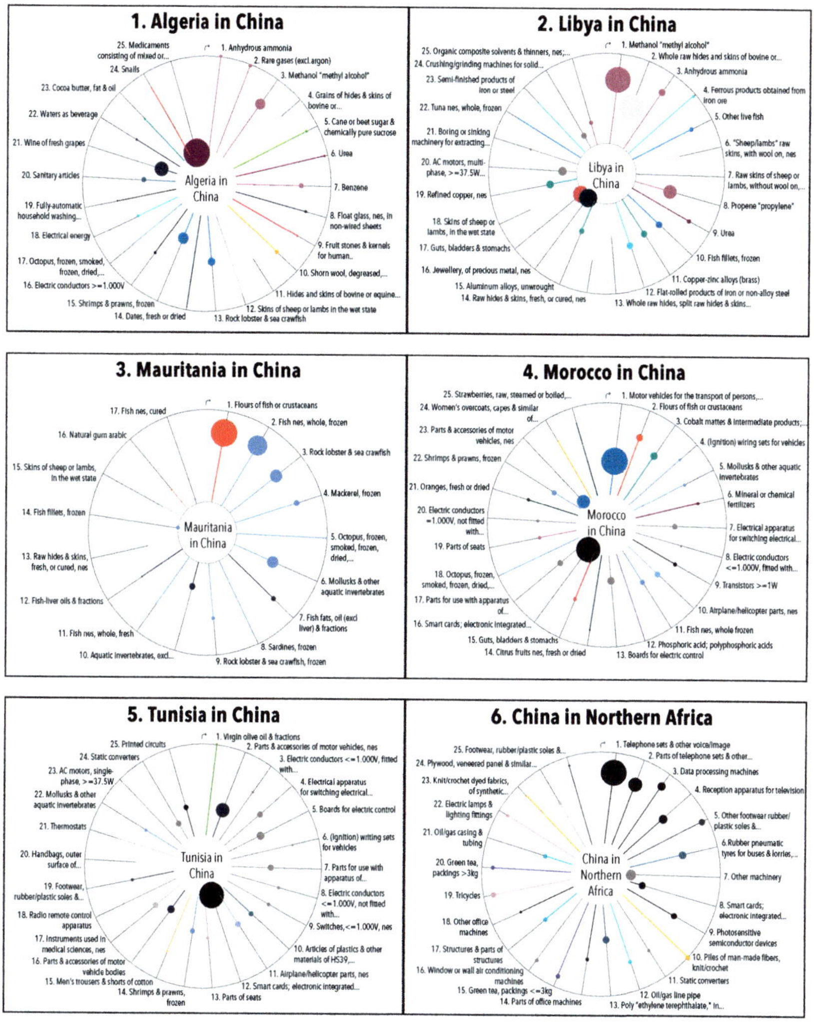

Source: ITC 2020. Decreux, Y., and J. Spies. 2016.

[1] Potential export is calculated as supply × demand (corrected for market access) × bilateral ease of trade. Supply and demand are projected based on GDP and population forecasts, demand elasticities, and tariffs. The supply component is based on the projected market share corrected for global tariff advantages of the country in each product. The demand component is based on projected imports augmented by expected growth of GDP per capita adjusted for the tariff advantages and bilateral distance. Ease of trade is based on the ratio of actual trade between an exporter and its market relative to their hypothetical trade if the exporter had the same share in this market as it has in world markets.

REFERENCES

Ali, M. 2020. "Pakistan-China FTA: Second Time's the Charm?" *Pakistan Today*, January. https://profit.pakistantoday.com.pk/2020/01/27/pakistan-china-fta-second-times-the-charm.

Allard, C., J. C. Kriljenko, J. Gonzalez-Garcia, E. Kitsios, J. Trevino, and W. Chen. 2016. "Trade Integration and Global Value Chains in sub-Saharan Africa: In Pursuit of the Missing Link." Africa Department, IMF. https://www.imf.org/external/pubs/ft/dp/2016/afr1602.pdf.

Anderson, J. E., and E. van Wincoop. 2003. Gravity with Gravitas: A Solution to the Border Puzzle. *American Economic Review* 93 (1): 170–92.

Asia Infrastructure Development Bank (AIIB). 2021. https://www.aiib.org/en/index.html.

Balassa, B., and M. Noland. 1989. "Revealed Comparative Advantage in Japan and the United States." *Journal of International Economic Integration* 4 (2): 8–22.

China FTA Network. 2021. Ministry of Commerce, People's Republic of China. http://fta.mofcom.gov.cn/english/index.shtml.

China–Arab States Cooperation Forum (CASCF). 2021. https://www.cgtn.com/special/3d3d514f7a45544d304a336277566d55.html.

Custodio, L. 2020. "Mining Companies Stand to Win From Peru-China FTA that Neglects Environment." Dialogo Chine, September. https://dialogochino.net/en/extractive-industries/37440-mining-companies-stand-to-win-from-peru-china-fta-that-neglects-environment.

Decreux, Y., and J. Spies. 2016. "Export Potential Assessments." International Trade Centre. https://exportpotential.intracen.org.

Didier, T., and M. Pinat. 2017. "The Nature of Trade and Growth Linkages." World Bank Policy Research Working Paper 8168, World Bank, Washington, DC. https://documents1.worldbank.org/curated/en/900341502818068705/pdf/WPS8168.pdf.

Duke Global Health Innovation Center. 2021. "Launch and Scale Speedometer." https://launchandscalefaster.org/covid-19/vaccinemanufacturing.

Eaton, J., and S. Kortum. 2002. "Technology, Geography and Trade." *Econometrica* 70 (5): 1741–79.

Fernández, A., M. W. Klein, A. Rebucci, M. Schindler, and M. Uribe. 2015. "Capital Control Measures: A New Dataset." IMF Working Paper 15/80, International Monetary Fund, Washington, DC.

Forum on China–Africa Cooperation (FOCAC). 2021. http://www.focac.org/eng.

Ghafar, A., and A. Jacobs. 2019. "Beijing calling: Assessing China's Growing Footprint in North Africa." Brookings Doha Center Policy Briefing, September. https://www.brookings.edu/research/beijing-calling-assessing-chinas-growing-footprint-in-north-africa.

Google Trends. Maghreb and China. Retreated from https://trends.google.com/trends/on June 17, 2021.

Green Belt and Road Initiative Center (GBRIC). 2021. https://green-bri.org.

International Comparison Program (ICP). 2021. World Bank. https://www.worldbank.org/en/programs/icp.

International Monetary Fund (IMF), Direction of Trade Statistics. 2020. https://data.imf.org/?sk=9d6028d4-f14a-464c-a2f2-59b2cd424b85.

International Monetary Fund (IMF), Direction of Trade Statistics. 2021. https://data.imf.org/?sk=9d6028d4-f14a-464c-a2f2-59b2cd424b85.

International Trade Center (ITC). 2020. Export Potential Maps. https://exportpotential.intracen.org.

Johns Hopkins SAIS China–Africa Research Initiative. 2020. http://www.sais-cari.org.

Kireyev, A., B. Nandwa. L. Ocampos, B. Sarr, R. Al Amine, A. Auclair, Y. Cai, and others. 2019. "Economic Integration in the Maghreb: An Untapped Source of Growth." IMF Departmental Paper 2019/02/08. https://www.imf.org/en/Publications/Departmental-Papers-Policy-Papers/Issues/2019/02/08/Economic-Integration-in-the-Maghreb-An-Untapped-Source-of-Growth-46273.

Lafargue, F. 2018. "The Economic Presence of China in the Maghreb: Ambitions and Limits. Observatory of the Arab-Muslim World and the Sahel." Note 294/FRS/OBSARCRISE of October 29. https://www.frstrategie.org/sites/default/files/documents/programmes/observatoire-du-monde-arabo-musulman-et-du-sahel/publications/en/294.pdf.

Meddeb, H. 2021. "The Hidden Face of Informal Cross-Border Trade in Tunisia After 2011." May, Carnegie Middle East Center. https://carnegie-mec.org/2021/05/27/hidden-face-of-informal-cross-border-trade-in-tunisia-after-2011-pub-84621.

Ministry of Commerce (MOFCOM), PRC. 2021. China FTA Network. http://fta.mofcom.gov.cn/english/fta_tanpan.shtml.

Organization for Economic Cooperation and Development (OECD). 2018a. "Morocco in Global Value Chains: Results and Statistical Recommendations from the Integration of Morocco in the Trade in Value Added Database." https://www.oecd.org/sti/ind/measuring-trade-in-value-added.htm.

Organization for Economic Cooperation and Development (OECD). 2018b. "Trade in Value Added: China." https://www.oecd.org/en/topics/sub-issues/trade-in-value-added.html.

Organization for Economic Cooperation and Development (OECD). 2021. "Global Value Chains." https://www.oecd.org/sti/ind/global-value-chains.htm.

Riera, O., and Ph. Paerzold. 2020. "Global Value Chains and Trade in the EBRD Regions." https://www.ebrd.com/what-we-do/economic-research-and-data/cse-economists/global-value-chains-and-trade-in-ebrd-regions.html.

Rudolf, M. 2021. "China's Health Diplomacy during COVID-19." SWP Comment, No. 9, January. https://www.swp-berlin.org/en/publication/chinas-health-diplomacy-during-covid-19.

The North Africa Post. 2020. "A China-Owned Garment Manufacturer Invested in a High-Tech Sock, Hosiery, and Lingerie Facility in Morocco." https://northafricapost.com/42519-new-chinese-textile-unit-in-casablanca-to-create-650-jobs.html.

UNCTAD. 2021. "Revealed Comparative Advantage." https://unctadstat.unctad.org/EN/RcaRadar.html.

World Bank. 2013. "Methodology." World Integrated Trade Solutions (WITS). Online Trade Outcomes Indicators. User's Manual. https://wits.worldbank.org/methodology.html.

World Bank. 2019. "Belt and Road Economics: Opportunities and Risks of Transport Corridors." https://www.worldbank.org/en/topic/regional-integration/publication/belt-and-road-economics-opportunities-and-risks-of-transport-corridors.

World Bank. 2020. World Integrated Trade Solutions (WITS). https://wits.worldbank.org.

World Bank. 2021. "International Debt Statistics." https://www.worldbank.org/en/programs/debt-statistics/ids.

World Trade Organization (WTO). 2020. "Trade in Value-Added and Global Value Chains Profiles. Explanatory Notes." https://www.wto.org/english/res_e/statis_e/miwi_e/explanatory_notes_e.pdf.

World Trade Organization (WTO). 2021. "Trade in Value-Added and Global Value Chains. China." https://www.wto.org/english/res_e/statis_e/miwi_e/cn_e.pdf.

Yotov, Y. V., R. Piermartini, J. A. Monteiro, and M. Larch. 2016. *An Advanced Guide to Trade Policy Analysis: The Structural Gravity Model*. Geneva: World Trade Organization.

Zoubir, Y. 2019. " China's relations with the Maghreb countries: the preponderant place of Algeria." Confluences Méditerranée 2019/2 (No. 109). https://www.cairn.info/revue-confluences-mediterranee-2019-2-page-91.htm?ref=doi.

Zoubir, Y. 2020. "Expanding Sino–Maghreb Relations: Morocco and Tunisia." Chatham House Brief (February). https://www.chathamhouse.org/2020/02/expanding-sino-maghreb-relations.

CHAPTER 5

Spillovers: Examining the Economic and Financial Links between China and Africa

Shushanik Hakobyan, Mariya Brussevich, Diego Cerdeiro, Eugenio Cerutti, Mattia Coppo, Benjamin Hunt, Papa N'Diaye, Chris Papageorgiou, Andrea Pescatori, Katsiaryna Svirydzenka, Nico Valckx, and Fan Zhang

INTRODUCTION

Over the past 20 years, China has become an increasingly important global economic player and has greatly expanded its economic ties to Africa, becoming the continent's largest trading partner and source of foreign direct investment (FDI). During 2020–22, China was the destination for about 13 percent of Africa's exports and the source of 16 percent of the continent's imports (up from about 3 percent each in 2000). FDI flows from China accounted for about 10 percent of overall FDI flows and about 9 percent of overall inward FDI stocks in 2020–21 (Chapter 3).

Given China's increasingly important role in the global economy, including in Africa, it is therefore unsurprising that the magnitude of spillovers from the country has significantly increased. Previous literature has identified *trade linkages* as the main channel of transmission of shocks originating from China, with large effects for net commodity exporters (for example, see Furceri, Jalles, and Zdzienicka [2017]). Financial developments in China come with spillovers as well, but so far this mainly reflects the country's important role in trade and commodity markets rather than its integration in global financial markets or direct financial linkages it has with other countries.

As the second-largest economy after the United States (at current exchange rates),[1] China's share in world GDP reached 18 percent in 2022, up from 3.5 percent in 2000. Its exports and imports rose from about 3 percent of the world total in the late 1990s to about 16 percent and 11 percent, respectively, by 2022. In this rise to prominence, China's demand for commodities has grown

[1] In purchasing power terms, China is already the largest economy.

even faster, with corresponding repercussions for commodity prices. For instance, the country's share of base and precious metals in global imports increased from 5 percent in 2000 to 20 percent in 2022.

This rise of China in trade and commodity markets, however, has not been accompanied by a commensurate rise in its role in international financial markets, reflecting, in part, the relatively gradual liberalization of the country's capital account. For instance, it accounted for only 2 percent of global portfolio investment holdings and 8 percent of global direct investments in 2022, and the share of Chinese renminbi in allocated global reserves and foreign exchange turnover was only 2 percent and 4 percent, respectively. At the same time, China has become a global creditor, including by providing financing through the Belt and Road Initiative. About $926 billion was invested in Belt and Road projects worldwide and $209 billion in Africa from 2013 to 2022.[2]

This chapter examines key stylized facts about Africa-bound spillovers from China, with new contributions in three areas. First, it illustrates how shocks in China affect Africa in a general equilibrium setting where the initial effect through trade linkages could be amplified through other transmission channels, including relative price changes, demand, and financial channels. Second, it updates and extends the previous empirical findings on the effect of China on commodity prices. Third, it provides empirical estimates of financial spillovers from China to foreign exchange and equity markets in Africa.

More specifically, the IMF's G20 Model (Andrle and others 2015) is used to simulate the potential effect on Africa of three scenarios for policy settings in China: (1) large public investment-led fiscal stimulus, comparable in magnitude with that observed after the global financial crisis; (2) a moderate fiscal package, as observed during the COVID-19 crisis; and (3) a continued rebalancing from investment to consumption.

The results suggest that large fiscal stimulus in China would boost growth in African countries, with a particularly large effect on low-income and fragile economies. In contrast, a rebalancing from investment to consumption would have minor negative growth effects on most African economies in the short term while benefiting eastern and fragile economies and hurting commodity exporters in the medium term.

The chapter then zooms in on the effects of Chinese industrial production (IP) growth on commodity prices, covering 1992–2020. The empirical approach is based on quantile regression techniques to account for extreme commodity price movements and a small vector autoregression (VAR) model to allow for dynamic interactions between the model variables. The findings suggest that China's IP has a major effect on commodity prices and that the effect is larger in times of extreme volatility in commodity markets. Furthermore, from the VAR model, Chinese IP shocks appear to have a more significant and

[2] American Enterprise Institute China Global Investment Tracker (https://www.aei.org/china-global-investment-tracker).

longer-lasting effect on commodity prices than IP shocks in the euro area or the United States.

Finally, the chapter sheds new light on how economic and financial developments in China affect foreign exchange and equity markets in Africa. Although the magnitude of financial spillovers from China has increased, the effect is still smaller than that coming from the euro area or the United States and often lower than that from the larger African countries. This is consistent with the fact that the financial linkages between China and Africa are still much smaller than their trade linkages.

The rest of the chapter first establishes stylized facts about China's role in goods trade, commodity markets, and portfolio investment flows in the pre-pandemic period, focusing on the China–Africa linkages. This is followed by estimating spillovers from China to Africa, by first using a computable general equilibrium model, then focusing on the effect of Chinese IP growth on commodity prices, and finally examining spillovers from China to foreign exchange and stock markets in Africa.

TRADE LINKAGES

As China's role in world trade increased dramatically over the past two decades, its trade linkages with Africa intensified as fast or even faster, making the country the most important trading partner for sub-Saharan Africa (IMF 2014c). China's

Figure 5.1. China's Trade with Africa and Other Economies
(Percent of world trade)

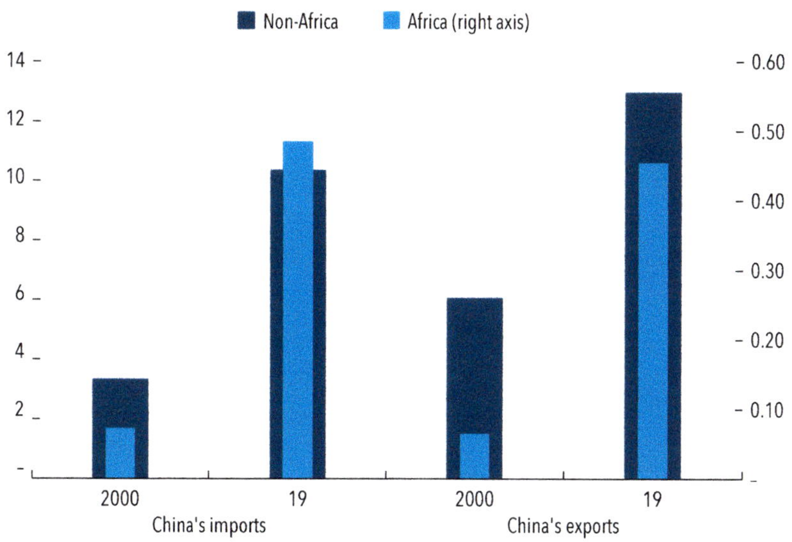

Sources: Direction of Trade Statistics; and authors' estimates.

imports rose from 3–4 percent of the world total in the early 2000s to about 11 percent by 2019 (Figure 5.1). Its imports from Africa increased at a slightly faster pace, albeit from a lower base, reaching nearly ½ percent of global imports by 2019. A similar pattern is observed in China's exports—both to the world in aggregate and to African economies in particular.

When analyzed from the perspective of individual African countries, the role China plays in African imports is relatively homogeneous (Figure 5.2, panel 1). For the median African country, China's role as a supplier has increased steadily

Figure 5.2. African Countries' Trade Integration with China
(Percent of total exports/total imports)

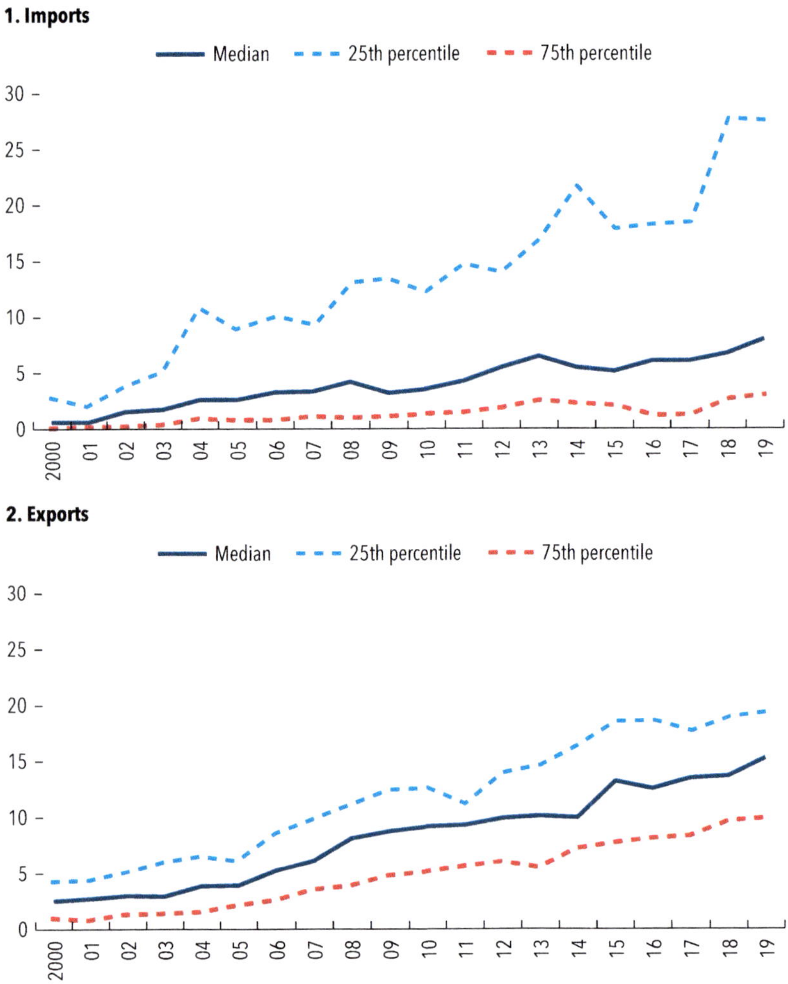

Sources: Direction of Trade Statistics; and authors' estimates.

from about 3 percent to over 15 percent of total imports between 2000 and 2019. This pattern is common across African countries, as evidenced by the relatively tight interquartile range of the distribution. But on exports, China's importance as a destination varies substantially. In aggregate, Africa's exports to China grew from $4.8 billion in 2000 to $92.5 billion in 2019. Although China's importance as an export market increased for the median country from about 1 percent in 2000 to about 10 percent of total exports in 2019, the increase has been far more pronounced for certain countries (Figure 5.2, panel 2). For a country at the 75th percentile of the distribution, its importance as an export market increased from a mere 4 percent of total exports in 2000 to over one-fourth (28 percent) in 2019.

To a large extent, the increased importance of China as an export market for certain countries reflects its growing demand for commodities. In fact, the top two Harmonized System two-digit commodities African countries export to China are mineral fuels and oils, and ores (Figure 5.3, panel 1). With certain exceptions, this pattern of exports to China is in fact similar to Africa's overall exports to the world (Figure 5.3, panel 2).

A similar, partial overlap is observed between Africa's top import products from China and Africa's overall top import products (Figure 5.3, panels 3 and 4). Africa is especially reliant on China in certain product categories, for example, mechanical appliances and electrical machinery. Chinese imports make up over one-fifth of total African imports in these categories.

China and Africa have also become more important to each other in both direct and indirect supply-chain channels. The case is starker for China as a direct and indirect supplier of inputs that end up being used in African exports. China's contribution to Africa's gross exports has increased from about 0.5 percent to about 1.5 percent from 2000 to 2019 (Figure 5.4). Africa's direct and indirect contribution to China's gross exports has also increased, although from an even lower base and far more modestly—from 0.3 percent to 0.5 percent of China's gross exports. These low figures reflect the region's room to further and better integrate into global value chains (Allard and others 2016).

Figure 5.3. China and Africa-Main Goods Exports

(Harmonized System [HS] two-digit classification, 2017, billions of US dollars)

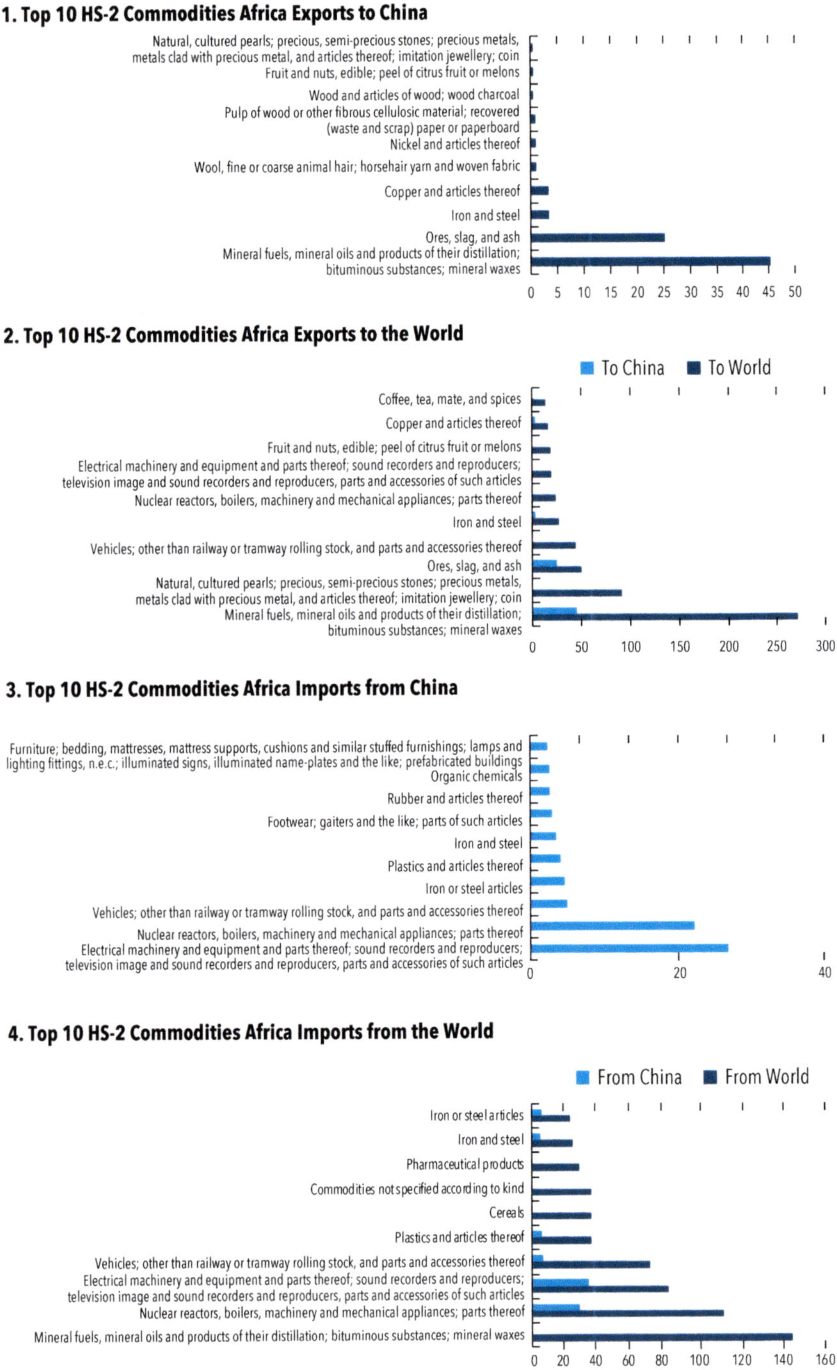

Sources: UN Comtrade; and authors' estimates.

Figure 5.4. Direct and Indirect Export Linkages

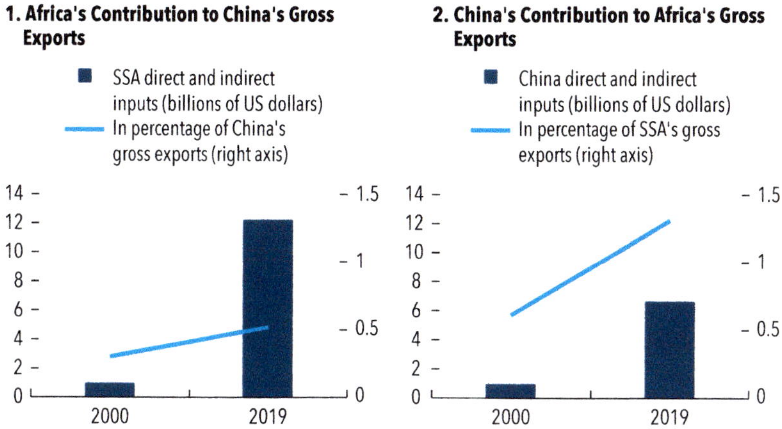

Sources: Eora World Input-Output database (Lenzen and others 2012, 2013); and authors' estimates.
Note: SSA = sub-Saharan Africa.

COMMODITY TRADE LINKAGES

Over the past 20 years, China has become an increasingly important global commodity importer, with growing demand for commodities. This includes both imports for domestic demand that could not be satisfied by domestic production and imports to process commodities for reexport. According to the World Bureau of Metals, China's share of global consumption of lead, aluminum, and copper rose from 10–13 percent in 2000 to 46–57 percent in 2019. In fact, China's share of global trade has increased dramatically across all types of commodities. Based on UN Comtrade imports data, the country's share of global agricultural commodity imports increased from 7 percent in 2000 to 12 percent in 2019 (with a higher share in nonfood), from 3 percent to 11 percent for energy commodities (mainly oil and petroleum products), and from 5 percent to 18 percent for base and precious metals (Figure 5.5). This implies that today changes in total commodity demand from China tend to have a major effect on commodity prices. Conversely, major commodity exporters, including many in Africa, have become more dependent on Chinese demand.

Figure 5.5. China's Share in Global Commodity Trade
(Percent)

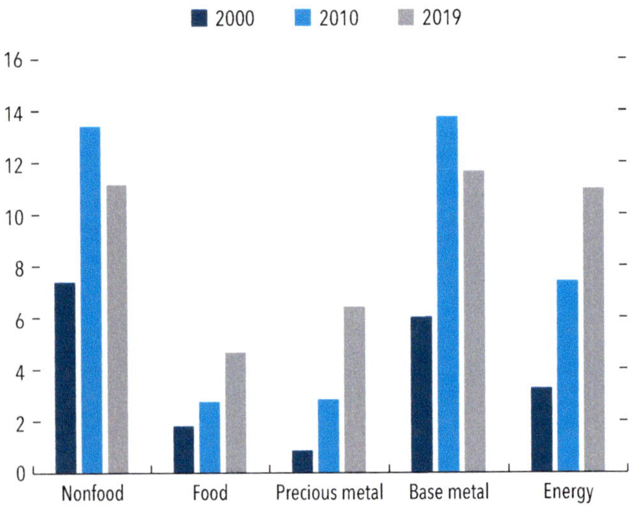

Sources: UN Comtrade; and authors' estimates.

In Africa, commodity trade and production are concentrated in a few resource-rich countries. However, on a global scale, African countries do not account for a large share of trade (except for certain markets such as gold and gemstones). More specifically, agricultural commodities from sub-Saharan Africa accounted for 3.8 percent of global agricultural trade, and metals and energy (oil) commodities accounted for 7.6 percent and 4.9 percent of global trade in 2019, respectively. In agricultural commodities, countries in Southern Africa (Namibia, South Africa, Zambia, Zimbabwe) are the major sub-Saharan exporters—notably of cereals, wheat, and beef (Figure 5.6). For metals and minerals, Democratic Republic of the Congo, South Africa, and Zambia are the major sub-Saharan exporters—especially of copper, aluminum, nickel, and tin. Angola and Nigeria are the most important fossil fuel exporters from Africa, along with Libya in North Africa.

Across most commodity groups, China is a major destination for African exports. China's share of African countries' commodity exports has gradually risen over time from 4 percent in 2000 to 25 percent in 2019, whereas its share of world trade increased from 4 percent to 15 percent over the same period. In 2019, China was the largest export destination for sub-Saharan forestry products

Figure 5.6. Commodities: Regional Production, 2019
(Percent)

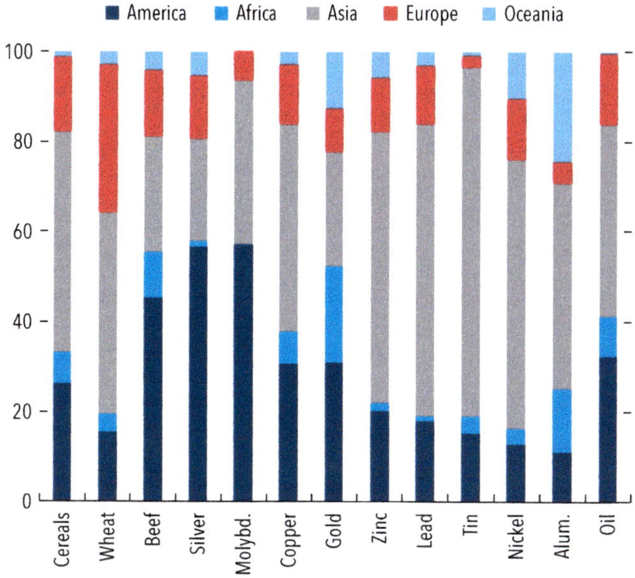

Sources: World Metals Bureau, Food and Agriculture Organization; and authors' estimates.

(40 percent), metals and minerals (27 percent), pearls and gemstones (27 percent), and oil (31 percent). It was the second most important destination for agricultural commodities (6.7 percent) after the Netherlands (10 percent). Other important destinations for sub-Saharan agricultural exports are other European Union (EU) countries (24 percent) and the United States (5.4 percent) (Figure 5.7, panel 1). In metals and minerals, the United Arab Emirates (for gold), the EU (for a broad range of base and precious metals), and Switzerland (two-thirds of which is for gold) each account for 12–15 percent of sub-Saharan exports (Figure 5.7, panel 2). In energy (oil), other important destinations are the EU (24 percent) and India (15 percent).

As a source of demand for Africa's commodity exports, shocks to growth in China and shifts in its composition could entail significant spillovers to Africa. The evidence of such spillovers from Chinese demand to commodity prices is examined later in the chapter.

Figure 5.7. Sub-Saharan Africa's Major Trade Partners, 2019

1. Agricultural Commodities

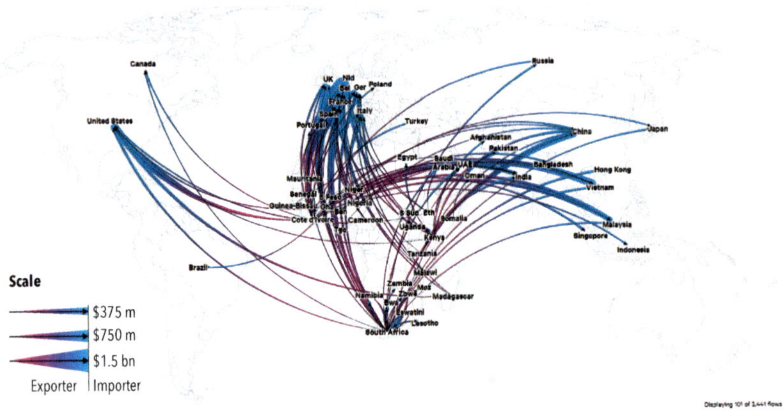

2. Metals and Minerals Commodities

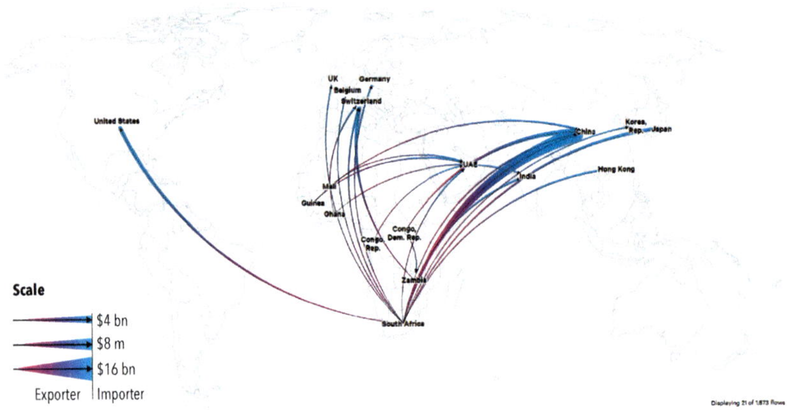

Sources: UN Comtrade, visualization by Resourcetrade.earth.
Note: The boundaries, colors, denominations, and any other information shown on the maps do not imply, on the part of the International Monetary Fund, any judgment on the legal status of any territory or any endorsement or acceptance of such boundaries.

FINANCIAL LINKAGES

Unlike trade flows, China's financial nonbank linkages both globally and with Africa are still more limited, although they have been growing from low levels over the past decades. In line with China's gradual capital account liberalization that initially focused on FDIs, total FDI flows from China to the rest of the world grew from about 0.6 percent of China's GDP in 2005 to over 1 percent of GDP in 2021. FDI flows from China to Africa, in turn, grew from 1.3 percent of total inflows in 2005 to over 6.3 percent in 2021 (see Chapter 3). Because it relates to banks, claims of Chinese banks are quite significant in some countries (see Box 5.1). Chinese bond and equity market flows into Africa—which only started in 2000—still remain relatively limited.

Zooming in on portfolio investments, China's contribution to global portfolio investment flows is still relatively modest. With total portfolio investment assets reaching almost $646 billion in 2019, China accounted for only 1 percent of global portfolio investment holdings. Nevertheless, China's portfolio holdings have more than doubled since 2015, after its accelerated capital account liberalization since the global financial crisis. Africa, as a destination for Chinese portfolio investment, accounted for less than 0.15 percent of China's total portfolio outflows in 2019 (Figure 5.8, panel 1). East Asia is the fastest-growing

Figure 5.8. Gross Foreign Portfolio Investment Flows

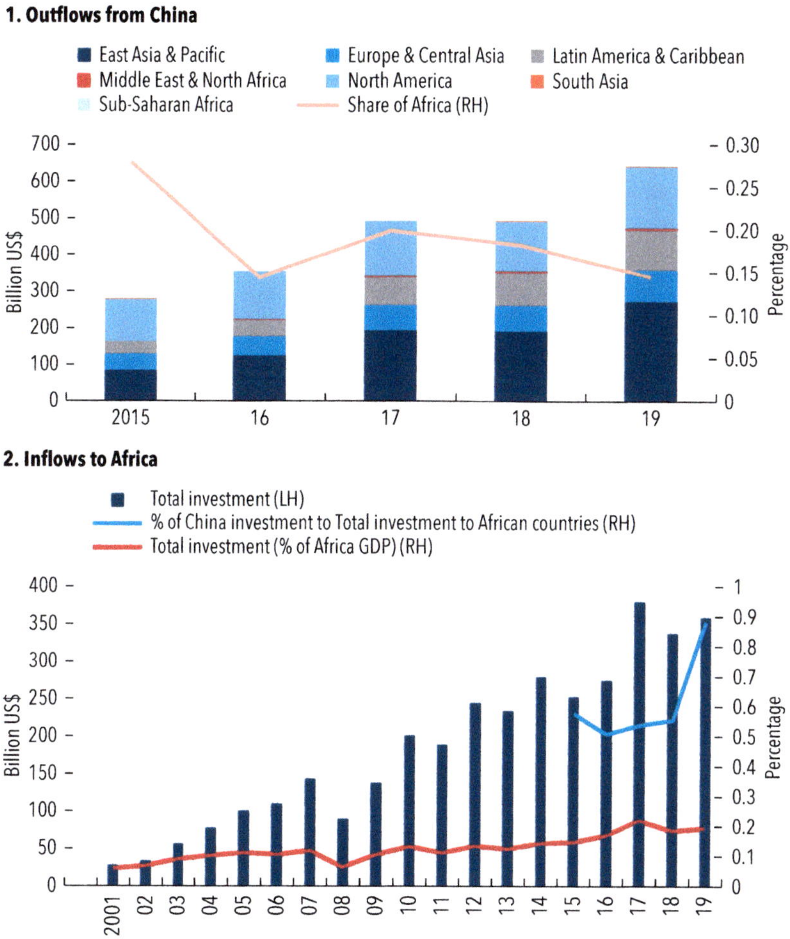

Sources: Coordinated Portfolio Investment Survey; authors' estimates.

destination for Chinese foreign portfolio investment, followed by North America and Latin America (Box 5.1 reviews the global role of Chinese banks).

Although still relatively low, gross foreign portfolio investments to Africa grew more than tenfold over the past two decades (Figure 5.8, panel 2).[3] Foreign portfolio inflows increased from 0.05 percent to 0.2 percent of GDP. Chinese investors began entering African bond and equity markets in the beginning of the 2000s. By 2019, China's engagement in private capital markets had expanded to only 1 percent of all portfolio holdings in Africa. This suggests that in contrast to China's key engagement channels with Africa—trade and official loans, private capital flows—foreign direct and portfolio investments—still play a negligible role in Africa–China economic relations (refer to Chapter 3 on FDI and Chapter 6 on official debt).

By destination, sub-Saharan Africa accounted for the largest share of portfolio flows to the continent from China and the rest of the world (Figure 5.9, panel 1). China's presence in North Africa's bond and equity markets expanded to 2 percent of foreign portfolio inflows (Figure 5.9, panel 2).[4] Nevertheless, foreign portfolio investment remains a small share of GDP in North Africa (see Chapter 4).

Frontier and emerging market economies were the main beneficiaries of foreign portfolio inflows from China, whereas flows to other developing countries in Africa are still nascent and highly volatile (Figure 5.9, panels 3 and 4). Among the largest beneficiaries, Mauritius has the longest-standing engagement with portfolio investors from China. Foreign portfolio investment from China to other major destinations, including Côte d'Ivoire, Ghana, Morocco, and South Africa, began picking up only during the past decade (Figure 5.10). In 2019, Ghana successfully issued a \$3 billion eurobond, with China accounting for more than 10 percent of the total issuance. This put Ghana at the forefront of China's investor engagement in Africa.

[3] The analysis in this section relies on a sample of 30 countries, reporting data on foreign portfolio investment inflows through the IMF's Coordinated Portfolio Investment Survey: Algeria, Angola, Cabo Verde, Cameroon, Chad, Côte d'Ivoire, Ethiopia, Gabon, Gambia, Ghana, Kenya, Liberia, Libya, Madagascar, Mali, Mauritius, Morocco, Mozambique, Namibia, Nigeria, Rwanda, Senegal, Seychelles, Sierra Leone, South Africa, Tanzania, Togo, Tunisia, Uganda, and Zambia.

[4] North African countries in the sample include Algeria, Morocco, and Tunisia.

Figure 5.9. Gross Foreign Portfolio Investment Flows by Country Group

1. Inflows to Sub-Saharan African Countries

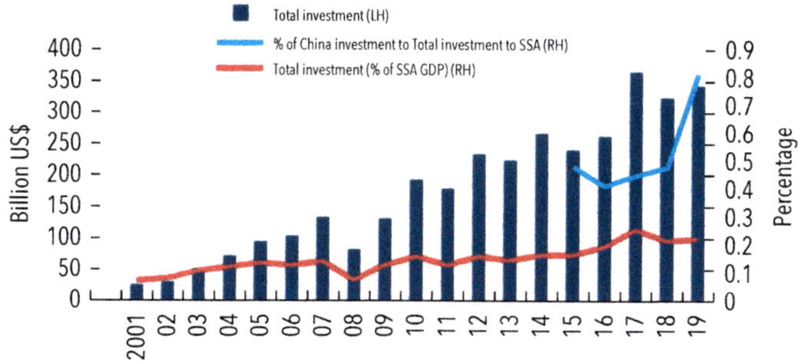

2. Inflows to North African Countries

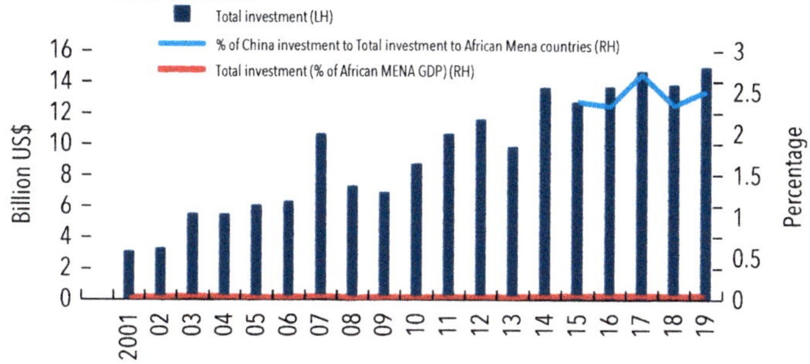

3. Inflows to African EM and Frontier Countries

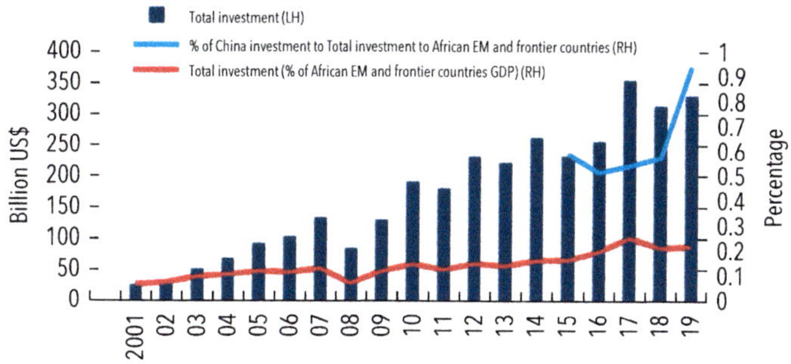

4. Inflows to Other African Developing Countries

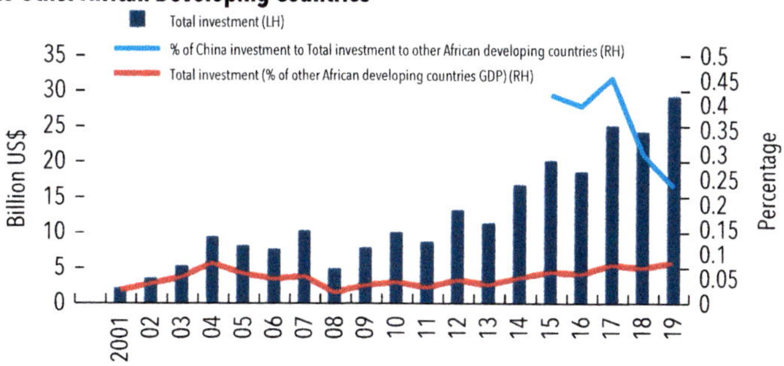

Sources: Sources: Coordinated Portfolio Investment Survey; and authors' estimates.
Note: Total investment flows include equities and short- and long-term debt securities.
EM = emerging markets; SSA = sub-Saharan Africa; MENA = Middle East and North Africa.

Figure 5.10. Foreign Portfolio Investment Flows from China: Top Five Recipient Countries

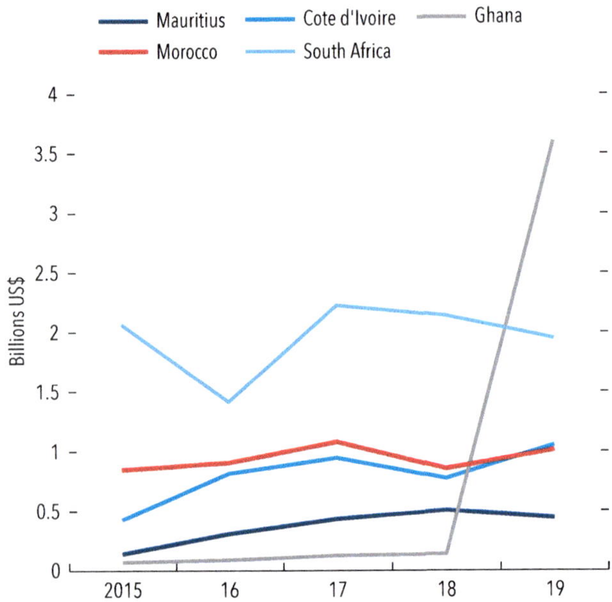

Sources: Coordinated Portfolio Investment Survey; and authors' estimates.

In terms of composition, in 2018, more than 76 percent of China's foreign portfolio investment in Africa was in debt securities. Within the debt security portfolio, 70 percent was long-term debt, as in the case of Ghana's eurobond (Figure 5.11). China's participation in African equity markets remains limited. Among the top 10 recipients of Chinese foreign portfolio investments in Africa, only Ghana, Kenya, Liberia, Mauritius, and South Africa received equity investment from China, totaling $1.5 billion in 2018. Short-term debt securities, mainly consisting of Treasury bills, account for only a small fraction of total foreign portfolio inflows from China.

FDI flows from China to Africa are also small and highly correlated with foreign portfolio investment flows (Figure 5.12). This suggests that well-established equity and bond markets may encourage higher FDI inflows by providing an opportunity for investors to list their companies on the local stock market.

Can conventional "push" and "pull" factors explain the increase in Chinese portfolio investment inflows to Africa over the past two decades? Generally, evidence is mixed on the role of global push factors, such as interest rate and growth differentials, and domestic pull factors, such as debt-to-GDP ratios and stock

Figure 5.11. Composition of Foreign Portfolio Investment Flows from China: Top 10 Recipient Countries, 2018

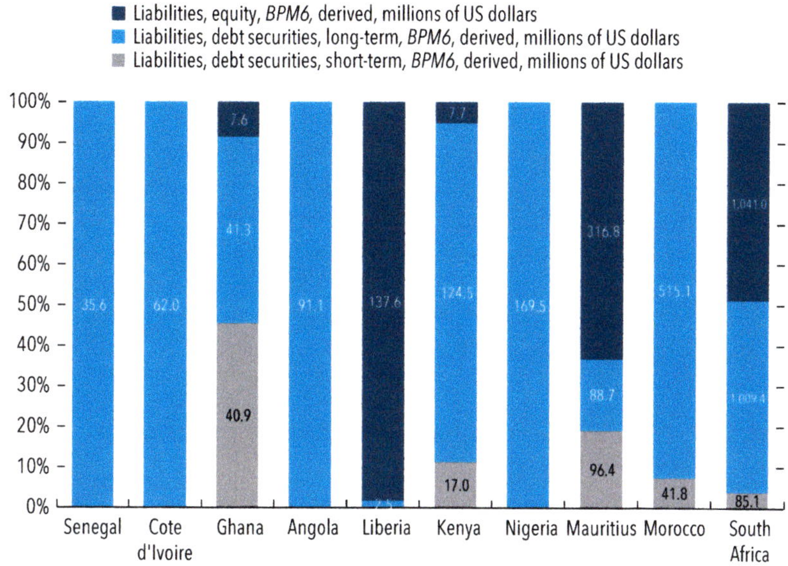

Sources: Coordinated Portfolio Investment Survey; and authors' estimates.
Note: *BPM6* = *Balance of Payments and International Investment Position Manual, 6th Edition*.

Figure 5.12. Correlation between Foreign Direct and Foreign Portfolio Investment Flows from China, 2018

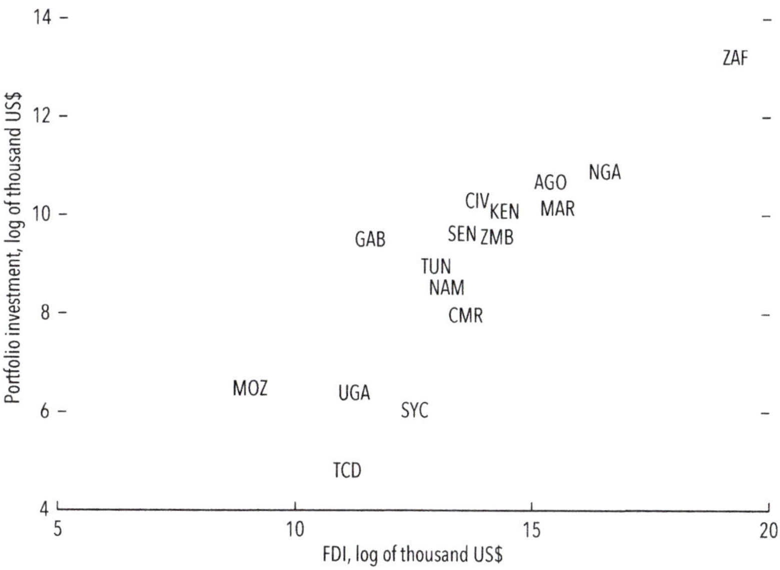

Sources: United Nations Conference on Trade and Development; Coordinated Portfolio Investment Survey; and authors' estimates.
Note: Figure uses International Organization for Standardization (ISO) country codes.
FDI = foreign direct investment.

market development, in driving portfolio inflows to African countries.[5,6] For Chinese investors, the conventional push and pull factors may play an even smaller role in determining the destination and magnitude of portfolio investment flows. Among the 10 largest recipient countries of Chinese portfolio investments, 5 are major commodity exporters: Angola, Côte d'Ivoire, Liberia, Nigeria, and South Africa, signaling that established trade and direct investment links could be key predictors of Chinese foreign portfolio flows to the African continent.

Despite the steady presence of African countries in foreign capital markets, foreign portfolio investment inflows remain volatile and are prone to large global shocks and changes in risk appetite, as reflected during global and emerging market crises. During the market turmoil in the first seven months of the COVID-19 pandemic, African countries witnessed an unprecedented episode of bond and equity fund outflows (Figure 5.13). Market response to the pandemic was at least three times larger than the global financial crisis episode.

Figure 5.13. Cumulative Foreign Portfolio Flows in African Countries
(Percent GDP since the start of each episode)

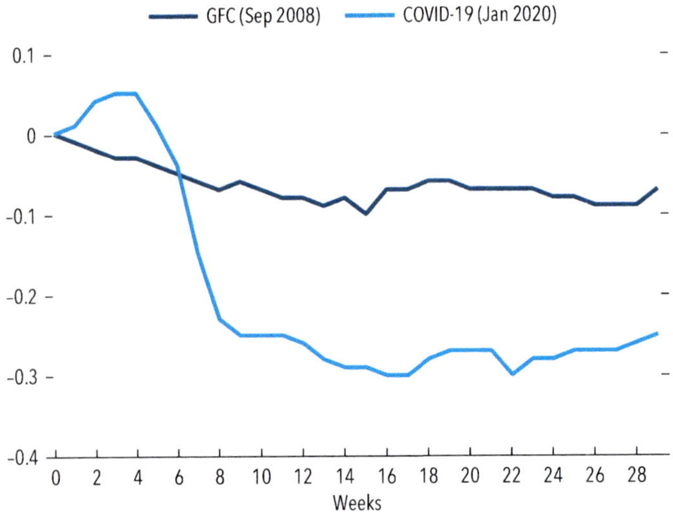

Sources: EUROPACE AG/Haver Analytics; IMF, World Economic Outlook; and authors' estimates.
Note: GFC = global financial crisis.

[5] IMF (2014c) documents mixed evidence on the role of push and pull factors in increasing global portfolio investment flows to a set of sub-Saharan African frontier and emerging countries, in part due to low quality of data used in the analysis.

[6] Volatile macroeconomic and political conditions, underdeveloped financial markets (World Bank 2020), and restrictions on capital flows explain the overall low engagement of foreign investors in African equity and bond markets. For instance, the Economic Community of Central African States, Democratic Republic of the Congo, Madagascar, Nigeria, and Seychelles have capital flow management measures in place, including surrender and repatriation requirements.

Box 5.1. Understanding the Global Role of Chinese Banks

Chinese banks have constituted the largest banking system in the world since 2016, with substantial cross-border claims on emerging markets. Although this top position among major global banking systems is mostly driven by their domestic activity, Chinese banks have also been expanding abroad at a great speed (Cerutti and Zhou 2018). As of mid-2018, they represented about 7 percent of total cross-border bank lending and reported claims on 176 of 185 borrower countries/jurisdictions, according to the Bank for International Settlements locational banking statistics. More precisely, Chinese banks lend to 135 of 143 emerging market and developing economies and to 30 of 31 advanced economies.[1] Moreover, 63 emerging market and developing economies already borrow more from Chinese banks than from any other country's banking system, highlighting that even though very small relative to their domestic claims, Chinese banks' foreign claims are substantial, especially for many borrowing emerging market and developing economies (Table 5.1.1).

The market share of Chinese banks on cross-border bank lending to emerging market and developing economies has been increasing—even during the COVID-19 crisis—and reached 26 percent of the total in the second quarter of 2020 (Figure 5.1.1). Although the largest share of Chinese banks is among Asia–Pacific borrowers at about 38 percent, their share within Africa and Middle East borrowers is just 19 percent. Nonetheless, about 30 of the 63 emerging market and developing economies that borrow more from Chinese banks than from any other bank nationality are in Africa and Middle East.

TABLE 5.1.1.

Measures of Global Relevance by Bank Nationality: Top Cross-Border Creditors and Market Share
(As of June 2018)

	CN Banks	JP Banks	US Banks	UK Banks	CH Banks	FR Banks
Borrowers Worldwide (185):						
Number of borrower countries	176	136	156	175	179	175
Total credit (billion US dollars)	2,101	4,540	3,318	2,808	1,875	3,341
Share in total outstanding (percent)	7.1	15.4	11.3	9.5	6.4	11.3
Number of countries for which banks are the top creditor	66	11	11	5	7	16

Measures of Global Relevance by Bank Nationality: Top Cross-Border Creditors and Market Share
(As of June 2018)

	CN Banks	JP Banks	US Banks	UK Banks	CH Banks	FR Banks
Borrowers in Advanced Economies (31):						
Number of borrower countries	30	30	30	31	31	31
Total credit (billion US dollars)	488	2,953	2,215	2,081	1,164	2,715
Share in total outstanding (percent)	2.4	14.8	11.1	10.4	5.8	13.6
Number of countries for which banks are the top creditor	0	3	1	0	1	6
Borrowers in Emerging Market and Developing Economies (143):						
Number of borrower countries	135	98	115	133	137	133
Total credit (billion US dollars)	919	434	277	303	120	312
Share in total outstanding (percent)	23.7	11.2	7.1	7.8	3.1	8.1
Number of countries for which banks are the top creditor	63	6	9	5	4	10

Source: Cerutti, Casanova, and Pradhan (2023).
Note: CN = China; JP = Japan; US = The United States; UK = The United Kingdom; CH = Switzerland; FR = France.

Figure 5.1.1. Cross-border Bank Lending by Chinese Banks
(Share of total, percent)

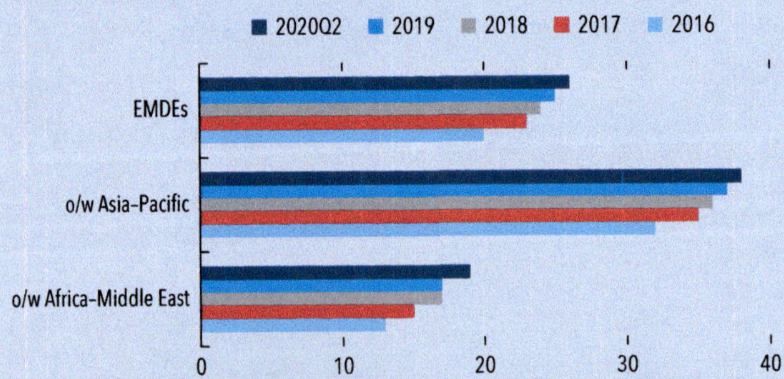

Sources: Bank of International Settlements locational banking statistics (by nationality).
Note: EMDEs = Emerging Market and Developing Economies; o/w = of which.

As Cerutti, Koch, and Pradhan (2018) highlight, accounting for the global network of foreign affiliates is key to understanding banks' global presence.

Across all bank nationalities, only about 60 percent of their cross-border lending is extended from their home country.[2] Like most other banking systems, a substantial part of Chinese banks' cross-border lending originates from affiliates operating outside the borders of China. Banks lend across borders from loans booked from the home country of their headquarters but also from the lending by their affiliates (branches or subsidiaries) located abroad (in either financial centers or third countries).

Although Chinese banks' global reach resembles that of advanced countries' banks, a few differences exist, with the factors associated with their expansion. Chinese banks seem to perceive distance (a proxy of information asymmetries) to their borrowing emerging market and developing economies as less of a barrier than other emerging market and developing economy banks, and more like the US and European banks. With respect to traditional measures like trade, foreign direct investment, and portfolio flows, interesting differences exist. The Chinese banks' positive correlation between cross-border bank lending and trade with emerging market and developing economies stands out. It is much stronger than the trade-lending relationship exhibited by Japanese and European banks and is more in line with patterns exhibited by the US banks. On the other hand, unlike all other banking systems, Chinese banks' past portfolio investment is negatively correlated with cross-border lending to emerging market and developing economy borrowers. This seems linked to China's capital outflow restrictions and the fact that Chinese portfolio investment is mostly narrowly distributed within a few advanced economies. In fact, when lending to advanced economy borrowers, strong complementarities with portfolio investment emerge. Finally, only weak evidence exists on the relationship between Chinese foreign direct investment and cross-border lending.

Source: Eugenio Cerutti based on Cerutti, Casanova, and Pradhan (2023).

[1] See Cerutti, Casanova, and Pradhan (2023) for methodological details. Reported aggregate figures cover, among other banks, the three policy banks (China Development Bank, the China Export–Import Bank, and the Agricultural Development Bank of China) as well as China's four largest commercial banks by assets that are state owned (Industrial and Commercial Bank of China, Bank of China, China Construction Bank, and Agricultural Bank of China).

[2] This is not a minor detail. Failing to account for the network of affiliates could drive assertions of hidden debt, as is the case of Horn, Reinhart, and Trebesch (2020) when comparing estimated bilateral Chinese cross-border lending using the Bank for International Settlement locational statistics by residence and those from other loan-based sources capturing the borrowing from cross-border banks using more of a nationality perspective (for example, Chinese banking group perspective).

EMPIRICAL ESTIMATES OF THE EFFECTS OF CHINA SHOCKS ON AFRICA

The growing importance of China–Africa trade and financial linkages, as discussed earlier, imply that any developments in China are likely to have a significant effect on Africa. Spillovers from China have been studied extensively, especially since the aftermath of the 2008 crisis (for example, see Cashin, Mohaddes, and Raissi 2016; Furceri, Jalles, and Zdzienicka 2017; Lakatos and others 2017; Dieppe and others 2018). Spillovers from China have been the topic of various

IMF spillover reports (IMF 2011, 2012, 2014a) and regional economic outlooks (IMF 2014b, 2015, 2016a). This section first illustrates how shocks in China affect Africa through the lens of a macro model, before zooming in on the effect of China on commodity prices and financial spillovers from China.

Spillovers through the Lens of a Macro Model

Although earlier papers on spillovers from China focused on the role of the country's fiscal stimulus in lifting global growth, after the global financial crisis, the emphasis shifted to studying the possible effects of a slowdown (see also Cashin, Mohaddes, and Raissi 2016). Furceri, Jalles, and Zdzienicka (2017) provide empirical evidence of the growing spillover effects from China, with trade linkages remaining the main transmission channel and net commodity exporters being particularly exposed to developments in China. The significantly larger exposure through commodity prices is a consistent finding in the model-based analysis by Dieppe and others (2018, for example, chart 38). Dieppe and others (2018) also confirm the Furceri, Jalles, and Zdzienicka (2017) finding that trade links are overall a preeminent transmission channel.[7]

Closest to the approach used here and with a focus on Africa is the work by Lakatos and others (2017). Using a computable general equilibrium model, the paper finds that an average 1 percentage point annual slowdown of China's GDP growth is expected to result in 1.1 percentage point GDP growth decline in sub-Saharan Africa. When the slowdown is accompanied by rebalancing toward consumption and the services sector, however, the net effect is an increase in sub-Saharan Africa's GDP of 4.7 percent.[8] The positive effect of rebalancing is explained by the fact that in their underlying data (Global Trade Analysis Project (GTAP) v. 9, corresponding to the year 2011), private consumption in China is relatively more intensive in imported commodities than investment.[9] Using microsimulations, the authors also conclude that rebalancing would help reduce

[7] More subtly, Mano (2016) shows that China's move up the value chain—defined as a shift toward higher-tech sectors—has the potential to generate positive spillovers to lower-income countries because their comparative advantage in lower-tech manufacturing is reinforced and they can benefit from cheaper imports of higher-tech goods. Ahmed and others (2019) focus on the spillovers from a severe tail scenario of financial stress in China. Although their empirical methods already find growing and sizable spillovers from such a scenario, especially for emerging markets, the estimated global losses are amplified in simulations that account for financial transmission channels.

[8] Rebalancing is defined as a shift in final demand from investment to consumption of about 11 percentage points of GDP and an increase of the share of services in GDP, also of about 11 percentage points of GDP. The approach and results by Lakatos and others (2017) underscore the importance of looking at rebalancing more broadly because a slowdown in Chinese investment taken in isolation has been estimated to have negative effects on sub-Saharan Africa's export growth, with an elasticity of about 0.6 (Drummond and Liu 2015).

[9] This is footnote 7 in Lakatos and others (2017): GTAP v. 9 data indicate that in 2011, private consumption in China was relatively more intensive in imported commodities than the formation of gross fixed capital. The biggest component of the formation of capital goods in China is construction services (54 percent), which are not much traded. These data are consistent with the World Input-Output Database (WIOD) database, where the share of imports in final consumption (5 percent) is only slightly lower than the share of imports in gross fixed capital investment (6 percent).

poverty by lifting—to varying degrees—the incomes of lower-income households in all sub-Saharan African countries.

This section uses the IMF's G20 Model to simulate the potential effect of different Chinese policy scenarios on sub-Saharan African countries.[10] We consider three scenarios. As a starting point, the first scenario borrows from historical experience by mimicking an aggressive public investment-led fiscal stimulus in China, such as the one observed in the wake of the global financial crisis. The second scenario assumes a more moderate fiscal package as observed during the COVID-19 crisis. The third and final scenario assumes a continued rebalancing from investment to consumption in the Chinese economy.

In the first scenario, a "global financial-crisis-style" fiscal response assumes that China implements a fiscal stimulus that amounts to 5 percent of GDP each year for two consecutive years, similar to the actual size and duration of the fiscal response observed during the global financial crisis, with about two-thirds invested in infrastructure. The results suggest such a fiscal stimulus in China would boost output in the examined African countries by between 0.1 and 0.5 percentage points in the first and second years (Figure 5.14, panel 1).[11] The effect would be particularly large in low-income and fragile African economies, with an increase in output between 0.4 and 0.5 percentage points, even if endogenous monetary policy responds to the rise in external demand by increasing policy rates.[12] If monetary policy does not respond and instead keeps domestic interest rates on hold, adding policy support to the positive external demand shock, the effect would be doubled on average (Figure 5.14, panel 2).

In the second scenario, a less aggressive fiscal stimulus is assumed in China. The fiscal package approximates the authority's response in fighting the COVID-19 crisis. It assumes an overall fiscal package of about 5 percent of GDP for one year, of which about half is spent on infrastructure. Under this scenario, growth in sub-Saharan African economies would be 0.1–0.5 percentage points higher in the first year, whereas the effect in the second year is largely muted, should domestic interest rates be adjusted (Figure 5.14, panel 3). The spillover is most significant in low-income and fragile economies and smallest in

[10] The G20 Model is a global structural model of the world economy, capturing international spillover and key economic relationships among the household, corporate, and government sectors, including monetary policy (Andrle and others 2015). The exercise conducted in this section follows the approach described in Dizioli, Hunt, and Maliszewski (2016) and IMF spillover analysis (IMF 2016b).

[11] The African economies being examined include oil and resource exporting countries (Angola, Ghana, Nigeria, Zambia), East Africa (Kenya, Rwanda, Tanzania, Uganda), countries in fragile situations (Burkina Faso, Burundi, Central African Republic, Democratic Republic of the Congo, Comoros, Côte d'Ivoire, Eritrea, Guinea, Guinea-Bissau, São Tomé and Príncipe, Sierra Leone, Togo), middle-income countries (Botswana, Cabo Verde, Lesotho, Mauritius, Namibia, Senegal, Seychelles, Eswatini) and low-income (Ethiopia, Gambia, Madagascar, Malawi, Mozambique) countries, other energy exporters (Cameroon, Chad, Republic of Congo, Equatorial Guinea, Gabon), and other Western African Economic and Monetary Union countries (Benin, Mali, Niger).

[12] Each country is individually specified with its own monetary policy and exchange rate regime, for example, fixed exchange rate, or inflation targeting. In the simulations where endogenous monetary policy does not react, all monetary policy reactions are turned off; in the simulations in which endogenous monetary policy responds to external shocks, it would react according to the country specifics.

Figure 5.14. IMF's G20 Model Simulation Results

(Percent deviation from baseline)

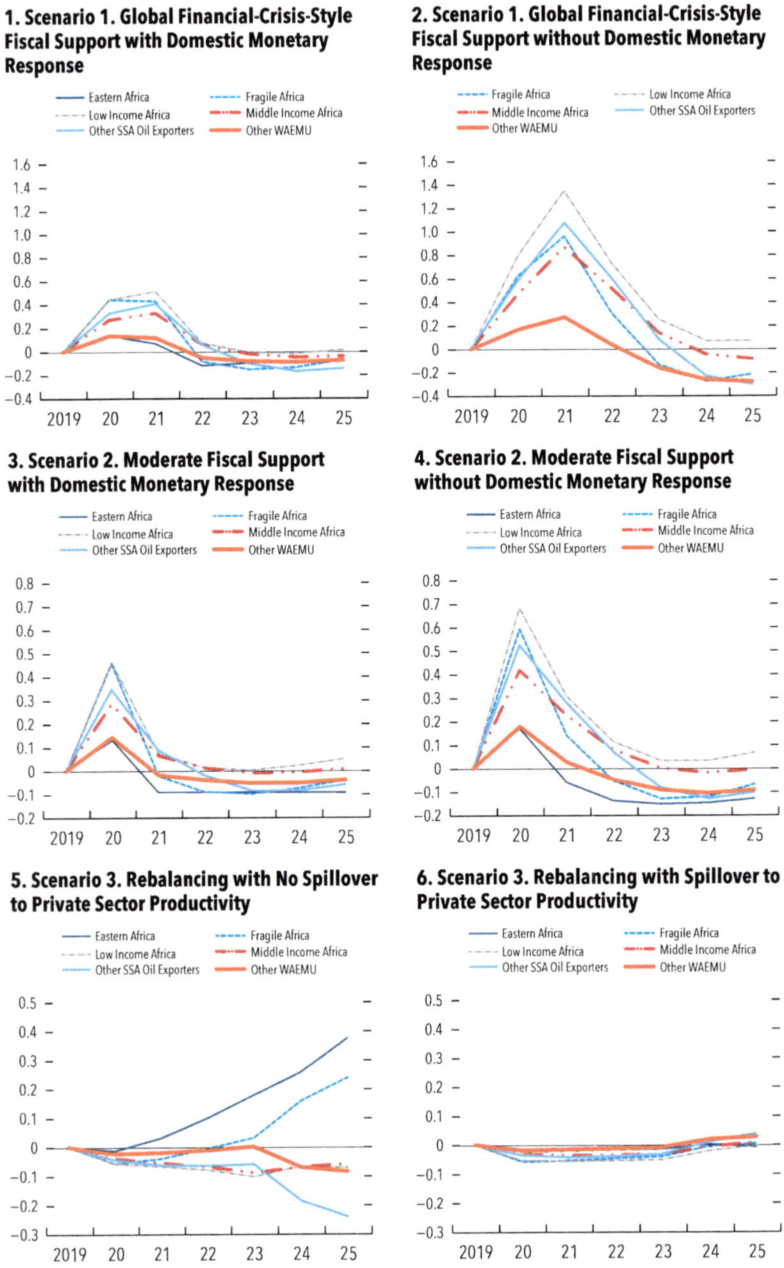

Source: Authors' estimates.

Note: SSA = sub-Saharan Africa; WAEMU = Western African Economic and Monetary Union.

East African economies and members of Western African Economic and Monetary Union because its member economies are more diversified and less dependent on commodity exports. The effect is marginally higher when domestic monetary policy does not respond to this positive terms-of-trade shock (Figure 5.14, panel 4).

The third scenario assumes rebalancing through a gradual but permanent reduction in the level of public investment by 7.5 percentage points of GDP over a five-year horizon, with a 1.5 percent decline each year. The decrease in public investment is offset by transfers to liquidity-constrained Chinese households, with a resulting one-for-one permanent increase in private demand. That is, the shock is fiscally neutral. Because investment is gradually replaced by household consumption in China, the demand for imported goods generally falls because consumption is less import intensive. However, the spillovers vary with the nature of China's public investment. Assuming public investment is neutral with regard to private sector productivity—for example, because the cuts focus on inefficient investment projects with little effect on the public capital stock—the rebalancing toward private consumption is expected to have a minor negative growth effect in most African economies (Figure 5.14, panel 5). If instead, the reduction in public investment is assumed to lower private sector productivity going forward (Figure 5.14, panel 6), the effect on sub-Saharan African economies is expected to be small in the short term. In the medium term, eastern and fragile African economies are likely to benefit from China's rebalancing because import demand for consumption gradually increases, whereas commodity exporters in the region are likely to experience a negative growth effect because the demand for energy and commodities gradually declines, resulting in a persistent negative terms-of-trade shock associated with the decline in commodity prices.

Effect of China's Demand on Commodity Prices

The model simulations as discussed earlier highlight the special role of commodities in understanding China–Africa spillovers, in line with the existing literature which finds that Chinese domestic demand affects global commodity prices, especially metals and crude oil prices. Kolerus, N'Diaye, and Soborowski (2016), using daily data from specific markets and Ordinary Least Squares (OLS) and panel data techniques, find that a 1 percent increase in Chinese IP leads to a 5–7 percent rise (over one year) in metals and fuel prices, and surprise increases (as a deviation from the previous consensus growth figure) in Chinese IP cause metal- and fuel-price increases of up to 2.5 percent (on a daily basis). Roache and Rousset (2015) show that besides IP, Chinese credit growth has an important effect on some base metal commodities—arguably because some commodities may serve as collateral for lending. Ahuja and Nabar (2012) examine the effect of Chinese fixed asset investments and find that a 1 percentage point slowdown in investment is associated with a 0.1 percentage point reduction of global growth, especially affecting commodity exporters with relatively less diversified economies.

This section presents new evidence on the effects of Chinese growth on commodity prices, using two different analytical approaches and the most recent monthly data covering 1992–2020. The first approach uses single equation regressions, looking at the effects of both realized and surprise Chinese IP growth on commodity prices, utilizing OLS and quantile regression techniques.[13] Hence, the results not only unveil the mean effect but also examine any effect of Chinese growth on extreme commodity price movements. The second approach uses a small VAR model, allowing for dynamic interactions between the variables in the model, which may not be captured by single equation regressions.

In both approaches, in addition to Chinese IP growth, the models include the US and European IP growth, which allows controlling for growth shocks to commodities from other large commodity-importing countries or regions.[14] Tests indicate that IP growth correlations are very low, allowing to separately identify the effect of Chinese IP growth. Instead of examining individual commodity prices, which may be affected by particular (idiosyncratic) supply, demand, and trading (liquidity) conditions, the analysis first examines broader indices covering a range of agricultural (food, raw materials, and industrial goods), metals (base and precious), and energy (oil, natural gas, and coal) commodities, before looking into individual commodities. This way, any observed, statistically significant effect may have broader macroeconomic relevance across a range of goods and trading partners.

Overall, China's IP appears to have a major effect on commodity indices and contributes even more strongly to large upward and downward commodity price movements. The coefficient of realized Chinese IP growth in models with broad commodity indices is positive and significant in the OLS model and larger in the quantile regression model (see the "ALL" bars in Figure 5.15, panel 1). A 1 percent (standardized) shock to Chinese IP growth translates into a 1.3 percent increase in real commodity prices on average. In an upswing (downturn), the effect of Chinese IP growth on broad commodity prices is slightly above (below) 2 percent. This suggests that Chinese IP growth has even stronger effects on commodity prices in the tails of the distribution than on average commodity price changes and hence may cause both upside and downside commodity price risks. For upside risks, this seems to stem from shocks to IP growth (the unexpected part), which is significant, whereas the average and downside risk effect seems more associated with the expected IP growth part, because the IP growth shock coefficient is not significant in those specifications (see the "ALL" bars in Figure 5.15, panel 2).[15]

Chinese IP growth is especially associated with upside risk to food and energy but not with downside risks for any specific commodity subgroup (Figure 5.15, panel 1). The significance of Chinese IP growth on average commodity prices (the "mean" bars representing OLS coefficients) comes through in various broad

[13] To distinguish between expected and surprise growth, a simple regression approach is adopted—taking growth surprises as the residuals of a model where IP is regressed on lagged values (up to 12 lags). Other ways to decompose IP growth into expected and new effects rely on consensus or official forecasts. Our approach instead relies on a simpler time-series pattern, exploiting the autoregressive nature of the series.

[14] In further tests, the VIX and a broad stock market index were added to control for global financial conditions, but this did not materially affect the results.

[15] See the full set of results in Annex Tables 5.1.1–5.1.3.

commodity subgroups—industrial goods, base metals, and energy (crude oil). IP growth shocks appear to account for the significance of the food and energy (coal) components (Figure 5.15, panel 2), while, in addition, they exert a significant upward effect on raw materials and precious metals (but no effect on average prices or downside risk to commodity prices, except for coal but with the wrong sign). This suggests that the average effect of IP growth is mainly associated with the expected part of Chinese IP growth.

Among agricultural commodities, wheat and sunflower and soybean oil prices are most significantly subject to upside risk to Chinese IP growth shocks, whereas poultry and pork prices are subject to significant downside risks (Figure 5.15, panel 3). IP growth shocks also have a strong average effect (in OLS models) on groundnuts, soy oil, and beef prices. Among metals, shocks in Chinese IP growth seem to contribute significantly to large increases in lead, tin, gold, silver, and palladium prices. In a subsample starting in 2010, it also contributes to large price increases in iron ore and silver (Figure 5.15, panel 4).

Figure 5.15. Effect of Chinese Industrial Production (IP) on Commodity Indices and Prices

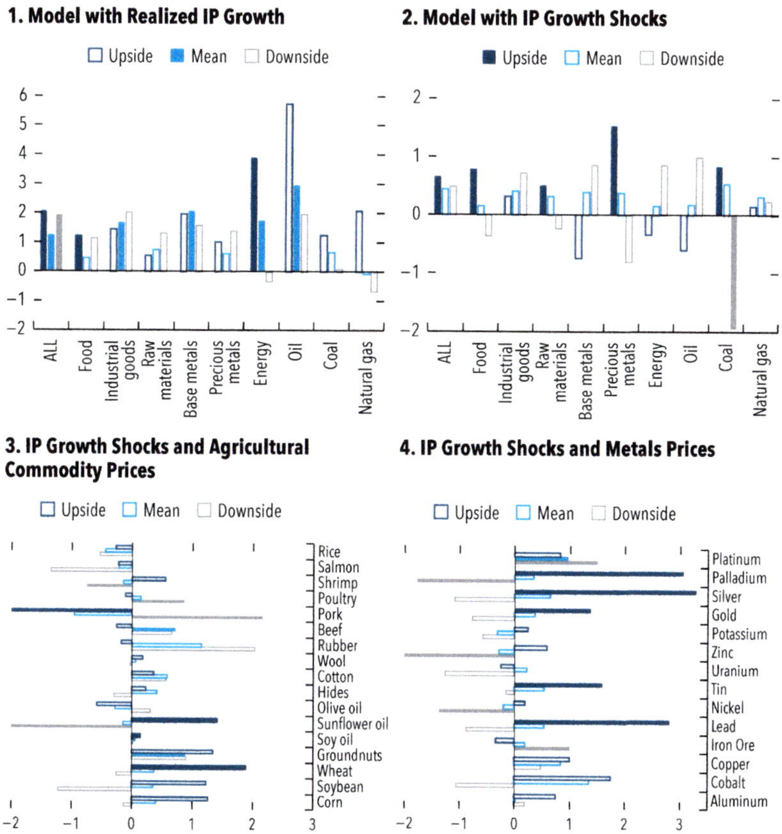

Source: Authors' calculations.

As a further sensitivity check, we test whether, over time, commodity prices may have become more sensitive to Chinese IP growth (or surprises), by looking at the sample starting in 2010 (an alternative approach, interacting the IP variable with its share in world GDP, yields similar results). The results suggest more significant average effects from Chinese IP growth with various broad commodity groups since 2010 (food, industrial goods, and base metals) but no significant upside or downside risk effects (yet there is a higher downside risk coefficient for Chinese IP growth surprises with the overall commodity price index and with some individual commodities but not with particular commodity subgroups).

Finally, the impulse response functions from a VAR model with the US, euro area, and Chinese IP, the US dollar real effective exchange rate and various commodity price indices show that Chinese IP shocks appear to have a more significant and longer-lasting effect on commodity prices than euro area or US IP shocks (Figure 5.16).[16] This suggests that shocks to growth in China produce stronger commodity price spillovers than other large countries' growth, reaching up to 3 percent after one year—slightly below the estimate in Kolerus, N'Diaye, and Soborowski (2016). In the same vein, the variance decomposition suggests that Chinese IP explains a larger share of the model's variance than other countries' IP and, in the longer term, this becomes the dominant factor.[17]

Financial Spillovers from China

Previous studies find that developments in China affect financial markets in both emerging and advanced economies, with the foreign exchange and equity markets affected most acutely (Mwase and others 2016). Furthermore, the effect is more pronounced for bad news than for good news and works largely through risk aversion and global commodity prices. This section examines the financial spillovers from China using the Diebold and Yilmaz (2014) Connectedness Index that

[16] For completeness, US dollar real effective exchange rate shocks have a strong but short-lived negative effect on commodity prices, reflecting the role of the US dollar as an invoicing currency, whereas shocks to commodity prices themselves have a significant effect. We also added oil prices, VIX, and a broad stock market index as additional factors in a larger VAR model, but this did not change the results (stock prices' impulse response function coefficients were never significant). Oil price shocks appear to follow a similar effect pattern as commodity price shocks themselves, which suggests that they move closely together, and VIX had initially a small negative effect.

[17] Results for VARs with different commodity price subindices (both impulse response functions and variance decompositions) convey a similar message (Annex Figures 5.1.1 and 5.1.2). Especially for food commodities and across all energy indices, Chinese IP growth appears to exert an increasing influence over time. Moreover, the impulse response results confirm the higher sensitivity of energy, especially oil and gas, to Chinese IP growth shocks than other commodity price subindices. Although the maximum effect of a 1 percent shock to Chinese IP on commodity prices overall is about 3 percent, it reaches 6 percent for energy prices.

Figure 5.16. Vector Autoregression Model Results

1. Impulse Response of Broad Commodity Price Index to Shocks

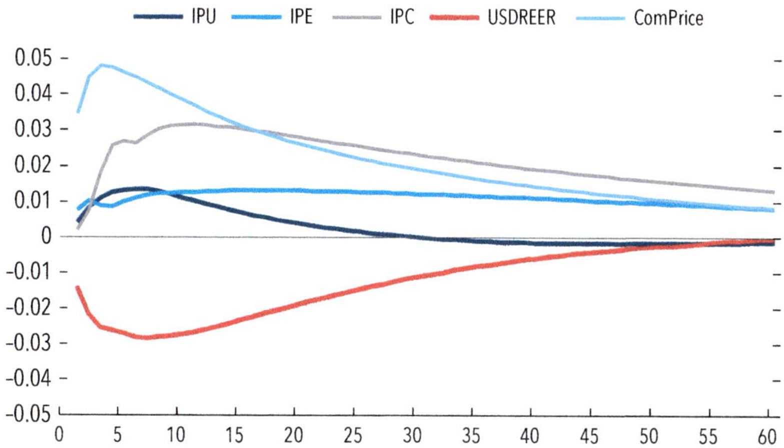

2. Variance Decomposition of Broad Commodity Price Index to Cholesky Factor Shocks

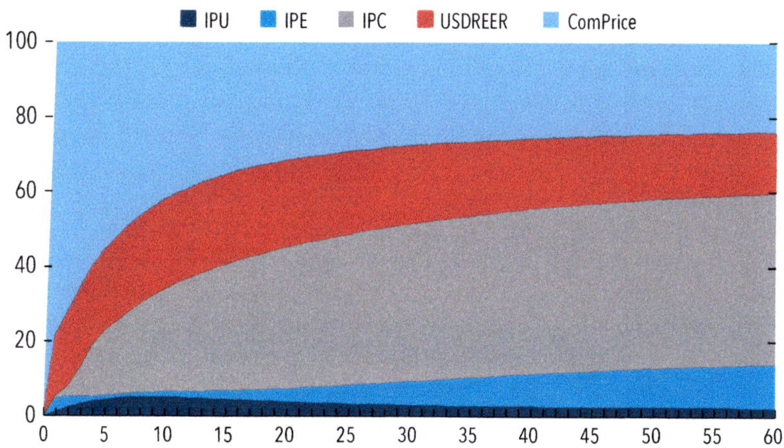

Source: Authors' calculations.
Note: The horizontal axis represents periods after the shock, with each period corresponding to months. Figure on the left shows the generalized impulse response functions of the broad commodity price index to a one-standard deviation increase in respective shocks. Figure on the right shows the percentage of variance explained by each shock. ComPrice = log of selected commodity price subindex; IP* = log industrial production with C = China, E = euro area, and U = US; USDREER = USD real effective exchange rate.

measures interdependence of asset returns and volatility.[18] The model is estimated based on daily data for two asset markets (local currency stock market and bilateral exchange rate vis-à-vis the US dollar) in China, 13 sub-Saharan African countries (Angola, Ethiopia, Gabon, Ghana, Kenya, Mauritius, Nigeria, Rwanda, Senegal, South Africa, Tanzania, Uganda, Zambia), and 4 North African countries (Djibouti, Libya, Morocco, Tunisia). Data for the euro area and the Chicago Board Options Exchange Volatility Index (VIX) are included as additional external comparators.

The analysis focuses on the period starting January 1, 2015, when financial spillovers from China first came to the fore, after (1) the first stock market correction on June 10, 2015; (2) the move to a new exchange rate regime on August 11; (3) the second stock market correction on August 24; and (4) the sharp fall in the Chinese stock market on the opening day of 2016, which triggered a suspension of all trading under a new circuit breaker system.

Empirical evidence from Diebold and Yilmaz (2014) suggests that developments in China's equity and foreign exchange markets have an effect on the returns and volatility of equity and foreign exchange markets in sub-Saharan and North Africa. Shocks in Chinese financial markets account for between 0.5 percent and 4.5 percent of the share of the forecast error variance in African financial markets on average and between 4 percent and 15 percent at the point of maximum spillovers (Annex Tables 5.1.4 and 5.1.5).

The effect seems to have increased in the past six years (Figure 5.17). The average share of the unexpected volatility because of shocks in China increased from 0.5 percent in 2015 to just under 2.5 percent in 2018–2020 in sub-Saharan Africa and just under 3.5 percent in North Africa. For stock returns, the average share of the forecast error variance due to China increased from about 1 percent in 2015 to 3 percent in 2020 in sub-Saharan Africa and up to 4.5 percent in 2020 in North Africa.

Typically, the exchange rate reacts more in countries with more developed financial institutions and markets, such as Mauritius, Morocco, South Africa, and Tunisia (Annex Figure 5.1.3; Svirydzenka 2016) because greater depth of such markets allows for easier transmission of financial shocks from China. Of the top 10 recipients of the portfolio investment flows from China (Figure 5.11), those

[18] Diebold and Yilmaz (2014) Connectedness Index defines country *j*'s spillover to (or connectedness with) country *i* as the fraction of the H-day-ahead forecast error variance of country *i*'s asset price that can be accounted for by innovations in the country *j*'s asset price, based on a daily VAR and using generalized variance decomposition (see Mwase and others [2016] for further details). Given that shocks can lead to both an adjustment in asset price level and a spike in the uncertainty about it, the study focuses on the co-movements in both asset returns and asset volatilities. Asset return is defined as the difference in the natural log of stock prices and exchange rates. Volatility is defined as the log of the annualized daily standard deviation based on the spread between high and low prices during the day (Alizadeh, Brandt, and Diebold 2002; Diebold and Yilmaz 2012), for example, for any country *i* on day *t*:

$$\text{volatility}_{it} = \ln \langle 100 \sqrt{365 \{0.361 [\ln(P_{it}^{\max}) - \ln(P_{it}^{\min})]^2\}} \rangle.$$

Given that volatilities tend to be distributed asymmetrically with positive skew, it is necessary to take logs to ensure approximate normality, which is one of the VAR assumptions. The VAR is estimated over a rolling 150-day window with three lags, and the forecast is done 10 days ahead. Given the large set of variables, the VAR is estimated using the elastic net shrinkage technique.

Figure 5.17. Financial Market Co-movement with China
(Share of forecast error variance due to China for an average country)

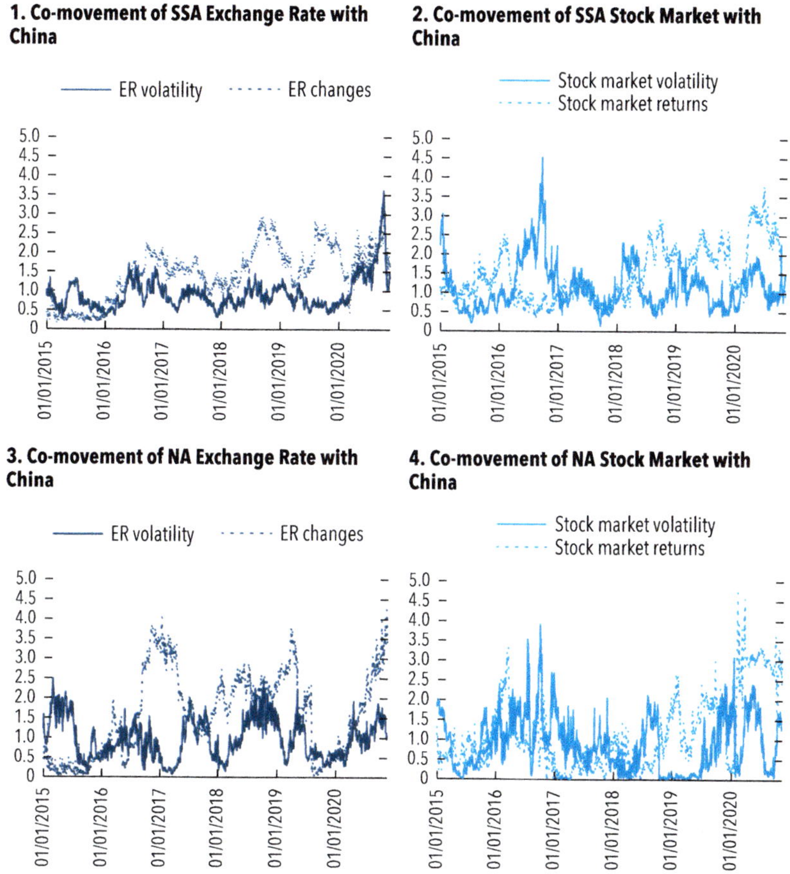

Source: Authors' estimates.
Note: ER = Exchange rate, NA = North Africa, SSA = sub-Saharan Africa, VIX = Chicago Board Options Exchange Volatility Index.

where these flows tend to go into the equity market tend to see larger stock market spillovers from China, such as Ghana, Kenya, Mauritius, and South Africa (Annex Tables 5.1.4 and 5.1.5).

That said, the effect of financial developments in China on sub-Saharan and North African financial markets is still small. On average in 2020, African exchange rates and stock markets reacted three times more to unexpected shocks in the euro area exchange rate and stock market, with stock market volatility spillovers four times those of China's (Figure 5.18, Annex Tables 5.1.6 and 5.1.7). Furthermore, in 2020, African stock markets reacted two times more to spikes in global risk aversion as proxied by the VIX than to shocks in China. Regional financial hubs, such as Morocco and South Africa, also seem to play a much larger role in affecting African financial markets than China.

Figure 5.18. Spillovers from China versus from Euro Area and VIX
(Share of forecast error variance due to China for an average country)

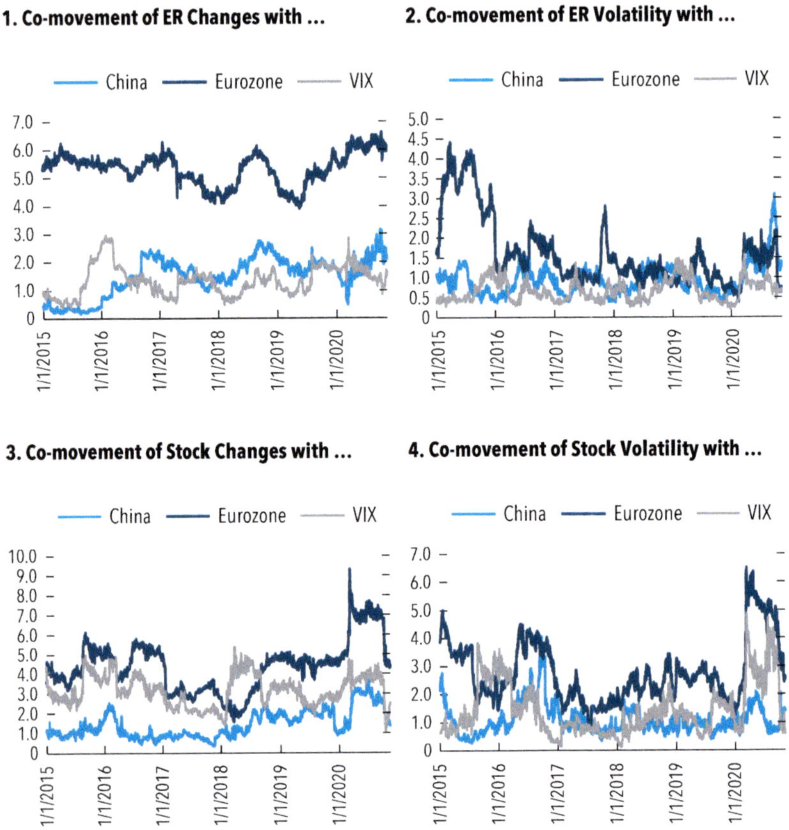

Source: Authors' calculations.
Note: ER = exchange rate; VIX = Chicago Board Options Exchange Volatility Index.

In 2020, average spillovers from South Africa to the region were five times higher than China's for stock market volatility and three times higher for stock market returns and exchange rate volatility. Morocco's effect was twice as high as that of China (Figure 5.19, Annex Tables 5.1.6 and 5.1.7). The smaller role of China and the larger role of other global and regional players in financial spillovers to Africa are not surprising, given the traditionally stronger economic and financial ties of the region to Europe and the still-limited financial linkages with China.

Figure 5.19. Spillovers from China versus from South Africa and Morocco
(Share of forecast error variance due to China for an average country)

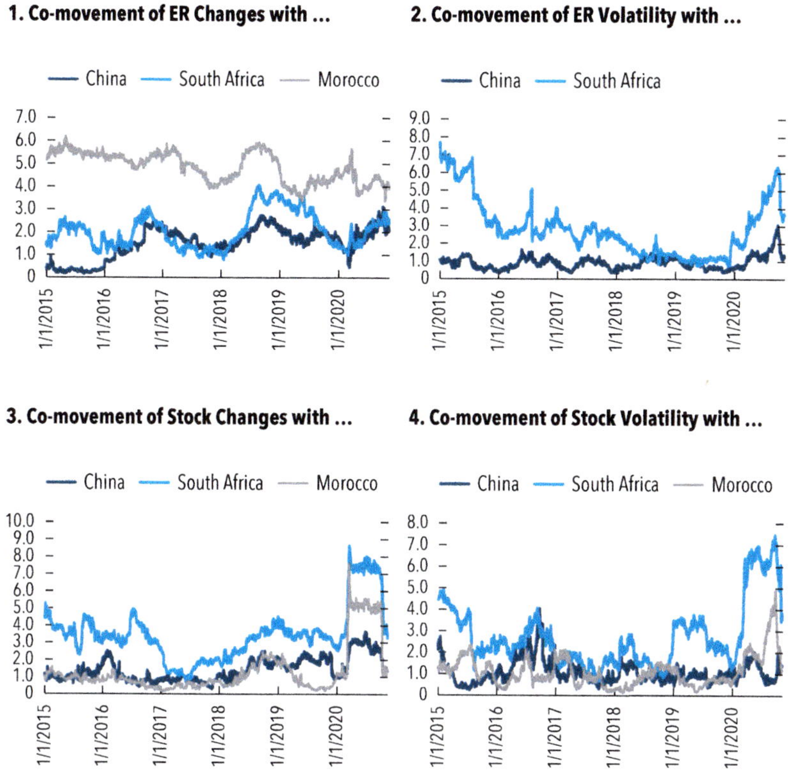

Sources: Authors' estimates.
Note: ER = Exchange rate, VIX = Chicago Board Options Exchange Volatility Index.

CONCLUSION

This chapter shows that economic and financial developments in China have significant spillovers into African economies, mainly through the effect on trade and commodity markets. In particular, large public investment-focused fiscal stimulus in China tends to boost growth in African countries. The largest effect of such stimulus is on low-income and fragile economies, whereas the smallest would be on more diversified economies, which are less dependent on commodity exports (East African and Western African Economic and Monetary Union member countries). Conversely, as China rebalances its economy away from investment and toward consumption, African countries most dependent on commodity exports are likely to experience a small negative effect, whereas the more diversified countries would likely benefit.

The chapter also shows that China's role in commodity markets is nonlinear and varies with the level of volatility in commodity markets. In particular, China's effect on commodity prices is stronger when volatility is high, with its demand amplifying large upward and downward commodity price movements. When compared with other economies, such as the United States and the euro area, Chinese IP shocks appear to have a more significant and longer-lasting effect on commodity prices than IP shocks in the euro area or the United States.

Finally, the empirical findings suggest that although the magnitude of China's spillovers to foreign exchange and equity markets in Africa has increased since 2015, it remains limited. This reflects the relatively limited direct financial linkages between China and Africa.

ANNEX 5.1. SPILLOVERS FROM CHINA TO AFRICA

ANNEX TABLE 5.1.1.

Commodity Price Ordinary Least Squares Regressions
(Coefficients and p values)

	With Realized IP Growth (Coefficients and *p* values)					With IP Growth Shocks (Coefficients and *p* values)				
	USIP	**Euro IP**	**China IP**	**$R_{2adj.}$**	**N. Obs.**	**USIP**	**Euro IP**	**China IP**	**$R_{2adj.}$**	**N. Obs.**
Broad index	0.496	3.555	1.257	0.927	331	−0.440	1.407	0.437	0.924	331
	0.640	0.000	0.053			0.469	0.003	0.282		
Broad excl gold	0.633	3.827	1.302	0.926	331	−0.409	1.522	0.459	0.923	331
	0.563	0.000	0.048			0.518	0.003	0.297		
Nonfuel index	−0.877	1.857	0.811	0.933	331	−0.706	0.800	0.331	0.933	331
	0.257	0.001	0.115			0.061	0.008	0.172		
Agricultural index	−0.587	1.453	0.561	0.909	331	−0.292	0.487	0.253	0.908	331
	0.502	0.010	0.153			0.447	0.137	0.231		
Food	−0.731	1.629	0.448	0.886	331	−0.349	0.532	0.155	0.885	331
	0.465	0.010	0.299			0.411	0.127	0.526		
Industrial goods	−0.410	3.414	1.688	0.930	331	−1.254	0.879	0.407	0.928	331
	0.723	0.000	0.038			0.051	0.140	0.340		
Raw materials	0.036	1.592	0.735	0.929	332	−0.050	0.090	0.316	0.927	344
	0.969	0.019	0.182			0.909	0.841	0.283		
Metals index	−0.574	2.487	1.456	0.922	331	−1.317	0.710	0.319	0.922	331
	0.646	0.003	0.116			0.031	0.168	0.360		
Base metals	−0.290	3.918	2.071	0.922	331	−1.726	1.218	0.380	0.921	331
	0.836	0.000	0.049			0.029	0.104	0.474		
Precious metals	−0.757	0.265	0.606	0.873	332	−0.869	−0.019	0.372	0.877	344
	0.622	0.725	0.476			0.070	0.968	0.315		
Energy index	2.080	5.338	1.746	0.905	331	−0.388	1.700	0.155	0.900	331
	0.249	0.000	0.086			0.697	0.050	0.838		
Coal	−2.363	3.467	0.657	0.932	332	−1.817	3.189	0.526	0.935	344
	0.292	0.079	0.564			0.039	0.002	0.450		
Natural gas	0.001	1.700	−0.080	0.868	331	0.852	1.019	0.310	0.870	331
	1.000	0.466	0.956			0.400	0.318	0.632		
Oil APSP	3.499	6.749	2.959	0.879	332	−0.591	1.684	0.172	0.870	344
	0.125	0.001	0.021			0.614	0.120	0.861		

Source: Authors' estimates.
Note: Table reports the coefficient (first line) and *p* values (second line) of industrial production (IP) growth and IP growth shocks in OLS regressions (1992:01–2020:08) with respective commodity price indices using a year-over-year growth (shock) specification. IP growth and IP growth shocks are measured in standardized form, as the year-over-year growth rate (or shock to the growth rate), divided by the standard deviation of the IP growth rate. OLS models also include (but not reported here) constant, lags of commodity price changes and change in the USD real effective exchange rate, besides the US, euro area, and China IP growth (or growth shocks). APSP = average petroleum spot price (average of West Texas Intermediate, Brent and Dubai light crude oil); IP = industrial production; N. Obs = number of observations; R^2_{adj} = adjusted R-squared.

ANNEX TABLE 5.1.2.

Commodity Price Quantile Regressions with Realized IP Growth *(Coefficients and p values)*

	Lower Quantile (*q* = 0.10) (coefficients and *p* values)				**Upper Quantile (*q* = 0.90)** (coefficients and *p* values)				
	USIP	**Euro IP**	**China IP**	**$R^2_{adj.}$**	**USIP**	**Euro IP**	**China IP**	**$R^2_{adj.}$**	**N. Obs.**
Broad index	2.376	3.852	1.935	0.754	1.232	2.289	2.057	0.722	331
	0.248	0.005	0.138		0.578	0.116	0.111		
Broad excl gold	1.477	4.028	1.004	0.752	1.319	1.533	2.195	0.720	331
	0.520	0.013	0.497		0.559	0.306	0.095		
Nonfuel index	−0.044	2.168	1.165	0.733	0.619	1.442	0.771	0.747	331
	0.981	0.070	0.183		0.756	0.187	0.370		
Agricultural index	−1.224	2.681	1.552	0.675	−2.024	0.819	1.001	0.732	331
	0.502	0.051	0.172		0.306	0.492	0.107		
Food	−0.838	1.503	1.129	0.652	−1.528	0.843	1.216	0.703	331
	0.712	0.360	0.349		0.454	0.476	0.145		
Industrial goods	−0.224	3.199	2.034	0.703	−1.026	3.972	1.454	0.755	331
	0.914	0.027	0.191		0.728	0.026	0.382		
Raw materials	0.337	0.916	1.319	0.716	0.792	0.901	0.545	0.769	332
	0.764	0.142	0.165		0.686	0.471	0.517		
Metals index	1.652	1.965	1.086	0.695	−1.833	2.114	0.941	0.743	331
	0.469	0.226	0.511		0.502	0.250	0.609		
Base metals	−1.263	4.879	1.585	0.677	3.665	0.960	1.962	0.751	331
	0.689	0.007	0.520		0.324	0.673	0.358		
Precious metals	2.857	−1.215	1.381	0.595	−0.349	0.291	1.015	0.670	332
	0.214	0.483	0.384		0.919	0.872	0.568		
Energy index	0.103	6.698	−0.355	0.691	5.905	2.238	3.890	0.717	331
	0.977	0.013	0.881		0.114	0.378	0.065		
Coal	−2.169	1.264	0.103	0.652	−5.175	6.032	1.252	0.815	332
	0.536	0.707	0.963		0.131	0.015	0.435		
Natural gas	0.644	0.056	−0.676	0.648	4.002	1.405	2.078	0.691	331
	0.823	0.982	0.796		0.543	0.781	0.378		
Oil APSP	1.052	9.296	1.969	0.651	3.806	3.807	5.739	0.676	332
	0.816	0.010	0.461		0.511	0.301	0.151		

Source: Authors' estimates.
Note: Table reports the coefficient (first line) and *p* value (second line) of industrial production (IP) growth in quantile regressions (1992:01–2020:08) with respective commodity price indices, using a year-over-year growth specification. IP growth is measured in standardized form, as the year-over-year growth rate, divided by the standard deviation of the IP growth rate. Quantile regressions include (but not reported here) constant, lags of commodity price changes, and changes of the USD real effective exchange rate, in addition to the reported US, euro area, and China IP growth rates. APSP = average petroleum spot price (average of West Texas Intermediate, Brent and Dubai light crude oil); IP = industrial production; N. Obs = number of observations; R^2_{adj} = adjusted R-squared.

ANNEX TABLE 5.1.3.

Specific Commodities' Sensitivity to Chinese Industrial Production (IP) Growth Shocks
(Coefficients and p values, $R^2_{adj.}$)

	"Agricultural Commodities (Coefficients and *p* Values, R2 adj)"					
	OLS		**Downside**		**Upside**	
Corn	0.400		−0.128		1.264	
	0.548	0.882	0.905	0.585	0.206	0.721
Soybean	0.355		−1.218		1.237	
	0.493	0.887	0.179	0.553	0.198	0.725
Wheat	0.370		−0.251		1.891	
	0.582	0.863	0.840	0.543	0.060	0.685
Groundnuts	0.883		0.899		1.350	
	0.079	0.896	0.293	0.651	0.233	0.705
Soy oil	0.061		0.022		0.147	
	0.136	0.889	0.761	0.666	0.015	0.691
Sunflower oil	−0.136		−2.172		1.426	
	0.859	0.900	0.025	0.648	0.022	0.774
Olive oil	−0.276		0.309		−0.575	
	0.476	0.905	0.597	0.648	0.494	0.713
Hides	0.418		−0.293		0.235	
	0.519	0.848	0.711	0.628	0.777	0.612
Cotton	0.581		0.572		0.362	
	0.262	0.917	0.520	0.618	0.647	0.781
Wool	0.067		−0.021		0.183	
	0.904	0.912	0.974	0.665	0.844	0.756
Rubber	1.152		2.038		−0.174	
	0.201	0.894	0.205	0.583	0.912	0.736
Beef	0.718		0.661		−0.253	
	0.100	0.844	0.383	0.619	0.779	0.632
Pork	−0.958		2.171		−4.068	
	0.331	0.724	0.082	0.493	0.017	0.540
Poultry	0.150		0.870		−0.104	
	0.518	0.864	0.020	0.661	0.828	0.624
Shrimp	−0.140		−0.753		0.553	
	0.699	0.836	0.127	0.560	0.294	0.632
Salmon	−0.215		−1.345		−0.221	
	0.712	0.818	0.224	0.534	0.887	0.599
Rice	−0.441		−0.532		−0.264	
	0.338	0.873	0.553	0.570	0.737	0.712

	"Base and Precious Metals (Coefficients and *p* Values, R2 adj)"					
	OLS		**Downside**		**Upside**	
Aluminum	0.021		0.188		0.752	
	0.967	0.891	0.777	0.667	0.202	0.703
Cobalt	1.353		−1.052		1.754	
	0.363	0.911	0.539	0.594	0.418	0.786
Copper	0.844		0.483		0.994	
	0.227	0.902	0.580	0.660	0.396	0.741
Iron ore	0.195		1.003		−0.337	
	0.207	0.874	0.001	0.631	0.214	0.690
Lead	0.543		−0.880		2.814	
	0.490	0.889	0.271	0.594	0.004	0.765
Nickel	−0.196		−1.369		0.194	
	0.845	0.905	0.142	0.623	0.886	0.779
Tin	0.543		−0.143		1.596	
	0.364	0.914	0.833	0.629	0.091	0.776
Uranium	0.230		−1.260		−0.243	
	0.676	0.925	0.242	0.632	0.888	0.784
Zinc	−0.277		−2.301		0.589	
	0.742	0.916	0.085	0.640	0.563	0.797
Potassium	−0.303		−0.575		0.251	
	0.491	0.964	0.339	0.763	0.508	0.875
Gold	0.369		−0.773		1.373	
	0.283	0.881	0.184	0.630	0.002	0.685
Silver	0.645		−1.091		3.292	
	0.282	0.848	0.403	0.523	0.000	0.708
Palladium	0.347		−1.772		3.059	
	0.708	0.884	0.025	0.672	0.021	0.692
Platinum	0.964		1.499		0.823	
	0.058	0.876	0.042	0.658	0.296	0.685

Source: Authors' estimates.

Note: Table reports the coefficient (first line) and *p* value and adjusted R^2 (second line) of Chinese IP growth shocks in OLS and quantile regressions (1992:01–2020:08) with respective commodity prices, using a year-over-year growth specification. IP growth shocks are measured in standardized form, as the year-over-year shock to the growth rate, divided by the standard deviation of the IP growth rate. OLS and quantile regression models also include (but not reported here) constant, three lags of commodity price changes and log differences of the USD real effective exchange rate, besides the US, euro area, and China IP growth shocks. Unexpected IP growth (growth shock) is derived from residuals of a simple regression model, where changes in IP are regressed on lagged values (up to 12 lags). The full sample contains 344 observations in each regression. OLS = Ordinary Least Squares.

ANNEX TABLE 5.1.4.

Maximum Spillovers from China, Jan. 1, 2015–Nov. 11, 2020
(Share of forecast error variance)

	ER Changes	ER Vol	Stock Changes	Stock Vol
SSA				
Angola	6.2	4.5		
Ethiopia	4.6	6.9		
Gabon	7.3	7.9		
Ghana	4.8	6.7	9.1	7.5
Kenya	5.3	5.0	7.4	
Mauritius	6.9	4.3	7.1	4.2
Nigeria	10.3	4.6	5.3	10.4
Rwanda	14.7		9.4	
Senegal	7.6			
South Africa	11.7	10.0	11.7	10.5
Tanzania	9.5	9.3	6.3	5.0
Uganda	4.4	5.5		
Zambia	7.0	6.1	4.7	
North Africa				
Djibouti	6.5	6.6		
Libya	8.5	5.3		
Morocco	8.3		9.4	6.3
Tunisia	7.5			

Source: Authors' estimates.
Note: ER = exchange rate; SSA = sub-Saharan Africa; vol = volatility.

ANNEX TABLE 5.1.5.

Average Spillovers from China, Jan. 1, 2015–Nov. 11, 2020
(Share of forecast error variance)

	ER Changes	ER Vol	Stock Changes	Stock Vol
SSA				
Angola	1.4	0.7		
Ethiopia	0.7	0.9		
Gabon	2.3	0.7		
Ghana	0.7	1.0	1.0	1.0
Kenya	0.6	0.8	2.0	
Mauritius	1.4	0.7	1.0	0.7
Nigeria	0.8	0.9	1.3	1.3
Rwanda	1.6		1.0	
Senegal	2.2			
South Africa	4.7	1.3	4.4	2.2
Tanzania	1.0	1.6	0.7	0.6
Uganda	0.9	0.6		
Zambia	0.7	0.9	0.6	
North Africa				
Djibouti	0.9	1.2		
Libya	0.8	0.7		
Morocco	2.9		1.1	0.8
Tunisia	1.8			

Source: Authors' estimates.
Note: ER = exchange rate; SSA = sub-Saharan Africa; vol = volatility.

ANNEX TABLE 5.1.6.

Maximum Outward Spillovers, Jan. 1, 2015–Nov. 11, 2020
(Share of forecast error variance)

	ER changes	ER vol	Stock changes	Stock vol
China	3.1	3.1	3.6	3.9
Eurozone	6.6	4.4	9.3	6.5
VIX	3.0	1.6	5.4	4.9
SSA				
Angola	2.1	5.1		
Ethiopia	1.2	2.9		
Gabon	6.4	6.0		
Ghana	1.9	2.0	2.1	2.7
Kenya	1.5	1.9	4.1	
Mauritius	2.2	3.8	7.9	2.8
Nigeria	4.2	4.1	2.4	2.8
Rwanda	3.7		2.8	
Senegal	6.2			
South Africa	4.1	7.7	8.6	7.5
Tanzania	1.5	3.8	2.6	3.1
Uganda	2.7	4.3		
Zambia	1.6	3.8	2.5	
North Africa				
Djibouti	2.0	2.9		
Libya	1.9	2.3		
Morocco	6.2		7.6	4.9
Tunisia	5.1			

Source: Authors' estimates.
Note: ER = exchange rate; SSA = sub-Saharan Africa; vol = volatility.

ANNEX TABLE 5.1.7.

Average Outward Spillovers, Jan. 1, 2015–Nov. 11, 2020
(Share of forecast error variance)

	ER changes	ER vol	Stock changes	Stock vol
China	1.6	0.9	1.5	1.1
Eurozone	5.3	1.6	4.4	2.8
VIX	1.3	0.6	3.2	1.4
SSA				
Angola	0.6	1.5		
Ethiopia	0.6	1.2		
Gabon	3.5	2.6		
Ghana	0.6	0.9	0.7	1.1
Kenya	0.6	1.0	1.1	
Mauritius	0.8	1.4	0.8	0.9
Nigeria	0.7	1.7	1.0	1.1
Rwanda	0.6		0.6	
Senegal	3.3			
South Africa	2.1	2.8	3.5	2.8
Tanzania	0.7	1.4	0.8	1.1
Uganda	0.8	1.4		
Zambia	0.6	1.4	0.9	
North Africa				
Djibouti	0.7	1.0		
Libya	0.9	1.1		
Morocco	4.9		1.3	1.1
Tunisia	2.9			

Source: Authors' estimates.
Note: ER = Exchange rate; SSA = sub-Saharan Africa; vol = volatility.

Annex Figure 5.1.1. Small Vector Autoregression (VAR) Models with Different Commodity Prices: Impulse Response Functions

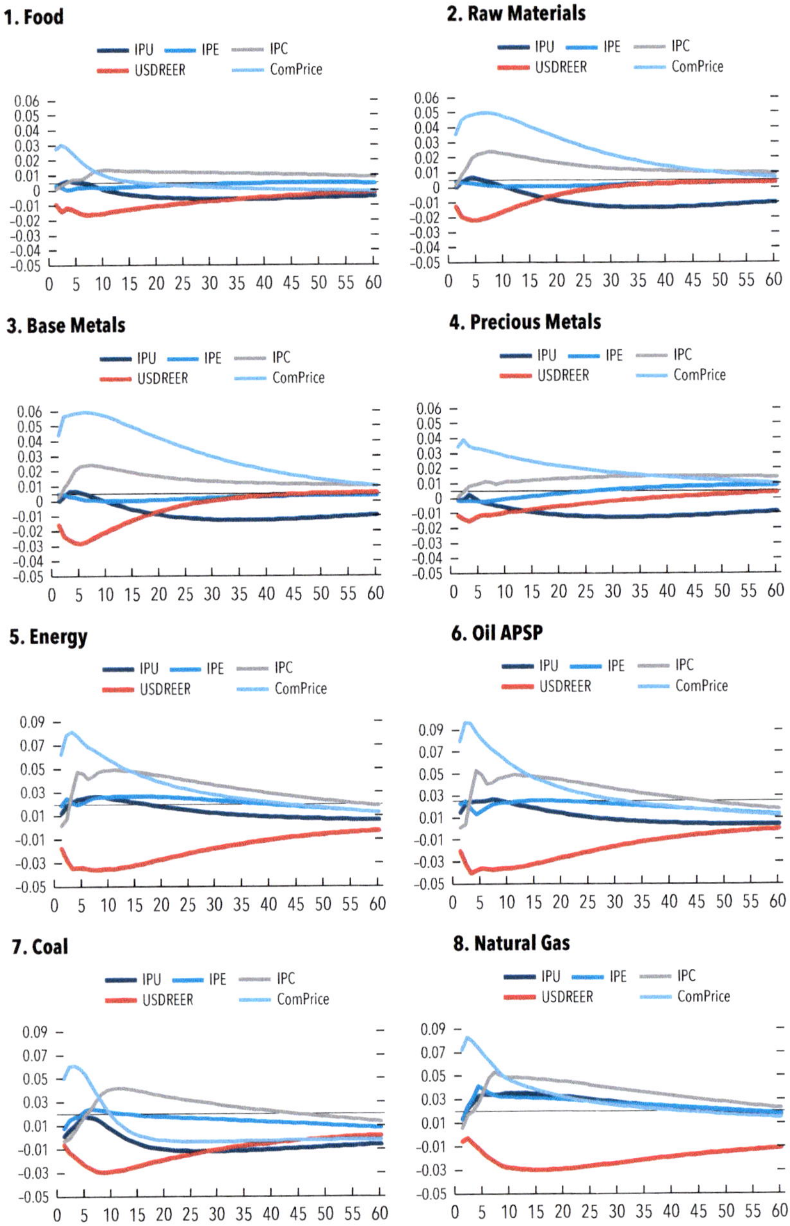

Sources: Primary Commodity Price System data, Haver; and authors' estimates.

Note: The horizontal axis represents periods after the shock, with each period corresponding to months. Figures show the generalized impulse response functions of the selected commodity price subindex to a one-standard deviation increase in respective shocks. APSP = average petroleum spot price (average of West Texas Intermediate, Brent and Dubai light crude oil); ComPrice = log of selected commodity price subindex; IP* = log industrial production with C = China, E = euro area, and U = US; USDREER = log of USD real effective exchange rate. Impulse response functions show the response of the respective VAR's commodity price index to shocks using a generalized Cholesky shock factorization. VAR contains IP series, USD REER, and the selected commodity price subindex (ComPrice).

Annex Figure 5.1.2. Vector Autoregression Models with Different Commodity Prices: Variance Decompositions

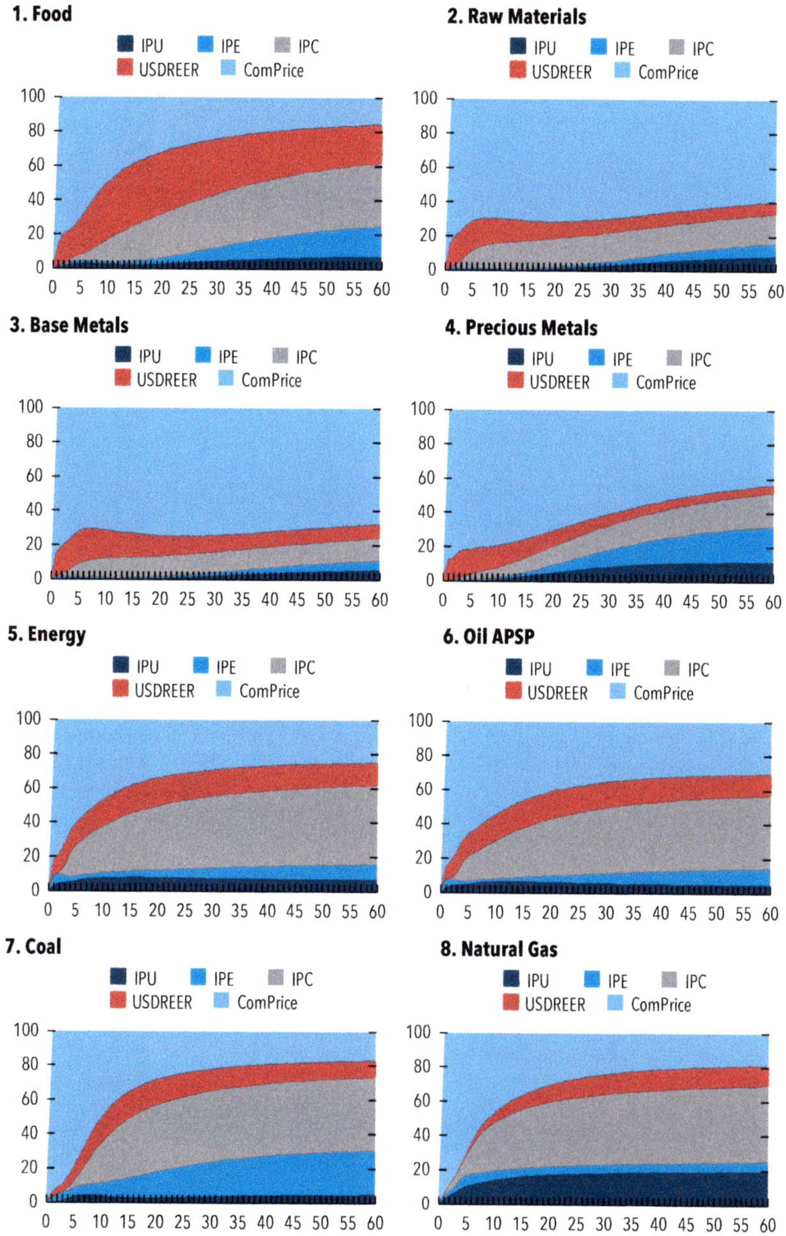

Sources: Primary Commodity Price System data, Haver; and authors' estimates.
Note: The horizontal axis represents periods after the shock, with each period corresponding to months. Figures show the percentage of variance explained by each shock. ComPrice = log of selected commodity price subindex; IP* = log industrial production with C = China, E = euro area, and U = US; USDREER = USD real effective exchange rate. Figures show variance decompositions of vector autoregression models, which include the US, euro area and China IP growth, USD REER, and the selected commodity price subindex (ComPrice), using a Cholesky factorization with degrees of freedom correction.

Annex Figure 5.1.3. Exchange Rate Co-movement with China and Financial Development

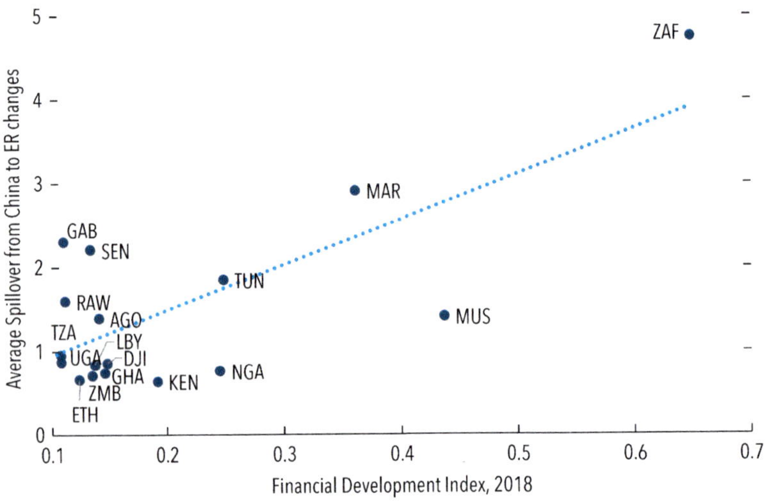

Sources: Svirydzenka 2016; and authors' estimates.
Note: Figure uses International Organization for Standardization (ISO) country codes. ER = exchange rate.

REFERENCES

Ahmed, S., R. Correa, D. A. Dias, N. Gornemann, J. Hoek, A. Jain, E. Liu, and others. 2019. "Global Spillovers of a China Hard Landing." International Finance Discussion Paper 1260, Board of Governors of the Federal Reserve System, Washington, DC.

Ahuja, A., and M. S. Nabar. 2012. "Investment-Led Growth in China: Global Spillovers." IMF Working Paper 12/267, International Monetary Fund, Washington, DC.

Alizadeh, S., M. W. Brandt, and F. X. Diebold. 2002. "Range-Based Estimation of Stochastic Volatility Models." *Journal of Finance* 57 (3): 1047–92.

Allard, C., J. I. Canales Kriljenko, J. R. Gonzalez-Garcia, E. Kitsios, J. P. Trevino, and W. Chen. 2016. "Trade Integration and Global Value Chains in Sub-Saharan Africa: In Pursuit of the Missing Link." IMF Departmental Paper 16/05, International Monetary Fund, Washington, DC.

Andrle, M., P. Blagrave, P. Espaillat, K. Honjo, B. Hunt, M. Kortelainen, R. Lalonde, and others. 2015. "The Flexible System of Global Models—FSGM." IMF Working Paper WP/15/64, International Monetary Fund, Washington, DC.

Cashin, P., K. Mohaddes, and M. Raissi. 2016. "China's Slowdown and Global Financial Market Volatility: Is World Growth Losing Out?" IMF Working Paper 16/63, International Monetary Fund, Washington, DC.

Cerutti, E., C. Koch, and S.-K. Pradhan. 2018. "The Growing Footprint of EMDE Banks in the International Banking System." *BIS Quarterly Review*, December.

Cerutti, E., C. Koch, and S.-K. Pradhan. 2020. "Banking Across Borders: Are Chinese Banks Different?" IMF Working Paper 20/249, International Monetary Fund, Washington, DC.

Cerutti, E. and H. Zhou. 2018. "The Chinese Banking System: Much More than a Domestic Giant." VoxEU, February 9.

Diebold, F. X., and K. Yilmaz. 2012. "Better to Give than to Receive: Forecast-Based Measurement of Volatility Spillovers." *International Journal of Forecasting* 28 (1): 57–66.

Diebold, F. X., and K. Yilmaz. 2014. "On the Network Topology of Variance Decompositions: Measuring the Connectedness of Financial Firms." *Journal of Econometrics* 182 (1): 119–34.

Dieppe, A., R. Gilhooly, J. Han, I. Korhonen, and D. Lodge. 2018. "The Transition of China to Sustainable Growth—Implications for the Global Economy and the Euro Area." European Central Bank Occasional Paper Series No. 206, European Central Bank, Frankfurt.

Dizioli, A., B. Hunt, and W. Maliszewski. 2016. "Spillovers from the Maturing of China's Economy." IMF Working Paper 16/212, International Monetary Fund, Washington, DC.

Drummond, P., and E. X. Liu. 2015. "Africa's Rising Exposure to China: How Large Are Spillovers through Trade?" *International Advances in Economic Research* 21: 317–34.

Furceri, D., J. T. Jalles, and A. Zdzienicka. 2017. "China Spillovers: New Evidence from Time-Varying Estimates." *Open Economies Review* 28 (3): 413–29.

Horn, S., C. M. Reinhart, and C. Trebesch. 2020. "China's Overseas Lending." NBER Working Paper 26050, National Bureau of Economic Research, Cambridge, MA.

International Monetary Fund (IMF). 2011. "People's Republic of China: Spillover Report for the 2011 Article IV Consultation and Selected Issues." IMF Country Report 11/193, Washington, DC.

International Monetary Fund (IMF). 2012. *2012 Spillover Report*. Washington, DC, July.

International Monetary Fund (IMF). 2014a. *IMF Multilateral Policy Issues Report: 2014 Spillover Report*. Washington, DC, June.

International Monetary Fund (IMF). 2014b. *Regional Economic Outlook: Asia and the Pacific*. Washington, DC, April.

International Monetary Fund (IMF). 2014c. *Regional Economic Outlook: Sub-Saharan Africa*. Washington, DC, October.

International Monetary Fund (IMF). 2015. *Regional Economic Outlook: Asia and the Pacific*. Washington, DC, May.

International Monetary Fund (IMF). 2016a. *Regional Economic Outlook: Asia and the Pacific*. Washington, DC, May.

International Monetary Fund (IMF). 2016b. *World Economic Outlook: Chapter 4 Spillovers from China's Transition and from Migration*. Washington, DC, October.

Kolerus, C., P. N'Diaye, and C. Saborowski. 2016. "China's Footprint in Global Commodity Markets." IMF Spillover Notes 6, International Monetary Fund, Washington, DC.

Lakatos, C., M. Maliszewska, I. Osorio-Rodarte, and D. Go. 2017. "China's Slowdown and Rebalancing: Impacts on Sub-Saharan Africa." *Journal of Economic Integration* 32 (4): 759–803.

Lenzen, M., K. Kanemoto, D. Moran, and A. Geschke. 2012. "Mapping the Structure of the World Economy." *Environmental Science and Technology* 46 (15): 8374–81.

Lenzen, M., D. Moran, K. Kanemoto, and A. Geschke. 2013. "Building Eora: A Global Multi-regional Input-Output Database at High Country and Sector Resolution." *Economic Systems Research* 25 (1): 20–49.

Mano, R. 2016. "Quantifying the Spillovers from China Rebalancing Using a Multi-Sector Ricardian Trade Model." IMF Working Paper 16/219, International Monetary Fund, Washington, DC.

Mwase, N., P. N'Diaye, H. Oura, F. Ricka, K. Svirydzenka, and Y. Zhang. 2016. "Spillovers from China: Financial Channels." IMF Spillover Notes 5, International Monetary Fund, Washington, DC.

Roache, S. K., and M. Rousset. 2015. "China: Credit, Collateral, and Commodity Prices." HKIMR Working Paper 27/2015, Hong Kong Institute for Monetary Research.

Svirydzenka, K. 2016. "Introducing a New Broad-Based Index of Financial Development." IMF Working Paper 16/5, International Monetary Fund, Washington, DC.

World Bank. 2020. *Global Financial Development Report 2019/2020: Bank Regulation and Supervision a Decade after the Global Financial Crisis*. Washington, DC.

CHAPTER 6

Sub-Saharan Africa's Public Debt to China

Seung Mo Choi, Xiangming Li, and Ivohasina Razafimahefa

INTRODUCTION

Over the past two decades, China has become a key economic partner for sub-Saharan Africa. It is the region's largest bilateral trading partner and a major source of infrastructure financing. At the same time, China has also become a major bilateral creditor to sub-Saharan African countries. In recent years, because the region has been buffeted by significant global economic shocks, some African countries have faced significant challenges in servicing their public debt. It is in this context that sub-Saharan African countries' debt to China has received increased attention. However, consistent and comparable data on sub-Saharan Africa's debt owed to China are scarce, and the discussion often draws on disparate data sources based on differing concepts. This chapter aims to fill this gap by presenting key features of sub-Saharan Africa's debt to China based on data that are consistent with IMF methodology, and hence comparable across countries.

This chapter is organized as follows. The second section sets the stage by discussing data sources, their coverage, and how they compare with other data sets. The third section briefly reviews research on sub-Saharan Africa's debt to China. The fourth section analyzes the structure and size of the stock of sub-Saharan Africa's public debt to China, and the fifth section looks at debt-service patterns. The sixth section presents information on the different lenders and borrowers, and the seventh section concludes.

Rachel Lyngaas and Francine Nyankiye provided significant contributions to this chapter. Vivek Arora provided many invaluable comments.

Data Sources and Coverage

The data set used in this chapter includes country-level data for the public debt of 45 sub-Saharan African countries that was owed to China at the end of 2020.[1] The data were shared by country authorities with IMF staff teams and were adjusted through iterations between both sides to ensure accuracy and consistency with the standard IMF–World Bank definition of public and publicly guaranteed (PPG) debt as specified in the Debt Sustainability Framework. PPG debt comprises debt contracted or guaranteed by the public sector.[2] In the following sections, the terms "total public debt" and "external public debt" refer to PPG debt from the borrowing countries' side. On the creditor side, the data cover debt owed to official Chinese creditors—government (financed by the national budget) and loans by Export–Import Bank of China (EXIM)—and to commercial Chinese creditors.[3]

How do the data used in this analysis compare with other well-known data sets such as the World Bank's International Debt Statistics (IDS), the Chinese Loans to Africa (CLA) database (Johns Hopkins University China–Africa Research Initiative [JHU CARI]), and AidData (William & Mary Global Research)? Although the data sets are complementary, they are based on different concepts. The World Bank data, like the data in this chapter, use the PPG definition and cover information on outstanding external debt. Because they are based on countries' self-reported information, there are differences across countries in the coverage of lenders and borrowers. The data set in this chapter adjusts

---

[1] The 45 sub-Saharan African countries include Angola, Benin, Botswana, Burkina Faso, Burundi, Cabo Verde, Cameroon, Central African Republic, Chad, Comoros, Democratic Republic of the Congo, Republic of Congo, Côte d'Ivoire, Equatorial Guinea, Eritrea, Eswatini, Ethiopia, Gabon, The Gambia, Ghana, Guinea, Guinea-Bissau, Kenya, Lesotho, Liberia, Madagascar, Malawi, Mali, Mauritius, Mozambique, Namibia, Niger, Nigeria, Rwanda, São Tomé and Príncipe, Senegal, Seychelles, Sierra Leone, South Africa, South Sudan, Tanzania, Togo, Uganda, Zambia, and Zimbabwe.

[2] Public and publicly guaranteed debt includes both external and domestic debt. The public sector includes central, state, and local governments; social security funds and extra budgetary funds; the central bank and the public enterprises controlled by the government. Public financial corporations are excluded. Also excluded are nonfinancial public enterprises that can borrow without a guarantee from the government, do not carry out uncompensated quasi-fiscal activities, and have an established track record of positive operating balances (IMF 2018). In some instances, data availability may limit the coverage, including, for instance, arrears/payables to Chinese contractors that may exist. Other definitions for debt of the public sector are used by the IMF as described in Public Sector Debt Statistics Guide for Compilers and Users (https://www.elibrary.imf.org/downloadpdf/book/9781616351564/9781616351564.xml).

[3] China's foreign aid is provided in three forms: (1) grants, (2) interest-free loans financed by the national budget, and (3) preferential loans provided by the Export–Import Bank of China (EXIM), as designated by the Chinese government (Chinese Foreign Aid, cidca.gov.cn [http://www.cidca.gov.cn/2018-08/06/c_129925064_3.htm]). Other than the central government, only EXIM is considered an official lender by the Chinese authorities. Other Chinese lenders, such as China Development Bank, are considered by China as commercial creditors. See, for example, "Written Interview with Finance Minister Liu Kun on G20 Debt Agenda (http://www.mof.gov.cn/en/Cooperation/mulid/202011/t20201120_3626593.htm)," November 20, 2020.

countries' self-reported information for methodological consistency. The CLA data coverage is close to the PPG concept, but it reflects loan *commitments* and not the actual outstanding debt stock. The AidData is also based on loan *commitments* and on a broader coverage than the PPG concept, including a wider set of borrowers.

The data used for this chapter are based on the standard definition of sovereign PPG debt according to the IMF definition used for debt sustainability analysis. It represents outstanding debt, reflecting actual disbursements and repayments. As noted previously, the data are reported by country authorities to IMF staff teams, which may have been adjusted after the discussions between both parties to ensure conformity with the definition of PPG debt. This data set also includes information on projected debt service, as reported by the authorities to IMF staff teams, which is additional information relative to other data sets. Furthermore, this data set provides information, for some countries, about the main Chinese creditor entities as well as on concessionality.[4] In addition, the data set also covers domestic debt, which other data sets generally do not cover. Including domestic debt is essential to understand the overall composition of debt in sub-Saharan Africa and the relative contribution of China to sub-Saharan Africa's debt.

The World Bank's IDS also uses the PPG debt definition for external public debt (Table 6.1).[5] Our data set and IDS paint a broadly similar picture of external debt, but they have some differences because of different collection methods and coverage. The IDS reflects debtor-country self-reported data, whereas our data set reflects further iterations for consistency with the definition. Such iterations often involve the treatment of borrowing by majority state-owned enterprises (also referred to as nonfinancial public enterprises in this chapter), which in general is included in PPG debt unless they present limited fiscal risks. The treatment of debt owed by special purpose vehicles may also differ for similar reasons. On the borrower side, this data set covers all 45 sub-Saharan African countries, whereas the IDS covers the 41 sub-Saharan African countries that have borrowed from the World Bank and are obliged to report into the World Bank Debtor Reporting System.[6] Our data set also differs from the IDS by including some information on Chinese creditor entities and on the concessionality of the loans. In broad comparison, IDS reports that sub-Saharan Africa's debt to China stood at $75.4 billion at the end of 2020, fairly close to our data set, with total debt of $71.5 billion.

[4] Concessionality increases with the grant element of a debt, which is the difference between the present value of debt and its nominal value, expressed as a percentage of the nominal value of the debt (IMF 2018).

[5] The World Bank's IDS is based on the World Bank Debtor Reporting System from member countries that have received loans from the World Bank. It collects external debt only and contains two main categories: (1) public sector debt and publicly guaranteed private debt and (2) aggregated non-guaranteed private sector debt. The public sector includes the central and local government, central banks, and autonomous institutions, such as financial and nonfinancial corporations (World Bank 2020).

[6] The IMF sub-Saharan Africa definition excludes Djibouti and Somalia.

Another significant data source is the CLA database that was initially compiled by the JHU CARI (Brautigam and Hwang 2020) and currently managed by Global China Initiative. Data are collected systematically from websites and news aggregators, covering, among others, publications and announcements of governments of China and Africa, as well as company filings and bond prospectuses at the securities and exchanges (Database Methodology Guide Book and the China–Africa Loan Database Research Guidebook). The CLA data set aligns broadly with the IMF's PPG debt in its coverage of lenders and borrowers. One difference in the coverage of borrowers is the treatment of state-owned enterprises, joint ventures (JVs), and special purpose vehicles. Our data set includes the debt owed by majority government-owned state-owned companies and JVs and excludes state-owned enterprises that do not pose risks to the government budget. Conversely, the CLA takes the liability proportionate to government's stake for state-owned enterprises, JVs, and special purpose vehicles. More importantly, unlike our data set that covers outstanding debt resulting from disbursements and repayments, the CLA database covers loan commitments. The CLA data set also does not contain elements essential for estimating the outstanding debt stock, such as disbursements, repayment, or arrears. To illustrate, the CLA data set includes loan commitments by China to sub-Saharan African countries of $136.5 billion over 2000–19, almost double the outstanding debt stock from our data. A helpful distinguishing feature of the CLA is its categorization of individual loan and project information by sector (for example, transport), as well as loan terms (interest rate, maturity, and grace period), which could be used to estimate concessionality.

A third important data source is AidData's Global Chinese Development Finance Dataset by William & Mary Global Research Institute. The AidData data set covers a broader concept of financing than the other data sets, because it includes not only PPG debt but also grants, loans to the private sector that do not carry a public guarantee, and nonguaranteed loans to joint ventures that have a minor government stake (Brautigam and Huang 2021; Custer and others 2021). It is also broader than the CLA because it includes amounts in umbrella agreements, which may or may not become concrete loan agreements for specific projects, the basis for subsequent disbursements.[7] In addition, some of these umbrella agreements and their materialized project-level agreements may be simultaneously recorded in the database, so summing both umbrella and project-level agreements may cause double counting.[8] Similar to the CLA, AidData (https://www.aiddata.org/data/aiddatas-global-chinese-development-finance-dataset-version-3-0) is also

[7] Brautigam and Huang (2021) discuss the difference between the Johns Hopkins University China–Africa Research Initiative's CLA database and the William & Mary AidData.

[8] "Framework Agreements (umbrella agreements) are issued by a variety of official sector institutions in China. Because of the nature of the Tracking Underreported Financial Flows methodology, the method used for AidData compilation, the subsidiary projects/transactions approved and financed under these types of umbrella agreements are likely captured elsewhere in the dataset." (Custer and others 2021.)

TABLE 6.1.

Sub-Saharan Africa's Debt to China: Comparison of Data Sources

	IMF SSA Public and Publicly Guaranteed Debt to China (Authors' Data)	World Bank International Debt Statistics	Chinese Loans to Africa Database	AidData Global Chinese Development Finance Dataset
Scope	Domestic and external outstanding debt stock	External only outstanding debt stock	Loan commitments to specific projects by China	Financial flows commitments from China, including general umbrella agreements, which might not become specific project commitments (the basis for disbursement)
Creditor coverage	All entities, including domestic and external	All external entities	All Chinese entities	All Chinese entities
Recipient country coverage	All SSA countries	Countries that have borrowed from the World Bank	All African countries	All countries around the world
Recipient entity coverage	Public and publicly guaranteed debt	Public and publicly guaranteed debt	Public and publicly guaranteed debt	All types of entities
• of which, public enterprises (including joint ventures and special purpose vehicles)	Includes only majority owned but excludes public financial corporations	Includes only majority owned and includes public financial corporations	Commitments allocated in proportionate to the government stake	Full amounts for all
• granularity	Country aggregate	Country aggregate	Project-level information	Project-level and umbrella agreement-level information, including identifiers on loans or grants
Types of financing	Stock of outstanding debt	Stock of outstanding debt	Loan commitments, which include amount that might not have been disbursed, and does not reflect any repayment or accumulation of arrears or interest payments	Loan and aid commitments
Terms	Includes some country-level average grant element data	None	Includes interest rate, duration, grace period information	Includes interest rate, duration, grace period information
Debt service	Includes historical and projected flows	Includes historical flows	None	None
Collection methodology	Country reporting, discussed with IMF staff	Country self-reporting	Public sources	Public sources

Sources: IMF 2018; Brautigam and Hwang 2020; World Bank 2020; and Custer and others 2021.
Note: SSA = Sub-Saharan Africa.

commitment-based and does not cover information on debt stock, service, or arrears. In terms of time period, the latest version covers 2000–21 in the version published in November 2023 and includes total Chinese commitments to African countries of $330 billion (excluding umbrella agreements that represent general credit lines between China and the recipient countries without actual projects)—almost double the amount in the CLA, which has a longer time span. Similar to the CLA, AidData categorizes loans by sector, which is not a feature of our data set.

RESEARCH RELATED TO SUB-SAHARAN AFRICA'S DEBT OWED TO CHINA

Research on Chinese lending to sub-Saharan African countries has addressed different aspects, including its effect on the region's economies and issues that may arise during debt treatments. Some notable papers in the recent literature are discussed briefly in the following section.

One strand of analysis seeks to estimate the overall size of African debt to China (sometimes including debt owed by the private sector with no government guarantees). For example, Horn, Reinhart, and Trebesch (2021) conclude that China became the world's largest official creditor to Africa by 2017, surpassing the credits to sub-Saharan Africa from the World Bank or the IMF. They estimate "direct lending by the Chinese state and state-owned Chinese entities to private and public sector recipients" using AidData as the main data source for the period 2000–17, when Chinese overseas lending increased rapidly, and referencing other data sources, including the CLA. Given that these data sources record loan commitments, the authors estimated the debt stock by 108 countries globally of $392 billion by assuming that all loan commitments were fully disbursed.[9] When comparing their data with IDS data, the authors drop loans to private recipients and all umbrella agreements. Based on their own analysis, the authors conclude that the IDS significantly under-reports. Some of these differences, however, may be explained by the fact that the authors' work uses AidData, which is commitment-based. Therefore, it includes some amounts that may not have been disbursed. In addition, it covers loans to the countries that have not borrowed from the World Bank and, hence, are not required to report to IDS, as well as loans to the private sector that are not guaranteed by the government and thus not in the IDS (Brautigam and Huang 2021).

A second strand of literature studies trends in China's lending and debt cancellation and restructuring in Africa. Acker and Brautigam (2021) found that China committed $153 billion to African public sector borrowers over 2000–19, at least 80 percent of which went to finance infrastructure projects (such as transport, power, telecommunications, and water). Excluding a significant amount of refinancing of projects in Angola in 2016, the value of signed annual

[9] Horn, Reinhart, and Trebesch (2021) project disbursements and repayments based on available information and assumptions on loan terms, arrears, and debt restructuring.

commitments peaked in 2013. The subsequent moderation reflected concerns over debt sustainability. In recent years, new commitments shifted toward countries that are less vulnerable or "countries that had not previously asked Chinese banks for debt relief." The study also notes that Angola was the largest sub-Saharan African borrower from China and accounted for 70 percent of China's resource-secured lending in the region. Acker, Brautigam, and Huang (2020) document that changes in interest rates and principal reductions ("haircuts") are rare, with debt write-offs being limited mainly to zero-interest loans. The more common approach to debt treatment is to extend maturities or repayment periods. This approach has its roots in China's domestic laws, which seek to discourage local governments from failing to repay loans to domestic banks. This logic appears to have been extended to external debt treatment. They find little evidence of asset seizures and, despite contract clauses requiring arbitration, the use of courts to enforce payments or the application of interest rate penalties.

A third strand of literature examines how public debt to China is associated with macroeconomic performance in sub-Saharan Africa. Dollar (2016) concludes that China's deepening economic engagement (including through foreign direct investment) has largely been associated with better economic performance in Africa.

KEY FEATURES OF SUB-SAHARAN AFRICA'S PUBLIC DEBT OWED TO CHINA

This section presents some key facts on sub-Saharan Africa's public debt to China, drawing on the data set prepared for this analysis. Because the data set describes the actual debt stock, rather than the estimated debt stock or loan commitments, it can be used in a complementary manner with existing data sets to analyze the implications of sub-Saharan Africa's debt to China.

Levels and Shares

At the end of 2020, sub-Saharan Africa's public debt to China was $71.5 billion, equivalent to 4.3 percent of sub-Saharan African GDP (Figure 6.1). The level was broadly unchanged from 2019 ($71.0 billion). The data are based on the standard IMF definition of PPG debt. In particular, the debt by state-owned enterprises that is not explicitly guaranteed by the government and poses limited fiscal risk to the government is excluded.[10]

This amount is also close to the IDS aggregate of sub-Saharan Africa's public debt to China ($75.4 billion).[11]

[10] The exclusion of state-owned enterprises is based on the list of criteria described in the Guidance Note on the Bank-Fund Debt Sustainability Framework for Low Income Countries (https://www.imf.org/en/Publications/Policy-Papers/Issues/2018/02/14/pp122617guidance-note-on-lic-dsf).

[11] Seven sub-Saharan African countries (accounting for $1.4 billion in our data set) are not covered by IDS.

Figure 6.1. Sub-Saharan African Countries: Public Debt to China, 2020
(Billions of US dollars)

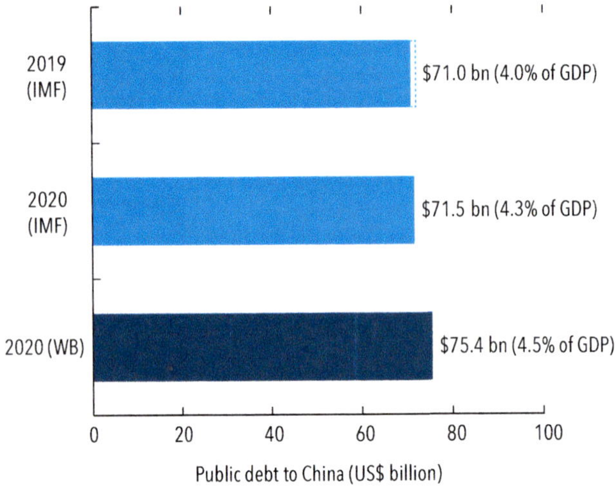

Sources: IMF data set and country authorities; and World Bank, International Debt Statistics.
Note: IMF data include all 45 sub-Saharan African countries. World Bank data exclude Equatorial Guinea, The Gambia, Guinea-Bissau, Namibia, São Tomé and Príncipe, Seychelles, and South Sudan.

In relative terms, sub-Saharan Africa's public debt to China accounts for only a small share of the region's total PPG external and domestic debt, at about 7.3 percent. Out of this, about three-quarters (5.4 percent) is owed to Chinese official creditors, whereas 1.9 percent is owed to commercial creditors (such as China Development Bank [CDB]).[12]

Taking a broader perspective of sub-Saharan Africa's indebtedness and using other more aggregated data sources that cover earlier years, one sees that increased borrowing domestically and from foreign commercial lenders contributed the lion's share of the near tripling in sub-Saharan Africa's total public debt between 2010 and 2020, accounting for 50 and 30 percent, respectively (Figure 6.2). Official bilateral debt, including debt to China, accounted for only about 7 percent of the increase.

Within official bilateral debt of sub-Saharan African countries, China accounts for 57 percent of the total, making China the largest bilateral creditor to the region. To put this in context, this chapter breaks down the region's total public debt, which stood at 57 percent of sub-Saharan African GDP at the end of 2020 (Figure 6.3). External and domestic debt each account for about half of the region's total public debt. Among external creditors, bilateral official creditors

[12] The Chinese government classified Chinese Development Bank as a commercial creditor.

Figure 6.2. Sub-Saharan Africa: Sources of Public Debt Increase, 2010–20
(Billions of US dollars)

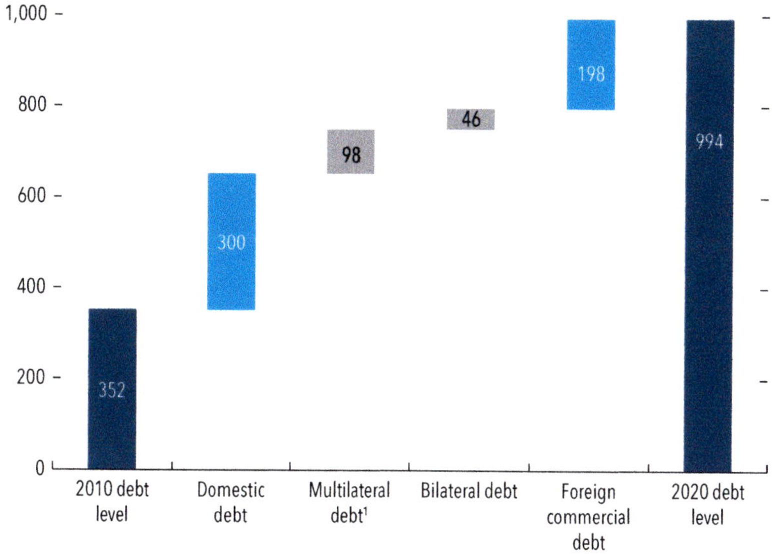

Sources: IMF WEO database; and World Bank International Debt Statistics.
[1] Includes regional development banks.

Figure 6.3. Sub-Saharan Africa's Public Debt, End of 2020
(Percent, unless otherwise indicated)

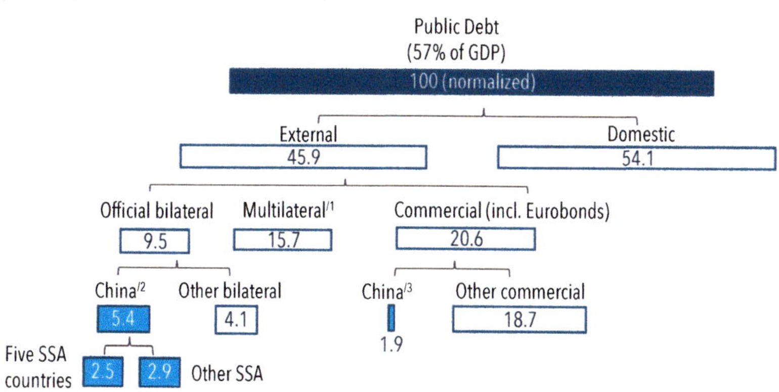

Source: IMF and country authorities.
[1] Includes regional development banks.
[2] Does not include the China Development Bank.
[3] Includes the China Development Bank.

account for a relatively small share of 20 percent, whereas commercial creditors (including Eurobond holders) account for about 50 percent and official multilateral creditors for about 30 percent of the total.

China's large share in sub-Saharan Africa's official bilateral debt partly reflects the decline of official development assistance—since the mid-2000s (Figure 6.4).

Meanwhile, the share of debt to China differs markedly across sub-Saharan African countries (Figure 6.5). On a simple average, 14 percent of external public debt is owed to China, with a range of 0–65 percent and a median of 10 percent; similarly, China's share in official bilateral debt ranges from 0 to 100 percent, with a simple average of 47 percent and a median of 50 percent.

Figure 6.4. Sub-Saharan Africa: Net Official Development Assistance Received

(Percentage of sub-Saharan Africa's GDP)

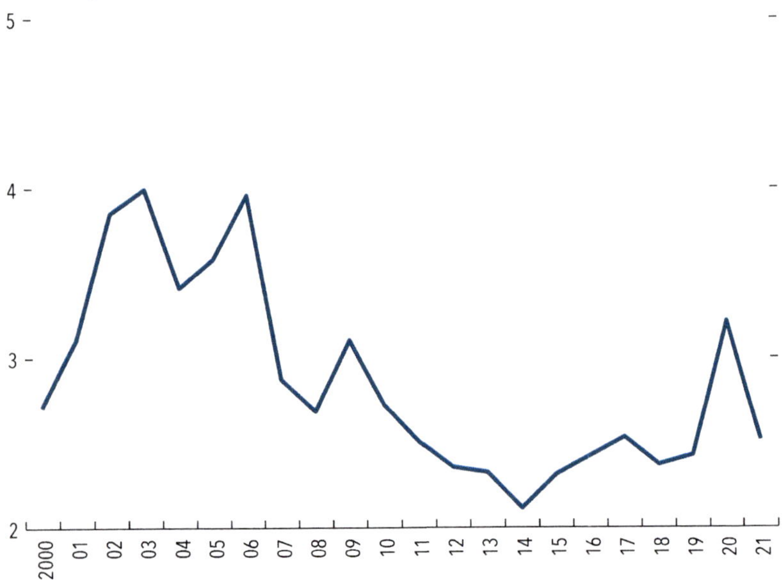

Sources: World Development Indicators; World Bank; and World Economic Outlook, IMF, October 2022.

Figure 6.5. Sub-Saharan African Countries: Public Debt to China, End of 2020

1. Public Debt to China

(Percentage of external public debt)

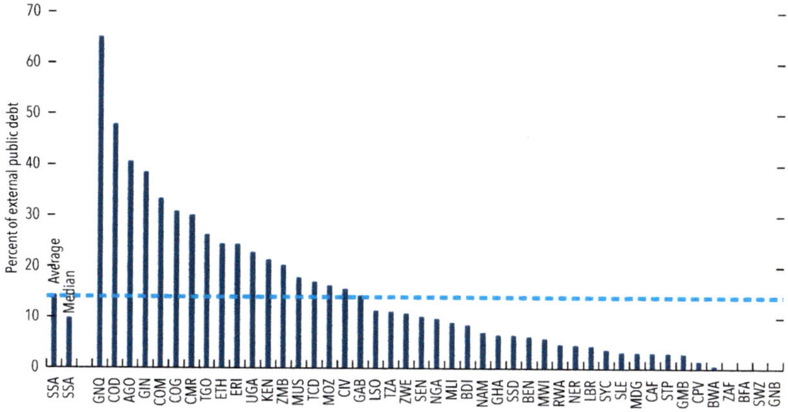

2. Public Debt to China's Official Sector[1]

(Percentage of official bilateral public debt)

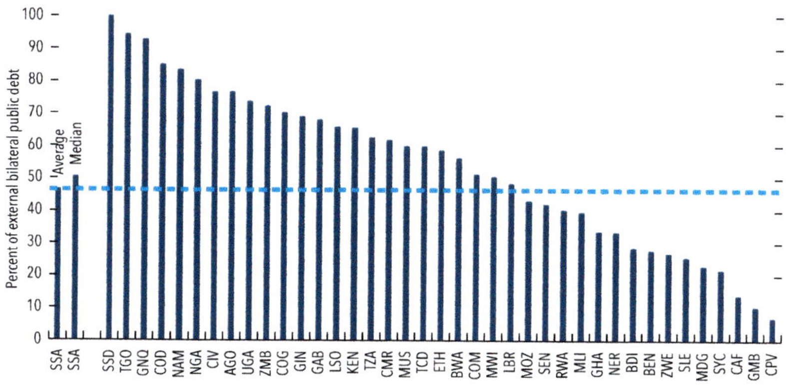

Source: IMF data set and country authorities.

Note: Figure uses International Organization for Standardization (ISO) country codes. SSA = Sub-Saharan Africa.

[1] Does not include the China Development Bank.

CONCENTRATION

The concentration of China's exposure to sub-Saharan African countries is also noteworthy (Figure 6.6). Five countries accounted for almost 60 percent of the region's public debt to China, and 10 countries owed nearly 80 percent. Among the top five, Angola accounted for almost 30 percent of sub-Saharan Africa's debt to China; Ethiopia and Kenya accounted for about 10 percent each, followed by Cameroon and Nigeria with about 5 percent each.

Figure 6.6. Sub-Saharan African Countries: Public Debt to China by Country, 2020
(Billions of US dollars)

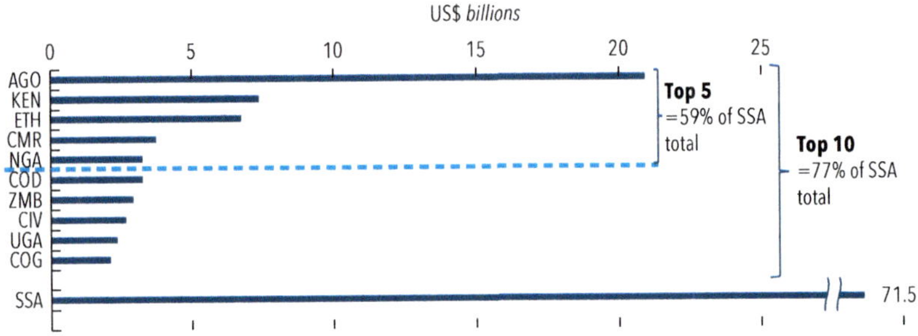

Sources: Country authorities; and IMF data set.
Note: Figure uses International Organization for Standardization (ISO) country codes.

Sub-Saharan Africa Public Debt Service to China

In this section, creditors are categorized into four groups: (1) multilateral, (2) bilateral excluding all Chinese lending entities (such as EXIM), (3) commercial, excluding all Chinese lending entities (such as CDB), and (4) China, including all Chinese lending entities. The analysis is based on these four creditor groups because of the lack of granular data distinguishing debt service between Chinese lending institutions (for example, EXIM versus CDB).

Patterns of sub-Saharan African countries' debt service to China broadly mirror those in the debt stock, with some slight differences. Based on the creditor groups noted in the previous section, commercial creditors (excluding China) accounted for the largest share (more than half) of the region's projected public external debt service due during 2022–26, followed by official multilateral creditors, China, and official bilateral creditors (Figure 6.7).

Figure 6.7. Projected External Debt Service by Creditor, 2022-26[1]
(Sub-Saharan Africa aggregates, percentage)

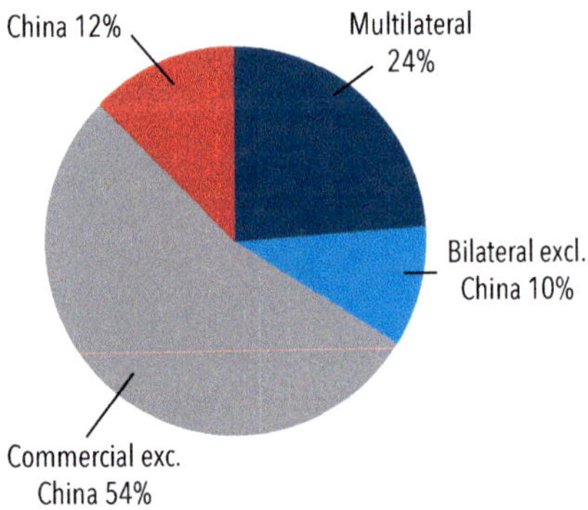

Sources: Country authorities; and IMF data set.
[1] "China" category includes both official and commercial lenders, as disaggregated debt-service data are not available. Projected in 2021 using data through 2020.

China's share in the projected external debt service of sub-Saharan Africa—including EXIM, CDB, and other Chinese lending entities—was relatively small, at 12 percent. The projected annual average sub-Saharan Africa's debt service due to China for 2022–26 was equivalent to 0.2 percent of (annual) projected GDP, 1.9 percent of (annual) projected fiscal revenues (including grants), and 7.7 percent of (annual) projected international reserves (Figure 6.8). Within sub-Saharan

Figure 6.8. Sub-Saharan African Countries: Annual Public Debt Service to China, 2022-26

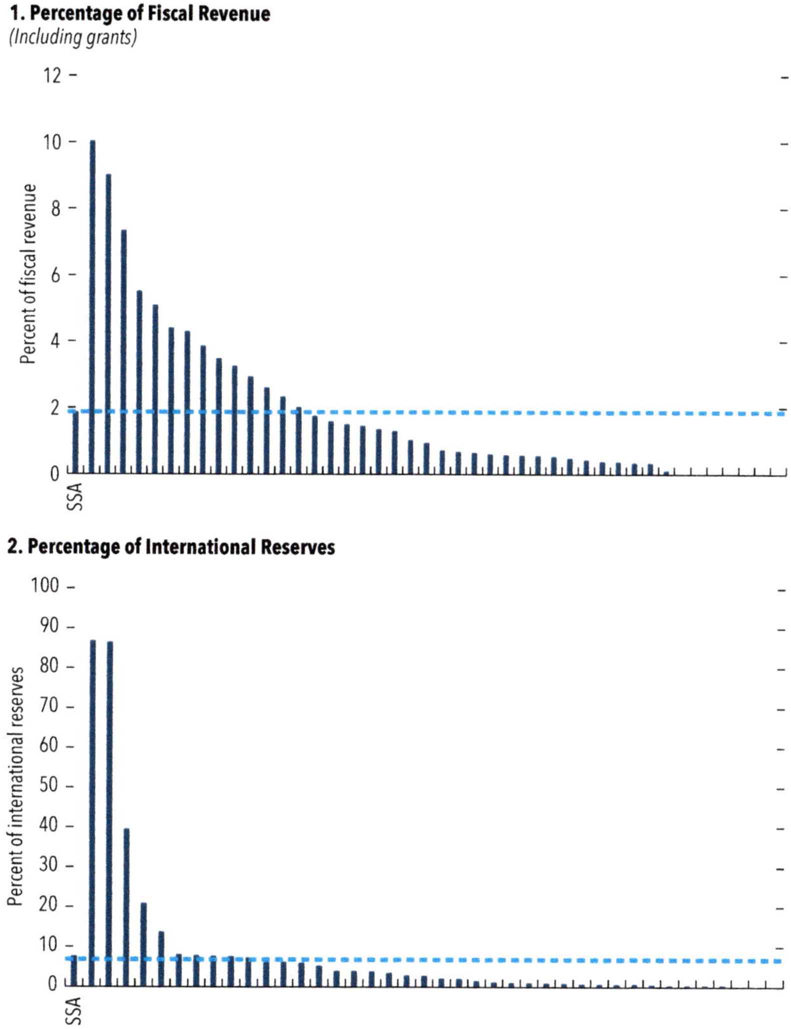

Source: IMF data set and country authorities.
Note: The 2022-26 annual average of projected debt service is divided by the 2022-26 annual average of projected fiscal revenue (panel 1) or international reserves (panel 2). The dotted lines show simple averages across sub-Saharan African countries. Country names are omitted to avoid sensitivity. SSA = Sub-Saharan Africa.

Africa's bilateral external debt service, however, China accounted for about 60 percent, broadly similar to the share of sub-Saharan Africa's debt stock to China. The large share of China in sub-Saharan Africa's bilateral debt service highlights the importance of China in debt treatment and related discussions, with regard to addressing pressures arising from bilateral debt.

Similar to the case of debt stock, the share of projected debt service to China differed widely across sub-Saharan African countries. Compared with an average of 12.5 percent of external debt service, the range was 0–74.1 percent, with a median of 8.8 percent. As a share of GDP, debt service to China ranged from 0–2.2 percent of GDP (Figure 6.9). As a share of fiscal revenue and international reserves, sub-Saharan African countries' debt service to China is in the 0–10 percent and 0–90 percent range, respectively (Figure 6.8). Larger economies in sub-Saharan Africa have a higher proportion of debt service due to commercial creditors (excluding Chinese lending entities such as CDB) and a lower proportion due to China (including EXIM, CDB, and other Chinese lending entities). Starting from the left quartile in Figure 6.10, for sub-Saharan African countries in the bottom quartile by GDP size, about 60 percent of their debt-service payments are due to multilateral creditors. As the economic size of the country grows, the shares of multilateral and bilateral debt service decrease and that of commercial debt service rises, given that larger economies have

Figure 6.9. Sub-Saharan Africa: Annual Public Debt Service to China, 2020-26

(Percentage of GDP)

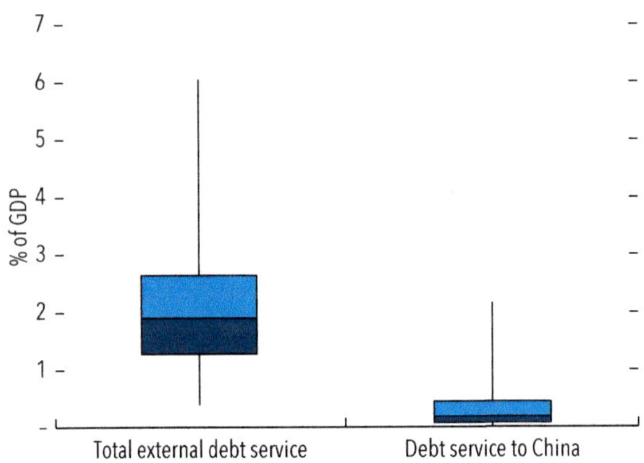

Source: IMF data set and country authorities.
Note: The end points show minimum and maximum. The middle line in the box represents the median. The box represents the first and third quartiles.

Figure 6.10. Creditor Share in External Debt Service per GDP Quartile, 2022-26[1]

(Sub-Saharan Africa aggregates, percentage)

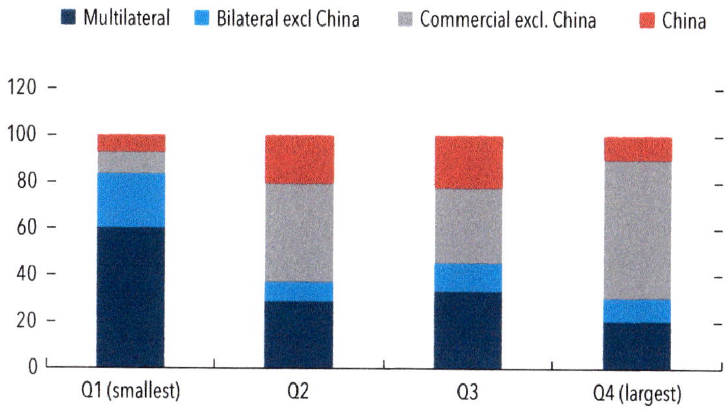

Source: IMF data set and country authorities.

[1] Q1 corresponds to the quartile group of countries with the smallest GDP.

greater access to international financial markets. In sum, the share of debt service to China is small for countries in the bottom and top quartiles but is relatively larger for countries in the second and third quartiles.

As for debt stock, sub-Saharan African countries' projected debt service due to China was concentrated in a few countries (Figure 6.11). However, the set of countries with the highest projected debt service was not exactly the same as those with the highest debt stock. Six countries accounted for about 60 percent of sub-Saharan Africa's projected debt service due to China during 2022–26: Ethiopia (17 percent), Kenya (14 percent), Zambia (12 percent), Cameroon (7 percent), Uganda (5 percent), and Mozambique (4 percent). Of these countries, Cameroon, Ethiopia, and Kenya were the countries with the largest debt stock due to China, but Uganda and Zambia were not. Meanwhile, Angola and Nigeria were among the top five countries by debt stock to China but were not among those with the highest debt service due to China during 2022–26. These differences reflect country-specific circumstances, such as the nature and terms of the loans and any debt rescheduling that had taken place by the end of 2020.

Figure 6.11. Sub-Saharan Africa's Public Debt Service to China by Country, 2022–26

1. Debt Service to China, 2022–26
(Percentage)

2. Debt Service to China, 2022–26
(Millions of US dollars)

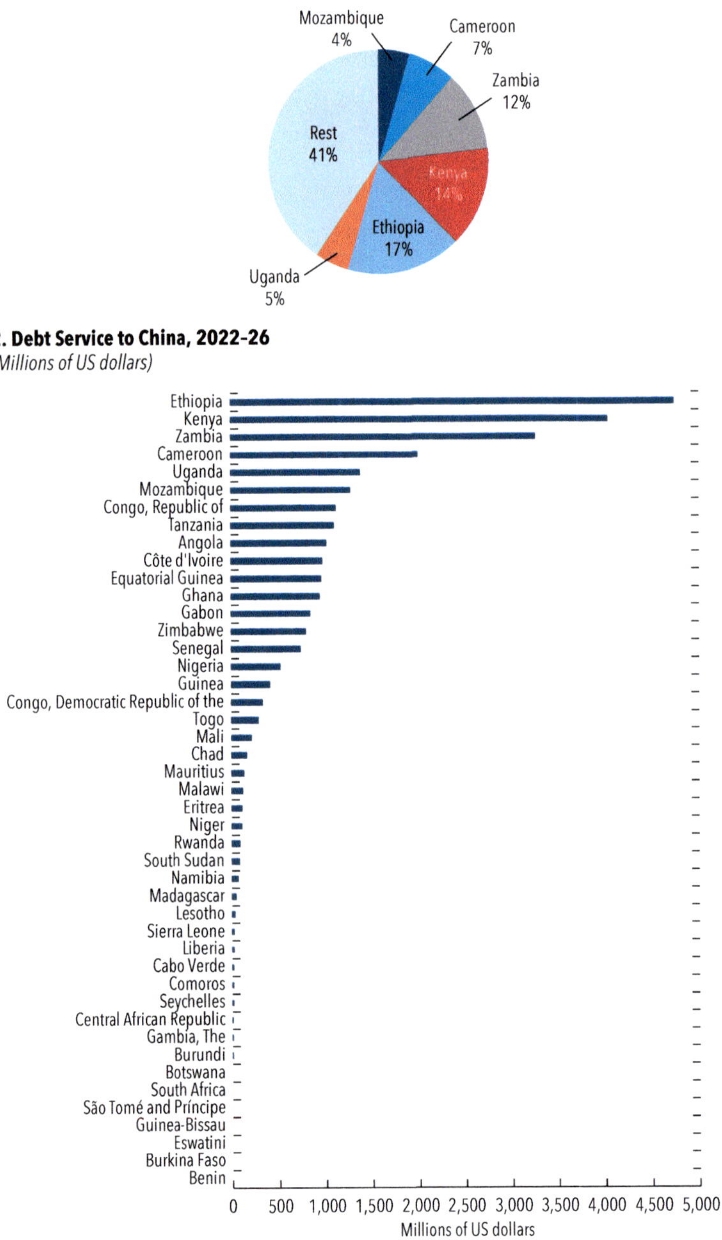

Sources: Country authorities; and IMF data set.

LENDERS AND BORROWERS

Chinese Lenders

Most of sub-Saharan Africa's public debt to China is owed to EXIM (about 60 percent) and CDB (about 20 percent), whereas a small amount is owed to the Chinese government (Figure 6.12). Based on the type of creditor, Chinese official creditors hold almost three-quarters of sub-Saharan Africa's public debt to China. The government and EXIM account for more than 80 percent of sub-Saharan Africa's public debt to Chinese official creditors, whereas the rest is owed to unidentified official lenders. The total commercial creditors, including CDB, account for about one-quarter of sub-Saharan Africa's public debt to China. As noted, the Chinese authorities consider only loans from the government and EXIM as official.

Sub-Saharan African Borrowers

Borrower information is incomplete in this data set, covering only about 70 percent of the debt stock. Based on available information, sub-Saharan African governments account for the majority of the PPG debt to China, at 60 percent. Meanwhile, state-owned enterprises hold 10 percent (Figure 6.13). Of the debt by state-owned enterprises, about two-thirds are guaranteed by governments. The remaining debt by state-owned enterprises has no explicit guarantee but is included in PPG debt because of fiscal risks as discussed in the previous sections. Information regarding the entities responsible for the remaining 30 percent of sub-Saharan Africa's public debt owed to China is unavailable.

Sub-Saharan Africa's public debt to China is mainly owed by resource-intensive countries (of which there were 23 in our sample). Oil exporters (including Angola) account for about 45 percent and non-oil resource-intensive countries for 35 percent (Figure 6.14). Non-resource-intensive countries account for 20 percent.[13]

Figure 6.12. Sub-Saharan Africa's Public Debt Service to China: By Lenders, End of 2020

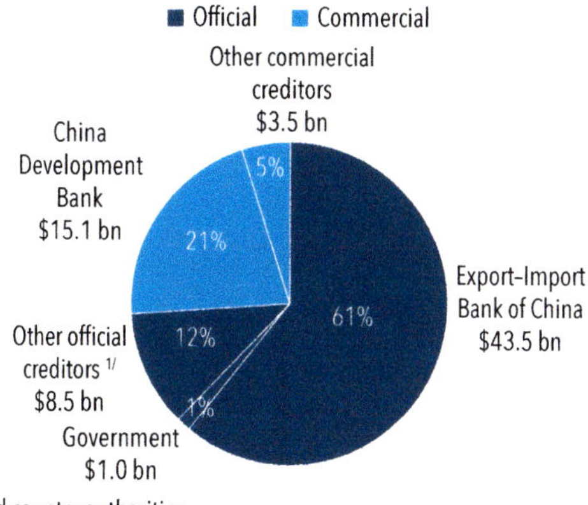

Source: IMF data set and country authorities.
[1] Includes "unknown public creditors" that may be the Export-Import Bank of China or the government.

[13] Across sub-Saharan Africa oil exporters, about 15 percent (simple average) of public debt is owed to China. For other country groupings, the average is about 7 percent.

Figure 6.13. Sub-Saharan Africa's Public Debt to China: By Borrowers, End of 2020

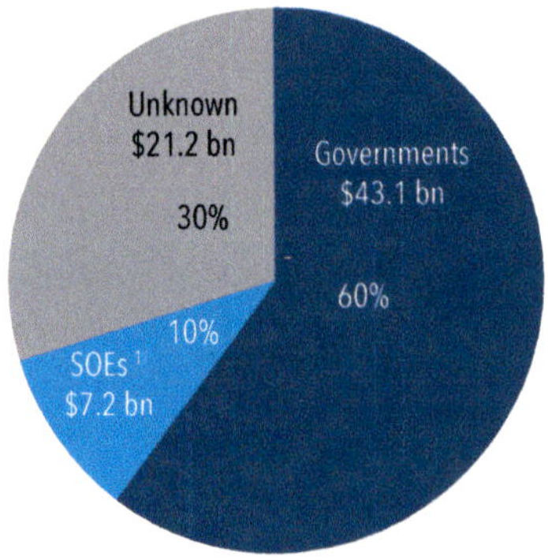

Source: IMF data set and country authorities.
Note: SOEs = state-owned enterprises.
[1] Includes state-owned enterprises deemed government liabilities, even though not explicitly guaranteed.

Figure 6.14. Sub-Saharan Africa's Public Debt to China: By Resources Intensity, End of 2020

1. US Dollars

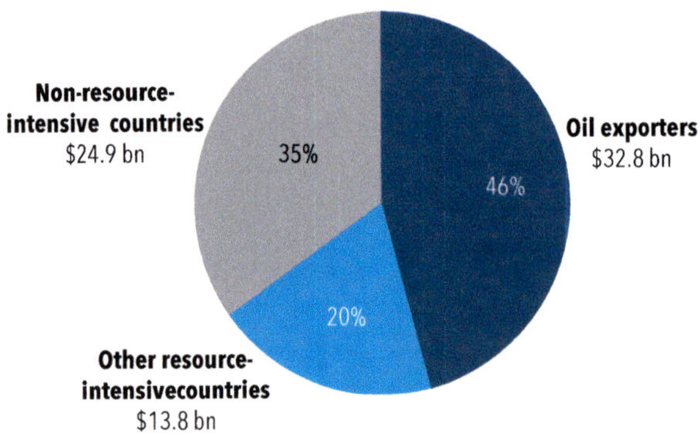

2. Percentage of Public Debt
(Simple average across countries)

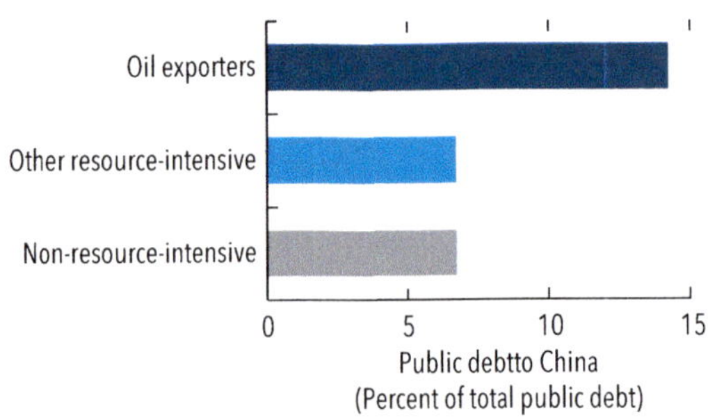

Sources: Country authorities; and IMF data set.

More than 40 percent of debt to China was owed by countries with high debt vulnerabilities, namely countries in or at high risk of debt distress (Figure 6.15). However, even for countries with high debt vulnerabilities, public debt to China represented less than 10 percent of total public debt. There are no clear patterns indicating whether more vulnerable countries have borrowed more from China than from other creditors. Looking at total public debt in 2010 and China's lending (which accelerated from 2010), there is also no clear indication that China's lending has been concentrated on the countries that already have high debt burdens (Figure 6.16). In addition, the increase in public-debt-to-GDP ratio (2010–20)

Figure 6.15. Sub-Saharan Africa's Public Debt to China: By Debt Rating, End of 2020

1. US Dollars

2. Percentage of External Public Debt
(Simple average across countries)

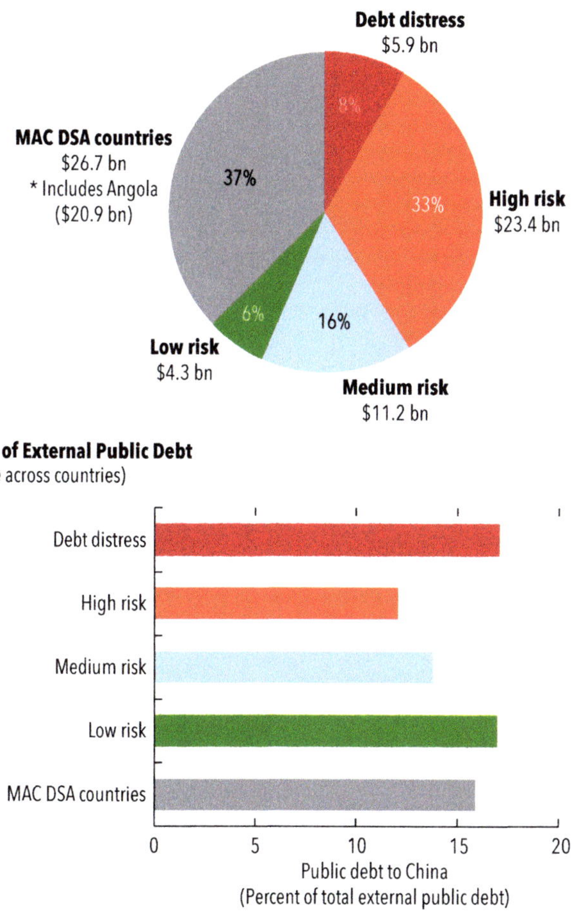

Sources: Country authorities; and IMF data set.
Note: Debt sustainability analysis ratings as of the end of 2020. MAC DSA = market-access countries debt sustainability analysis.

Figure 6.16. Sub-Saharan Africa's Public Debt in 2010 and Public Debt to China in 2020

The initial debt level is not correlated with Chinese lending

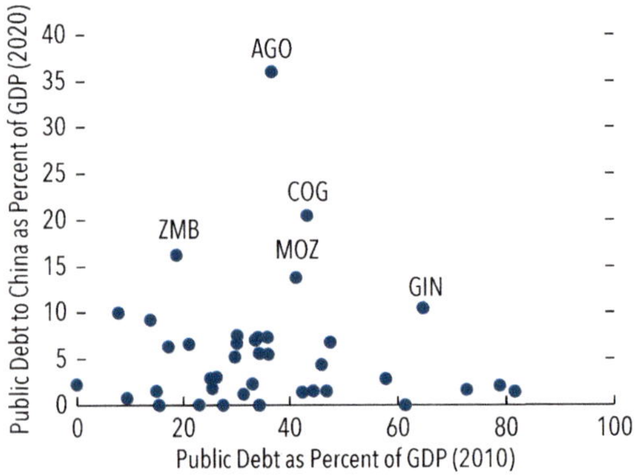

Source: IMF data set and country authorities.
Note: Figure uses International Organization for Standardization (ISO) country codes.

Figure 6.17. Sub-Saharan Africa's Public Debt, Change during 2010–20 and Public Debt to China in 2020

The correlation of debt increases and lending from China is weak.

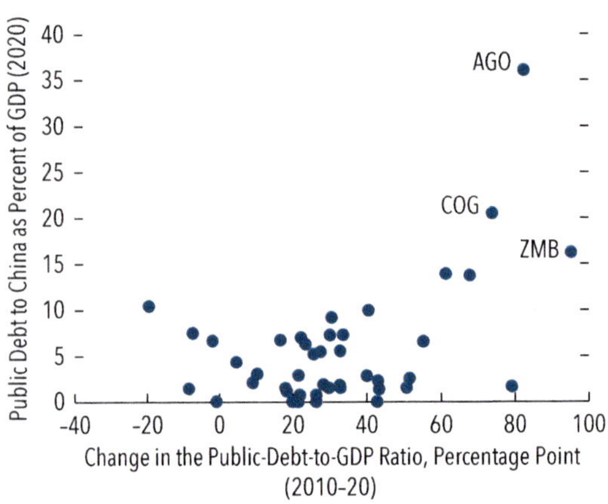

Source: IMF data set and country authorities.
Note: Figure uses International Organization for Standardization (ISO) country codes.

and debt to China as a ratio to GDP (2020) are compared (Figure 6.17).[14] Again, the figure shows there is no clear relationship between the two variables, consistent with the observation at the aggregate level noted previously (Figure 6.2) that

[14] This implicitly assumes that debt to China in 2010 was negligible in the absence of country-level data. The assumption is consistent with a pickup of Chinese lending after 2010 (Acker and Brautigam 2021; Horn, Reinhart and Trebesch 2021).

debt to China was not the main contributor to the recent debt-to-GDP ratio increase in sub-Saharan African countries.

Although information on concessionality of public debt to China was available for only 15 countries in this data set, concessionality appeared to be higher for: (1) countries in debt distress or at high risk of debt distress and (2) low-income countries, particularly for the lending from EXIM (Figure 6.18). The average concessionality of China's lending to sub-Saharan Africa was about 15 percent; EXIM provided more concessional lending than CDB.

Figure 6.18. Sub-Saharan Africa's Public Debt to China: Average Concessionality, End of 2020

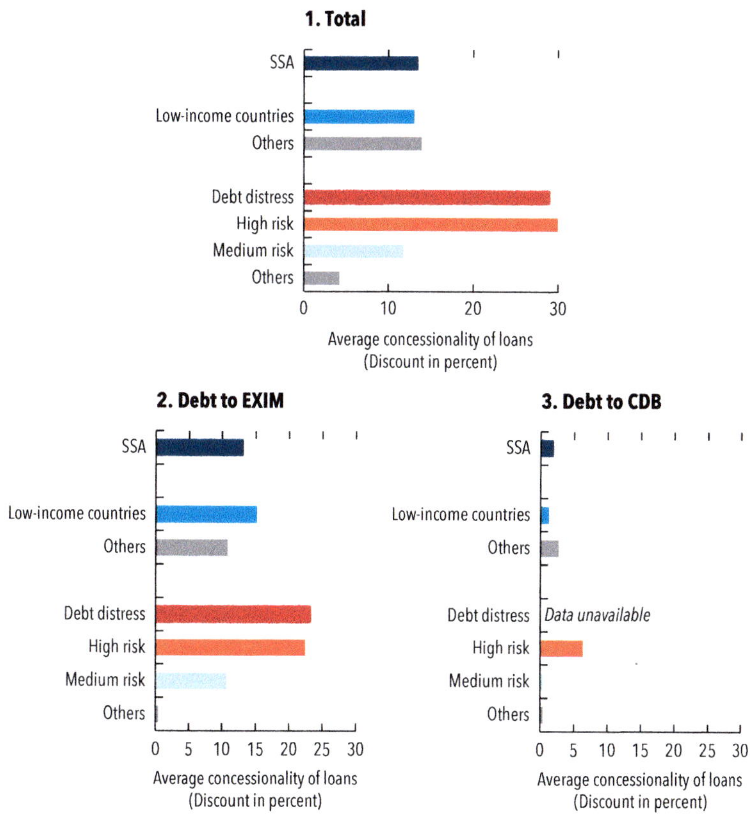

Sources: Country authorities; and IMF data set.
Note: Debt sustainability analysis ratings as of the end of 2020. SSA = Sub-Saharan Africa; CDB = China Development Bank; EXIM = Export-Import Bank of China.

CONCLUSION

This chapter has discussed different features of sub-Saharan African countries' public debt to China at the end of 2020. The raw input data have been self-reported by sub-Saharan African countries, but the final data set reflects the results of iterations between IMF staff and the authorities to ensure accuracy and consistency with the standard IMF–World Bank Debt Sustainability Framework debt definitions. The data set thereby fills a gap in the existing literature on this topic by providing a set of data on sub-Saharan Africa's debt to China that are consistent with the statistical concepts used in public debt sustainability analysis. It also complements other data sources, including the commitment-based data sets such as CLA and AidData that have no outstanding debt stock information, or the IDS, which has a slightly different coverage than the authors.

The stylized facts from this data set reveal that China accounts for a relatively small share of total public debt in sub-Saharan Africa but a significant share of the region's official bilateral debt. At the end of 2020, sub-Saharan Africa's outstanding public debt to China amounted to $71.5 billion, equivalent to 7.3 percent of its total public debt. Of this, official bilateral debt owed to China was $53 billion, which accounted for 57 percent of sub-Saharan Africa's total official bilateral debt. This, in part, reflects the decline of official development assistance from the traditional bilateral donors since 2010, particularly in proportion to sub-Saharan Africa's GDP. Given that the official bilateral debt is an important subject of negotiation in debt treatment, China has an important role in such negotiations. Meanwhile, domestic debt and non-Chinese external commercial debt accounted for 54.1 percent and 18.7 percent of total sub-Saharan Africa's PPG debt, respectively, far larger than official bilateral debt (including China) of 9.5 percent.

This data set also shows that China's share in official bilateral debt differs markedly across sub-Saharan African countries. The region's public debt to China is highly concentrated; five of the countries account for about two-thirds of the total. Resource-intensive countries held a dominant share of about 80 percent of PPG debt owed to China. China is susceptible to sub-Saharan Africa's public debt vulnerabilities, but no distinct pattern emerges to link such vulnerabilities with Chinese lending. Sub-Saharan African debt service to China broadly mirrored the patterns of the debt stock to China. The slight differences in patterns of concentration reflect the varying terms of debt, including with respect to maturity, as well as rescheduling.

This data set can provide the IMF with a basis for a deeper analysis of issues discussed in the literature.[15] Future work could include examining the association between public debt to China and macroeconomic performance in sub-Saharan Africa, for example, using Dollar (2016) as a starting point. A potential area for investigation is the relationship between sub-Saharan Africa's debt to China and trade or foreign direct investment from China. In addition, although this data set lacks information on collateralization and debt restructuring patterns, future work can seek to collect more information on these trends, perhaps referring to Acker and Brautigam (2021).

---

[15] Because the data set contains confidential country-level information, detailed data cannot be published.

ANNEX 6.1. COMPARISON WITH OTHER DATA SOURCES

The data on sub-Saharan Africa's public debt to China discussed in this chapter are relatively close to the World Bank IDS database (Annex Figure 6.1.1). Although they are not identical, their differences do not appear systemic.

The JHU CARI's CLA data set records new loan commitments (flow), not repayments or cancellations. The CLA is therefore not directly comparable with the data. Because commitments are larger than disbursements and the CLA does not capture repayments, the cumulative commitments during 2000–19 reported in the CLA exceed the debt stock reflected in the data set for most countries (Annex Figure 6.1.2). Overall, these cumulative commitments and the debt stock in the data are positively associated. For example, Angola has the highest cumulative commitments during 2000–19 in CLA and the highest debt stock to China in this data among sub-Saharan African countries.

William & Mary AidData also shows a positive association with these data, although the association appears to be weaker than that of CLA data (Annex Figure 6.1.3). As an example of the positive association, Angola has the highest cumulative commitments among sub-Saharan African countries during 2000–17 in AidData.

Annex Figure 6.1.1. Sub-Saharan African Countries: Public Debt to China by Country, 2020

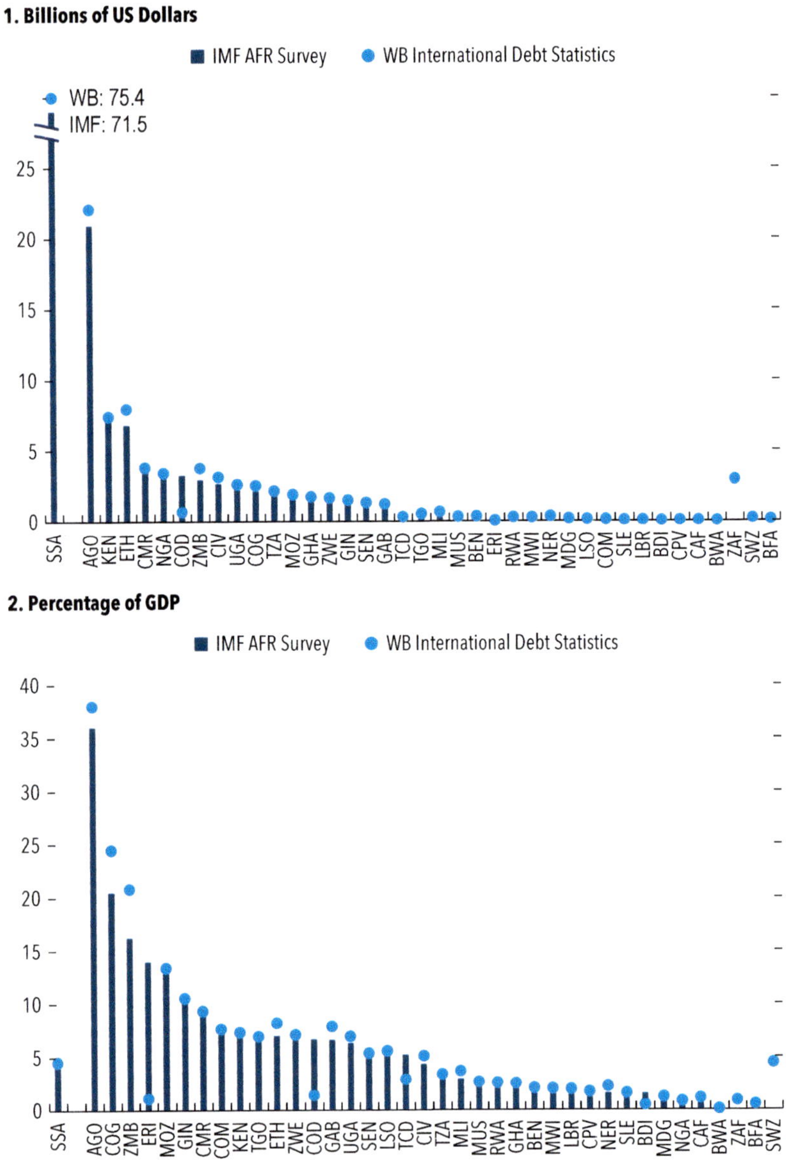

Sources: Country authorities; World Bank, International Debt Statistics; and IMF data set.
Note: Figure uses International Organization for Standardization (ISO) country codes. WB = World Bank, AFR = African Department.

Annex Figure 6.1.2. Sub-Saharan African Countries: Public Debt to China by Country, 2020

1. Billions of US Dollars

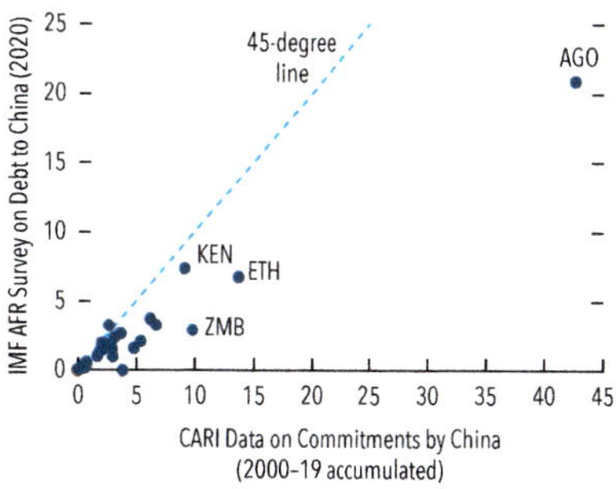

2. Percentage of GDP

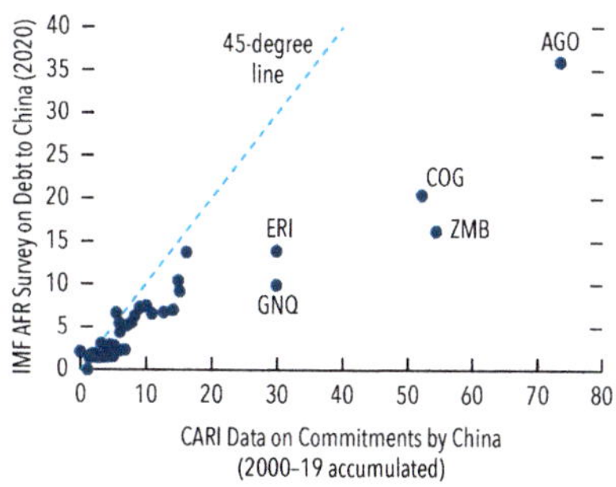

Sources: Country authorities; Johns Hopkins University China-Africa Research Initiative; and IMF data set.
Note: Figure uses International Organization for Standardization (ISO) country codes. AFR = Africa; CARI = China Africa Research Initiative.

Annex Figure 6.1.3. Sub-Saharan African Countries: Public Debt to China by Country, 2020

1. Billions of US Dollars

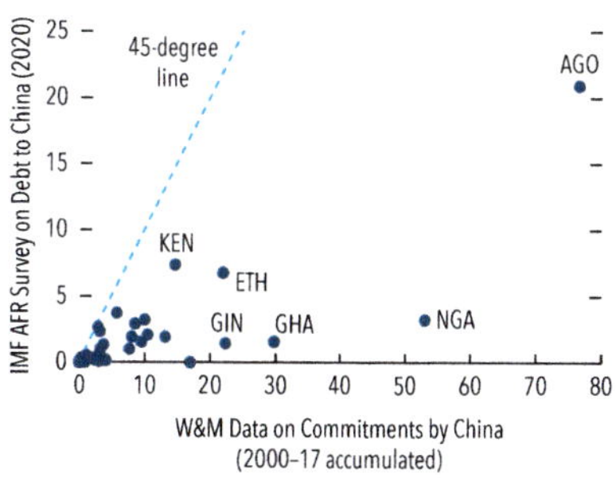

2. Percentage of GDP

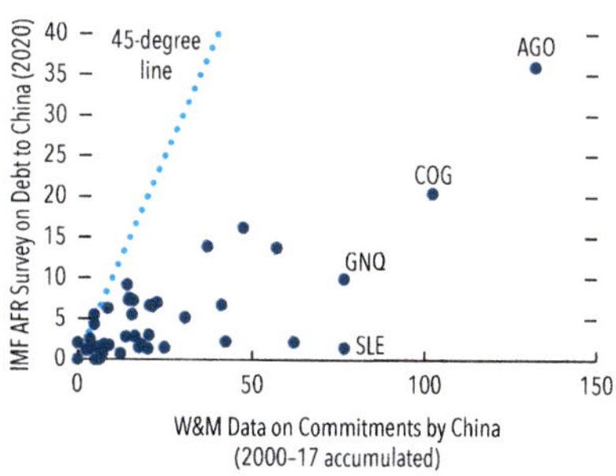

Sources: IMF data set and country authorities; and William & Mary AidData.
Note: William & Mary AidData is the sum of loans, export buyer's credit, and export seller's credit. Figure uses International Organization for Standardization (ISO) country codes. AFR = African Department; W&M Data = William & Mary AidData.

REFERENCES

Acker, K., and D. Brautigam. 2021. "Twenty Years of Data on China's Africa Lending." China Africa Research Initiative Briefing Paper, School of Advanced International Studies, Johns Hopkins University, Washington, DC. https://static1.squarespace.com/static/5652847de4b033f56d2bdc29/t/605cb1891cb0ff5747b12167/1616687497984/BP+4+-+Acker%2C+Brautigam+-+20+Years+of+Data+on+African+Lending.pdf.

Acker, K., D. Brautigam, and Y. Huang. 2020. "Debt Relief with Chinese Characteristics." China Africa Research Initiative Working Paper 2020/39, School of Advanced International Studies, Johns Hopkins University, Washington, DC. https://papers.ssrn.com/sol3/papers.cfm?abstract_id=3745021.

Brautigam, D., and Y. Huang. 2021. "What Is the Real Story of China's 'Hidden Debt'?" China–Africa Research Initiative Briefing Paper 6, School of Advanced International Studies, Johns

Hopkins University, Washington, DC. https://static1.squarespace.com/static/5652847de4b033f56d2bdc29/t/61774f9037cd225dc2cdf4d7/1635209104652/V5+%28FINAL%29+-10-25-+Briefing+Paper+6+-+Brautigam+and+Huang+-+AidData.pdf.
Brautigam, D., and J. Hwang. 2020. *China–Africa Loan Database Research Guidebook.* Baltimore: China–Africa Research Initiative, Johns Hopkins University
Custer, S., A. Dreher, T. B. Elston, A. Fuchs, S. Ghose, J. Lin, A. Malik, and others. 2021. *Tracking Chinese Development Finance: An Application of AidData's TUFF 2.0 Methodology.* Williamsburg, VA: AidData at William & Mary. https://www.aiddata.org/publications/aiddata-tuff-methodology-version-2-0.
Dollar, D. 2016. *China's Engagement with Africa: From Natural Resources to Human Resources.* Washington, DC: John L. Thornton China Center, Brookings Institution.
Horn, S., C. Reinhart, and C. Trebesch. 2021. "China's Overseas Lending." *Journal of International Economics* 133 (C): 1–32. https://www.sciencedirect.com/science/article/pii/S0022199621001197.
International Monetary Fund (IMF). 2018. *Guidance Note on the Bank-Fund Debt Sustainability Framework for Low Income Countries.* Washington, DC.
World Bank. 2020. *Debtor Reporting System (DRS): What It Measures.* Washington, DC.

CHAPTER 7

Fintech in China and Africa

Longmei Zhang, Yibin Mu, Tao Sun, and Amadou Sy

INTRODUCTION

The digital revolution and rapid technological advances are reshaping the payments and financial landscape globally. Fintech has developed with speed in emerging market economies, such as China, and in low-income countries in Africa, because the many millions of financially underserved people in these regions fuel enormous demand. In contrast, demand for fintech has been comparatively lower in advanced economies with well-developed financial services.

Despite similarities in the rapid adoption of fintech, China and African countries have followed their own distinct path of fintech development, which was to a significant extent driven by different initial conditions, such as levels of digital infrastructure, e-commerce, and business models. Although a selected group of countries in Africa has quickly become a leader in mobile payments, with clear gains for financial inclusion and payment efficiency, China has rapidly broadened the scope and depth of fintech from mobile payments to a much wider range of financial services.

In African countries, fintech services started with and continue to be dominated by mobile payments and remittances, which are mostly provided by telecommunication companies. This is mainly because internet and electricity access in the region remains limited and costly, but mobile payments are still possible using feature phones.[1] Hence, telecom companies are the prominent players to promote fintech. In China, fintech began with payments to facilitate e-commerce and social media platforms and soon expanded beyond payments to include lending, wealth management, insurance, and credit rating. The main fintech players are e-commerce giants and social networks, which have created a comprehensive fintech ecosystem with hundreds of millions of users. Today, fintech is integrated into people's daily lives, such as public transportation, health care, and education.

Comparing China and African countries illustrates significant potential for further fintech development in Africa. Despite its achievements so far, sub-Saharan Africa still has immense potential to expand the scope and depth of

[1] A feature phone is a type or class of mobile phone that retains the form factor of earlier generations of mobile telephones, with press-button-based inputs and a small non-touch display. Feature phones are sometimes called "dumb" phones, when compared with modern touchscreen smartphones.

digital financial services and develop e-commerce as in China. Mobile payments and remittances are now ubiquitous in African countries, but progress has been uneven, with countries such as Kenya, Nigeria, and South Africa attracting most of the investments in fintech start-ups. Digital lending is growing but remains at a very early stage, and further development could help reduce the high financing cost, in particular for SMEs, and facilitate poverty reduction and enhance growth.

China and African countries' experiences in fintech development are also useful for other emerging market economies and low-income countries, highlighting the potential for them to leapfrog their digital transformations.[2] Despite their differences, experiences in the two regions illustrate how countries can leverage technology and foster their own fintech development path based on the level of digital infrastructure and development stage. Fintech can help promote financial inclusion, improve payment efficiency, and spur financial innovation. Countries should also develop regulatory and legal standards to safeguard financial stability and protect consumers before fintech players become more dominant.

This chapter examines fintech development in China and Africa by answering the following questions: How has fintech emerged? What path have the two regions followed? How have regulatory and legal standards evolved? What are the lessons from China's experience for the future development of fintech in Africa?

FINTECH IN CHINA

Over the past two decades, China has risen to prominence as a global fintech front-runner. Fintech firms provide services including payments, microlending, wealth management, insurance, and credit ratings, as well as technology services for everyday life, such as public transportation, health care, and education. This success reflects a confluence of factors, including a large financially underserved population,[3] well-established digital infrastructure, and thriving use of e-commerce and social networking. China's experience also illustrates the power of new technologies to reduce costs and address information asymmetry,[4] the role of policy support to develop the digital economy, and the choice of a "light regulatory touch" early in fintech development. However, as the sector matured and a few large fintech players grew very large and established their own ecosystems, new concerns emerged for financial stability, fair market competition, data security, and privacy protection. To manage the associated risks, the Chinese

[2] Fintech development in India offers important and insightful lessons to developing countries but is beyond the scope of this chapter.

[3] In 2011, account ownership among adults was 64 percent in China, compared with more than 90 percent in Japan, Korea, and Germany. (World Development Indicator.)

[4] In traditional banking, loan origination can be expensive reflecting the cost of due diligence, that is, to verify the borrower's repayment capacity. In fintech, the credit risk assessment can be automated through machine learning models using borrower's digital footprints, such as payment history and e-commerce transaction records.

government's regulatory tightening since 2019 highlighted the critical need for setting regulatory parameters that balance innovations and risks.

Fintech Development

The origins of China's fintech industry can be traced back to mobile payments for nascent e-commerce firms to facilitate online transactions. And its subsequent wide-ranging path deviates from the experiences of fintech firms in other countries, which have frequently focused on one or a few core businesses with no integration across business lines.

China's fintech development began with third-party mobile payments, led by Alipay. In 2004, e-commerce was in its infancy, and consumers had little trust in online merchants. In response, Alibaba introduced Alipay, an escrow account in which clients pay Alibaba first, and the money is transferred to the merchant only after the customer confirms receipt of the purchase. The number of Alipay users has surged quickly, from 440,000 at the beginning of 2005 to more than one billion today. The application of Alipay has been expanded from Alibaba to general online shopping and offline shopping through QR codes. In 2019, for instance, mobile payments accounted for 66 percent of total transactions in China (23 percent for cash and 7 percent for cards) and 59 percent of total transaction value (16 percent for cash and 23 percent for cards) (Figure 7.1).[5] In general, mobile payments are mostly used for small transactions, whereas bank cards (including both debit and credit cards) are more commonly used for large transactions. The mobile payment space is highly concentrated, with the two leading players, Alipay and WeChat Pay, accounting for more than 90 percent of the market share.

With the popularity of mobile payment, fintech firms expanded into the microlending business. Taking advantage of the considerable number of existing users on their platforms, firms established virtual banking business units to lend to small online merchants, and later to consumers. Leveraging real-time data, the three leading virtual banks—MYbank of Ant Group, WeBank of Tencent Group, and XWBank of Xiaomi Group—provide loans to millions of small firms and consumers annually, more than 80 percent of which have no credit history. Virtual banks' loans are significantly smaller than those of traditional banks, shorter in duration, and mostly used for operational rather than long-term investments (Huang and others 2020). Hence, virtual bank lending has so far complemented traditional banking by reaching underserved customers. Despite the expansion, aggregate fintech lending remains minor compared with traditional banks, accounting for less than 0.2 percent of total banking assets in 2019.[6]

Fintech firms have also developed their credit rating businesses by harnessing big data. Ant Financial provides "Zhima credit scores" for Alipay users based on consumer payment data on the Alipay platform, filling a void left by a lack of

[5] 2019 PBC Survey.

[6] For more information, see https://www.leadleo.com/pdfcore/show?id=5f9b7d062d5b87c723f999d1.

Figure 7.1. Retail Payment Landscape in China

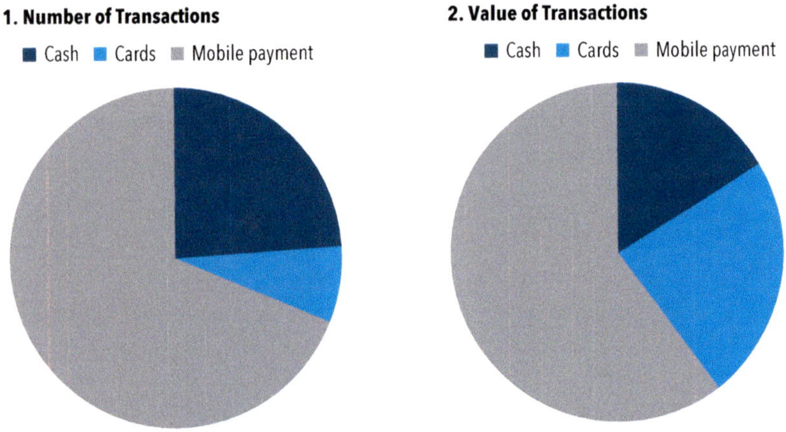

Source: 2019 People's Bank of China survey.

individual credit scoring in China. Users with higher "Zhima credit scores" can enjoy benefits such as deposit waivers when renting a bike, borrowing a book, or staying at a hotel. This rating information is also provided to traditional banks in the provision of joint consumer loans, which surged to RMB2 trillion ($300 billion) in 2019 (Caixin 2019).

After the lending business, fintech firms have further ventured into wealth management. In 2013, Ant Financial launched an online money market fund, Yu'e Bao, which taps into unused funds in Alipay accounts with an investment threshold of just RMB1 ($0.15). These funds are pooled and invested in money market funds and bank deposits. Customers can withdraw money almost immediately, track accrued interest daily, and use money in the account for payments through Alipay. Alipay's ease of use helped the platform to rapidly expand its user base and funds under management, and Yu'e Bao has become the world's largest money market fund in just a few years since its launch. By the end of 2017, the number of users swelled to 474 million (about 30 percent of the population) and funds under management rose to RMB1.6 trillion ($250 billion), 2.5 percent of total bank deposits. Since 2018, because of the tightened regulations, sector development stalled.

Fintech insurance has also grown rapidly, though it remains small compared with traditional insurance companies. Fintech giants have taken advantage of large existing users in the ecosystem to distribute products by traditional insurance companies. Some have launched their own insurance products. For example, in October 2018, Ant Financial launched "Xianghubao," and participants surged to 20 million within a few months, though its business discontinued in January 2022 because of its emerging risk and regulatory tightening. Insurance income also accounts for a small share of fintech revenue in general.

Peer-to-peer lending (P2P) experienced a boom-and-bust cycle along with regulatory changes. Separately from the large fintech companies, China

Figure 7.2. China: Number of Peer-to-Peer Lending Platforms

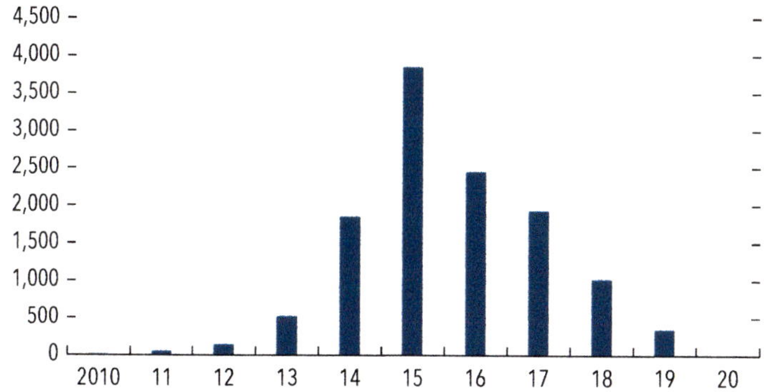

Source: Statista.

experiences a rapid growth of P2P platforms. P2P platforms, as opposed to credit intermediaries provided by virtual banks, are information intermediaries because they gather information, evaluate credit, facilitate information exchange, and match borrowers and lenders. The rise of these P2P firms reflected the increasing credit demand from small and micro enterprises and individuals, and by growth in the supply of funds from retail investors. In 2014, the return for retail investors was five times the bank deposit rate (Lee and Bao 2022). Total P2P transaction volume reached RMB2.06 trillion ($310 billion) by the end of 2016, equivalent to 12 percent of total bank loans extended in 2016 (People's Bank of China [PBC]). The maturity of these loans is short, averaging 5 to 8 months; the average rate of return was 10.5 percent. However, the number of P2P platforms has fallen significantly since 2017 amid regulatory tightening, and the sector had largely been eliminated by 2020 (Figure 7.2).

Drivers of Fintech

A large financially underserved population is a key prerequisite to the fintech boom. During its early days, limited investment channels and interest rate caps combined with banks' preference to lend to state-owned enterprises and large firms provided fertile ground for Chinese fintech firms to expand.

A well-established digital infrastructure is critical for the development of fintech and the digitalization of the economy. Investment in digital infrastructure has been especially important in enabling the growth of digital industries and the digital economy. Reflecting continued government investment, China's digital infrastructure is broadly comparable with that of advanced economies. For example, the connecting speed of fixed broadband is 39 megabits per second, downloading speed 12 megabits per second, higher than those in advanced economies, such as France. The population using smartphones in China reached 84 percent of the total population in 2020, making it one of the highest in the world (Boku 2021).

Light regulation at the early stage of fintech allowed room for innovation. When fintech first emerged in China, government regulation was very accommodating. The financial regulators have long taken supportive policies to promote digital technology and digital finance since the early 2000s. For example, Alipay received the official license of payment only a few years after the business started. In July 2015, 10 central governmental departments issued the "Guiding Opinions on Promoting the Sound Development of Internet Finance." These efforts facilitated the boom of new industries. The public's relatively low level of concern about data security and privacy protection, coupled with lax regulation, has aided China's rapid digital development.

Big data and new technology in artificial intelligence and cloud computing have given fintech firms the competitive advantage in financial services. Big data, including traditional (such as gender, age, location, profession, business) and proprietary information (or digital footprints), could help in credit risk assessment, in the absence of financial history and collateral assets (Holmström 2018). Digital technologies, such as cloud computing and artificial intelligence, enable Big Tech companies to process massive numbers of loan applications quickly and update risk assessment dynamically based on real-time data. For example, MYbank has developed the "310 lending model," which allows borrowers to complete loan applications online in three minutes, obtain approval in one second, and with zero human intervention. Furthermore, the big data and machine learning approach enables Big Tech lenders to restructure loans quickly at large volumes, which significantly reduces operating costs.

The horizontal and vertical integrations with the broader economy resulted in significant economies of scale, economies of scope, and network effects. Apart from the horizontal expansion from payment to other financial services, large fintech firms in China have developed an ecosystem encompassing people's daily lives, from e-commerce, logistics, and health care to entertainment. By harnessing digital technology to promote both horizontal and vertical integrations, large fintech firms achieved significant economies of scale and network effects (Figure 7.3).

Figure 7.3. Horizontal and Vertical Integrations

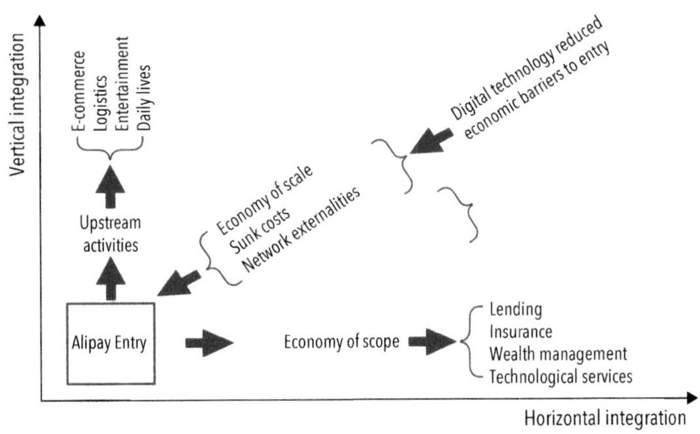

Source: Authors.

Implications of Fintech

Fintech has increased efficiency and promoted financial inclusion, but it has also led to challenges related to financial stability, market competition, data security, and privacy protection.

Large fintech firms have provided diverse financial services and created ecosystems by amassing large customer bases over commerce, gaming, and social network businesses. The application of new technologies has made transaction costs significantly lower and borrowing easier, particularly for small firms and low-income households, which were previously underserved.[7] The "contact-free feature" of the business process, from customer acquisition to loan underwriting and restructuring, made the digital lending model especially resilient during the COVID-19 pandemic.[8]

The rise of fintech is also reshaping the landscape of China's financial system. Traditional banks are losing ground in traditional retail payment services and are increasingly becoming the fintech payment provider's middle or back office. In addition, traditional banks outsource credit risk analysis to virtual banks in their joint loans. Alipay and WeChat Pay have become de facto part of payment infrastructure, with systemic importance because of their dominant market shares.

Successful integration and network effects have resulted in dominant market players. Horizontal and vertical integrations have propelled a few large fintech firms, such as Alipay and WeChat Pay, to critical mass, a point which the value of new users of participating in the platform exceeds the cost of participation (Moazed and Johnson 2016).[9] As a result, large fintech firms have set up both online payment platforms and offline payment markets with millions of merchants and billions of consumers in a two-sided market.[10] Fintech services have become an indispensable part of economic and social life underpinned by economies of scale and of scope and the associated network effects.

[7] Fintech has reduced costs, improved efficiency, and promoted financial inclusion. In the early 2000s when bank-based payment systems were dominant in China, to place an e-commerce order, consumers had to repeatedly key in personal information (bank name, card number, customer name, and branch at which the account was opened) and spend several minutes to complete transactions. To address this pain point, fintech leveraged almost zero-cost mobile app QR codes to serve merchants in online and offline commerce markets, allowing consumers and merchants to complete transactions within seconds (Sun and Rizaldy 2023). This fintech solution also greatly increased the number of users, including those who were previously financially underserved or excluded in China.

[8] Digital banks were able to remotely evaluate borrowers and sustain lending during the pandemic, facilitating the business continuity, sales growth, and financial inclusiveness of micro and small enterprises (Sun and others 2021).

[9] Because of high fixed costs, payment networks often need to sign up a minimum number of users (often referred to as the "critical mass") for the total value of the network to exceed its operating costs (CPSS 2012).

[10] A two-sided market is an intermediary (https://en.wikipedia.org/wiki/Intermediary) economic platform having two distinct user groups that provide each other with network benefits (Rochet and Tirole 2003).

Meanwhile, financial stability risks arose on multiple fronts:

- In the payment space, reflecting their market dominance in retail transactions, any operational failures of Alipay and WeChat Pay could disrupt payment services and compromise China's payment infrastructure. The closed-loop transactions between Alipay and WeChat Pay and hundreds of banks, in the early days, operated outside the purview of the central bank, posing operational and settlement risks.
- Online wealth management products, such as Yu'e Bao, have expanded at an unprecedented pace. The total assets of Yu'e Bao increased to a historical high of RMB1.69 trillion ($250 billion) in the second quarter of 2018. The growing size has posed challenges in fund management and entails significant liquidity risk.
- Virtual banks raised credit risks. By adopting a new way to analyze credit risk based on big data and AI, virtual banks have not experienced economic downturn and their resilience remains to be evaluated. In the meantime, the rapid lending was accompanied by surging leverage, raising concerns about credit risk. Some virtual banks follow a capital-light model through asset-backed securities and joint loans with commercial banks, resulting in liquidity and credit risks.
- Many Chinese P2P platforms themselves directly initiated loans to borrowers and raised funds from investors, that is, they did not focus on providing financial services. Instead, they were directly engaged in financing and lending activities (Huang 2018). Severe information asymmetry results in high uncertainty surrounding China's P2P lending industry (Shao and Bo 2022).
- The internal controls of some small payment firms are weak, posing risks of embezzlement and fraud. Limited clarity on the size and nature of financial transactions, combined with challenges regulating and supervising service providers and ensuring proper customer due diligence, has raised anti-money laundering and combating the financing of terrorism (AML/CFT) concerns.
- The close integration across different segments of financial services also exacerbates risk spillovers across the financial services chain, amplifying losses in the event of a downturn. For commercial banks, because they are increasingly relying on fintech firms for operational support, including credit risk analysis, questions exist related to insufficient internal monitoring of these services and potential spillover from the instability of fintech providers.
- Fintech firms have also led to duopoly market structure and privacy protection challenges. To grow their customer bases, fintech firms have expanded to achieve economies of scale and scope. These firms have created obstacles, such as data silos, which have resulted in market dominance. Meanwhile, some small fintech firms have led to unintentional and even intentional data

leaks to third parties. These leaks have raised public concerns about data security and privacy protection.

In sum, the initial rapid expansion in the light regulatory environment has raised risks to China's fintech system. The rapid expansion of fintech firms has, to some extent, reflected regulatory arbitrage, for example, the development of Yu'e Bao has benefited from the interest rate ceilings imposed on commercial bank deposits, which should not be allowed under the "same risk, same activity, same regulation" principle. Users, banks, and regulators have increasingly stressed the risks to market competition, data security, privacy protection, cybersecurity, and AML/CFT.

Regulatory Shift and Challenges

To address the rising risks in fintech firms, China's regulatory authorities tightened regulatory oversight, a major shift from the accommodative stance that prevailed during the early days of fintech development.

Financial regulation started with introducing a licensing requirement for payment services. In June 2010, the PBC mandated that nonbank online payment institutions obtain payment licenses to operate in China. Furthermore, banking and securities regulators required licenses on banking and securities services provided by fintech firms. In 2011, Alipay and WeChat Pay secured the payment license. In 2014, Alipay became a business unit of Ant Financial, which received approval from various regulators for additional financial services licenses.[11]

New fintech regulatory policies were then initiated. In a series of announcements from June 2015 to October 2016, authorities laid out a comprehensive overarching framework, defining who and how they will regulate each business activity within the "internet finance" industry, putting more checks and balances on fintech companies' business practices. These announcements focus on compliance, funding models, and consumer protection. In 2017, a new fintech committee was formed to coordinate between different financial regulators and industry participants.

AML/CFT requirements were introduced for fintech firms. In July 2016, the PBC required nonbank online payment institutions to apply AML/CFT preventive measures, including customer due diligence obligations, and establish a real name customer identification system.[12] In response, Alipay and WeChat Pay established account-opening requirements, for instance, by asking users to register

[11] Ant Financial secured banking and insurance licenses from the China Banking and Insurance Regulatory Commission (formerly known as CBRC and CIRC before they were merged in March 2018), fund and security licenses from the China Securities Regulatory Commission, and micro-credit licenses from local governments.

[12] The People's Bank of China (PBC) issued "Measures for the Administration of Online Payment Services by Nonbank Online Payment Institutions" in July 2016. Following these measures, Alipay needs to implement real-name verification, check the valid ID card as required, keep a copy or photocopy of the valid ID card, and establish a unique customer identification code.

information (name, identification card, address, and occupation) using mobile phone numbers and emails. These efforts, along with escrow accounts, have resulted in the establishment of a digital ID system, which made it easier to provide safer and faster payment services to Alipay users. More recently, China has strengthened the national AML/CFT frameworks, including through legal reform, to bring the online lending sector within the AML/CFT regime.[13] However, weaknesses persist in application of market entry controls and risk-based supervisory engagement.

Regulatory requirements were tightened to ensure customer funds security. Because Alipay and WeChat Pay have built a de facto small debit system in more than 200 banks in 2016, the PBC has required nonbank payment institutions since early 2017 to transfer 100 percent of customer funds from banks as reserves at the PBC by 2019.[14] Alipay and WeChat, like all other nonbank online payment institutions, transferred 100 percent of customer funds from banks to the reserve account at the PBC.[15] This policy has effectively protected the security of customer funds from any potential misuse and liquidity risks of the third-party payment providers.

A unified national clearing system was strengthened to better manage online payment services transactions initiated by nonbank online payment institutions. Nets Union Clearing Corporation (Nets Union) was found in March 2017 to settle transactions of nonbank online payment institutions. The Nets Union is responsible solely for the transaction information flow and platform operation, and the payment is settled by the PBC.[16] This has effectively broken the previous closed loop between fintech payment providers and banks and greatly improved information transparency and settlement security.

The regulatory tightening then spread to fintech wealth management. With the growing size of money market funds, regulators began to tighten policies,[17] including requiring purchase and redemption limits to prevent liquidity risks. Since May 2017, Yu'e Bao has implemented purchase quota restrictions four

---

[13] Administrative measures for anti-money laundering and combating the financing of terrorism of internet finance institutions.

[14] For instance, in January 2017, the PBC issued the "Notice on Matters Concerning the Implementation of the Centralized Depository of Customer Reserves of Nonbank Online Payment Institutions." In June 2018, the PBC issued the "Notice on Matters related to the Centralized Deposit of All Customer Reserve Funds of Nonbank Online Payment Institutions."

[15] The total balance of nonbank online payment institutions (including Alipay and WeChat Pay) in the PBC reached RMB1.99 trillion ($305 billion, equivalent to 6.1 percent of total reserves at the PBC) in September 2021.

[16] Nets Union was established by the Payment and Clearing Association of China and is subject to the supervision and regulation of the PBC. The company is 37 percent owned by seven subordinate entities of the PBC. Nets Union is responsible for operating China's Nonbank Payment Institutions Internet Payments and Clearing Platform, which is the nationwide platform for the settlement of transactions by nonbank online payment institutions involving bank accounts.

[17] For instance, the China Securities Regulatory Commission and the PBC promulgated "The Measures for the Supervision and Administration of Money Market Funds" in February 2016.

times to restrict new inflows into the fund. As a result, the total assets of Yu'e Bao declined from a historical high of RMB1.69 trillion ($250 billion) in the second quarter of 2018 to RMB780.8 billion ($120 billion) in the second quarter of 2021.[18] Moreover, the China Securities Regulatory Commission issued the "Interim Regulations on the Supervision of Important Money Market Funds (Draft for Comment)" in January 2022 to impose more strict and prudential regulatory requirements for significant money market funds.

Fintech lending practice has also been under scrutiny. To manage the potential risks arising from virtual banks' asset-backed security issuance and joint loans with commercial banks, regulators have taken tightening policies on both fronts. In 2020, regulators imposed a leverage ratio cap of 16 for microlenders, which resulted in a significant reduction in asset-backed security issuance. On joint loans with traditional banks, fintech lenders will need to contribute at least 30 percent of capital from January 2022, compared with the previous 1–2 percent. This would significantly raise the amount of capital fintech firms need for their lending business. In addition, the regulator has capped how much capital commercial banks can commit to online lending in cooperation with tech platforms. For online consumer loans, caps are also introduced to prevent overborrowing by young people and low-income households. Regulatory tightening greatly reduced the risks of regulatory arbitrage.

Recent regulatory changes call for large fintech firms to be regulated as financial holding companies. The PBC designated Ant Financial as one of the financial holding company pilots and drafted measures in 2019 requiring that financial holding companies hold levels of capital commensurate with the scale of their assets and risk level.[19] In September 2020, China's State Council approved regulations that would introduce licensing procedures for financial holding companies and, potentially, capital requirements. In addition to adhering to capital requirements for financial holding companies, Ant Financial has gradually transformed its business from directly providing financial services to aggregating and selling technological services to its users. Its name also changed from Ant Financial to Ant Group.[20]

A new paradigm of fintech financial regulation is now emerging. After years of exploration, a new regulatory framework is gradually being established. Financial businesses, in general, must be licensed to operate. For each line of business, fintech firms would be subject to the "same business, same rules" as traditional financial institutions. To prevent cross-sector risks, firewalls must be set up between various parts of the business, such as insurance and wealth management, and the direct link between nonbanks and banking information services must be

[18] Yu'e Bao's limits on purchases were released in April 2019.

[19] In July 2019, the PBC promulgated "Trial Measures for the Supervision and Administration of Financial Holding Companies (Draft for Solicitation of Comments)" to strengthen the regulation of financial holding companies.

[20] In mid-2020, Ant Financial changed its name to Ant Group, emphasizing that it is a tech, rather than a financial services company.

severed. Large fintech firms with multiple lines of financial services were restructured as financial holding companies (PBC 2018).

Regulation also strengthened antitrust and data protection. China's State Administration for Market Regulation has published draft rules (https://www.cnbc.com/2020/11/13/china-faces-the-challenge-of-keeping-big-tech-in-check.html) aimed at preventing monopolistic practices by internet platforms and launched a probe into Alibaba over such practices. In October 2021, China released a draft personal data protection law to regulate how companies process user data. To address potential data monopoly, the credit and consumer rating information of platform companies is separated from lending business, and the government is building a centralized credit registry that collects and provides information to all financial institutions.

The government has also taken a hawkish stance toward crypto assets. Domestic crypto-asset exchanges have been shut down because they were deemed speculative and did not provide benefits to the real economy. The PBC does not accept initial coin offerings or other types of crypto tokens as payment instruments. Trading Bitcoin in RMB is prohibited, whereas trading Bitcoin with foreign currencies is discouraged. In 2020, China further banned crypto-related mining activities, partly also to reflect the high energy intensity of these activities.

In sum, financial regulation must be tailored to the developmental stage of fintech and balance risks and benefits. In the early days, China's "light touch" regulatory approach worked well, allowing the industry to experiment and develop. Later, despite the introduction of the licensing framework in 2005, overall regulation has been relatively accommodative. However, the Chinese government's recent regulatory crackdown indicates a significant shift in policy stance amid rising concern about financial stability, unfair competition, and privacy infringement. China's experience demonstrates the importance of constantly evolving regulations as the fintech sectors grow in size and complexity. In the process, it is also critical to facilitate a smooth transition of fintech companies and minimize the broad economic and financial effect of regulatory changes. As China enhanced the development of its fintech regulatory framework, it also actively pursued the development of a central bank digital currency (CBDC) to promote financial inclusion, improve efficiency, and safeguard monetary sovereignty (Box 7.1).

Box 7.1. Central Bank Digital Currency in China

Rapid fintech development driven by the private sector provided a solid foundation for the introduction of a central bank digital currency. Since 2014, the People's Bank of China (PBC) has researched central bank digital currency, and many pilots have been tested since 2019. In the process, the central bank worked closely with the private sector in setting objectives and designing the overall framework.

Objectives. The main policy goals are to promote financial inclusion,[1] improve payment efficiency, strengthen payment system resilience,[2] ensure monetary sovereignty, and enhance competition (PBC 2021).

Design. The e-CNY is essentially the digital form of cash. It will substitute cash in M0 and bears no interest in the current phase. The PBC would provide issuance and redemption of the e-CNY to commercial banks and other payment providers in the first tier, who would then circulate and distribute the e-CNY to their end users in the second tier. Such a two-tier system could leverage the private sector's technology and resources, facilitate innovation through private sector competition, and help avoid potential competition between the e-CNY and bank deposits.

Public-private partnership. Intermediaries can also be selected as development partners. China, for instance, has collaborated with nine banks, including MYbank and WeBank (through which e-CNY can be accessed by Alipay and WeChat Pay users), to develop payment solutions and functions that have been added to and tested as part of the e-CNY ecosystem.

Business model. The PBC does not charge intermediaries or users for e-CNY transactions, and intermediaries cannot charge individual users in the e-CNY project. However, intermediaries have the choice of charging merchants. The PBC views this as a substantial incentive for firms to enter the market and thus keep the fees in check (Soderberg and others 2022).

Managed anonymity. e-CNY follows the principle of "anonymity for small value and traceability for high value" (PBC 2021).

The PBC is likely to adopt a "loosely coupled" design to allow for payments and transfers without a bank account. Furthermore, it has ruled out a distributed ledger technology as an option for e-CNY (mainly because of its limited capacity and scalability) and has mandated centralized management. To address concerns that the e-CNY could leak personal information, the PBC ensures that the e-CNY follows China's Personal Information Protection Law and offers hardware for low-value transactions without any information collected.

Potential cross-border payments. Although the e-CNY will mostly be used for domestic transactions initially, it could also be used for cross-border payments in the future. For instance, the PBC has launched the technical testing of cross-border payments in e-CNY in the mainland and Hong Kong and has explored the interconnectivity between the e-CNY system and Hong Kong's Faster Payment System to support the HKD settlement needs of local residents and merchants in Hong Kong.

Legal amendment. China is preparing for a general revision to the PBC Law (draft), which suggests that Chinese currency includes both physical and digital forms (e-CNY), confirming the legal tender status of e-CNY.

Pilots. Since 2019, the e-CNY pilots have been launched in 23 cities and in the Beijing Olympic Games and expanded into broader use cases, with commercial banks and internet companies promoting account opening and usage. The e-CNY app is now available for download to smartphones. As of August 31, 2022, the pilot areas in 15 provinces and municipalities had recorded 360 million e-CNY transactions with a total value of RMB100.04 billion, and over 5.6 million stores had accepted payment in e-CNY (PBC 2022). Pilot designs have so far aimed to promote financial inclusion (for example, serving visually impaired users), green behavior (for example, encouraging carbon reduction businesses), and digital transformation (for example, promoting targeted fiscal transfer). Further adoption of e-CNY requires payment service providers to leverage digital technology, target use cases, develop business models, and comply with legal and regulatory requirements (Sun and Rizaldy 2023).

e-CNY app for the Beijing 2022 Olympic Winter Games. The app was designed to ensure efficiency, inclusiveness, safety, and innovativeness. Foreign visitors could open an e-CNY wallet without a Chinese bank account, using their foreign or temporary Chinese mobile numbers, and pay by connecting to their VISA cards. The latter ensured a zero balance in the e-CNY app when visitors left China. The PBC continuously adds functions to the app.

Potential implications for monetary policy transmission. The effects of e-CNY on monetary policy transmission are expected to be relatively small. The strengthening of transmission channels through increased competition and wholesale funding relies on a significant substitution of bank deposits for central bank digital currency, which may not materialize (Das and others 2023). Furthermore, by increasing financial inclusion, the e-CNY may strengthen monetary policy transmission because previously excluded individuals who are nearly unaffected by monetary policy may now become involved. However, this effect depends on the share in overall savings and lending of the financially excluded population in China.

Financial stability implications. In theory, the e-CNY should help reduce the maintenance and transaction costs of cash while also addressing counterparty risk from private third-party payment providers, improving stability and safety. Some disintermediation and decentralization of financial services are possible, but such risks are mitigated by the two-tier system and the proposed upper limit on e-CNY balance and transaction amount. The e-CNY may also reduce the risk of bank runs during times of stress because its digital form could facilitate PBC liquidity provisions.

"Managed anonymity" should also help protect privacy while ensuring the implementation of regulations for anti-money laundering and combating the financing of terrorism.

[1] The proportion of adults in China with a bank account was 64 percent in 2011; see World Bank and People's Bank of China (2018).

[2] The most crucial policy goal is to make e-CNY function as a backup to existing digital payment solutions, according to the PBC.

FINTECH IN SUB-SAHARAN AFRICA

Technology is transforming the sub-Saharan African financial landscape. The rapid growth of mobile network operators after the privatization of the telecommunication sector in many sub-Saharan African countries has helped catalyze the use of new technology in the financial system over the past 30 years. The transformational effect of fintech has been strong in the region given its initial low level of bank penetration and underdeveloped financial market infrastructure, including a limited number of bank branches and automated teller machines (ATMs). Positive gains have included broader financial inclusion, greater financial sector efficiency, and lower transaction costs. Policymakers have an opportunity to scale up such gains while carefully considering the associated challenges.

Fintech Development in Sub-Saharan Africa

Experiences with Mobile Payments and Recent Trends and Developments

Unlike in China, mobile payments dominate fintech in sub-Saharan Africa, and this region is the most reliant on this technology worldwide. Sub-Saharan Africa is the second in the world in registered mobile money accounts per capita and leads all regions on mobile money agent outlets and on the volume and value of mobile money transactions (Figure 7.4).

Mobile payments have underpinned a radical change in the delivery of financial services in sub-Saharan Africa. Mobile money innovation, adoption, and usage have grown rapidly albeit at different paces. East Africa continues to lead the region in adoption and usage rates, although progress is also rapid in other regions. Although overall financial depth remains below global levels, mobile money is emerging as an engine of growth and technological enabler that fosters financial inclusion and economic development. Data from the Global Findex Database indicate that in 2021, about 55 percent of adults in sub-Saharan Africa had an account at a bank or regulated institution such as a credit union, microfinance institution, or a mobile money service provider compared with 76 percent globally and 71 percent in developing economies. Ten years earlier, account

Figure 7.4. Sub-Saharan Africa Mobile Money (December 2021)

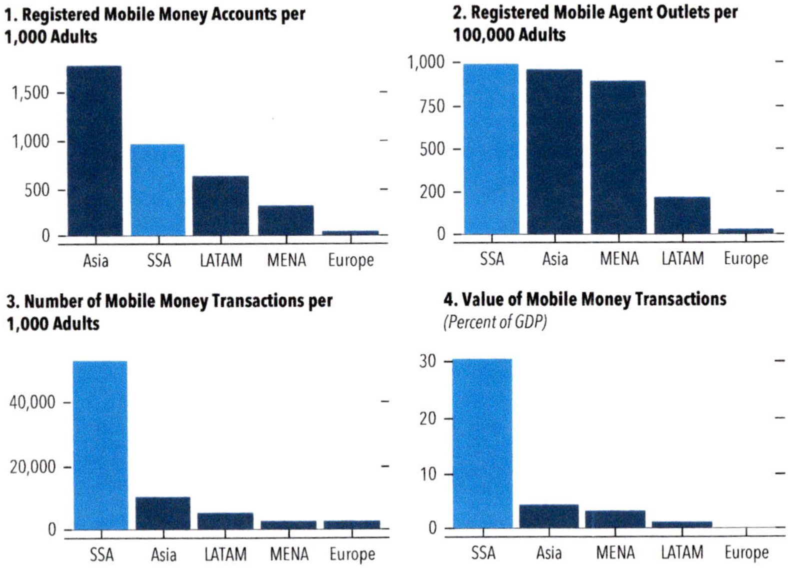

Source: IMF's Financial Access Survey.
Note: LATAM = Latin America and the Caribbean; MENA = Middle East and North Africa; SSA = Sub-Saharan Africa.

ownership was 23 percent in sub-Saharan Africa compared with 55 percent globally and 63 percent in developing economies.[21]

Mobile money accounts have now overtaken traditional bank accounts in sub-Saharan African economies and the region stands out for its use of mobile money. The growth in account ownership over the 2011–21 decade highlighted in the previous section can be attributed to the rapid development of mobile money, and in 2021, the share of adults having a mobile money account in sub-Saharan Africa (33 percent) was three times higher than the global average of 10 percent.

Fintech is accelerating financial inclusion in sub-Saharan Africa. The cost of transferring remittances to Africa is much higher compared with other regions (FSB 2023). Making it cheaper and easier to send money may seem like a modest innovation, but this innovation of mobile payments has had a profound effect on households' ability to transfer money, pay for bills, and deposit and borrow funds using mobile phones. The Global Findex Database shows that the use of mobile money accounts is no longer limited to person-to-person transactions (see Figure 7.5). In 2021, about 15 percent of adults in sub-Saharan Africa used their mobile money accounts to save (the same share that used a formal account at a bank or other financial institution) and seven percent of adults used the same technology

[21] For more information, see https://www.worldbank.org/en/publication/globalfindex.

Figure 7.5. Uses of Mobile Money in Sub-Saharan Africa

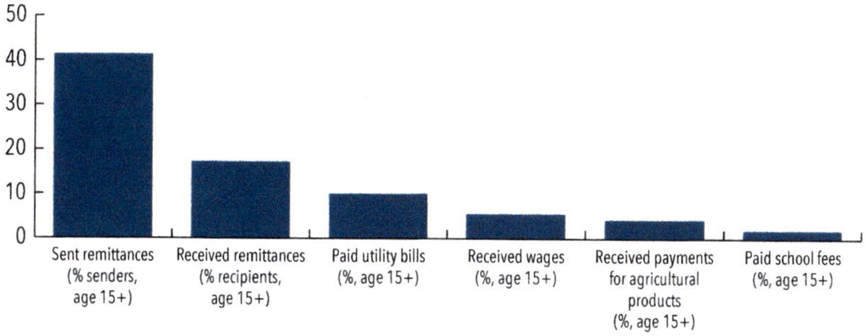

Source: Global Findex Database.

to borrow. Mobile payment services have also improved the ability to deal with shocks such as pandemics, allowing businesses to better coordinate their activities and connect to the broader financial system.

Mobile payments proved particularly useful in managing the COVID-19 pandemic in sub-Saharan Africa. Governments leveraged the technology to improve the effect of their social safety net programs when in-kind transfers (such as food vouchers or in cash payments) were difficult or impossible to deliver. This is the case in refugee camps, for instance, but also during the COVID-19 pandemic. The Novissi (which translates to "solidarity" in the Ewe language) cash transfer program in Togo, for instance, distributed more than $22 million through mobile payments to 600,000 citizens who lived in urban areas during COVID-19.[22] To target rural areas, the program used satellite imagery, mobile data, and artificial intelligence to estimate individual wealth, the idea being that poorer people use cell phones less often, receive more calls than they make, and have lower mobile money balances.

The COVID-19 pandemic and social restriction policies have spurred the use of digital payments in the developing countries and China. The Findex Global Database indicates that of the 18 percent of adults in developing economies who paid utility bills directly from an account, about one-third did so for the first time after the beginning of the COVID-19 pandemic. Even in China, which is much more advanced on the use of digital payments, the data show that of the 82 percent of adults that made a digital merchant payment in 2021, about 11 percent (over 100 million adults) made one for the first time during the pandemic. In India, over 80 million adults made their first digital merchant payments after the start of the pandemic.

Innovation by mobile network operators coupled with an enabling regulatory environment helped kick-start the rapid growth of mobile payments in

[22] The Novissi Program was financed by the World Bank under the West Africa Unique Identification for Regional Integration and Inclusion Program to support social protection delivery systems and data-driven methods for prioritizing the poorest in Togo.

sub-Saharan Africa (Sy and others, 2019). Studies point to the leading role played in Kenya by Safaricom and Vodafone, and the former UK Department for International Development in the development of mobile money services in sub-Saharan Africa with the launch of M-PESA in 2007 (M for mobile, pesa means *money* in Kiswahili). Importantly, the regulatory space given by the Central Bank of Kenya helped support the growth of this new technology (Figure 7.6).

There is a complementarity between mobile network operators, mobile service providers, and banks. Mobile money operators rely on banks to manage their "float," the balance of e-money, physical cash, or money in a bank account that a mobile agent can immediately access to meet customer demands to purchase or sell electronic money. For instance, in 2020, mobile network operator Orange collaborated with Bancassurance company NSIA to open a bank in Cote d'Ivoire (Orange Bank Africa) that targets micro savings and credit. Customers of mobile money company Wave in Senegal can use prepaid credit cards provided by United Bank of Africa Bank to debit their accounts.[23]

The extent of horizontal and vertical integrations seen in China has not yet taken place in sub-Saharan Africa. Mobile payments are being used for domestic transfers, such as paying utility bills, receiving wages, and payments for goods and services (Figure 7.5). Increasingly, this technology is also being used to pay taxes in several countries, such as Cameroon and Kenya. In Kenya, savings and loans services (M-SHWARI) are available to M-PESA, and the government has experimented with the issuance of a retail bond through mobile phones (M-AKIBA). However, the region is far from the level of horizontal and vertical expansions seen in China, and the ecosystem remains dominated by mobile network operators and banks. Nevertheless, fintech remains the sector that attracts most funding for

Figure 7.6. Funding Raised by Start-Ups in Africa, by Sector, 2022

Source: Africa: The Big Deal Start-Up Deals Database.
Note: AI = XX; IoT = XX.

[23] Source: Orange and NSIA launch Orange Bank Africa to provide greater access to financial services and improve the financial inclusion of people living in West Africa–Newsroom Orange Groupe (https://newsroom.orange.com/orange-and-nsia-launch-orange-bank-africa-to-provide-greater-access-to-financial-services-and-improve-the-financial-inclusion-of-people-living-in-west-africa).

start-up companies in Africa (mostly to Nigeria and South Africa) much more than other sectors such as e-commerce. The sector has raised $2.3 billion, or about 53 percent of the total in 2021 compared with 49 and 43 percent in 2020 and 2019, respectively (Figure 7.6).

- Countries are also at various levels of fintech development. Data from start-ups, for instance, show that Nigeria, South Africa, and Kenya dominate the sector in terms of the number of start-ups and funding raised (Disrupt Africa Team 2023). Start-up data show that payments and remittances account for 48.7 percent of the total, and lending and financing for 19.3 percent. Although "fintech is a truly pan-African phenomenon," only three countries account for more than three-fourths of total start-ups in 2023: Nigeria with 36 percent, South Africa with 23.3 percent, and Kenya with 16.9 percent. Ghana and Uganda are distant fourth and fifth with 5.8 percent and 4.8 percent, respectively.

Drivers of Fintech in Africa

The success of mobile payments in sub-Saharan Africa is driven by several factors:

First, unfulfilled demand for payment services is large, given low bank penetration and financial market infrastructure. For instance, the cost of opening branches remains prohibitively high and financial inclusion low and very few people have access to means of payment beyond cash such as checks or credit and debit cards. Providing cash and servicing ATMs remain a challenge outside urban areas.

Second, access to reliable and affordable electricity and internet services are still challenging in most countries. In this context, the privatization of state-owned telecommunication companies and the advent of privately owned mobile operators coupled with the relatively large penetration of affordable 2G mobile devices in the region provided a technological platform that can be used by mobile money agents. In fact, mobile money agents in sub-Saharan Africa outnumber ATMs and bank accounts because mobile network operators have developed strong profitable networks of agents to deliver mobile money services, including cash-out services. This strategy is now being adopted by some banks, such as in Nigeria, which are launching their agent-banking networks to offer digital financial services.

Challenges of Developing Fintech in Africa

The proliferation of mobile payment services indicates fintech's potential to broaden further financial inclusion in sub-Saharan Africa. Despite this success, challenges to the development of fintech beyond mobile payments persist. These include:

- Low electricity and internet connectivity: Although about 78 percent of urban populations have access to electricity in the region, the share is only

28 percent of the region's rural population (2019, World Bank data). A traditional cellular network is still not available in some rural areas. Greater investment is needed for more reliable and affordable electricity and internet connections, especially in the rural areas. The low provision of electricity and penetration of cellular and internet networks (World Bank data indicates that 50.6 and 36 percent of the population has access to electricity and internet, respectively, in sub-Saharan Africa compared with 100 percent and more than 73.5 percent, respectively, in China), particularly in rural Africa (https://www.worldbank.org/en/news/press-release/2019/10/17/achieving-broadband-access-for-all-in-africa-comes-with-a-100-billion-price-tag), suggest that fintech still has significant growth potential. Amid low fiscal revenues, governments will have to explore development finance options, including development banks and public-private partnerships.

- Slower mobile technology: Most mobile payments still rely on slow cellular networks (such as 2G and 3G), feature phones rather than smartphones, and SMS messaging, unlike in China where smartphones and internet access are ubiquitous. Cell towers are often far from the fiber cable network and cannot transmit a stronger and faster signal. Expanding the digital ecosystem and linking mobile payments to other services such as e-commerce will necessitate a higher provision of faster and reliable mobile and internet services, as well as the use of smartphones. It is interesting that Chinese phones are the most used in sub-Saharan Africa because manufacturers have tailored them to the region as they are of low cost but with practical functions. Affordable feature phones with basic features and multiple SIM card slots allow customers to arbitrage between different mobile network operators. Chinese company Transsion is reported to control 44.3 percent of the African market and another Chinese firm, Oppo, accounts for 8.3 percent.[24]
- Low literacy rates: With about 66 percent of the population (ages 15 and above) in sub-Saharan Africa able to read and write, the success of mobile payments has been driven by active communication campaigns, as in Mozambique, and adapted technology. For instance, networks of agents help improve financial literacy and applications with SMS and vocal messaging are relatively easy to use.
- Gender gap: Identifying the drivers of the gender gap in financial inclusion, including in mobile money accounts would help guide policymakers. Data from the Findex Global Database indicate that although the gender gap in account ownership has decreased globally from 2001 to 2021, the reverse has been observed in the sub-Saharan Africa where the gap rose to 12 percent from 5 percent over the decade, triple the global average and double that of other developing regions. However, this trend masks important country differences with countries such as South Africa, where women have

[24] For more information, see https://www.scmp.com/news/china/article/3138003/chinese-telecoms-firms-dial-africa-last-big-growth-market-phones.

more financial accounts than men, and others where the gap is above 20 percent. There are also encouraging developments recently, and during 2017–21, the growth in mobile money account ownership and usage was higher among women compared with the men in sub-Saharan Africa. Still, women in the region lag behind men in using their accounts for other services than person-to-person transactions such as saving, merchant payments, and utility payments.[25]

- Narrow scope: So far, the use of mobile money is still concentrated on person-to-person payments. Person-to-business, business-to-business, and government-to-business payments are rarely transferred through mobile money. For instance, governments can benefit from the use of mobile money as a tool for tax collection. Digital payments of tax can also have benefits in helping reduce the perception of corruption (Ouedraogo and Sy 2022).
- Operational risks: The growth of mobile payments and of other types of fintech has put to the fore the existence of associated risks such as fraud and more generally of cybercrime. For instance, mobile money companies can be vulnerable to data breaches because of improperly encrypted communications.
- Identification systems: Identification systems are required for AML/CFT reasons in order to open mobile money accounts. The region is also relying on the deployment of mobile technology to establish or improve national identification systems. Countries that have introduced such systems, such as India and Peru, where they cover 99 percent of the adult population, have found them to offer an affordable tool to provide benefits in areas such as financial inclusion, social protection, migration, and coping with natural disasters (World Bank 2017). Skeptics, however, point to privacy concerns and subsequent uses beyond their original purposes.
- Taxation: In sub-Saharan Africa, taxes on mobile transactions and on the telecom sector have been proliferating in recent years because policymakers are attempting to increase domestic revenue mobilization and because the sector is profitable and growing (Gupta and others, 2017). These include customs duties on capital equipment and handsets, diverse regulatory fees, high corporate income tax, and value-added tax rates, or telephone call excises. The increased fiscal revenues need to be weighed against the costs of constraining the growth of the fintech sector and the associated financial inclusion benefits.
- Regulation: Because sub-Saharan Africa is dominated by small value payments, proportionality—the balancing of risks and benefits against costs of regulation and supervision—is important and regulators can focus on specific

[25] For more information, see Majorie Chalwe-Mulenga and Gerhard Coetzee (2021), https://www.cgap.org/blog/findex-2021-insights-boosting-financial-inclusion-in-africa.

challenges such as price and financial stability, consumer protection frameworks, cyber-risk, agent transparency, increasing financial literacy, and improving financial integrity. In AML/CFT, efforts are needed to encourage proper application of preventive measures (for example, customer due diligence).

Central Bank Digital Currencies in Africa

African countries such as in Ghana, Nigeria, and South Africa are increasingly paying attention to CBDCs.[26]

Nigeria's eNaira

The Central Bank of Nigeria officially launched the eNaira on October 25, 2021. The eNaira, just like cash, is a liability of the central bank. It is a digital form of the Nigerian national currency, the Naira, to which it is pegged at parity. It is stored in digital wallets and can be used for payment transactions and transferred digitally to other eNaira wallets.

The expected benefits of the eNaira, according to the central bank, include (1) broader financial inclusion, (2) the facilitation of remittances at reduced cost, and (3) increased formalization of the Nigerian economy.[27]

The retail wallet downloads initially surged for a few weeks before tapering off. As of the end of November 2021, the total number of retail eNaira wallets amounted to about 860,000, equivalent to 0.8 percent of Nigeria's active bank accounts. Merchant wallet downloads reached about 100,000 at the end of June, equivalent to about one-eleventh of the number of merchants with point-of-sale terminals. However, most wallets appear to remain inactive except for a limited window of weeks of surging activity. The average value of an eNaira transaction was 923 million naira per week—0.0018 percent of the average amount of M3 as of the end of November 2021 (Ree 2023).

Ghana's e-Cedi[28]

In August 2021, Ghana signed an agreement with its chosen technology partner, G+D, for its pilot project, which was expected to conclude at the end of 2021. Its statement announced that this forms part of the "Digital Ghana Agenda," seeking to digitize government services in the country. The e-Cedi forms part of an agenda to reduce the use of physical cash while "ensuring a secure and robust payment infrastructure."

Ghana's pilot study will aim to consider user experiences, security, legal aspects, and effects on monetary policy and existing payment systems. Another

---

[26] A forthcoming IMF paper will focus on central bank digital currency and digital payments in Africa.

[27] For more information, see J. Ree (2021), https://www.imf.org/en/News/Articles/2021/11/15/na111621-five-observations-on-nigerias-central-bank-digital-currency.

[28] For more information, see https://www.bog.gov.gh/wp-content/uploads/2021/08/CBDC-Joint-Press-Release-BoG-GD-3.pdf.

priority is likely to be financial inclusion, within Ghana's previously stated aim of an "ambitious infrastructure development program for the ICT Sector," with Ghana's Ministry of Communications having pledged back in 2017 to develop "a national broadband infrastructure and total connectivity for the unserved and underserved."

The pilot has been divided into three phases: "design, implementation, and pilot." The pilot program will test e-Cedi using diverse social and demographic groups while using multiple vehicles including mobile apps and smart cards.

South Africa

South Africa does not have near-term plans to launch a CBDC, and it started its feasibility study in May 2021, seeking "to investigate if it would be feasible, appropriate, and desirable for the South African Reserve Bank to issue a CBDC to be used for retail purposes." Findings will help determine "whether to pursue the issuance of a South African CBDC." Even if the study suggests that CBDC may be "feasible and/or desirable," it does "not necessarily imply that it will be pursued."

In addition, the South African Reserve Bank is participating in "Project Dunbar," an initiative sponsored by Bank for International Settlements Innovation Hub, together with the Reserve Bank of Australia, Bank Negara Malaysia, and the Monetary Authority of Singapore. This initiative is testing the use of CBDCs for cross-border payments using a common platform. This is supposed to eliminate the need for intermediaries and reduce the time and cost of transactions.

CONCLUSION

By drawing out lessons from the experiences of fintech development in Africa and China, this chapter synthesizes lessons for countries when they consider promoting fintech development.

Fintech firms can stimulate the supply of new payment services and functionalities and create business opportunities, but they can also create new sources of risks, such as financial and operational risks. The development of fintech in Africa and China benefited from a combination of factors: harnessing various digital technologies, targeting clear use cases, developing sustainable business models, and complying with regulatory and legal requirements. The development of fintech in Africa and China has also resulted in new challenges, such as liquidity and credit risks, data security and privacy protection, and data silos and market dominance.

Fintech firms should meet the requirements of legal and regulatory policies on licensing, management of customer funds, and AML/CFT and data security. Innovations in these three areas should work together to provide room for movement along the indifference curve and payment technology frontier to the reach risk–cost efficiency frontier (Figure 7.7).

Figure 7.7. Risks, Costs, and Efficiency of Fintech Development

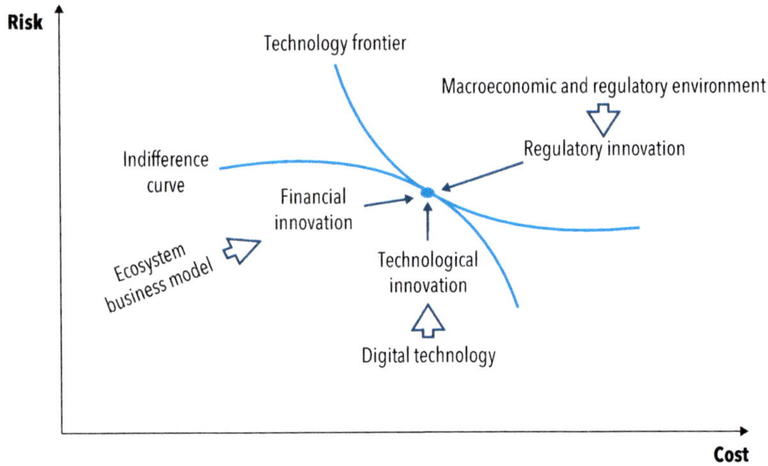

Source: Authors, based on Berger, Hancock, and Marquardt (1996).
Note: The axes measure risks and costs of fintech development: the vertical axis measures a weighted sum of risks, and the horizontal axis measures a weighted sum of costs borne by all the parties. The convex shape of risks and costs reflects the usual assumption of diminishing marginal returns–as risks get lower and lower (moving toward the horizontal axis), the marginal costs of further reductions in risks increase.

Country authorities in Africa and China, and more broadly in other regions, could work with fintech firms to promote technological, financial, and regulatory innovations, as well as manage risk and cost. Under this framework, improvements in digital technology can help move the payment technology frontier for processing payments, reducing costs, and speeding settlement to reduce risks. Financial innovation can help evaluate credit and liquidity risks and reduce costs. Regulatory policies can diminish risks and costs and ensure long-run efficiency by preventing crises.

ANNEX 7.1.

EMPIRICAL EVIDENCE FROM MOBILE MONEY USAGE IN AFRICA: MOBILE MONEY CAN GENERATE FINANCIAL RESILIENCE

A growing body of research is emerging with a consistent finding: households can better respond to unforeseen difficulties when they have access to mobile money. When an unexpected negative event—such as a flood or a child falling ill—occurs, households with mobile money can rely on the easy and affordable transfer of money from family and friends, even if they are living far away.

In Kenya, a study (Suri and Jack 2016) that uses a difference-in-difference technique has shown that the effect of mobile money on a household's resilience can be sizable. Households that had access to M-PESA (Kenya's mobile money platform) during a negative event—such as unexpected extreme weather conditions or illness in the family—were better able to respond and did not have to reduce their spending on food and related goods in response to the event. This is because mobile money helps risk-sharing among the community or family irrespective of location, strengthening these informal insurance networks.

In related work (https://www.pnas.org/content/109/26/10257) that also uses a difference-in-difference methodology (Suri, Jack, and Stoker 2012), researchers looked at the effects of a health shock and found households that used M-PESA were able to spend more on health-related expenses while also keeping up with other household payments. Households that did not use M-PESA financed their health-related expenses by cutting down on nonfood expenses, including withdrawing their children from school. Similar results have been found in other contexts using randomized control trials in Mozambique (Batista and Vicente 2021) and Uganda (Wieser and others 2019), where difference-in-difference and instrumental variable estimation strategies were used, respectively.

Mobile Money Can Facilitate Higher Savings for Households

Mobile money can also be helpful for financial resilience because it facilitates saving. In Kenya, researchers used instrumental variables to find (https://blogs.worldbank.org/en/impactevaluations/does-mobile-money-mobilize-savings-yes-guest-post-alev-gurbuz) that mobile money usage led households to save more. Households with mobile money accounts were 16–22 percent more likely to save and their average household savings increased by 15–21 percent, the equivalent of $2.7 to $3.7 per month (Gurbuz 2017).

Mobile Money Facilitates Transparency and Formalization

Mobile money electronically records all transactions, which improves the security of payments as well as their transparency, the consequences of which could be far-reaching on the economy. Greater transparency of earnings, transactions, and remittances could greatly improve tax collection. A mature mobile money system could also foster formalization of the economy (https://voxeu.org/article/economics-mobile-money), integrating informal sector users into formal banking and insurance, and allowing for stronger links to the government through social protection schemes, tax collection, and other government programs (Aron and Muellbauer 2019).

In the Long Term, Mobile Money Can Affect Occupation Decisions

Mobile money and the ability to receive money easily and safely from social networks at a distance have been found to change the way that individuals within households make decisions around their occupation. In Kenya, researchers (Suri and Jack 2016) used a difference-in-difference methodology to examine the long-run effects of M-PESA usage and found that higher access to mobile money changed occupation choices, especially among women. The study estimated that approximately 185,000 women moved from agriculture to small-scale retail thanks to access to M-PESA.

Similarly, access to mobile money led to a shift from farm-based work to self-employment in Uganda (Wieser and others 2019) and migration from rural to urban areas where the income is higher in Mozambique (Batista and Vicente 2018). The latter was because mobile money increased individuals' trust that they could easily and safely remit money to their families in the rural areas.

Long-Term Effects on Poverty and Women

Research from Kenya (Suri and Jack 2016) found that access to mobile money increased per capita household consumption and savings and therefore reduced the rate of poverty. This increased consumption translated to a movement of 196,000 households out of extreme poverty—equivalent to 2 percent of all households in Kenya. Long-term effects are examined in this study by running a follow-up survey in 2014 for households that saw relatively large increases in agent access between 2008 and 2010. The effects were largest in female-headed households, which highlight how the effect can be amplified when technology is given to female household leaders. The researchers posit that mobile money could give women in male-headed households, who are also usually secondary income earners, more financial independence. Agent density—the number of agents operating in a specific area—played a key role. Increased agent density was linked to 3 percent of women in both female- and male-headed households taking up business or retail occupations over farming.

REFERENCES

Aron, J., and J. Muellbauer. 2019. *The Economics of Mobile Money: Harnessing the Transformative Power of Technology to Benefit the Global Poor.* Oxford: Center for the Study of African Economics.

Batista, C., and P. C. Vicente. 2018. "Is Mobile Money Changing Rural Africa? Evidence from a Field Experiment." NOVAFRICA Working Papers 1805.

Berger, A. N., D. Hancock, and J. C. Marquardt. 1996. "A Framework for Analyzing Efficiency, Risks, Costs, and Innovations in the Payments System." *Journal of Money, Credit and Banking* 28 (4): 696–732.

Boku. 2021. "Mobile Wallets Report 2021." https://boku.mobilewallet.report.

Caixin, P. 2019. https://weekly.caixin.com/2019-10-25/101475419.html.

Committee on Payment and Settlement Systems (CPSS). 2012. "Innovations in Retail Payments. Report of the Working Group on Innovations in Retail Payments. Bank for International Settlements." Basel.

Das, M., F. Nakamura, J. Otten, G. Soderberg, J. Sole, and B. Tan. 2023. "Implications of CBDCs for Monetary Policy Transmission." IMF Fintech Notes 2023/009, International Monetary Fund, Washington, DC.

Disrupt Africa Team. 2023. *Finnovating for Africa: Reimagining African Financial Services Landscape.* Nairobi: Disrupt Africa.

Financial Stability Board (FSB). 2023. *G20 Roadmap for Enhancing Cross-border Payments Consolidated Progress Report for 2023.* Basel.

Gupta, S., M. Keen, A. Shah, and G. Verdier, eds. 2017. *Digital Revolutions in Public Finance.* Washington, DC: International Monetary Fund.

Gurbuz, A. 2017. *Mobile Money and Savings in Rural Kenya.* Alipay. https://finance.sina.cn/usstock/hlwgs/2009-07-13/tech-icczmvun8328349.d.html?fromtech=1&from=wap.

Holmström, B. 2018. Keynote speech at Toulouse School of Economics, October 10, Toulouse, France.

Huang, R. H. 2018. "Online P2P Lending and Regulatory Responses in China: Opportunities and Challenges." *European Business Organization Law Review* 19 (1): 63–92.

Huang, Y., L. Zhang, Z. Li, H. Qiu, T. Sun, and X. Wang. 2020. "Fintech Credit Risk Assessment for SMEs: Evidence from China." IMF Working Paper 20/193, International Monetary Fund, Washington, DC.

Lee, J., and Y. Bao. 2022. *The Rise, Fall and Future of P2P Lending Platforms in China: The Role of Policy, Law, and Enforcement.* http://dx.doi.org/10.2139/ssrn.4300276.

Moazed, A., and N. Johnson. 2016. *Modern Monopolies: What It Takes to Dominate the 21st Century Economy.* New York: Macmillan.

Ouedraogo R., and A. N. Sy. 2022. "Digitalization, Corruption, and Trust in Tax Officials in Africa." In *Good Governance in Sub-Saharan Africa: Opportunities and Lessons*, edited by IMF, M. Neuwiak, A. Segura-Ubiergo, and A. Wane. Washington, DC: IMF. https://doi.org/10.5089/9781513584058.071.

People's Bank of China (PBC). 2018. *Financial Stability Report.* Beijing: China Financial Publishing House.

People's Bank of China (PBC). 2021. "Progress and Research Development of e-CNY in China." http://www.pbc.gov.cn/en/3688110/3688172/4157443/4293696/2021071614584691871.pdf.

People's Bank of China (PBC). 2022. "Pressing Ahead with the Pilot Program of E-CNY R&D." http://www.pbc.gov.cn/en/3688006/4671762/4688130/index.html.

Ree, J. 2023. "Nigeria's eNaira, One Year After." IMF Working Paper 23/104, International Monetary Fund, Washington, DC.

Rochet, J., and J. Tirole. 2003. "Platform Competition in Two-Sided Markets." *Journal of the European Economic Association* 1 (4): 990–1029. https://doi.org/10.1162/154247603322493212.

Shao, S., and H. Bo. 2022. "Behavioural Aspects of China's P2P Lending." *European Journal of Finance* 28 (1): 30–45.

Soderberg, G., M. Bechara, W. Bossu, N. X. Che, S. Davidovic, J. Kiff, I. Lukonga, and others. 2022. "CBDC Behind the Scenes: Emerging Trends, Insights, and Policy Lessons." IMF Fintech Note 2022/004, Washington, DC. https://www.imf.org/en/Publications/fintech-notes/Issues/2022/02/07/Behind-the-Scenes-of-Central-Bank-Digital-Currency-512174.

Sun, T., A. Feng, Y. Wang, and C. Chang. 2021. "Digital Banking Support to Small Businesses amid COVID-19: Evidence from China." IMF Global Financial Stability Note 2021/02, International Monetary Fund, Washington, DC.

Sun, T., and R. Rizaldy. 2023. "Some Lessons from Asian E-Money Schemes for the Adoption of Central Bank Digital Currency." IMF Working Paper WP/23/123, International Monetary Fund, Washington, DC.

Suri, T., and W. Jack. 2016. "The Long-Run Poverty and Gender Impacts of Mobile Money." *Science* 354 (6317): 1288–92. https://doi.org/10.1126/science.aah5309.

Suri, T., W. Jack, and T. M. Stoker. 2012. "Documenting the Birth of a Financial Economy." *Proceedings of the National Academy of Sciences* 109 (26): 10257–62.

Sy, A., R. Maino, A. Massara, H. Perez-Saiz, and P. Sharma. 2019. *FinTech in Sub-Saharan African Countries: A Game Changer?* Washington, DC: IMF.

Wieser, C., M. Bruhn, J. Kinzinger, C. Ruckteschler, and S. Heitmann. 2019. "The Impact of Mobile Money on Poor Rural Households: Experimental Evidence from Uganda." World Bank Policy Research Working Paper 8913, World Bank, Washington, DC.

World Bank. 2017. *The State of Identification Systems in Africa*. Washington, DC.

World Bank. 2018. "Toward Universal Financial Inclusion in China: Models, Challenges, and Global Lessons." Washington, DC.

CHAPTER 8

Strengthening Policy Frameworks and Capacity: International Experience and Toolboxes

Alfred Schipke and Ling Hui Tang

INTRODUCTION

Several global economic shocks have increased vulnerabilities, leaving countries with high debt levels and high gross financing needs. Some nations have already undertaken debt restructurings. As of September 2024, about 50 percent of the 68 low-income countries (LICs) globally were classified as at high risk of debt distress or in debt distress, according to the IMF–World Bank Debt Sustainability Framework for Low-Income Countries. Given that 18 of those LICs are in sub-Saharan Africa, these challenges are significant for the economic relationship between Africa and China (see also Chapter 6). At the same time, these issues underscore the importance of strengthening policy frameworks and fostering capacity development. President Xi Jinping had already emphasized this at the second Belt and Road Forum in April 2019, noting that an overarching framework requires high project quality, fiscal sustainability, governance standards, open procurement, and private sector participation.[1]

The IMF has developed several toolkits that are useful for countries aiming to strengthen policy frameworks to maximize the benefits of investments and financing, while minimizing risks. The following section provides an overview of relevant frameworks. Global shocks (for example, sharp and prolonged movements in commodity prices or pandemics) can adversely affect the debt sustainability of LICs. Also, because investment decisions are made about an uncertain future, they can lead to debt overhangs. Hence, it is important to

This chapter benefited from inputs and comments from the IMF's Strategy and Policy Review Department (SPR). Particular thanks go to Guillaume Chabert and Mark Flanagan. It also reflects inputs and helpful comments from Debra Adams, Virginia Alonso, Cigdem Aslan, Dora Benedek, Hamid Davoodi, Dan Devlin, Michael Hardy, Robert Kokoli, Waikei Raphael Lam, Anamaria Maftei, Mario Mansour, Tewodaj Mogues, Clement Ncuti, Ian Parry, Graham Prentice, Fazeer Rahim, Michelle Stone from the IMF Fiscal Affairs Department as well as Hui He from the Institute for Capacity Development.

[1] Speech at the Belt and Road Forum for International Cooperation in April 2019.

have frameworks in place that consider such adverse outcomes and, if necessary, allow for orderly and speedy resolutions. Here, good practices and international experience can be useful for Africa and China. In this chapter, the second section provides an overview of relevant IMF fiscal frameworks, whereas the third section presents some international experiences with lending abroad, including issues related to collateralized transactions. The fourth section highlights the importance of capacity development, and the fifth section concludes.

USEFUL FRAMEWORKS

Ensuring that investments and financing contribute to growth and job creation requires supportive macroeconomic policy frameworks. Here, fiscal policy and debt sustainability are critical for reducing risks for both African countries and China. In addition, international experience offers guidance on good lending policies.

Fiscal Framework

Strong fiscal frameworks can ensure that African countries get the best "bang for the buck" and minimize fiscal risks. Fiscal reforms have been underway for decades in many African countries, with many benefiting from IMF technical assistance in these areas (see IMF 2018a). These reform efforts should be continued and, in several areas, accelerated, especially in public financial management institutions, risk management, revenue policy and administration, and the use of fiscal rules.[2] Here, it is also important to assess the spending needs to reach the Sustainable Development Goals (SDGs).

Public Financial Management Institutions

Budgetary institutions, particularly public investment management institutions, are critically important because they can improve the effective allocation and efficiency of public investment (Dabla-Norris and others 2013; Fainboim, Last, and Tandberg 2013; IMF 2015). Policies and capacity-building efforts should aim to strengthen the credibility, unity, and comprehensiveness of the budget (Box 8.1).

Sound policymaking requires fiscal transparency and good governance. The principles embedded in the IMF Fiscal Transparency Code can be a useful guide,

[2] Other important areas include transparency and accountability, strong analytical and policy-design capacity at ministries of finance and line ministries, strong budget execution systems (including IT systems), and adoption of international standards for fiscal reporting.

Box 8.1. Key Principles for Effective Budgetary Institutions

- **Budget comprehensiveness** ensures that governments take a holistic view of their expenditures. This approach means that all expenditure decisions, including investment, are considered together, leading to better prioritization among competing items regardless of the funding channel (for example, public–private partnerships). In addition, public investment is authorized by the legislature and disclosed in the budget documentation, thereby enabling adequate oversight.
- **Budget unity** ensures that decisions about individual investment projects take into account both immediate capital outlays and future operating and maintenance costs.
- **Safeguarding investment** ensures sufficient appropriations to cover the total project cost, avoiding any ad hoc diversions by the executive and costly project overruns because of inadequate funding.
- **Multiyear budgeting** keeps capital spending transparent and predictable over the medium term.

Source: *IMF Manual on Fiscal Transparency*—Chapter III. Open Budget Preparation, Execution, and Reporting (https://www.imf.org/external/np/fad/trans/manual/sec03a.htm).

focusing on clearly defining the roles and responsibilities of different government entities, making information on fiscal accounts publicly available, and ensuring data integrity.[3]

Countries should adopt and implement sound medium-term budgetary frameworks (MTBFs) with realistic and targeted expenditure policies, fully aligned with resource envelopes (Allen and others 2017). The design of the MTBF should be tailored to rationalize the size and horizon of scaled-up public investment and its financing, given the available fiscal space. A well-developed MTBF would help improve the predictability of resources and provide budget managers at different levels with adequate planning certainty.

Strong public investment management institutions can enhance the efficiency and productivity of public investment (Presbitero 2016; Gonguet and Jin 2017; Weisfeld 2017). Public investment institutions are a subset of the broader framework of budget institutions that govern the public financial management

[3] The IMF's Fiscal Transparency Code is the international standard for disclosure of information about public finances. The Code comprises a set of principles built around four pillars: (1) fiscal reporting, (2) fiscal forecasting and budgeting, (3) fiscal risk analysis and management, and (4) resource revenue management. See https://www.imf.org/external/np/fad/trans/Code2019.pdf.

process. Priorities vary across country groups but generally involve the following:

- Ensuring fiscal sustainability and effective coordination (for example, phasing in investment gradually commensurate with countries' absorptive capacity) to guide sustainable and adequate levels of public investment.
- Ensuring the allocation of capital spending to the most productive sectors and projects through careful cost–benefit analysis and risk assessment, with a clear pipeline of approved projects.
- Strengthening project implementation through transparent budget execution and procurement processes.
- Ensuring accountability and integrity in project management to ensure value for money.
- Systematically strengthening the management of public–private partnerships (PPPs) to contain related fiscal risks (IMF 2016).

Box 8.2 outlines the key components of the IMF Public Investment Management Assessment (PIMA) Framework.

Box 8.2. Public Investment Management Assessment (PIMA) Framework

The PIMA Framework assesses public investment management practices. The key components include the following:

- Institutions assessment: Evaluates 15 institutions or practices involved in the three key stages of the public investment cycle—planning, allocation, and implementation. It also assesses three cross-cutting institutions: the legal framework, IT systems, and staff capacity.
- Institutional design and effectiveness: Focuses on assessing both the institutional design ("what is on paper") and effectiveness ("what is in practice") of public investment management practices.
- Assessment process: Involves conducting a thorough assessment based on data requirements, conducting meetings with key stakeholders, analyzing dimensions, and preparing a detailed report outlining findings and recommendations for reform.
- Action plan for reform: The PIMA Framework aims to identify key bottlenecks in public investment management and develop an action plan for reform to enhance the efficiency and effectiveness of public investment practices.

Hence, the PIMA Framework provides a structured approach to evaluating and improving public investment management systems, with a focus on enhancing transparency, accountability, and the optimal use of resources in the public sector. In 2021, the PIMA climate-focused module was introduced to highlight the climate-responsive dimension of the PIMA.

Source: *PIMA Handbook: Public Investment Management Assessment, 1st Edition* (https://www.imf.org/en/Publications/Books/Issues/2022/07/12/PIMA-Handbook-Public-Investment-Management-Assessment-1st-Edition-50166) (imf.org) and Policy Paper Strengthening Infrastructure Governance for Climate-Responsive Public Investment (https://www.imf.org/en/Publications/Policy-Papers/Issues/2021/12/22/Strengthening-Infrastructure-Governance-for-Climate-Responsive-Public-Investment-511258).

Risk Management

Sound fiscal risk-management practices can help limit the fiscal risks associated with large-scale investment, thereby safeguarding macroeconomic stability. A better understanding of these risks would not only allow governments to curb their exposures but also enable them to take mitigating measures and allocate budget provisions when appropriate (IMF 2016). Moreover, greater transparency and effective risk-management practices can underpin credibility and market confidence, which in turn could attract more trade and investment.

African countries with limited disclosure of risks should prioritize monitoring and the development of macro-fiscal sensitivity analysis, especially to understand the fiscal implications of indicative shocks and the scaling-up of public investment (Weisfeld 2017). For resource-rich countries, a careful and realistic assessment of the implications of major swings in commodity prices is critical. Efforts should also be made to construct a basic financial balance sheet, initially focusing on debt liabilities and liquid financial assets, with progressive recognition of other financial assets and liabilities. These countries generally need to improve their understanding and disclosure of major contingent liabilities such as guarantees, PPPs, and disaster insurance schemes. Because countries collect more information on sources of risk and build their analytical capacity, it is useful to construct alternative macro-fiscal scenarios based on plausible shocks to a range of macroeconomic variables underpinning their fiscal forecasts, using more advanced techniques, including probabilistic forecasting methods (IMF 2016).

African countries would benefit from expanding their toolkits for fiscal risk management and adopting instruments to transfer, share, or provision for risk. Priorities will depend on the country's level of development and capacity, specific exposures, and the cost–benefit trade-off of mitigation measures. Reporting and accounting for all investment projects, including commitments and actual flows, should be the first step. In general, LICs can benefit most from stronger direct controls over exposures, including legally binding limits and centralized authorization of guarantees, PPPs, subnational and state-owned enterprise borrowing, and other explicit contingent liabilities. African frontier and emerging market economies with basic risk management in place could make more effective use of risk mitigation and transfer tools such as partial guarantees, risk-based fees, disaster reinsurance, and hedging instruments to incentivize better risk management and reduce their exposure when risks materialize.

To accomplish this, it is important to introduce institutional arrangements to support an integrated fiscal risk-management system. The appropriate organizational setup would depend on country-specific factors, but Box 8.3 lists some good practices.

Box 8.3. Good Practices of Institutional Arrangements for Fiscal Risk Management[1]

- **Establishing a central risk oversight body.** For low-income and emerging market countries, centralizing the monitoring and management of overall fiscal risk in a single body is advantageous (Cebotari 2008). This allows for an assessment of aggregate risk exposures across the government and the identification of any systemic relationships and interactions between risks. It also facilitates the examination of whether risks from various sources offset each other (and therefore may not require mitigation). This role can be assigned to a specific unit or a high-level oversight committee.
- **Establishing central controls over major risks.** A central authorizing entity (for example, Ministry of Finance or a cabinet committee) should approve contracts that expose the government to various fiscal risks, particularly when a decision is made to cap exposure to specific risks. These risk exposures (for example, guarantees) should be benchmarked against traditional policy instruments and accounted for in the budget.
- **Defining clear accountabilities.** Individual departments and line ministries should be accountable for identifying, estimating, analyzing, and monitoring specific fiscal risks within their functions. Oversight functions, such as the oversight of the subnational governments, state-owned enterprises, public–private partnerships, and any other sources of significant risk, should be centralized under the Ministry of Finance.

Source: IMF Fiscal Risk Management (https://www.imf.org/en/Topics/fiscal-policies/Fiscal-Risks).

[1] Governments can outline the preconditions to take on specific fiscal risks (such as loans, guarantees, public–private partnerships, and so on). For example, the sponsoring public entities should demonstrate the investment project cannot be financed on reasonable terms without government loans or guarantee.

Comprehensive, reliable, and timely fiscal data covering all public entities, stocks, and flows are important to strengthen the oversight of the broader public sector. The central government should require quarterly financial statements and audited year-end statements from public entities whenever possible and monitor performance against these financial targets. Monitoring these fiscal risks enables the government to take corrective measures against unsustainable policies undertaken by units outside the central government, in a manner consistent with transparency, governance, and accountability arrangements.

The management of PPPs is an integral part of the overall public investment management framework. PPPs and traditionally procured projects follow a similar three-stage cycle (planning, allocation, and implementation) and share common management features. To ensure PPPs deliver efficiency gains for African countries while keeping their fiscal costs and risks under control, an effective regulatory framework is important. This framework should include several key elements (Box 8.4).

Box 8.4. Key Elements for an Effective Public–Private Partnership Regulatory Framework

- **Good projects.** All public investment projects, whether public–private partnership (PPP) or traditional procurement, should go through a two-step process. First, there should be a clear investment strategy to select public investment projects based on national priorities and cost-benefit analysis. Second, once the projects are selected, it should be determined whether a PPP or traditional public procurement is more efficient, that is, provides better value for money. Spending decisions should be consistent with budgetary restrictions to ensure fiscal sustainability and take into account the long-term fiscal implications of investment projects.
- **Good institutions.** It is essential that the Ministry of Finance manages a "gateway process" for PPPs that gives it sufficient control over PPPs at each stage of the process, including contract renegotiation. At any point in the process, the Ministry of Finance should be able to stop projects that are fiscally unaffordable. A dedicated PPP unit, with specialized and capable staff, can be helpful in managing this process. It can also be useful for the Ministry of Finance to establish ceilings on both the stocks and flows of PPPs to help control fiscal risks.
- **Good laws.** Preferably, a PPP law should be adopted to provide a clear, fair, and predictable legal environment for the private sector. The legal framework should also clarify the roles and responsibilities of all relevant parties in PPP transactions. A dedicated PPP law can be helpful in this regard because it has been associated with lower rates of contract renegotiation (Guasch 2004).

- **Good budgeting, accounting, and reporting practices.** These should aim to achieve full and transparent disclosure of all future budgetary costs and fiscal risks from PPPs. The effect of PPPs on future government outlays should be incorporated into debt sustainability analysis and the medium-term fiscal framework. The use of commitment appropriations in the budgetary process, which authorize governments to commit public resources for future years, can also be helpful in drawing attention to the future costs of PPPs.

The IMF–World Bank PPP Fiscal Risk Assessment Model (PFRAM) is a useful tool to analyze government costs and risks in individual PPP projects for China and African countries. PFRAM is an Excel-based analytical tool that assesses the potential fiscal costs and risks arising from PPP projects based on international accounting and statistics standards, including International Public Sector Accounting Standards 32 and the *IMF Government Finance Statistics Manual 2014*. It generates standardized outcomes based on project-specific and macroeconomic data, which include: project cash flows; fiscal tables/charts on a cash and accrual basis; debt sustainability analysis with and without the PPP project; sensitivity analysis of main fiscal aggregates to changes in macroeconomic and project-specific parameters; and a summary risk matrix of the project.

The Excel template and user manual can be downloaded from the Infrastructure Governance site (http://www.imf.org/external/np/fad/publicinvestment).

Source: IMF 2006.

Revenue Policy and Administration

Robust revenue policies and administration are essential for African countries to mobilize revenues, enabling necessary spending while ensuring fiscal sustainability.

Tax competition among African countries can ultimately lead to revenue losses in all countries, theoretically prompting scope for tax coordination. However, experience from other regions suggests significant obstacles to agreements on tax levels, such as tax rates, because of differing interests and preferences among countries (see Keen and Konrad [2013]).[4] In the case of the West African Economic and Monetary Union, taxation policies of companies, value-added taxes, and excises are already coordinated through regional directives with floors

[4] Beyond interests and preferences, countries also face constraints, such as (1) different tax systems and regulations that are hard to harmonize, (2) political considerations (or geopolitical tensions) that lead to restrained or volatile decision making, (3) limited resources that hinder the implementation and enforcement of complex agreements, and so on.

on tax rates. Agreements to limit the scope for international tax planning are easier to reach,[5] as are agreements that restrict the use of tax incentives.[6]

To address some of these issues, the Belt and Road Initiative Tax Administration Cooperation Mechanism,[7] a multilateral tax cooperation mechanism under the Belt and Road Initiative, was established in April 2019. It includes tax authorities from about 36 countries and regions, including African countries. Its objective is to facilitate cross-border trade and investment and help resolve tax disputes (Box 8.5). Another platform for coordinating taxes in Africa is the African Tax Administration Forum.

Box 8.5. The Belt and Road Initiative Tax Administration Cooperation Mechanism (BRITACOM)

BRITACOM consists of the Council, the Secretariat, the BRI Tax Administration Cooperation Forum (BRITACOF), the BRI Tax Administration Capacity Enhancement Group, and the Advisory Board. The permanent secretariat is in Beijing. The head of the Revenue Service of Georgia is currently the chair of the BRITACOM Council,[1] and Mr. Wang Daoshu, deputy commissioner of the State Taxation Administration (STA) of China, is currently the executive secretary of the BRITACOM Secretariat.[2]

BRITACOM holds annual BRITACOF conferences. The first BRITACOF conference was held in Wuzhen, China, in April 2019 and produced the so-called Wuzhen Action Plan organized along six themes: (1) annual BRITACOF conference together with a Business and Industry Tax Dialogue, (2) rule of law and tax certainty, (3) tax dispute resolution, (4) building tax administration capacity, (5) streamlining tax compliance, and (6) digitalization of tax administration. Subsequent conferences took place in 2021, 2022, and 2023.

[1] For more information, see https://www.britacom.org/xw_7086/jzdt/202309/t20230911_1129744.html.

[2] For more information, see https://www.britacom.org/jzgk/secretariat.

---

[5] The G20/Organisation for Economic Co-operation and Development Inclusive Framework on Base Erosion and Profit Shifting initiative, for example, already covers many Belt and Road Initiative countries as members.

[6] In the European Union, for example, State Aid rules that limit subsidies also apply to certain beneficial tax provisions. Moreover, there is a voluntary agreement to abstain from certain practices deemed as harmful tax competition (https://www.consilium.europa.eu/en/council-eu/preparatory-bodies/code-conduct-group). Tax agreements also help in (1) fighting tax avoidance/evasion (information exchange, anti-abuse rules, and so on); (2) preventing double taxation (allocating taxing rights); (3) enhancing legal stability for taxpayers; and (4) avoiding discrimination (equitable treatment for cross-border activities).

[7] For more information, see https://www.britacom.org/jzgk/council.

In general, establishing anti-avoidance rules and addressing cross-country tax mismatches might be important. For instance, countries lacking strong transfer pricing regulations and thin capitalization rules could benefit from their introduction or strengthening. Such measures can reduce the risk and scope of revenue losses from international tax planning. Although international coordination on these issues is useful, countries can also implement many of them unilaterally. However, it will be important to consider interactions with any existing double taxation agreements.

Many countries will need to strengthen their tax administrations (see also IMF and World Bank 2023). These reforms align with the reform programs that many countries should pursue regardless of China's engagement, but investment and financing flows from China provide an additional incentive (see Box 8.6).

Box 8.6. Priority Tax Administration Reforms

- Undertake an objective diagnostic assessment of the capability of the tax administration against international good practices, such as with the Tax Administration Diagnostic Assessment Tool[1] instrument, to prioritize and guide the scope of reforms. Make use of international capacity development support[2] in implementing the reforms.
- Understand trends in the country's tax gap. Tools are available to estimate the overall tax gap, the compliance gap, the policy gap, and their subcomponents.[3]
- Strengthen headquarters capacity to ensure it has the analytical capacity to assess risks to the tax system and guide the organizational responses to them. This requires assigning sufficient resources and developing the capacity to develop segment- and function-based risk compliance management strategies, especially where China will bring new types of cross-country investment.
- Amend legislation to ensure that tax administrations have the powers to access information and deal with more sophisticated types of transactions.
- Expand information gathering and sharing, especially between tax and customs administrations. If tax incentives are provided, their costs should be accounted for (as "tax expenditures") and taxpayers should be required to report their use to the tax administration, so that the cost of these incentives can be assessed against the economic benefits gained from providing them.
- Establish (or strengthen) large-taxpayer offices to manage the most sophisticated taxpayers that will engage in the most complex cross-border transactions.

- Consider establishing medium-taxpayer offices to manage those taxpayers that are smaller than large taxpayers but still significant in terms of revenue. Many importers and exporters involved with transactions generated by the Belt and Road Initiative will be in this segment.
- Bolster information technology to improve efficiency of processing, reduce the compliance burden on taxpayers, and provide the information needed to identify risks and assess responses.
- Increase the capability of staff to adopt modern tax administration approaches.[4]

[1] See TADAT.org.

[2] Including from the Belt and Road Initiative, through Virtual Training to Advance Revenue Administration (VITARA—Organization https://www.imf.org/en/Capacity-Development/Training/ICDTC/Courses/VITARA-ORG), or other international capacity development resources.

[3] See the IMF's Revenue Administration–Gap Analysis Program for Value-Added Tax: https://www.imf.org/en/Publications/TNM/Issues/2017/04/07/The-Revenue-AdministrationGap-Analysis-Program-Model-and-Methodology-for-Value-Added-Tax-Gap-44715.

[4] VITARA is a series of online training modules supporting tax administrators around the world to build their knowledge and understanding of critical features of modern tax administration. VITARA is a joint initiative of Inter-American Center of Tax Administrations, Intra-European Organisation of Tax Administrations, IMF, and Organisation for Economic Co-operation and Development. See: https://www.imf.org/en/Capacity-Development/Training/ICDTC/Search?sortby=Relevancy&sortdir=Descending&keywords=VITARA.

A major challenge for customs administrations is ensuring effectiveness and efficiency, balancing between controls undertaken at the borders and inland, the balancing of enforcement with trade facilitation, and the need for modern transit procedures. This will require improvements to customs staffing and infrastructure to:

- *Reduce processing times:* Customs administration procedures should be modernized, predictable, fast, cost-effective, easily accessible, and understandable, based on international standards and good practices. Customs controls should be fair, effective, and efficient, based on risks assessed using intelligence from various sources, and selective by mode of transport and reliability of economic operators.
- *Prioritize border controls:* To ensure the fast passage of goods and means of transport across the borders, only essential controls should be performed at the borders. All other controls, including financial (revenue related) controls, should be undertaken at inland clearance facilities to eliminate unnecessary and expensive waiting times at the borders.[8]

[8] In addition to inland clearance, a formal post-clearance audit operation is key because this is a fundamental part of the customs' compliance mechanisms.

- *Facilitate transit:* Customs transit procedures cover both goods and means of transport proceeding from the national borders to an inland clearance facility (inland/national transit) and goods proceeding from one external border station to another one. The former is normally a national procedure, whereas the latter can be national or based on bilateral or a wider, international arrangement.[9] A regional arrangement is more desirable, creating standard procedures and opportunities to lower both administrative burdens and clearance time.

Many African countries would benefit from organizing their tax system reform efforts under the umbrella of a medium-term revenue strategy (see IMF 2019). The core elements of a medium-term revenue strategy are shown in Box 8.7 (IMF, OECD, United Nations, and World Bank 2016).

Fiscal Rules

Fiscal rules, if properly calibrated and implemented, can help correct a deficit bias prevailing in many African countries and ensure fiscal sustainability by imposing a long-lasting constraint on fiscal policy. The rules can create room for predictable

Box 8.7. Core Elements of a Medium-Term Revenue Strategy

Developing a broad consensus on medium-term revenue goals should be a government-led effort that reflects societies' expectations of public sector and expenditure needs. It should be an inclusive process that is ideally reflected in a medium-term budget and formal documents—including the medium-term revenue strategy document.

Reform of the tax system through a carefully sequenced overhaul of key elements. This includes a redesign of tax policy settings, a reform of the revenue agencies, and strengthening of the legal framework.

Governments must lead the tax system reform—a country-owned objective—from the highest level. Most success factors depend on government decisions: strategic goals, governance, political support, timeframe of effort, reform management process, communication, and institutionalization.

External support is often needed to help formulate and implement the medium-term revenue strategy. The other Belt and Road Initiative participants and existing donors and technical assistance providers could provide support for countries with lower capacity.

Source: IMF 2019.

[9] Adopting the Customs Convention on the International Transport of Goods under Cover of TIR Carnets (TIR Convention) might be useful. They provide international transit arrangements and guarantees, but so far, few African countries have ratified them.

levels of investment by limiting policymakers' discretion and anchoring expectations (Balassone and Franco 2000; Schaechter and others 2012; Eyraud and others 2018). Best practices in designing and implementing fiscal rules are outlined in Box 8.8.

Assessing the Spending Needs for the Sustainable Development Goals

Achieving the SDGs in African countries aligns closely with broader objectives of strengthening inclusive and sustainable economic growth. Fiscal policy can serve key goals, such as macroeconomic stability and long-term development objectives, and integrating the attainment of the SDGs into policy frameworks

Box 8.8. Best Practices for Fiscal Rules

Best practices for fiscal rules foster effective economic governance and sustainable public finances. They include:

- *Feasible and stable fiscal plans:* Fiscal rules should be linked to feasible and stable fiscal plans that guide government spending and revenue decisions.
- *Flexibility in response to shocks:* Fiscal rules should incorporate flexibility mechanisms to allow for adjustments in response to unexpected economic shocks or crises.
- *Transparent fiscal anchors:* Clear and transparent fiscal anchors should be established to provide guidance on the government's fiscal policy objectives and constraints.
- *Risk-based rules:* Implementation of risk-based rules that ensure a path to debt sustainability and the accumulation of fiscal buffers to mitigate risks associated with fiscal policy decisions.
- *Checks and balances:* Establishment of checks and balances within the fiscal framework to promote accountability, transparency, and oversight of government fiscal decisions.
- *Quality of government finance statistics*: Improving the quality of government finance statistics, including enhancing fiscal reporting, adopting accrual accounting methods, and moving toward a comprehensive public sector balance sheet approach for better monitoring of government actions and risk exposures.

Incorporating these best practices into fiscal rule design and implementation can enhance the government's effectiveness of its fiscal frameworks, promote fiscal discipline, and ensure sustainable public finances in the long term.

Source: Caselli and others 2022.

contributes to the latter objective. This dual focus of fiscal policy is essential in an environment in which African countries are navigating the challenges of high debt levels, large financing needs, and an imperative for sustainable growth.

The IMF SDG Costing Tool estimates the additional spending required to achieve SDGs by 2030 that are critical for human and physical capital development and for which expenditure policy plays a large role (Gaspar and others 2019; Carapella and others 2023). These include spending in social sectors and infrastructure. The analytical tool also provides guidance on the key cost drivers that need to be adjusted to make progress in the SDGs. This analysis can serve as input for macro-fiscal policy and as the basis for African countries' assessments on the needed revenue mobilization, financing, and expenditure efficiency gains to achieve core medium-term development objectives. Box 8.9 outlines the key approach to estimate the additional expenditure for the SDGs and the central findings.

Box 8.9. Assessing the Additional Spending Required for Sustainable Development Goals

- The IMF Sustainable Development Goal (SDG) Costing Tool's latest (third) edition (Carapella and others 2023) contains estimates for the additional spending needs for SDG3 (health), SDG4 (education), and targets within SDG6 (water and sanitation), SDG7 (electricity), and SDG9 (road infrastructure) for 173 countries, including 45 from sub-Saharan Africa.
- In the SDG costing methodology, the target performance in 2030 for a given country is determined by a combination of absolute targets derived from SDG indicators, and the use of values from income peers with the highest SDG outcomes. For example, in education, the student–teacher ratio to be achieved in 2030 by a country is the average student–teacher ratio of high-SDG4 countries among the income peers, whereas the target gross enrollment rate is 80 percent for all countries based on SDG4 targets.
- Globally, additional spending needed to achieve a strong performance in the selected SDGs in 2030 amounts to $3 trillion (3.4 percent of 2030 world GDP). Estimated at 16.1 percent of 2030 LIDC GDP, the average additional SDG cost of this income group is significantly higher than in Emerging Market Economies, who face additional spending amounting to 4.8 percentage points of their GDP in 2030.
- Sub-Saharan Africa is the region with by far the largest additional expenditure burden—at 19.4 percentage points of GDP—to achieve a good performance in the SDGs.

- The amounts the world will need to spend in addition to meet human versus physical capital development needs are about equal—1.7 percentage points of GDP in each case. Sub-Saharan Africa will need to spend 9.9 and 9.5 percent of the region's GDP on human and physical capital development, respectively.

FINANCING STRATEGIES

Another important aspect of bolstering macroeconomic stability is to ensure sound public financing strategies. Pre-existing debt vulnerabilities and countries' exposure to shocks need to be carefully accounted for in designing financing strategies. For governments with limited fiscal space beyond their baseline fiscal plans, a couple of possibilities could be explored:

- *Highly concessional support:* Combined with well-targeted and efficient investment that would boost growth, financing on highly concessional terms would have a lower effect on debt burden indicators. It is important to note that LICs under an IMF-supported program that are rated at high risk of debt distress or in distress cannot borrow on non-concessional terms (with some limited exceptions for priority projects), and the same applies for countries subject to the World Bank's sustainable development finance policy (see, for example, IMF 2021).
- *Foreign direct investment rather than lending:* This would have the advantage of not adding to countries' debt burdens while supporting economic growth. At the same time, to the extent that such direct investment was to come in the form of PPPs with a Chinese-backed entity taking the role of the private investor, care should be taken to ensure that financial risks for host governments are fully understood and contained, because PPPs are already a source of rising debt risks in LICs (IMF 2018a).
- *Other financial arrangements:* To reduce reliance on public sector funding, flexible and innovative financial arrangements could be encouraged to attract institutional investors for better risk sharing and improved project selection and execution. In particular, project equity contribution by the public sector could support syndicated bank loans and project bond issuance. Equity contribution from the host country may align incentives properly to reduce sovereign risks. Such equity contributions can both lower the risk of impairment and increase project quality control.

For African countries with some fiscal space, a careful examination would be needed to understand how the proposed borrowing would affect their debt burden indicators, taking into account the beneficial macroeconomic effects of the investment being financed. Financing should be structured to avoid creating or exacerbating debt vulnerabilities. Loan amounts could be calibrated to avoid breaching debt stock thresholds[10] (taking account of the beneficial macroeconomic effects of the investment), whereas grace periods and maturities can be structured to not add to debt-service requirements, or gross financing needs, in years where such requirements from outstanding debt are high already. For countries with a moderate risk of debt distress rating and under an IMF program, there may be limits on the total amount of concessional and non-concessional borrowing (to prevent debt from being pushed into a high-risk region).[11]

Because many African countries are highly exposed to a variety of shocks, there is a strong case for adding state-contingent features to new debt contracts.[12] By linking a country's debt-service payments to its ability to pay, state-contingent official loans can help enhance sovereign resilience when there is high uncertainty in returns on the investments being financed and the country is vulnerable to large exogenous shocks (IMF 2017b). This, in turn, increases fiscal space. State-contingent bonds could also be attractive for China—for instance, commodity-linked bonds would provide a natural hedge for China, which tends to be a net importer of commodities.

There are several options for state-contingent features. Commodity-exporting African countries exhibit highly volatile growth-interest rate differentials and primary balances. If loans to these countries could include a provision to reduce debt payments when commodity prices fall (and raise payments when commodity prices rise), this volatility could diminish. Similarly for low-income African countries with a volatile debt-to-GDP ratio, linking interest payments to GDP could help stabilize fiscal policy and provide much needed relief in times of stress. More generally, for other small open economies, debt payments could be linked to variables such as exports, trading partner GDP, bond spreads, or global volatility index. In the event of a large adverse shock, the automatic relief imbedded in the instrument would reduce the probability of sovereign default, which can be costly for both debtors and creditors.[13] In addition, given the increase of climate-related shocks, Climate Resilient Debt Clauses—as reflected, for example, in the initiative led by the United Kingdom in 2023—can provide countries with additional fiscal space at the time of the crises (see United Kingdom Government 2023).

---

[10] In the debt sustainability analyses for both market-access countries and low-income countries, debt burden indicators such as the ratio of debt to GDP are compared with thresholds. If an indicator is less favorable than the threshold, this is interpreted as a sign of heightened risk of debt distress.

[11] See *Public Debt Limits in IMF-Supported Programs* (http://www.imf.org/external/np/spr/2015/conc/index.htm).

[12] Some official bilateral creditors have already been extending loans with such features: Agence Française de Développement has, in the recent years, extended to seven African countries "countercyclical loans" in which the maturity period extends in the face of a large export shock. For a review of this experience, see Commonwealth Secretariat (2016).

[13] Maturity extension triggers could also be set as an export fall of, say, 10 percent; a decline in commodity prices of 20 percent; a natural disaster of given intensity (akin to the "hurricane clause" in Grenada's 2015 exchange bonds).

Box 8.10. Techniques Used by Chinese Lenders to Reduce Project Finance Risks

Chinese banks use different techniques to help reduce project risks:

- Chinese infrastructure funds, such as the Silk Road Fund, may provide equity stakes to reduce the banks' exposure.
- The China Export and Credit Insurance Corporation (Sinosure) may provide insurance for risky projects at a premium (typically 2–5 percent). Credit guarantees from project sponsors (for example, large Chinese state-owned enterprises) are sometimes provided to the lenders.
- Collateral arrangements such as concessions offered to lenders in the form of operating the infrastructure assets or providing commodity exports as collateral may be used. Chinese policy banks typically go together with the project sponsors (for example, Chinese companies) to bid for overseas projects in African countries, leveraging the knowledge and experience of these private firms.

The following risk mitigation techniques are reportedly used by Chinese policy banks:

	Instruments, contract design, collateral arrangement, and pricing
Select the viable project and price the risk properly	Thorough due diligence to ensure high-quality projects and price the loan based on project risk
Equity cushion from public sector	Government-owned infrastructure fund; economic cooperation fund between China and Association of Southeast Asian Nations (ASEAN) , United Arab Emirates (UAE), Eurasia
Credit insurance	Sinosure
Credit guarantee	Guarantee provided by project sponsors
Collateral	Commodity output (for example, oil or minerals), land leasing, right to operate the ports/highway/power stations
Contract design	Incentive-compatible equity ownership for better risk sharing

Source: IMF staff.

At the project level, many Chinese lenders have reportedly used different techniques to help reduce project finance risks (Box 8.10).

COLLATERALIZED TRANSACTIONS

An important question relates to the use of collateralized financing. The IMF and the World Bank suggest that collateralized lending can be beneficial to a developing country, but there are also pitfalls. Specifically, collateralized financing of projects where future revenue streams are directly linked to repayment under adequate disclosures that mitigate the risk of mispricing for both unsecured and secured creditors has the highest potential for benefiting the borrower and protecting the longer-term development relationship with creditors. In contrast, collateralized financing, even if related to a project, can cause more harm than good when one or more of the following criteria are met: (1) it does not improve borrowing terms, (2) it weakens debt sustainability, (3) it is not disclosed, and (4) it does not respect negative pledge clauses. Hence, it is important for both public lenders and borrowers to undertake a careful assessment when considering collateralization. For lenders, this would imply aligning decisions about collateralized transactions with existing G20 Operational Guidelines on Sustainable Financing (see IMF and World Bank 2023).[14]

GOOD PRACTICES FOR LENDING ABROAD

As discussed in the previous section, prudent and sustainable financing practices are vital for African countries to support macroeconomic and debt sustainability. For borrowers, prudent borrowing would fund investment toward a higher growth rate, thus helping them toward achieving the SDGs; excessive borrowing in turn could lead to debt distress, disrupting their development process. For China, prudent lending practices allow China's savings to be deployed in higher-return projects, while reducing the risks associated with such lending.

As international experience shows, there is not one single model for lending frameworks. At the same time, the international experience suggests that strong lending frameworks are critical. Frameworks can generally be organized along different dimensions and comprise (1) the governance and oversight of lending agencies, (2) procedures for internal risk assessments and controls, and (3) monitoring and reporting provisions (and transparency).

Debt Transparency

Debt transparency is essential to foster sustainable financing.[15] Without transparency about a borrower's exposures, creditors are less likely to make the right decisions, more likely to lend beyond a country's capacity to bear debt, and thus more likely to face debt resolution situations. Although each individual creditor may have an incentive not to reveal its exposure ("commercial interest"), collectively all are better off if transparency and accuracy of debt data are secured.

Several practices can promote strong transparency and accuracy of debt data. These include publishing information on exposures in a timely manner[16] (or at least sharing information with International Financial Institutions); regularly reconciling data between borrowers and creditors; publishing information on contractual clauses (for example, on the existence of collateral); and conducting a regular dialogue with other creditors (for instance, through the Paris Club). To

[14] See also G20 (2020).

[15] On debt transparency, see also IMF 2022.

[16] In line, for example, with data provision to the IMF for surveillance purposes.

accomplish these practices, a country first needs procedures for aggregating information from individual official creditor agencies (including delegation to an agency to do this).

Based on a 2019 IMF–World Bank survey of creditors, many have already achieved sound and strong practices in this area.[17] About half of the countries self-reported to have at least sound practices in terms of sharing information on existing and new lending. About one-third were assessed to have strong practices, reporting all aspects of terms as per Organization for Economic Cooperation and Development requirements and providing information for all lending agencies consolidated in one website.

Lenders' Internal Risk Assessment and Risk Management/Control

There are several important dimensions to risk analysis and control on the side of lenders. Risk analysis has both a microelement (what return will the project yield based on some assumptions) and a macroelement (whether the country generates enough foreign exchange to repay). Both need to be considered because it is possible to get the analysis at the project level perfectly right and still face a repayment problem because of a shock to a country's terms of trade. This could be a macro shock such as a sudden drop in oil prices or an increase in global risk aversion leading to higher interest rates or even capital outflows. In any of these cases, a country could be short of the foreign exchange needed to repay the loans. Risk control refers to how decisions are taken based on the risk analysis, how lending terms and decisions are related to the risk analysis, and how risks are managed on lenders' balance sheets.

Several practices/approaches can assist with effective risk control:

- ***Layered decision making.*** Setting the right controls on lenders can be critical. At a high level, this should cover: (1) defining the types of lending activities allowed and (2) overall and country exposure limits. In the context of individual loans, this involves setting procedures to determine when decisions are delegated. One good practice involves requiring all transactions above a certain size/risk threshold to be approved at a higher level in the governance structure (for example, the supervising ministry, instead of the lenders' Board of Directors).
- ***Tying terms and conditions to the level of risk.*** Usually, higher risk should lead to a higher interest rate to protect lenders from losses. However, to support development in LICs and mitigate debt crisis risks, many lenders have agreed to refrain from lending non-concessionally to countries at high

[17] *G20 Operational Guidelines for Sustainable Financing—Survey Results and Policy Recommendations,* Joint paper by the IMF and the World Bank, May 31, 2019. The survey had extensive participation by creditors, including by non-G20 members, with a total of 15 G20 members (covering 37 lending agencies) and 5 non-members of the G20 (covering 12 agencies) responded.

risk of distress.[18] This puts a focus on offering rates below market and longer grace and repayment periods. Of course, other terms and conditions also matter (including collateral, which can be highly problematic for borrowers).

- ***Provisioning requirements.*** Requiring a set aside for potential losses can prove a powerful tool to discourage risky lending (because it consumes lender resources). This entails the use of risk analysis matched to some methodology for determining loss-given default. On the latter, it is important to note that the IMF and World Bank have published guidance on how to calibrate a sustainable debt sustainability analysis for an LIC from an unsustainable starting point (IMF 2017a).[19] Guidelines on loss-given default should account for this.

Most sovereign creditors have strong practices for effective risk control. Based on the results of the G20 survey of country practices, more than 70 percent of the respondents appear to also have at least sound practices in terms of debt sustainability analysis guiding lending volumes and terms. An option used by one major creditor is to have lending agencies use a single interagency country risk-assessment system to inform lending decisions and terms while allowing each agency to have its own provisioning policy.

Creditor-Debtor Engagement (Debt Resolution Procedures)

The adoption of good information sharing as well as risk-assessment and risk-management/control practices is necessary but is not sufficient to ensure success. As history, however, reveals, it is also important to have frameworks in place to deal with potential debt distress issues.

Good lending practices should also encompass what to do when borrowers get into trouble and cannot repay. In such cases, timely resolution is of the essence, and it reduces costs borne by both the debtors and creditors. However, there is a well-documented tendency among lenders in these circumstances to address the situation—"too little and too late."[20] This, in turn, damages the borrowers and impairs both the borrowers' development and their overall capacity to repay creditors.

[18] *Recommendation of the Council on Sustainable Lending Practices and Officially Supported Export Credits*, Organization for Economic Co-operation and Development, November 2016 (http://www.oecd.org/officialdocuments/publicdisplaydocumentpdf/?cote=tad/ecg(2016)14&docLanguage=En).

[19] *Guidance Note on the Bank-Fund Debt Sustainability Framework for Low Income Countries*, Joint paper by the IMF and the World Bank, February 2018 (https://www.imf.org/en/Publications/Policy-Papers/Issues/2018/02/14/pp122617guidance-note-on-lic-dsf). In particular, see the section on Assessing Sustainability (pp. 46–47) for guidance to debt sustainability analysis for users in constructing a sustainable scenario from an "in distress" starting point.

[20] *Sovereign Debt Restructuring—Recent Developments and Implications for the Fund's Legal and Policy Framework*, April 2013 (https://www.imf.org/~/media/Websites/IMF/imported-full-text-pdf/external/np/pp/eng/2013/_042613.ashx).

To correctly orient and incentivize lenders in debt-resolution situations and facilitate sustainable outcomes, several key practices are necessary:

- ***Defined procedures for covering losses.*** In part, this relates to lenders' provisioning practices, but it also needs to cover circumstances where provisioning proves inadequate and a budgetary appropriation is needed (not an uncommon outcome because LICs are subject to large shocks and risks can shift quickly).
- ***Internal coordination procedures*** (covering lending agencies). This is a necessary condition for external coordination. Official lenders in a country need to speak with one voice in a restructuring process. This involves defining who is the negotiating authority and procedures to establish "red lines" for the negotiators to respect.
- ***Procedures for coordination with other external creditors.*** Coordination is critical in speeding up to reach agreement with every official creditor. It also minimizes holdout problems. Several approaches are possible.
- ***Where available, using the G20 Common Framework for Debt Treatment.*** This coordination mechanism ensures that all official bilateral creditors are organized in one single pool, share information among themselves, and can enforce comparability of treatment from other creditors, in particular private creditors.[21]
- ***Ad hoc coordination with the Paris Club*** (the approach initially taken by Korea and Brazil). Although membership has advantages which could be considered over time, these advantages can also be realized by participating in individual club treatments on an ad hoc basis. A key benefit is close coordination with IMF policies to achieve comparability of treatment for any non-participating creditors.
- Coordination can also be achieved by ***relying on debt advisors*** (for example, hired by the borrower). However, difficult issues such as trust between creditors, funding of legal and administrative costs of the advisor, and influence over potential holdout creditors would need to be satisfactorily addressed to secure success.
- ***Taking a leading role in organizing creditors.*** This raises the same issues as relying on advisors, especially in terms of managing holdouts. Moreover, it lacks some of the advantages of ad hoc cooperation with the Paris Club, particularly facilitating comparability of treatment (because IMF policies are not as well defined with respect to treatment of holdouts in this instance).
- ***Procedures for determining repayment capacity and securing adjustment by the borrowing country.*** Generally, debt resolution requires a careful

[21] In 2020, the G20 and Paris Club agreed to coordinate and cooperate on debt treatments for up to 73 low-income countries under the Common Framework for Debt Treatments. The framework aims to address sovereign debt sustainability and liquidity issues (see https://www.imf.org/-/media/Files/News/news-articles/english-extraordinary-g20-fmcbg-statement-november-13.ashx).

assessment of the macroeconomic outlook, and then involves a mixture of adjustment by the borrowing country and restructuring of loans by lenders to restore sustainability. Lenders have a very strong interest in seeing a feasible adjustment realized, because without it, their losses will be higher. The usual way is to both define the macro envelope and ensure that adjustment is implemented in an IMF program (for example, the Paris Club and the G20 Common Framework require this for a treatment). Alternative models of restructuring outside IMF programs have been prone to failure and can lead to repeat restructurings (for example, Belize).

CAPACITY DEVELOPMENT

Focusing on upgrading policy frameworks and adopting good international practices will ensure that resources are channeled to the most productive sectors and that risks are minimized. Strengthening policy frameworks, however, needs to go hand in hand with capacity development.

The IMF has been working with many countries in Africa and China—and stands ready to further increase its engagement—through technical assistance and training from six regional capacity centers in Africa,[22] the Africa Training Institute, the China–IMF Capacity Development Center (see Box 8.11), as well as technical assistance from the IMF Fiscal Affairs, Monetary and Capital Markets, the Strategy and Policy Review,[23] Legal and Statistics Departments, and the Institute for Capacity Development.

Box 8.11. The China–IMF Capacity Development Center

The China–IMF Capacity Development Center (CICDC) was established by the IMF and the People's Bank of China during the first Belt and Road Forum in May 2017 and formally inaugurated a year later at the joint People's Bank of China–IMF high-level conference on Macroeconomic and Financial Frameworks for the Successful Implementation of the Belt and Road Initiative. As part of the IMF's global network of regional capacity development centers, the CICDC provides IMF training to support government officials from China and countries associated with the Belt and Road Initiative (BRI) and beyond in effective institution-building and policymaking.

[22] The centers are Central Africa Regional Technical Assistance Center; East Africa Regional Technical Assistance Center, South Africa Regional Technical Assistance Center, West Africa Regional Technical Assistance Center (AFW), and West Africa II Regional Technical Assistance Center (AFW2).

[23] For example, the IMF worked closely with the Chinese Ministry of Finance on the development of the Belt and Road Initiative debt sustainability framework. See Chinese Ministry of Finance (2019).

As of January 2024, CICDC has conducted 96 courses/workshops for China and BRI countries, including 13 outside China in collaboration with IMF regional training centers/programs in Mauritius, Georgia, Austria, Central America, and the Caribbean. These included a workshop on the low-income countries debt sustainability framework and IMF policies for a group of BRI country officials and Chinese state lending agencies, and a workshop on sustainable infrastructure jointly delivered by staff from the IMF and the European Bank for Reconstruction and Development (EBRD). In its first five years of operation, the CICDC trained a total of 3,115 government officials, of which 672 came from 108 countries mainly in Africa, Asia, Central Asia, and Europe. Inside China, the CICDC trained 2,794 officials, of which 2,443 are from China and 352 are from BRI countries.

CONCLUSION

Several global shocks have increased vulnerabilities, and many countries in Africa face high debt levels and high gross financing needs. Looking ahead, policymaking will become even more challenging, especially because continued investments are necessary to foster growth and reduce poverty. These vulnerabilities and potential exposures to shocks must be carefully considered in designing future financing strategies. African countries with limited fiscal space would benefit from highly concessional support; foreign direct investment rather than lending; and other flexible, innovative, and transparent financial arrangements to reduce risks and reliance on public sector funding. The current challenges, however, also provide a unique opportunity to redouble efforts to strengthen policy frameworks to maximize the benefits of investments while minimizing risks.

Regarding fiscal policy frameworks, the IMF has developed several fiscal toolboxes and principles aimed at reducing vulnerabilities and improving the allocation of resources, which could be useful for African countries. These cover effective public financial management institutions, public investment management assessment frameworks, institutional arrangements for fiscal risk management, effective PPP regulatory frameworks, tax administration cooperation mechanisms, tax administration reforms, medium-term revenue strategies, and fiscal rules.

When it comes to good practices for lending abroad, there is no single model, but international experience suggests that strong lending frameworks are critical, especially concerning governance and oversight of lending agencies, procedures for internal risk assessment and controls, and monitoring and reporting. In the case of collateralized transactions, the G20 Operational Guidelines and a 2023 joint IMF–World Bank note also highlight that improved governance frameworks and enhanced technical capacity are critical to ensure that the benefits of collateralized transactions outweigh costs.[24]

[24] Please see *G20 Operational Guidelines for Sustainable Financing—Survey Results and Policy Recommendations*, Joint paper by the IMF and the World Bank, May 31, 2019.

At a time of heightened vulnerabilities, strengthening policy frameworks and institutions combined with capacity development is more important than ever. IMF practices and international experience provide guidance regarding Africa–China relationships, and in many areas, the IMF has been working with authorities in African countries and China through technical assistance and training from IMF Headquarters as well as through six regional capacity development centers in Africa, the Africa Training Institute, and the China–IMF Capacity Development Center and stands ready to increase its engagement.

REFERENCES

Allen, R., T. Chaponda, L. Fisher, and R. Ray. 2017. "Medium-Term Budget Frameworks in Selected Sub-Saharan African Countries." IMF Working Paper 17/203, International Monetary Fund, Washington, DC.

Balassone, F., and D. Franco. 2000. "Public Investment, the Stability Pact, and the Golden Rule," *Fiscal Studies* 21 (2): 207–29.

Carapella, P., T. Mogues, J. Pico-Mejia, and M. Soto. 2023. "How to Assess Spending Needs of the Sustainable Development Goals: The Third Edition of the IMF SDG Costing Tool." How-To Note 23/05, International Monetary Fund, Washington, DC.

Caselli, F., H. R. Davoodi, C. Goncalves, G. H. Hong, A. Lagerborg, P. A. Medas, A. D. M. Nguyen, and others. 2022. "The Return to Fiscal Rules." IMF Staff Discussion Note SDN/2022/002, International Monetary Fund, Washington, DC.

Cebotari, A. 2008. "Contingent Liabilities: Issues and Practice." IMF Working Paper 08/245, International Monetary Fund, Washington, DC.

Chinese Ministry of Finance. 2019. "Debt Sustainability Framework for Participating Countries of the Belt and Road Initiative." Beijing, April. http://m.mof.gov.cn/czxw/201904/P020190425513990982189.pdf.

Commonwealth Secretariat. 2016. *Extending Countercyclical Loans: Lessons from Agence Française de Développement.* London: Commonwealth Secretariat.

Dabla-Norris, E., J. Brumby, A. Kyobe, Z. Mills, and C. Papageorgiou. 2013. "Investing in Public Investment: An Index of Public Investment Efficiency." *Journal of Economic Growth* 17: 235–66.

Eyraud, L., X. Debrun, A. Hodge, V. D. Lledo, and C. A. Pattillo. 2018. "Second-Generation Fiscal Rules: Balancing Simplicity, Flexibility, and Enforceability." Staff Discussion Note 18/04, International Monetary Fund, Washington, DC.

Fainboim, I., D. Last, and E. Tandberg. 2013. "Managing Public Investment." In *Public Financial Management and Its Emerging Architecture*, edited by M. Cangiano, T. Curristine, and M. Lazare. Washington, DC: International Monetary Fund.

G20. 2020. *Collateralized Transactions: Key Considerations for Public Lenders and Borrowers.* Washington, DC: IMF and WB.

Gaspar, V., D. Amaglobeli, M. Garcia-Escribano, D. Prady, and M. Soto. 2019. "Fiscal Policy and Development: Human, Social, and Physical Investments for the SDGs." Staff Discussion Note SDN/19/03, International Monetary Fund, Washington, DC.

Gonguet, F., and H. Jin. 2017. "Improving Public Investment Management to Support BRI-Related Investment." Unpublished, International Monetary Fund, Washington, DC.

Guasch, J. L. 2004. *"Granting and Renegotiating Infrastructure Concessions: Doing It Right."* Washington, DC: World Bank.

International Monetary Fund (IMF). 2015. *Making Public Investment More Efficient.* Washington, DC.

International Monetary Fund (IMF). 2016. *Analyzing and Managing Fiscal Risks—Best Practices.* Washington, DC.

International Monetary Fund (IMF). 2017a. "Guidance Note on the Bank-Fund Debt Sustainability Framework for Low-Income Countries." Washington, DC, December.

International Monetary Fund (IMF). 2017b. "State-Contingent Debt Instruments for Sovereigns." IMF Policy Paper, May, International Monetary Fund, Washington, DC.

International Monetary Fund (IMF). 2019. "Medium-Term Revenue Strategy (An Update)." Presentation by Michael Keen at the Tenth IMF-Japan High-Level Tax Conference for Asian Countries in Tokyo April 26, 2019. Washington, DC.

International Monetary Fund (IMF). 2021. "Guidance Note on Implementing the Debt Limits Policy in Fund Supported Programs." Washington, DC, April. https://www.imf.org/en/Publications/Policy-Papers/Issues/2021/05/25/Guidance-Note-On-Implementing-The-Debt-Limits-Policy-In-Fund-Supported-Programs-460445.

International Monetary Fund (IMF). 2022. *Making Public Debt Public—Ongoing Initiatives and Reform Options*. Washington, DC.

International Monetary Fund (IMF), Organisation for Economic Cooperation and Development (OECD), United Nations (UN), and World Bank. 2016. "Enhancing the Effectiveness of External Support in Building Tax Capacity in Developing Countries." Prepared for submission to G-20 Finance Ministers, Washington, DC.

International Monetary Fund (IMF) and World Bank. 2023. "Collateralized Transactions: Recent Developments and Policy Considerations." Washington, DC, September 15.

Keen, M., and K. A. Konrad. 2013. "The Theory of International Tax Competition and Coordination." In *Handbook of Public Economics*, Vol. 5, edited by A. J. Auerbach, R. Chetty, M. Feldstein, and E. Saez, 257–328. Amsterdam: North Holland Publishing.

Presbitero, A. F. 2016. "Too Much and Too Fast? Public Investment Scaling-up and Absorptive Capacity." *Journal of Development Economics* 120: 17–31.

Schaechter, A., T. Kinda, N. Budina, and A. Weber. 2012. "Fiscal Rules in Response to the Crisis-Toward the 'Next-Generation Rules: A New Dataset.'" IMF Working Paper 12/187, International Monetary Fund, Washington, DC.

United Kingdom Government. 2023. *Climate Resilient Debt Clauses*. https://www.gov.uk/government/publications/climate-resilient-debt-clauses.

Weisfeld, H. 2017. "Fund Support for the Belt and Road Initiative—Perspectives on Countries that May Face Debt Challenges." Unpublished, International Monetary Fund, Washington, DC.

Index

Page numbers followed by *f* refer to figures. Page numbers followed by *t* refer to tables. Page numbers followed by *n* refer to notes.